AN INTRODUCTION TO
THE STUDY OF LITERATURE

Other books by the author:

An Outline History of English Literature

AN INTRODUCTION TO
THE STUDY OF LITERATURE

WILLIAM HENRY HUDSON

RUPA

Published by
Rupa Publications India Pvt. Ltd 2015
7/16, Ansari Road, Daryaganj
New Delhi 110002

Sales Centres:

Allahabad Bengaluru Chennai
Hyderabad Jaipur Kathmandu
Kolkata Mumbai

ISBN: 978-81-291-3597-1

First impression 2015

10 9 8 7 6 5 4 3 2 1

The moral right of the author has been asserted.

Printed by HT Media Ltd., Noida

Contents

Preface

The aim of this book is to set forth, in the simplest possible way, some of the questions to be considered and the principles to be kept in view in the systematic study of literature. Despite the large and ever increasing number of works which deal with special aspects of literature on the historical and critical sides, I believe that there is still a place for a compact and fairly comprehensive volume of this kind. This faith may indeed be taken for granted, as otherwise the book would not have been written. I should, however, add that the utility of the plan adopted in it has been established by practical experience, since much of its substance has already been used and tested in a course of lectures delivered before University Extension audiences at the Municipal Technical Institute, West Ham, and the Polytechnic, Woolwich. The fact that these lectures were followed with sustained interest, in the one case by upward of 500, in the other by over 100, listeners, of whom, while many were engaged in teaching, the majority were concerned with literature only as general readers, encourages me to think that the same matter, put into the form of a book, may prove equally helpful to a wider circle of students.

In the course itself, ample illustrations were provided of every point considered. In reducing the contents of twenty-five lectures to meet the requirements of a not too bulky volume, while adding a good deal that could not well be included in them, I have been compelled to omit quotations from and detailed analyses of particular works. I must therefore ask the reader to remember that this book is planned as a guide and companion to his own study, and that, while I hope it may be interesting and suggestive in itself, the value of the things said in it must ultimately be sought in their application.

It will be found that little place is given to questions of abstract aesthetics. These, as well as all details of a purely scholastic character, have been purposely avoided, as my desire throughout has been to make my volume of practical service to those students for whom literature is primarily a means of enjoyment and a help to life.

William Henry Hudson

NOTE TO THE SECOND EDITION

In the two and a half years since this book was published, much evidence has reached me from many quarters of its practical usefulness both to students of literature and to general readers. I am thus able to feel with satisfaction that the objects for which it was written, as explained in the original preface, have to some extent been attained. I have seen no occasion to make any changes in the text for this new edition; but I have added an appendix, in which I have said something more about the question of personality in literature, have dealt more fully with the treatment of nature in poetry, and have offered some suggestions for the study of the essay and the short story as forms of literary art. I hope that the value of the book may be increased by these additions.

1

Some Ways of Studying Literature

I. *The Nature and Elements of Literature.* What is Literature?—Literature and Life—The Impulses behind Literature—The Themes of Literature—The Classification of Literature—The Elements of Literature. II. *Literature as an Expression of Personality.* The Principle of Sincerity—The Man in the Book. III. *The Study of an Author.* Reading and Study—The Reading of Books and the Study of Authors—The Chronological Method of Studying an Author—The Comparative Method. IV. *Biography.* Its Abuse—And Use— The Need of Sympathy. V. *The Study of Style as an Index of Personality.* The Personal Interest of Style.

However loosely employed, the word literature commonly carries with it, alike in the language of criticism and in that of everyday intercourse, a clear suggestion of delimitation; in the one case as in the other a distinction is implied between books which in the literary sense are books, and those which in the same sense are not. But where is the boundary line to be drawn? The moment that question is raised our difficulties begin. In many instances there is, of course, no room for discussion. We should all agree about the place to which, for example, a railway guide or a manual of cookery, *Paradise Lost* or *Sartor Resartus* should respectively be assigned.

But as we approach the border-country from either side we pass into the region of uncertainty; and with this uncertainty the controversy as to the exact definition of literature commences. Shall we follow Charles Lamb, who (half humorously, it is true) narrowed the conception of literature to such an extent that he excluded the works of Hume, Gibbon, and Flavius Josephus, together with directories, almanacks, and 'draught-boards bound and lettered on the back'? Shall we adopt the view of Hallam, who under the general head of literature, comprised jurisprudence, theology, and medicine? Or, if Lamb seems to err on the one side and Hallam on the other, where between these two extremes is any just mean to be found? These are questions to which no final answer has yet been given, and it is fortunate therefore that they need not detain us here. We shall get what for our purposes should be an idea of literature at once sufficiently broad and sufficiently accurate if we lay stress upon two considerations. Literature is composed of those books, and of those books only, which, in the first place, by reason of their subject matter and their mode of treating it, are of general human interest; and in which, in the second place, the element of form and the pleasure which form gives are to be regarded as essential. A piece of literature differs from a specialised treatise on astronomy, political economy, philosophy, or even history, in part because it appeals, not to a particular class of readers only, but to men and women as men and women; and in part because, while the object of the treatise is simply to impart knowledge, one ideal end of the piece of literature, whether it also imparts knowledge or not, is to yield æsthetic satisfaction by the manner in which it handles its theme.

The study of literature, as thus conceived, is as far as possible removed both from the academic formalism and from the dilettante trifling, with one or other of which it has, in popular thought, been too often associated. Why do we care for literature? We care for literature primarily on account of its deep and lasting human significance. A great book grows directly out of life; in reading it, we are brought into large, close, and fresh relations with life; and in that fact lies the final explanation of its power. Literature is a vital record of what men have seen in life, what they have experienced of it, what they have thought and felt about those aspects of it which have the most immediate and enduring interest for all of us. It is thus fundamentally an expression of life through the medium of language. Such expression is fashioned into the various forms of literary art, and these in themselves will, in their proper place and time, enlist the attention of the student. But it is important to understand, to begin with, that literature lives by virtue of the life which it embodies. By remembering this, we shall be saved from the besetting danger of confounding the study of literature with the study of philology, rhetoric, and even literary technique.

To say that literature grows directly out of life is of course to say that it is in life itself that we have to seek the sources of literature, or, in other words, the impulses which have given birth to the various forms of literary expression. The classification of literature, therefore, is not conventional nor arbitrary. What we call the formal divisions of literature must be translated into terms of life, if we would understand how they originated, and what meaning they still have for us.

The great impulses behind literature may, I think, be grouped with accuracy enough for practical purposes under four heads: (1) our desire for self-expression; (2) our interest in people and their doings; (3) our interest in the world of reality in which we live, and in the world of imagination which we conjure into existence; and (4) our love of form as form. We are strongly impelled to confide to others what we think and feel; hence the literature which directly expresses the thoughts and feelings of the writer. We are intensely interested in men and women, their lives, motives, passions, relationships; hence the literature which deals with the great drama of human life and action. We are fond of telling others about the things we have seen or imagined; hence the literature of description. And, where the æsthetic impulse is present at all, we take a special satisfaction in the mere shaping of expression into forms of beauty; hence the very existence of literature as art.

Man, as we are often reminded, is a social animal; and as he is thus by the actual constitution of his nature unable to keep his experiences, observations, ideas, emotions, fancies, to himself, but is on the contrary under stress of a constant desire to impart them to those about him, the various forms of literature are to be regarded as only so many channels which he has opened up for himself for the discharge of his sociality through media which in themselves testify to his paramount desire to blend expression with artistic creation. Moreover, these impulses behind literature explain not only the evolution of the various forms of literature, but also our interest (for this is merely the reverse side of the same matter) in such forms. If we are constrained to make others the confidants of our thoughts and feelings, experiences, observations, imaginings, we are glad to listen while others tell us of theirs, especially when we are aware that the range of their commerce with life, the depth of their insight or passion, their power of expression, or all these things combined, will render their utterances of unusual interest and value; while our own delight in artistic beauty will make us readily responsive to the beauty in which a master-artist embodies what he has to say.

Of these four impulses, the last named, being a factor common to all kinds of literature, may for the moment be disregarded; for purposes of classification the other three alone count. Now, it is evident that these three impulses continually merge together in life. In describing what we have seen or imagined, for example, we are almost certain to express a great deal of our own thought and feeling; and again, any kind of narrative will be found almost necessarily to involve more or less description. As these impulses merge together in life, so they will merge together in literature, with the result that the different divisions of literature which spring from them will inevitably overlap. We simply distinguish them one from another, therefore—the lyric poem from the epic, the drama from the descriptive essay, and so on—as one or another of the generative impulses seems to predominate. It is in this way that we obtain a basis of classification.

It is, however, a basis only. To make our survey even approximately complete, we must go farther, and consider not only the impulses which produce literature, but also the subjects with which it deals. These, being almost as varied as life itself (for there is little in life which may not be made a theme for literature), may at first sight appear to defy any attempt to reduce them to systematic statement. But—still having regard only to practical purposes—we may perhaps venture to arrange them into five large groups: (1) the personal experiences of the individual as individual—the things which make up the sum-total of his private life, outer and inner; (2) the experiences of man as man—those great common questions of life and death, sin and destiny, God, man's relation with God, the hope of the race here and hereafter, and the like—which transcend the limits of the personal lot, and belong to the race as a whole; (3) the relations of the individual with his fellows, or the entire social world, with all its activities and problems; (4) the external world of nature, and our relations with this; and (5) man's own efforts to create and express under the various forms of literature and art. Looking at literature in the light of this analysis, and considering only the character of its subjects, we may thus distinguish five classes of production: the literature of purely personal experience; of the common life of man as man; of the social world under all its different aspects; the literature which treats of nature; and the literature which treats of literature and art.

By combining the results of these two lines of analysis, we get a fairly comprehensive scheme of classification, and one which, as will be seen, has the advantage of resting upon natural foundations. We have, first, the literature of self- expression, which includes the different kinds of lyric poetry, the poetry of meditation and argument, and the elegy; the essay and treatise where these are written from the personal point of view; and the literature of artistic and literary criticism. We have, secondly, the literature in which the writer, instead of going down into himself, goes out of himself into the world of external human life and activity; and this includes history and biography, the ballad and the epic, the romance in verse and prose, the story in verse and prose, the novel and the drama. And, thirdly, we have the literature of description, not in itself a large or important division, since description in literature is ordinarily associated with, and for the most part subordinated to, the interests of self-expression or narrative, but comprising in the book of travel, and the descriptive essay and poem, some fairly distinct minor forms of literary art.

Thus the various forms of literary expression fall into their places as natural results of common human impulses working themselves out under the conditions of art; and when we remember the great principle that a piece of literature appeals to us only when it calls into activity in us the same powers of sympathy and imagination as went into its making, the interest which such forms have for us is also explained.

It should further be noted, among the preliminaries of our study, that in all these divisions certain elements of composition are always present. There is in the first place, of course, the elements furnished by life itself, which constitute the raw material of any piece of literature—poem, essay, drama, novel. Then there are the elements contributed by the author in his fashioning of such raw material into this or that form of literary art. These may be roughly tabulated under four heads. First, there is the intellectual element— the thought which the writer brings to bear upon his subject, and which he expresses in his work. Secondly, there is the emotional element—the feeling (of whatever kind) which his subject arouses in him and which in turn he desires to stimulate in us. Thirdly, there is the element of imagination (including its lighter form which we call fancy), which is really the faculty of strong and intense vision, and by the exercise of which he quickens a similar power of vision in ourselves. These elements combine to furnish the substance and the life of literature. But however rich may be the materials yielded by experience, however fresh and strong may be the writer's thought, feeling, and imagination, in dealing with them, another factor is wanting before his work can be completed. The given matter has to be moulded and fashioned in accordance with the principles of order, symmetry, beauty, effectiveness; and thus we have a fourth element in literature—the technical element, or the element of composition and style.

II

It has been necessary to touch upon these somewhat abstract considerations in order to clear the way for what is to follow. We may now pass directly to matters of more immediate importance to the student, whose business is not with the theory of literature, but with literature itself.

If literature be at bottom an expression of life, and if it be by virtue of the life which it expresses that it makes its special appeal, then the ultimate secret of its interest must be sought in its essentially personal character. Literature, according to Matthew Arnold's much-discussed definition, is a criticism of life; but this can mean only that it is an interpretation of life as life shapes itself in the mind of the interpreter. It is with the critic or interpreter, therefore, that we have first to do. The French epigram hits the mark—'Art is life seen through a temperament,' for the mirror which the artist holds up to the world about him is of necessity the mirror of his own personality. The practical bearings of this fundamental truth must be carefully noted.

A great book is born of the brain and heart of its author; he has put himself into its pages; they partake of his life, and are instinct with his individuality. It is to the man in the book, therefore, that to begin with we have to find our way. We have to get to know him as an individual. To establish personal intercourse with our books in a simple, direct, human way, should thus be our primary and constant purpose. We want first of all to become, not scholars, but good readers; and we can become good readers only when we make our reading a matter of close and sympathetic companionship. 'Personal experience,' it has been rightly said, 'is the basis of all real literature'; and to enter into such personal experience, and to share it, is similarly the basis of all real literary culture. A great book owes its greatness in the first instance to the greatness of the personality which gave it life; for what we call genius is only another name for freshness and originality of nature, with its resulting freshness and originality of outlook upon the world, of insight, and of thought. The mark of a really great book is that it has something fresh and original to say, and that it says this in a fresh and independent way. It is the utterance of one who has himself been close to those aspects of life of which he speaks, who has looked at them with his own eyes, who by the keenness of his vision has seen more deeply into things, and by the strength of his genius has apprehended their meaning more powerfully than the common race of men; and who in addition has the artist's wonderful faculty of making us see and feel with him. 'A good book,' as Milton finely says in words which, however hackneyed, can hardly be too often repeated, 'is the precious life-blood of a master-spirit, embalmed and treasured up on purpose to a life beyond life.' To throw open our whole nature to the quickening influence of such a master-spirit, to let his lifeblood flow freely into our veins, is the preliminary step in literary culture—the final secret of all profitable reading.

It is important, then, that in all our dealings with books we should distinguish between what Carlyle calls the 'genuine voices' and the mere 'echoes'—between the men who speak for themselves and those who speak only on the report of others. 'I have read,' wrote Charlotte Brontë of Lewes's *Ranthorpe*, 'a new book; not a reprint, not a reflection of any other book, but a new book.' Charlotte Brontë clearly recognised the distinction upon which we are now insisting. We are not in the least obliged to despise the echoes and the reprints, or to say hard and contemptuous things of them, as is sometimes done; for provided they be good of their kind, they have their place and usefulness. But to safeguard ourselves against erroneous estimates, it is necessary to keep well in mind the essential difference between the literature which draws its life directly from personality and experience, and that which draws its life mainly at second hand from contact with the personality and experience of others. The literature which, in Turgenev's phrase, 'smells of literature,' is always to be classed below that which carries with it the native savour of life itself; and it is not with the bookish books of the world, no matter how great their technical excellence, but with those which are fullest of original vitality, that we are chiefly concerned.

Involved in this, yet calling for separate emphasis, is the great principle, first enunciated by Plato, that the foundation of all good and lasting work in literature is entire sincerity to oneself, to one's own experience of life, and to the truth of things as one is privileged to see it—that very quality of sincerity which was, it will be remembered, for Carlyle the essence of all heroic greatness. '*C'est moi qui ai vécu*,' wrote Alfred de Musset. The words may seem commonplace enough, but how many of us could honestly say as much? 'The value of the tidings brought by literature,' as George Henry Lewes rightly insists, 'is determined by their authenticity[…] We cannot demand from every man that he have unusual depth of insight or exceptional experience; but we demand of him that he give us of his best, and his best cannot be another's.' We can thus see why men who speak frankly for themselves in literature have always a chance of being listened to, while others of perhaps greater natural power, wider culture, and far more accomplished art, but of less candour and directness of utterance, are passed over or quickly forgotten. It is always a sure sign of literary decadence in an individual or age when this preference is not shown. Without sincerity, no vital work in literature is possible; and 'that virtue of originality that men so strive after,' as Ruskin says, 'is not newness…it is only genuineness.' Readers of Kingsley will remember how Alton Locke's first attempt at poetry took the shape of a South Sea Romance compounded of *Childe Harold* and the old missionary records, and how Sandye Mackaye, with a contemptuous 'What do ye ken about Pacifies? Are ye a cockney or a Cannibal Islander?' took the would be poet on a tour of inspection through Clare Market and St Giles's, on a foul, chilly Saturday night, showed him something of the actual tragedy of London's misery and sin, and at each new revelation of its horrors advised him curtly to 'write anent that.' The principle that, whether his range of experience and personal power be great or small, a man should write of that which lies at his own doors, should make it his chief business to report faithfully of what he has lived, seen, thought, felt, known, for himself, is one which the student of literature can never afford to lose sight of. The cleverness and brilliancy of many books which have not this essential quality of genuineness will often tempt him to neglect it. But the truth remains that the value of literature is in the measure of its authenticity.

Our study of literature thus begins in a very simple and humble way. We take a great book, and we try to penetrate as deeply as we can into its personal life. We make our reading of it, to the fullest extent possible to us, a matter of actual intercourse between its author and ourselves. We listen attentively to what he has to tell us, and we do our best to enter sympathetically into his thought and feeling. We note carefully how he looked at life, what he found in it, what he brought away from it. We observe how the world of experience impressed him, and how it is interpreted through his personality, strength and weakness, his very accent, as we become familiar with the character, outlook, strength, weakness, and accent of those with whom we talk in the flesh. We get to know the man as the man reveals himself in what he has written. The book lives for us in all the potency of his individuality.

This, then, is our starting point—the first step, as I have said, in the cultivation of the habit of good and profitable reading. And if it is objected that this is, indeed, an obvious view of literary culture, and one so generally recognized that there is no need to labour it, my reply is, that this is precisely one of those commonplaces of theory which we are only too apt to leave unutilized in practice. The moment we begin to talk about the systematic study of literature, the tendency sets in to think of something formal and pedantic, and to substitute for the true ideal of intimate and sympathetic inter-course the academic ideal of mere scholarship; it comes to be regarded as our main business, not to know our books in the sense in which we here speak of knowing them, but rather to know, down to the minutest particulars, everything that patient erudition and elaborate criticism have accumulated or found to say about them—a very different thing. Hence the necessity of dwelling even at some length upon this primary conception of good reading as fundamentally a direct contact between mind and mind, and of insisting that all other aspects of literary study are supplemental to, and not substitutes for, it.

With this conception before us, we can realize from yet another point of view, the vital relations of literature and life. What George Eliot said of art in general is specially true of the art of literature: it 'is the nearest thing to life; it is a mode of amplifying experience and extending our contact with our fellow-men beyond the bounds of our personal lot.' Thus literature makes us partakers in a life larger, richer, and more varied than we ourselves can ever know of our own individual knowledge; and it does this, not only because it opens up new fields of experience and new lines of thought and speculation, but also, and even more notably, because it carries us beyond the pinched and meagre humanity of our everyday round of existence into contact with those fresh, strong, and magnetic personalities who have embodied themselves in the world's great books.

III

Taking this as our point of departure, we must next seek to make our reading at once broader and more systematic. Between the mere reader of books and the student of literature the essential difference is not to be sought, as I am afraid it is very often sought, in the supposed fact that the one enjoys his reading and the other does not. The true difference is this, that the one reads in a haphazard and desultory way, while the other's reading is organised according to some regular order or plan. So long as we simply take a book here and a book there, as chance or the whim of the hour may dictate, we are merely readers. It is only when we introduce method into our reading that we become students.

Obviously, our most natural course is to pass directly from the reading of books to the study of authors. Our first aim being, as we have said, to establish personal relations with a man in his work, we begin by devoting ourselves to some one or other of his writings which may have a special kind of interest for us. But as students we cannot rest here. We want to realise the man's genius, so far as this is possible, in its wholeness and variety; and to this end we have to consider his works, not separately, but in their relations with one another, and thus with the man himself, the growth of his mind, the changes of his temper and thought, the influence upon him of his experiences in the world. Those records of himself which he has left us in his books are now no longer to be regarded as detached and independent expressions of his personality—isolated productions forming a mere miscellaneous aggregate of unconnected units, to be read without any sense of their affiliations one with another. They are rather to be taken as a corpus, or organic whole—not simply as his works, but as his work.

A telling illustration lies ready to hand in the case of Shakespeare. We may read, and we often do read, Shakespeare's plays without the slightest idea of sequence or method, jumping, let us say, from the *Comedy of Errors* to *King Lear*, and from the *Tempest* back to *A Midsummer Night's Dream*; and no one will deny that the keenest delight and a great deal of profit may be found in such random reading of them. But though in this way we may get to know much of Shakespeare, there is much that we cannot get to know. We have still to study these plays together as diverse expressions of one and the same genius; to compare and contrast them in matter and spirit, in method and style; to conceive them, alike in their similarities and in their differences, as products of a single individual power revealing itself, in different periods and in curiously varying artistic moods, now in one and now in another of them. Hence, manifestly the need of systematising our reading.

If, recognising this need, we raise the question of the course to be pursued, the answer is not far to seek. Clearly, the most natural and the most profitable of all plans of study that might be suggested is the chronological—the study of a writer's works in the order of their production. Taken in this way such works become for us the luminous record of his inner life and of his craftsmanship; and we thus follow in them the various phases of his experience, the stages of his mental and moral growth, and the changes undergone by his art. 'In order to know Balzac, and to judge him,' writes a French critic of that great novelist, 'we must arrange his works in the order in which they were produced.' It is now almost universally recognised that the true, in fact the only, way in which to study Shakespeare, if we would properly know and judge him, is similarly to arrange his works, so far as we can do so, in the order in which they were produced, since in this way we can obtain, as we can obtain by no other method, a substantial sense of those works as a progressive revelation of his genius and power. And what is thus now taken as a principle of practice in the study of Balzac and Shakespeare will be found to hold equally good in the study of every other writer who is worth systematic study at all.

To prevent misapprehension, it should, however, be added that when we speak in this way of a writer's work as a whole, it is generally with a certain amount of qualification. We may not always or usually mean literally everything that he produced, but simply everything that is really vital and important as an expression of his genius. Today there is something very much like a mania for the collection and preservation of every miscellaneous scrap which any great author allowed to remain unpublished, or perhaps threw aside as unworthy of publication; but the outcome of such indiscriminate enthusiasm has seldom any solid value. Even apart from these gleanings from the notebook and the waste-paperbasket (which here can hardly concern us), most writers, even the greatest, leave behind them a considerable body of published work, which is either tentative and experimental, or in which they are merely echoes of themselves, repeating less effectively what they have already said in other forms, and adding nothing to the sum total of their real contribution to the world's literature. Such secondary kind of work will always have its value for the special student intent upon the exhaustive investigation of a given author; but to begin with we may, in the vast majority of cases, safely disregard it.

In following the chronological method we shall find ourselves, it is evident, continually comparing and contrasting a man with himself. Our next step will be to sharpen our impression of his personality by comparing and contrasting him with others—with men who worked in the same field, took up the same subjects, dealt with the same problems, wrote under similar conditions, or who, for any other reason, naturally associate themselves with him in our minds. The student of Shakespeare almost inevitably turns to Shakespeare's greater contemporaries—to men like Marlowe, Jonson, Beaumont and Fletcher, Webster—and rightly feels that by marking the points at which the master resembled these other dramatists, and, the points in which he differed from them, he gains immeasurably in his realisation of the essential qualities of Shakespeare's genius and art. We throw a flood of fresh light upon Tennyson and Browning alike when we read them side by side. The fundamental features of the art of Sophocles and Euripides are brought into relief when we pass backward and forward from one to the other. Thackeray furnishes us with an illuminating commentary on Dickens, and Dickens does the same service for Thackeray. We have laid down the principle that in studying literature our first business is to enter into the spirit of our author, to penetrate into the vital forces of his personality. We need add no further illustrations to show how the comparative method will help us to do this. The doctrine that 'all higher knowledge is gained by comparison, and rests on comparison,'[1] is as true and important in the study of literature as in the study of science.

IV

In our study of the personal life in literature, we shall, of course, be greatly helped by the judicious use of good biography. Our

[1] Max Müller, *Lectures en the Science of Religin*, p. 12.

interest in the writings of any great author being once aroused, the desire will inevitably be stimulated to learn something of the man himself, as a man, beyond that which his work reveals to us. We shall be curious to see him in the social surroundings in which he lived, and in his daily converse with his fellows; to know the chief facts of his outward history—his ambitions, struggles, successes, failures—and the connection of his books with these; the way in which and the conditions under which such books were written; his intellectual habits and methods of work. Curiosity on such and similar points is entirely natural and legitimate, and we need not scruple to gratify it. We may well be grateful, therefore, for such massive and detailed narratives as we possess, for instance, of the lives of Milton, Johnson, Goethe, Scott, Tennyson; apart altogether from their interest simply as human documents (which is really a different matter), their direct literary value is inestimable, since we rightly feel that we can understand and enjoy the works of these men so much the better for the information they afford. And for every good piece of biographical writing, small or great, we shall be similarly thankful, and for the same reason. Side by side on our shelf with the books of any author we really care for, a place should thus certainly be made for a well-chosen account of his life.

It is necessary, however, to lay stress upon the twofold qualification which I have suggested; it is a good biography which alone can be of service to us, and this must be used judiciously and kept in its proper place. There is a great deal today which passes under the name of literary biography which yields little more than trivial gossip about those details of the private life of famous men with which the public has really no concern, and which the student is not in the least helped by knowing. 'Petrarch's house in Arqua, Tasso's supposed prison in Ferrara, Shakespeare's house in Stratford, Goethe's house in Weimar, with its furniture, Kant's old hat, the autographs of great men—these things,' as Schopenhauer rightly remarked, 'are gaped at with interest and awe by many who have never read their works.' Since Schopenhauer's time, the craze for mere personal detail, at once fostered and fed by a newspaper press which, in these matters, has lost all sense of reticence and decency, has developed to an extent which may fairly be described as alarming, as the puerile chatter with which even our so-called literary and critical periodicals frequently fill their pages only too eloquently proves.

We must not mistake our interest in the external facts of literary biography—which is generally an idle, often a vulgar interest—for an interest in literature itself; our knowledge of these things, however wide and accurate, for literary culture. This warning is opportune, for the danger lest we do so is real and urgent, and may beset us at times when we are least on our guard against it. The student of Carlyle, for instance—I take an example which at once suggests itself, and than which it would be difficult to select one more immediately to the point—will find much to his purpose in Froude's four volumes of biography; yet through the perusal of those volumes he may easily get himself entangled in the whole problem of Carlyle's home-life and domestic relationships, and in the mass of controversial literature which within recent years has unfortunately grown up about this. But the fact is that with this problem he, as a student of the great preacher and artist, has nothing whatever to do, and that thus all the hundreds of pages which have been written about it are for him little more than so much rubbish. Hence, as they add nothing of real significance to our knowledge of the essential personality and character of the author of *Sartor Resartus* and *Past and Present*, and as the mastery of them would at best involve an expenditure of time which could be much more profitably devoted to *Sartor Resartus* and *Past and Present* themselves, we shall do well, it is clear, to leave them severely alone. I am not one of those who believe that we are really better off for knowing no more than we are ever likely to know about the man William Shakespeare, actor, manager, playwright, frequenter of the Mermaid Tavern, citizen of Stratford; on the contrary, I quite frankly admit that I should be glad to have the greatest amount of detailed information about him in all these capacities. Yet I am bound to add that this feeling is more than half due to curiosity only; and if I were asked whether I think it probable that we should gain in the least in our insight into the essential Shakespeare—the Shakespeare of the plays—if we had as many particulars concerning his relations with Anne Hathaway as we have of Carlyle's relations with Jane Welsh, and were able to read the personal riddle, if personal riddle there be, of the *Sonnets*, I should answer with an unhesitating negative. And it is with Shakespeare the poet and dramatist, as it is with Carlyle the great prophet and consummate literary artist, that we ought rather, after all, to be concerned.

But because we are fully alive to the danger lest biography may too easily degenerate into idle and impertinent gossip about unimportant things, we need not therefore go with some critics to the other extreme of maintaining that biography is valueless, and that the student of a man's work should confine himself to that work, and has no proper interest in the man outside it. Distinguishing as we must between the reading of a biography simply as a piece of literature, which is one thing, and the reading of it in connection with and as a commentary upon an author's writings, which is another, we shall in the latter case welcome and utilise everything that really brings us into more intimate relationships with the genius and essential character of the man with whom we have to deal; all else may go. And in a good biography—as in Carlyle's own admirable essays—it will be found that a line is commonly drawn between the important, intrinsic, and fundamental aspects of experience and character and those which are merely trivial, superficial, and accidental. Of course it will often be difficult, in any given instance, to say exactly up to what point the personal material will be useful to us, and where it will cease to be so. Sometimes a seemingly insignificant fact will prove to be unexpectedly illuminating and suggestive; sometimes, on the other hand, phases of a man's career, important and interesting in themselves, will turn out on examination to have had so little to do with his work that on the literary side they will mean nothing. Hence, we must exercise our own tact and discretion. Much will depend upon the special objects we may for the moment have in view; a good deal also on the nature of the particular case. Thus, for instance, biographical detail will always occupy a prominent place in the study of Dante, whose writings can hardly be understood when detached from his life, and of Goethe, whose works, according to his own oft-quoted description of them, were but fragments of a great personal confession; while with Johnson, as every reader knows, the usual relations between production and biography are actually reversed, and instead of the life being read as a commentary upon the writings, the writings are read almost entirely in connection with the life. We can, therefore, lay down no hard and fast rule for the use of biography in literary study, nor is it necessary that we should try to do so. It will be well for us, however, to be on our guard against the rather widespread error of confusing means employed with end to be attained. Biography in itself is nearly always interesting and generally profitable. But the study of biography is not the study of literature, and should never be made a substitute for it.

In closing this section, let me insist that it is beyond all things necessary that we should cultivate a spirit of sympathy—at least of provisional sympathy—with our author. We cannot of course expect that our personal relations with all the great writers we may from time to time take up will be uniformly intimate and agreeable. Our own temperaments have to be reckoned with. Literature contains the revelation of many different personalities, and we ourselves have our well-marked leanings and antipathies. It is to no purpose then that the dogmatic critic tells us that we most perforce enjoy this or that author, admire this or that book, on pain of instant condemnation as hopelessly lacking in taste. No one has a right, thus, to impose his own judgment upon us; and honest likes and dislikes are never to be despised. We cannot force our temperaments; in literature as in life there are people whose greatness we may indeed recognise, but with whom we should find good fellowship altogether impossible; others, towards whom our feelings will be of positive repugnance. It is right to recognise this fact, and wise to accept its implications, if only that we may be saved thereby from the too common habit of indiscriminate or merely conventional admiration. Yet recognition of it should be accompanied by certain reserves. We must remember that many authors should prove interesting even when, and occasionally because, they are intellectual and moral aliens to us. We must remember, too, that it is precisely as it brings us into contact with many different kinds of personality, which often challenge our own, and thus increases our flexibility of mind, breadth of outlook, catholicity of taste and judgment, that the value of literature as a means of culture becomes so great. A certain amount of patience and persistency in our dealings with writers who at first rather repel than attract is therefore to be recommended. The fault may lie entirely with us—in prejudices which we ought to overcome; in mere inability to place ourselves at once at their point of view, or even to rise to the level of their thought and power. In any event, we may rest assured that without some amount of initial sympathy, we shall never understand an author's real character. To reach the best in literature, as in life, sympathy is a preliminary condition. Only through sympathy can we ever get into living touch with another soul.

V

It is while we are still dealing with literature on the personal side that style or expression first becomes important for us. It is very commonly supposed, indeed, that the formal element in literature is a matter for the specialist only. This is a serious mistake. Leaving the more technical and recondite aspects of the subject for the moment out of consideration, we have therefore to insist that the study of style is itself full of broad interest for every reader who seeks to enter into the human life in literature.

It is probable that we have all at some time or other had the experience of chancing upon a passage quoted without indication of authorship, and of exclaiming—'So and so must have written that.' In such a case, it is often not the thought that strikes us as familiar so much as the way in which the thought is expressed. The passage has somehow—we might be at a loss to say exactly how—a characteristic ring, like that of a well-known voice. However commonplace the idea, we feel sure that no one else would have put it just in that way. The choice of the words, the turn of the phrases, the structure of the sentences, their peculiar rhythm and cadence—these are all curiously instinct with the individuality of the writer. The thing said may have little to distinguish it, but the man has put himself into it nonetheless.

This is enough to show that style—I am using the word in its broadest sense—is fundamentally a personal quality: that, as Buffon's oft-quoted dictum has it, *le style est de l'homme même*. When Pope called it 'the dress of thought,' he failed entirely to recognise its essentially organic character, for he evidently conceived it as something apart from the man, which he could put on or take off at will. Style, as Carlyle says in one of his *Journals*, is not the coat of a writer, but his skin. There are authors, of course, who have deliberately shaped their utterance on the speech of stronger men, and set themselves to reproduce their very gestures and mannerisms; the tyro in letters is often, indeed, advised by teachers who know no better to take this or that master as his model. Moreover, the strongest and most original men are frequently deeply influenced by others, and carry traces of such influence in their style. But as sincerity is the foundation principle of all true literature, so is it the foundation principle of all true style. A man who has something really personal to say will seldom fail to find a really personal way in which to say it. Thought which is his own will hardly permit itself to be shaped into the fashion of some one else's expression. Imitation will always be significant as revealing the sources from which a writer who deals with life mainly at second-hand derives his inspiration; but it takes us in reality but a short distance beneath the surface even of his work. Imitate as he may, the native qualities of a man—his inherent strength and weakness—will ultimately show through, and he will of necessity write himself down for what he is. So profound a truth is it that 'every spirit builds its own house.'[2]

'Literature,' says one who was himself a great master of style, 'is the personal use or exercise of language. That this is so is…proved from the fact that one author uses it so differently from another…. While the many use language as they find it, the man of genius uses it indeed, but subjects it withal to his own purposes, and moulds it according to his own peculiarities. The throng and succession of ideas, thoughts, feelings, imaginations, speculations, which pass within him, the abstractions, the juxtapositions, the comparisons, the discriminations, the conceptions, which are so original in him, his views of external things, his judgments upon life, manners, and history, the exercises of his wit, of his humour, of his depth, of his sagacity, all these innumerable and incessant creations, the very production and throbbing of his intellect, does he image forth… in a corresponding language, which is as multiform as this inward mental action itself, and analogous to it, the faithful expression of his intense personality, attending on his inward world of thought as its very shadow; so that we might as well say that one man's shadow is another's as that the style of a really gifted mind can belong to any but himself. It follows him about as a shadow. His thought and feeling are personal, and so his language is personal.'[3]

I have made this long quotation chiefly with the view of further

---

[2]The following extract from one of our earliest English critics will be read with interest, because it shows that men were impressed by the personal quality of style as soon as they began to think about literature at all. 'Style is a constant and continual phrase or tenour of speaking and writing.[…] So we say that Cicero's style and Sallust's were not one, nor Cæsar's and Livy's, nor Homer's and Hesiodus', nor Herodotus' and Thucydides', nor Euripides' and Aristophanes', nor Erasmus' and Budeus' styles. And because this continual course and manner of writing or speech zheweth the matter and disposition of the writer's mind more than one or two instances can show, therefore there be that have called style the image of man (montis character). For man is but his mind, and as his mind is tempered and qualified, so are his speeches and language at large; and his inward conceits be the metal of his mind, and his manner of utterance the very warp and woof of his conceits' (Puttenham, The Arts of Englishe Pæsie, 1589).

[3]Newman, Lectures an Literature, in The idea of a University, §3.

elucidating the principle I am trying to make clear by putting it in language other than my own. One point touched upon by Newman is, however, worthy of special attention. He notes, it will be observed, that while the majority of men use the language of their time 'as they find it,' the man of genius subjects such language 'to his own purposes, and moulds it according to his own peculiarities.' This means that language always receives a certain fresh impress from the hands of every writer of strongly marked personality. As Dr Rutherford, Headmaster of Westminster, in speaking of the style of Thucydides, has well said: 'Just in proportion to the measure of individuality with which a man is gifted, does his use of the language of his race'—and we may add, of his period—'differ from the common or normal use'; and this difference is sometimes so great that 'we may know a language very well in an ordinary way, and yet be unable to enjoy perfectly some of the greatest writers in it.' In this fact we have another illustration of the intimate and inevitable relation of personality and style.

As even an uncritical reader, then, must recognise the individual quality in style, and as this is something which we are bound to feel with ever-increasing distinctness the more we think about it, the student will naturally be led to consider wherein, in any given case, this individual quality consists, and to look closely into the connection between the character of a writer's genius and thought, and the form of expression which he has fashioned for himself. To approach style in this way is to find in it not only the living product of an author's personality, but also a transparent record of his intellectual, spiritual, and artistic growth. Carefully examined, it will tell us much of his education; of the influences which went to shape and mould his nature; of the masters at whose feet he sat, and who helped him to find himself; of the books he lived with; of his intercourse with men; of the development and consolidation of his thought; of his changing outlook upon the world and its problems; of the modifications of his temper and of the principles by which he governed his art in the successive stages of his career. All the factors which combine in the making of a man will subtly play their parts in giving to his style its well-defined individuality of form and colour; all the phases of his outer and inner experience will register themselves in it. In the chronological study of his writings, therefore, it will become interesting to correlate the changes undergone by his style with contemporaneous changes in his matter and thought.[4] Even his defects of utterance, his limitations, his mannerisms, will thus have their value. Matter and expression being no longer thought of apart, as things which have no connection or at most only an accidental one, style will become for us a real index of personality, and the way in which a writer expresses himself a commentary upon what he says.

---

[4]The extraordinary changes which came over Shakespeare's style during the twenty years of his dramatic activity are familiar to all students of the plays. 'In the earliest plays the language is sometimes as it were a dress put upon the thought—a dress ornamented with superfluous care; the idea is at times hardly sufficient to fill out the language in which it is put; in the middle plays (*Julius Cæsar* serves as an example) there seems a perfect balance and equality between the thought and its expression. In the latest plays this balance is disturbed by the preponderance or excess of ideas over the means of giving them utterance. The sentences are close- packed; there are 'rapid and abrupt turnings of thought, so quick that language can hardly follow fast enough; impatient activity of intellect and fancy, which, having once disclosed an idea, cannot wait to work it orderly out" (Dowden, Primer of *Shakespeare*, p. 37). It is evident that these changes are simply the external expression of changes in thought and feeling. Shakespeare could no more have written *Cymbeline* in the style of *Love's Labour's Lost* than Carlyle could have written *Sartor Resartus* in the style of Washington Irving.

2

Some Ways of Studying Literature
(*concluded*)

I. *The Historical Study of Literature.* What is a National Literature? II. *Literature as a Social Product.* Literature and the Spirit of the Age—The Epochs of Literary History—Literature as the Product of Society. III. *Taine's Formula of Literary Evolution.* The Formula criticised—Interest of Literature on the Sociological Side. IV. *The Comparative Method in the Historical Study of Literature.* The Interaction of Races and Epochs in Literary Evolution—Illustration: Literary Relations of England and France—Another Illustration: Literary Relations of England and Germany—The Mediæval Revival. V. *The Historical Study of Style.* Illustration: the Growth of English Prose. VI. *The Study of Literary Technique.* Literature in the Making The Study of Genealogy and Antecedents—The Technical Study of Style—The Art of Literature and the Life of Literature—The True End of Technical Study.

As we pass from individual books to their authors, so by an equally natural transition we pass from an individual author to the age in which he lived, and the nation to which he belonged. We cannot go far in our study of literature before we realize that it involves the study of the history of literature. A great writer is not an isolated fact. He has his affiliations with the present and the past; and through these affiliations he leads us inevitably to his contemporaries and predecessors, and thus at length to a sense of a national literature as a developing organism having a continuous life of its own, yet passing in the course of its evolution through many varying phases. Thus in our study of literature on the historical side we shall have to consider two things—the continuous life, or national spirit in it; and the varying phases of that continuous life or, the way in which it embodies and expresses the changing spirit of successive ages.

First, what do we mean when we speak of the history of any national literature—of the history of Greek, or French, or English literature? The ordinary textbook may perhaps give us the impression that we mean only a chronological account of the men who wrote in these languages, and of the books they produced, with critical analyses of their merits and defects, and some description of literary schools and traditions, and of fluctuations in fashions and tastes. But in reality we mean much more than this. A nation's literature is not a miscellaneous collection of books which happen to have been written in the same tongue or within a certain geographical area. It is the progressive revelation, age by age, of a such nation's mind and character. An individual writer may vary greatly from the national type, and the variation, as we shall have to insist presently, will always be one of the most interesting things about him. But his genius will still partake of the characteristic spirit of his race, and in any number of representative writers at any given time, that spirit will be felt as a well-defined quality pervading them all.

We talk of the Greek spirit and the Hebrew spirit. By this we do not of course suggest that all Greeks thought and felt in the same way, that all Hebrews thought and felt in the same way. We simply mean that, when all differences as between man and man have been cancelled, there remains in each case a clearly recognised substratum of racial character, a certain broad element common to all Greeks as Greeks, and to all Hebrews as Hebrews. It is in this sense that we speak of the Hebrew and the Hellenic views of life, and compare and contrast them with one another. Now, as such

common qualities are most fully expressed in the literatures of the
two peoples—as Greek literature is the completest revelation of
the mind and character of the Greek race, and Hebrew literature
of the mind and character of the Hebrew race—it is through their
literatures that we really come to know these peoples best, alike in
their strength and in their limitations, and to learn at first hand what
they have contributed to the permanent intellectual and spiritual
possessions of the world.

We travel that we may see other nations at home—their 'cities
of men and manners, climates, councils, governments'; and this we
rightly conceive as an important agency in humane culture. The study
of literature is a form of travel; it enables us to move about freely
among the minds of other races; with this additional advantage that,
as Professor Barrett Wendell has happily said, it gives us the power
of travelling also in time. We become familiar not only with the
minds of other races, but with the minds of other epochs as well.

The history of any nation's literature, then, is the record of the
unfolding of that nation's genius and character under one of its
most important forms of expression. In this way literature becomes
at once a supplement to what we ordinarily call history and a
commentary upon it. History deals mainly with the externals of a
people's civilisation, portrays the outward manner of their existence,
and tells us what they did or failed to do in the practical work
of the world. But it is to their literature that we must turn if we
would understand their mental and moral characteristics, realise what
they sought and achieved in the world of inner activity, and follow
through the stages of their changing fortunes the ebb and flow
of the forces which fed their emotional energies and shaped their
intellectual and spiritual life.

II

We thus come to a singularly interesting and fertile line of
inquiry—the study of the literature of an age as the expression of
its characteristic spirit and ideals.

Even the most casual reader is soon struck by the many qualities exhibited in common by writers belonging to the same time, no matter how widely these may differ among themselves. There is perceptible among them a marked family likeness; or, as Shelley put it, 'a general resemblance under which their specific distinctions are arranged.'[5] We have said that in order to get a clear idea of the salient features of Shakespeare's genius and art it is necessary to compare and contrast him with his fellow playwrights. Though in doing this we shall at first be most strongly impressed by those outstanding elements in his personality which set him altogether apart from men like Marlowe, Jonson, Fletcher, Webster, we shall hardly fail presently to observe also in how many ways he nonetheless resembled them, as they in turn resembled each other. Taking them as a group, and considering alike the matter and texture of their work and its form and spirit, we shall find in them a predominant and unmistakable common note; we shall feel that these Elizabethan dramatists are united by a number of elementary characteristics which sharply distinguish them as a group from the men of Pope's time and the men of Wordsworth's time. It is these group characteristics which we have now to investigate if we would grasp the underlying principles and the historic significance of that large and intensely fascinating body of work which we call roughly the Elizabethan, or, more correctly, the English romantic drama, and if we would see that work in its vital relationships, not with this or that author only—Shakespeare or any other—but with the whole social world out of which it came. Hence, however much Shakespeare himself as a unit may interest us by the distinctive qualities of his individuality, attention to these must not be allowed to blind us to the fact that he too, like his companions and rivals, was after all the product and exponent of a particular phase of civilisation and culture, and that we may get far into the heart of the conditions and tendencies of his time if we devote ourselves to the consideration of the generic as well as to

---

[5]Preface to *Prometheus Unbound*.

the specific aspects of his writings.

Clear as this principle of historical interpretation should be, it may yet be well to illustrate it in a somewhat different way. If we place Pope side by side with Tennyson we shall of course be struck at once by the glaring contrast between the two poets, and our first impulse will probably be to regard this as merely a contrast of personality in the narrowest sense of that word. But as a contrast of personality only it cannot be entirely explained. The writings of both Pope and Tennyson everywhere bear, mingling with their individual qualities, the unmistakable impress of those impersonal forces of their respective epochs which combined to create what we describe as the *Zeitgeist* or Time-spirit of the age of Anne and the Victorian era; and if we should be troubled by any doubt as to the reality and importance of such Time-spirit, it will be dissipated on our observing that precisely where the two poets differ most radically from each other there they often remind us most distinctly of their contemporaries. Apart from all considerations of individual genius and temper, *The Rape of the Lock* could hardly have been born of the age which produced *The Princess*. Pope's mock epic belongs to the days of *The Spectator*, Tennyson's medley to those of Charlotte Brontë's novels and Mrs Browning's *Aurora Leigh*; which means that all the vast and far-reaching changes in the thought of a hundred years concerning women and their place in society and on many other matters, have to be taken into account in estimating the difference between two works which thus regarded become broadly typical of much beyond the individual poets' characters and intentions. In the same way, the *Essay on Man* and *In Memoriam* express the mood and speculation, the one of an epoch of facile and superficial optimism, the other of an epoch of heart-searching doubt and spiritual struggle, quite as clearly as they set forth respectively the thoughts and feelings of the poet-philosophers themselves. Once more, the contrast between Tennyson's intense love of nature and the conspicuous absence of any signs of such love in the town poetry of Pope is one that has to be interpreted on a wider basis than that furnished by any consideration of mere personal differences of taste and temper. It is a contrast which will be found to hold good as between all the poets of Tennyson's time as a class and all the poets of Pope's time as a class. The deep feeling for nature which is one of the most marked characteristics of our nineteenth century poetry as a whole is evidently, then, in large measure the product of a changing Time-spirit working more or less uniformly on many different minds, and tending at this point to bring them into a certain substantial harmony with one another.

As there is a common racial character in the literary productions of any given people, so therefore there is a common time character in the literary productions of such people at any given period. A nation's life has its moods of exultation and depression; its epochs now of strong faith and strenuous idealism, now of doubt, struggle, and disillusion, now of unbelief and flippant disregard for the sanctities of existence; and while the manner of expression will vary greatly with the individuality of each writer, the dominant spirit of the hour, whatever that may be, will directly or indirectly reveal itself in his work; since every man, according to Goethe's dictum, is a citizen of his age as well as of his country, and since, as Renan put it, 'one belongs to one's century and race even when one reacts against one's century and race.'

Thus, when we speak of periods of literature—of the literature of the age of Pericles or Augustus, of Louis XIV or the Revolution, of Elizabeth or Anne or Victoria—we have in mind something far more important than the establishment of such chronological divisions as may be arbitrarily made for the sake of mere convenience. Such phrases really refer to differential characteristics—to those distinctive qualities of theme, treatment, manner, spirit, tone, by which the literature of each period as a whole is marked, which are more or less pronounced in all the writers of that period, and by virtue of which these writers, despite their individual differences, stand together as a group in contrast with the groups formed by the writers of other periods.

We have, therefore, to study the literature of an age, as we study the writings of each separate author, as a great body of work expressing a common spirit under many diverse individual forms. We may of course do this, after the habit of many historians of literature, by looking no further than literature itself. Our chief object will then be to investigate the origin, growth, and decay of literary fashions and tastes, the formation of schools, the rise and fall of critical standards and ideals, the influence of particular men in initiating fresh tendencies and giving a new direction to literature, and so on; meanwhile keeping strictly to the literary phenomena themselves, and conceiving of these as explicable by reference only to such forces as lie within the field of literary activity. Of this narrower method of treatment I shall have something more to say presently. But those who care pre-eminently for the life which is in literature will scarcely be content to rest at this point of view. They will rather press on to examine the connection of the literature of the period under consideration with all the motive forces at work outside literature in the society of the time. If we ask, for example, why did our English writers produce and English readers enjoy, at the end of the sixteenth century, *The Faery Queens*, at the end of the seventeenth, *The Hind and the Panther*, at the end of the eighteenth, the poems of Burns and Cowper? or, Why did the age of Shakespeare find its main artistic outlet in the drama, and what were the causes which combined in the eighteenth century to bring about the decline of the drama and the rise of the modern form of prose fiction? or, How are we to account for the general coldness and aridity of the literature of Pope's time, and for the strong and often stormy passion which swept into poetry with the development of what we call Romanticism?, then we have to seek our answers in considerations which carry us far beyond all questions of literary taste and critical theories. The historian of literature may indeed object that with all these remoter problems he, as a student simply of literature, has really nothing to do; that his business is entirely with books as he finds them, and with such forces as lie, as I have put it, within the field of literary activity. We need not quarrel with those who take up such a position; rather, we may gladly allow them to do their own work in their own way, while we ourselves profit to the fullest extent by the results. At the same time we have to insist that the domain of literature cannot permanently be thus isolated, and that really to understand literature we have continually to get out of literature into the, life by which it is fed. As behind every book that is written lies the personality of the man who wrote it, and as behind every national literature lies the character of the race which produced it, so behind the literature of any period lie the combined forces—personal and impersonal—which made the life of that period, as a whole, what it was.

Literature is only one of the many channels in which the energy of an age discharges itself; in its political movements, religious thought, philosophical speculation, art, we have the same energy overflowing into other forms of expression. The study of English literature, for example, will thus take us out into the wide field of English history, by which we mean the history of English politics and society, manners and customs, culture and learning, and philosophy and religion. However, diverse the characteristics which make up the sum total of the life of an epoch, these, like the qualities which combine in an individual, are not, as Taine puts it, merely 'juxta-posed'; they are interrelated and interdependent. Our aim must therefore be to correlate the literature of any age we may take for consideration with all the other important aspects of the national activity of the time. In doing this we must of course remember that the age in question grew out of that which preceded it; that its own spirit and ideals were never fixed or settled, but were on the contrary in a continuous process of transformation; and, above all, that many different and often conflicting tendencies (some arising in natural reaction against others) are always to be found at work together in the civilisation of any period. This means that we have not only to investigate the literature of any given moment in connection with the then existing state of society, but have also to follow the movements of literature in their connection with contemporaneous movements and crosscurrents in other regions of life and thought.

Thus—to take a single illustration only, and this from a field which lies very near to the sympathies of every reader—the literature of the Victorian era, marvellously rich as it is in the range and variety of its purely personal interests, will gain immensely in significance and value if we study it in detail in its relations with the many-sided life and activities, with all the great intellectual and social movements and countermovements, of Victorian England—with the growth of democracy, humanitarianism, and the zeal for reform; with the enormous progress of science, and the profound disturbance of thought produced by this; with the immense industrial changes brought about in large part by the application of science to practical life; with the resultant struggle between materialism and idealism, upon both the theoretical and the practical sides; with the art revival; with the development of the romantic spirit prompting men to seek an imaginative escape into the past; with the later blending of this romantic spirit with the spirit of reform; and so on. Thus studied, Victorian literature, while never for a moment ceasing to appeal to us as the varied product of many different minds working independently upon the most divergent lines, will be found to exhibit fresh depths of interest and meaning as a revelation of the thoughts and feelings, the aspirations and ideals, the doubts and struggles, the faith and hope, of a great, intense, complex, and turbulent period of our history.

III

From my thus emphasising the immediate and necessary connection between the literature of an age and the general life out of which it grows, it may be inferred that I am to a certain extent following the lead of Taine, who attempted to interpret literature in a rigorously scientific way by the application of his famous formula of the race, the *milieu*, and the moment; meaning by race, the hereditary temperament and disposition of a people; by *milieu*, the totality of their surroundings, their climate, physical environment, political institutions, social conditions, and the like; and by moment, the spirit of the period, or of that particular stage of national development which has been reached at any given time. I must, however, hasten to add that I am no disciple of the brilliant French theorist. Suggestive as his method may be when employed carefully and with a full sense of its limitations, it is still clear that it breaks down completely at several important points. I do not now dwell upon the fact, which must be patent to every reader who takes up his *Literary History of the English People*, that Taine's interest is in reality not in literature as literature, but in literature as a document in the history of national psychology, and that thus, sub-ordinating as he does the study of literature to the study of society, he necessarily approaches the problem of their relationship from a point of view and with a purpose quite different from our own. Setting this consideration aside, I shall content myself with indicating two conspicuous defects of his method as it directly concerns the student of literature itself.

According to Taine's theory, all the individuals of a nation at any particular time are to be regarded simply as the products of the three great impersonal forces which he evokes to account for them; and thus the study of any author is reduced by him to an examination of the manner in which his genius and work express the combined action of the influences which play upon him in common with all his fellow countrymen and contemporaries. The initial error in this view, and it is one that goes far to vitiate it entirely, is its neglect of that essential factor of all really great literature upon which I have already laid so much stress—the factor of personality. In Taine's hands, the individual becomes little more than a sample of his race and epoch. Thus he practically overlooks the individual variation, or the qualities which differentiate a man from his surroundings; and this is a fatal mistake, since the greater the genius, the greater and the more important the individual variation, the differential qualities, are likely to be. It is the minor men of an age in whose work the general spirit of that age is most faithfully reflected, and by which it is transmitted with the least amount of personal colouring; a fact which shows that from the historical point of view these minor men will always have a special interest of their own. The strong man is most himself, is most independent of current influences, and it is in its application to his work, therefore, that the scientific formula will leave most unexplained. 'It has been said that the man of genius sometimes is such in virtue of combining the temperament distinctive of his nation with some gift of his own which is foreign to that temperament; as in Shakespeare, the basis is English, and the individual gift a flexibility of spirit which is not normally English.'[6]

So with the man of genius and the spirit of his time; we must make the fullest allowance for the individual gift, the marked and exceptional personal quality, which combines in him with the common characteristics of the world to which he belongs; and unless we do this—unless, in other words, we lay hold of precisely those features of his genius which are not to be accounted for by any reference to his race, surroundings, and period—we shall misunderstand him altogether. In the historic study of literature, then, we are quite as much concerned with variations from the predominant type as with the type itself. After investigating in the greatest detail the way in which the forces of an age entered as formative factors into the personality of any great writer, and helped to give direction and tone to his work, we are still brought back to that which no formula will elucidate, and no analysis explain—the original, mysterious, incommunicable element of personal genius itself. This we must be content to take as we find it; and however wide the lines of our subsequent inquiry, it is from this that we have to set out as our datum and point of departure.

In one other most important respect Taine's theory must be pronounced unsatisfactory. Neglecting the individual, he naturally neglects personality as an originating force. He notes the manner in which the age affects the author; the manner in which the author

[6]Jebb, *Classical Greek History*, p. 29.

affects the age he does not note. But the relation of literature and life is a double-sided relation; while the work of a great author is fed by the combined influences of his epoch, it enters again into that epoch as one of its most potent seminal elements. If we cannot understand Victorian literature unless we connect it with the large social and intellectual movements of Victorian civilisation, neither can we understand these movements themselves unless we realise how they were stimulated, or guided, or checked, by contemporary literature. The names of Tennyson and Browning, of Carlyle, and Ruskin, and Dickens—to take the most prominent examples only—are the names of men who counted enormously in the development of the Time-spirit of the world in which they lived. In our own study, therefore, we must be careful to keep this double-sided relationship always in view. We must regard the great writer as the creator as well as the creature of his time, and while keen to appreciate what the age gave to him, we must be equally solicitous to discover what in turn he gave to the age.

It is evident, then, that Taine's attempt to write the *Literary History of the English People* on the basis of a formula in which the fundamental element of individuality is practically ignored, was necessarily foredoomed to failure, and that, in the nature of things, no such scientific treatment of literary facts and problems can be other than disappointing, at any rate for the student of literature. It remains for us nonetheless to insist on the great interest and importance of the study of literature as literature on the sociological side. It is sometimes felt that to take literature in this way is to destroy our personal sense of the life in it; that when we adopt the historical method, great books, instead of being enjoyed as expressions of individual thought and feeling and master- pieces of art, come to be regarded rather as specimens to be analysed with critical disinterestedness, or classified and ticketed like the bones of dead animals in a museum of anatomy. One may well be pardoned for sympathising with such a misgiving. At the same time it should now be apparent that it is really founded upon a mistaken idea of the historic method and its results. To relate literature to the whole world of varied activity of which it is one expression, is not to destroy its living interest, but to make that interest broader and deeper; without ceasing to be essentially individual, literature thus comes to be more comprehensively human, as a record of the life of man as well as of the lives of men.

Moreover, by realizing the relativity of literature we gain a point of view from which every aspect of literary art becomes quickened for us into fresh significance. Henceforth we need not find any period of literary history wholly wanting in the quality of life. Much of the literature of the past must, on our first approach to it, necessarily seem to us both dull and unattractive—matter for the specialist, not for the general student. Thoughts, feelings, ideals change; the fashion of their utterance changes likewise; chasms yawn between us and bygone generations; and many a book which once held its readers spellbound seems a vapid and futile thing to us who belong to another age, and are touched by other modes of passion and other manners of speech. Our textbook writers and professional critics seldom acknowledge this, and by their failure to do so they often discourage young and untried students, who are apt to feel that their own inability to take a vital and personal interest in many books which figure prominently in the annals of literature is entirely due to some radical defect in themselves. This is not necessarily so. Of even the greater books of the past there are comparatively few which have not suffered more or less seriously, while all but the very greatest have suffered much, from the changes which are ever going on in life, fashion, taste; and it is at once idle and unwise to attempt to deny this fact or to shirk its obvious implications. But it is precisely here that the value of what we call the historic or sociological study of literature should become apparent. When we take up the historic point of view, we can carry every book, even the dullest, back into the life out of which it originally grew; we can place ourselves to some extent in the relations of its first readers with it; and the result is that the rich lifeblood of humanity begins to flow once more through its long dead pages. Forms of art, which to us are simply archaic—subjects and methods which can never now be revived—suddenly become of interest. If only as a record of what men once found potent to move, charm, console, inspire—if only as an example of what once seemed beautiful and engaging to them—literature which we might otherwise pass over as hopelessly deficient in every element of appeal reveals itself as worthy of close and sympathetic attention. It will live again for us if only by virtue of the life which was once in it.

IV

The comparative method, the importance of which in the study of individual authors has already been recognised, becomes of great service when we are dealing with literature historically; but after what I have said in discussing the relations of literature with the life of the race and age, this aspect of our subject hardly calls for elaboration. No one who passes from the literature of one nation or epoch to that of another nation or epoch will fail to be struck by the complete change in intellectual and moral atmosphere. Now, as the study of literature here as elsewhere means an effort to define and correlate phenomena which in casual reading we allow to remain vague and unconnected, it will be the business of the student as he pursues his inquiries along these wider lines, to note carefully and to formulate those fundamental differences which are frequently obscured by our paramount interest in individual authors, or are at most simply taken for granted. He will thus be led, for example, to consider the various ways in which the large, permanent themes of literature—love, hatred, jealousy, ambition, men's common joys and sorrows, the problems of life and destiny which were already old when literature began, and are as new as ever today—are taken up and handled, not merely by different great writers, but also by different peoples and at different times. He will observe how now one subject and now another comes to the front, and for a while holds the chief place in story and song, and he will investigate the causes of such ebb and flow of interest. He will mark the changes in temper, tone, emphasis, perspective, as he follows the same motive through its various forms of expression; the motive, say, of the love of man and woman, from Greek tragedy to mediæval romance, from the drama of the age of Shakespeare to that of the Restoration, from the prose fiction of the eighteenth to that of the nineteenth century, from the English novel to that of contemporary France. And discovering, moreover, that now one vehicle of expression and now another is for a time in the ascendant, he will endeavour to trace the history of the transformation and alternation of the great literary forms—such as the lyric, the drama, the novel—under changing conditions and in response to shifting conceptions of literary art, as they are freshly shaped to ever-varying uses by the masters of different nations and of different periods.

In his exploration of the vast field of study thus opened up—a field, it is clear, of almost inexhaustible interest—the reader will find one special line of inquiry particularly worthy of his attention.

Even if, our interest in literature being of the most narrowly personal kind, we set out with the purpose of confining ourselves to the writings of a single favourite author, we are certain sooner or later to discover that we shall never properly understand such author if we remain obstinately within the limits of his own personality and work. We are repeatedly reminded by him of the influence exerted upon his thought and style by the thought and style of other men, and to estimate him rightly we have to take account of such influence, to consider its sources, range, and significance, and to measure its extent for good or evil. And if, recognising the personal forces which helped to shape his character and art, we turn, as presently we shall of necessity be led to turn, to the question of his influence upon the thought and style of others, we shall come to see that our study of individual authors involves us everywhere in the study of the power exercised by mind upon mind. In precisely the same way, in the general evolution of literature, will the genius of one race or age be found to have influenced—sometimes slightly, sometimes to the extent of turning it aside from its natural course of development, and of almost destroying for a season its essential characteristics—the genius of another race or age; and thus, in our reading of the history of literature, we cannot go far before we find ourselves committed to the consideration of the various tributary streams, small or great, by which the literature of each country and each generation has been fed.

Even the briefest textbook of the literary history of Italy, France, or England, will tell us something of the enormous changes wrought during the period of the revival of learning by the enthusiastic study of the classics, which not only furnished artistic inspiration and set fresh models and standards of taste, but, by bringing men into living contact with the genius of Greece and Rome, and with a world of thought, feeling, and ideals, which was then entirely new to them, did much to emancipate their minds from the trammels of effete dogmatism, and to break up the intellectual and religious fabric of the Middle Ages. A fact of chief importance then in the genesis of the modern spirit and of modern literatures at the time of the Renaissance, this influence of pagan antiquity alike on form and on thought has to be followed through all their later developments as a constituent agency, varying greatly in the extent and intensity of its power, and in the modes of its manifestation, but never wholly lost; and thus the student of the history of literature has to inquire where and when it has been in the ascendant, and when and where it has waned. To seek the causes of these fluctuations, and to consider how far, at different epochs, classicism has proved fruitful of good by stimulating original activity and leading men to higher conceptions of art, and how far it has been detrimental by paralysing individual genius and turning literature into bypaths of pedantic theory and lifeless imitation.

Here, then, in one of the most familiar facts in the history of modern literatures we have an illustration of the profound influence exerted by the genius and art of one race upon those of other races.[7]

---

[7]For the sake of brevity I refer to the literatures of classical antiquity as if they constituted a single body of work, similar in character and of equal importance.

Another example is furnished by the interchange of influence during something like a century and a half, first between the literatures of France and England, and then between the literatures of England and Germany. Soon after the middle of the seventeenth century a variety of circumstances, political and other, combined to bring English genius under the sway of the genius of France. Thus we enter upon what the historian of our literature is accustomed to describe as the period of French influence. 'Until the time of Charles I,' English literature, 'in so far as it owed anything to external patterns of modern date, had been chiefly dependent upon Italy.' (The importance of Italian culture and art as a force in the English literature of the Renaissance is not, it may be said in passing, quite adequately recognised in this sentence.) 'This might have long continued but for the decay of Italian letters consequent upon the triumph of foreign oppression and spiritual despotism throughout the peninsula. France stepped into the vacant place....Ere long French ideas of style had pervaded Europe, and approximation to French modes was the inevitable qualification for the great mission of human enlightenment which was to devolve upon Britain in the succeeding century.'[8] Thus 'the dominant foreign influence on our literature, through the great part of the eighteenth century, was certainly French. By this declaration is not at all meant

To guard against misapprehension I should add that this is of course only a conventional and quite uncritical fashion of speech. One of the great mistakes in theory and practice down to comparatively recent times—as in the age of Boileau in France and in the age of Pope in England—has been the confusion of the original literature of Greece with the merely derivative and second-hand literature of Rome, and the consequent exaggeration of the claims of the latter. The 'classic' periods, so called, of all modern literatures show the fatal results of this error. In such periods the immediate source of inspiration has always been the literature of Rome; little has been known of Greek culture, and that little has come mainly through the medium of the Latins. Hence the discovery of the secret of true Hellenism in the second half of the eighteenth century helped greatly, in the hands of such men as Lessing, to destroy the tyranny of pseudo-classicism, and to proclaim the gospel of originality against imitation in literary art.

[8]Garnett, *The Age of Dryden*, p. 3.

that we did nothing but ape and imitate the French classics, though they were translated, or in some way, reproduced often enough. What is meant is that the direction and tone of our literature were to a large extent imparted by France, then, and just before then, at the height of its literary glory. Pope's work is thoroughly his own, and not to be confounded with that of anybody else at home or abroad; but in many respects that work would have been different had not Boileau, for instance, preceded him. And so elsewhere we see deeply impressed the influence of Racine, Voltaire, Rousseau.'[9] Here, in the ascendency of this French influence, we put our finger, as any historian of literature will tell us, upon one of the principal causes of the extraordinary transformation which English literature then underwent in matter, spirit, and style; and the English literature of the later seventeenth and earlier eighteenth centuries cannot therefore be understood without constant reference to the literature of France. But by the time we reach Voltaire and Rousseau (here classed as a French writer), we become aware of a fact not touched upon in the above quotation, but of very great significance for students of both French and English literatures—that another current of influence was now flowing fast and strong in a reverse direction, or from England into France. A period of pronounced Anglomania had begun, and the French mind was now busy absorbing English ideas and speculations on many subjects—on religion, philosophy, society, politics, and even the forms of literature. Voltaire's three years of exile in England are rightly described by Condorcet as of European importance, because it was by this direct contact with English life and thought that his spirit was first awakened to a sense of his mission as the apostle of intellectual liberty. 'Voltairism may be said to have begun from the flight of its founder from Paris to London. This...was the decisive hegira, from which the philosophy of destruction in a formal shape may be held seriously to date.'[10] Rousseau and Diderot alike derived much of their philosophy from thinkers like Locke, and of their literary

---

[9]J.W. Hales, *Folia Litteraria*, pp. 294, 295.
[10]John Morley, Voltaire, p. 44.

inspiration from such men as Richardson and Lillo, and from the whole domestic movement in English letters which these represented. And among the other great French writers of the period preceding the Revolution hardly one could be named whose work does not exhibit the most unmistakable evidence of his profound indebtedness to England. English literature was, in fact, as Hettner has said,[11] the real starting-point of the whole European movement of enlightenment in the eighteenth century and of the literature to which this movement gave birth. It was through their French interpreters, indeed, that English ideas became European and practically effective.[12] But if we are to follow the history of the revolutionary movement at large on the intellectual side, and of the rise and spread of revolutionary ideas and of the revolutionary spirit in literature, it is with England and English writers that we have to begin. Thus in the literatures of France and England from the middle of the seventeenth century to the close of the eighteenth, we shall find a continual revelation of the influence exerted, now on this side and now on that, by one national genius upon another; and thus, for the full comprehension of either French or English literature during this period, it is evident that they must be studied together.

Equally interesting will be the inquiry into the literary relations of England and Germany in the second half of the eighteenth century, particularly in respect of their reciprocal influences in the development of Romanticism. Here, in the first place, we shall have to note that, as men like Bodmer and Leasing will show us, English literature was a main power in the emancipation of Germany from

---

[11] *Literaturgeschichte des achtzehnten Jahrhunderts*, p. 9.

[12] "The literature of France has been to England what Aaron was to Moses, the expositor of great truths, which would else have perished for want of a voice to utter them with distinctness....The great discoveries in physics, in metaphysics, in political science, are ours. But scarcely any foreign nation except France has received them from us by direct communication. Isolated in our situation, isolated by our manners, we found truth, but we did not impart it. France has been the interpreter between England and mankind. In the time of Walpole, this process of interpretation was in full activity.'—Macaulay, *Essay on Walpole*.

AN INTRODUCTION TO THE STUDY OF LITERATURE ✧ 43

the long tyranny of French modes and of pseudo-classicism, and
thus in turning German genius inward upon itself and in preparing
the way for the rise of a truly national literature. Then we enter
upon a period of rapidly developing Romanticism, during which
the wild enthusiasm of 'young Germany' for those English writers
who had already caught up and expressed the romantic spirit is
everywhere felt as a predominant force. I am not now writing the
history of English influence upon German literature at this time,
but am simply trying to exhibit the interest of this history; and it
will therefore be quite enough for my purpose if I point out how
Percy's *Reliques of Ancient English Poetry* stimulated the study of folk-
poetry and the preference for the natural to the artificial in verse,
and how, inspired by them, Bürger wrote his ballads and Herder
produced his *Stimmen der Völker*, and formulated his theory of the
essential superiority of 'popular' poetry to all the productions of
refinement and art; how Mac-pherson's *Ossian* fired the imagination
with grandiose visions of a past world which had known nothing of
the petty conventions and restraints of 'civilization,' and thus gave a
fresh impetus to the movement for a 'return to nature' initiated by
Rousseau; how Shakespeare became the god of the idolatry of those
who had cast down the graven images of the artificial drama, was
proclaimed by Lessing as a new standard of dramatic art, and taken
by Goethe and Schiller as model and master. These few illustrations
will suffice to exemplify the extraordinary sway of English literature
in the earlier stages of developing German Romanticism. But ere
long the counter-current set in, and Germany began to return with
interest what she had borrowed from England. 'Whatever Germany
owed to us at that time of its so splendid regeneration,' writes Prof.
Hales, 'it repaid us, and still repays us, good measure, pressed down
and shaken together, and running over'; and a part reason for this
is indicated in the fact that 'the German impulse harmonised with
impulses that were already permeating England, and to these it gave
a stronger force and more successful action.'[13] Much of the influence

---

[13]*Folia Litteraria*, p. 296.

which the great English romantic writers derived directly from their
English predecessors was thus combined with the influences which
came originally from the same sources, but were now transmitted
to them by those Germans who had first been inspired by English
masters; as in the case of Scott, whose poetic genius was aroused both
by Percy's *Reliques* and by the ballads which Bürger had written under
the impulse of Percy, and whose novels are in part to be traced to
Goethe's *Goetz von Berlichingen*, itself an offspring of Shakespearean
enthusiasm. Hence, if English genius was an important factor in
the development of romantic German literature, German genius in
its turn was an important factor in the development of romantic
English literature; and to trace out the interplay of influences, to
estimate the value of the lendings and the borrowings between the
two peoples, would evidently prove a line of inquiry rich in interest
and fruitful of results.

Less important than the influence of one nation's genius upon
another, but still important, is that which from time to time is exerted
on the themes, temper, and fashions of literature by the genius of
some past age. This has already been exemplified by what has been
said about the influence of pagan antiquity, which might indeed
have been treated under the present head. Apart from this, the most
interesting illustration of the phenomenon in question is undoubtedly
the imaginative revival of the 'romantic' past, which began, roughly
speaking, about the middle of the eighteenth century, and the power
of which, though it reached its culmination and partly spent itself
in the great romantic outburst of the first three decades of the
nineteenth century, has still been conspicuous in nearly all European
literatures ever since. For something like a hundred and fifty years,
and especially during what is often termed the 'Augustan' period
of literature, general critical taste in England, largely moulded, as
we have said, on the principles of the dominant French or pseudo-
classic school, was in revolt against the whole spirit and method of
pre-Restoration literature. So little affinity was there between the
temper and ideals of the early eighteenth century and those of the

Elizabethan epoch or the Middle Ages that men for the most part turned away contemptuously from Chaucer and Spenser, treated Shakespeare as a rude genius totally wanting in refinement and art, and found in the word 'gothic,' which they used as synonymous with barbarous, a term of sweeping condemnation for whatever failed to satisfy the requirements of their new creed. The change from the temper thus revealed to that of the romantic period, with its enthusiastic admiration for precisely those gothic qualities which had formerly been spurned or ridiculed, was not, as I have already insisted, a change only in literary taste; it was correlated, as part cause and part effect, with various broad and comprehensive movements in life at large and with a general change in men's attitude to things. But in literature itself it was marked, among other ways, by a number of revivals—the revival of Spenser, the revival of Shakespeare, the revival of the old ballads—and by a return of the imagination to the Middle Ages with their romance, their chivalrous idealism, their supernaturalism. Classic antiquity had been reborn in the fifteenth century; the Middle Ages were reborn in the eighteenth. And so large a place does this mediæval or gothic Renaissance fill in the history of Romanticism from the time of Walpole, Chatterton, and Percy to that of Coleridge and Scott, and onward again to Ruskin, Rossetti, the Pre-Raphaelites, and William Morris, that historians of literature and art often confound the two, and treat mediævalism not only as a large feature of Romanticism, but even as entirely synonymous and coextensive with it. This is indeed a mistake; but the fact that it is so frequently and so naturally made serves to bring out the only points with which we are now concerned—the influence of the genius of the Middle Ages as expressed in their poetry, art, and religion, in some of the most important developments of modern literature, and the wide interest which this subject therefore possesses as a special theme for study.

V

Yet one other aspect of the historical study of literature may be indicated—the historical study of style. This is perhaps too technical a line of inquiry to appear at the outset very attractive to any but the specialist, but the general student may still be encouraged to give it some attention, since he will soon find that it has its broader as well as its more purely technical interest. On the principle already laid down that style, properly conceived, is not an accidental or arbitrary feature of literature, but an organic product of vital forces, some consideration of the larger movements of style from age to age, and of their significance, of the causes, literary and extra-literary, which have combined to bring them about, and of their connection with corresponding changes in the inner life of literature, will come to constitute an almost necessary part of our study of the literature of any given period. Whatever affects the inner life of literature will both directly and indirectly affect at the same time that outer organism which the inner life fashions for its manifestations. Thus, in the way in which he expresses himself no less than in what he has to express, every individual author will betray something of his affiliations with his age; and the form of his work, like the substance and tone of it, will, however personal to himself, find its place in the history of those comprehensive movements which, diversely as they may be represented in the writings of different men, are movements nevertheless in which they are all involved. In what has been said about style as an index of personality, all this has indeed been implied. To insist that Carlyle could never have written as he did had he been born into the age of Addison, that his prose is of the 'romantic,' not of the 'classic' kind, that it everywhere bears the unmistakable impress of those German influences of which we have recently spoken, is to indulge in mere commonplaces of criticism. But if these are facts too familiar to need elaborate restatement, their meaning must not be obscured by their familiarity. They show us that, individual as it is to the point of extra-vagance and mannerism, Carlyle's style does not wholly defy classification or stand outside the lines of historic development, but that, on the contrary, it was in part a product of the forces of his time and place and has to be considered therefore in its relations with them.

In order to bring out the larger interest of the historic study of style, I will suggest an illustration which, I think, should appeal even to students who may care little for details of mere technique. It is usual, as a glance at any textbook will tell us, to take the Restoration as the starting point of an entirely new order of things in the formal evolution of our prose literature. 'The Restoration,' as Matthew Arnold puts it, 'marks the real moment of birth of our modern English prose. It is by its organism—an organism opposed to length and involvement, and enabling us to be clear, plain, and short—that English prose after the Restoration breaks with the style of the times preceding it, finds the true law of prose, and becomes modern; becomes, in spite of superficial differences, the style of our own day.' That this statement, while in certain respects a little too emphatic and uncompromising, is still substantially correct, any reader can readily convince himself by comparing a page out of Hooker, or Clarendon, or Milton's *Areopagitica*, with a page out of Dryden, or Defoe, or Addison. The writing of the men of the latter group will strike him at once as characteristically modern; in structural principles, theirs is the kind of prose we still use; occasional archaisms will not prevent us from recognising that our own style stands in the direct line of descent from it. The prose of the earlier writers mentioned, on the other hand, is, it will be equally obvious, not our prose at all; often splendid in diction and various in its harmonies, it is for our taste altogether too cumbrous, unwieldy, and involved; it is manifestly built upon structural principles radically different from those which form the basis of our own prose writing.

Now, how are we to interpret this transformation of prose style in the period of its great metamorphosis? how explain substitution of the new prose which was rapidly taking shape in the closing decades of the seventeenth century for the old prose which had hitherto remained in almost undisputed possession of the field? It seems a much easier and more natural thing to write in the style of Addison than in the style of Milton, because Addison's prose is

the artistic development of real speech, while Milton's is scarcely
nearer to real speech than is his blank verse, and is in fact at its best
when in his own phrase it 'soars a little' into the higher regions of
eloquence and imagination. Why was it that the secret of naturalness
and simplicity had thus far eluded our greatest masters? and why
did it become an open secret, free to even the smallest men, in
the generation immediately following Milton's death? Well, the
history of the formation and establishment of the new prose after
the Restoration will, as we shall soon discover, carry us far afield
into the consideration of many co-operating causes, some of them
at first sight too remote from the question in hand to have had
any bearings upon it; among which may be mentioned, by way
of illustration:—the change from the poetic to the critical temper,
which was one of the most noteworthy characteristics of the time;
the spread of the spirit of common sense, of the love of definiteness
and perspicacity, and of the hatred of the pedantic and obscure; the
growth of science which greatly aided the general movement towards
precision and lucidity;[14] the eminently practical purposes to which
prose was now largely turned as an instrument of argument, persuasion,
satire, in an age of unceasing political and religious controversy; the
rise of a larger and more miscellaneous public to be addressed, and
of the resulting influence of the general reader, of women, of the
coffeehouse and the drawing-room; the desire for the de-specialisation
and popularisation of knowledge; the demand which thus grew up
for that kind of writing which could be easily produced to meet
the interests of the hour and as easily understood and enjoyed by

---

[14]Sprat pointed out how the Royal Society (incorporated by charter from
Charles II in 1662) had directly affected English style by exacting 'from all their
members a close, naked, natural way of speaking; positive expressions; clear senses;
a native easiness; bringing all things as near the mathematical plainness as they
can' (*History of the Royal Society*). That, under the influence of the critical spirit
of the time, much attention was now given to details of style is well illustrated
by the formation of a Committee, of which Dryden, Cowley, Sprat, and Waller
were members, 'to settle the language after the fashion of the French Academy.'

those for whom it was intended; the consequent output of a mass of pamphlets and of periodical literature in which the element of journalism and the pen of the ready writer are everywhere apparent; and—a point already noted—the influence of France, whose prose furnished to those who were thus prepared to appreciate its virtues and receive its guidance, an established model of just the qualities they were now most anxious to seek—ease, lucidity, sobriety, grace.[15]

It is manifest, therefore, that the great changes which our prose underwent during the ages of Dryden and Addison, and which had their parallels in analogous changes in the texture and form of verse, are to be understood only when they are studied in their connection with contemporary changes in the inner life of literature and with the whole complex of forces by which these were brought about. And similarly, if, passing from the early eighteenth to the early nineteenth century, we observe that a strong reaction had now set in against the limitations of the classic tradition in style—that in the hands of men like Wilson and De Quincey, and later, Carlyle and Ruskin, prose sought a freer movement, fuller harmonies, greater richness, warmth, and colour; then the development of this 'romantic' prose is once more to be considered in relation with the evolution of literature in general—that is, with the romantic movement in all

---

[15]Schlosser notes the importance of the fact that the writers of the early eighteenth century 'began to work for a very different public from that of their predecessors. They attempted to make easy, pleasant, and accessible all that had previously been regarded as serious, difficult, and unattainable' (History of the Eighteenth Century, I. 26). Addison, it will be remembered, was 'ambitious to have it said of ' him 'that he had brought philosophy out of closets and libraries, schools and colleges, to dwell in clubs and assemblies, at tea-tables and coffee-houses' (Spectator, No. 10). The hatred of narrow specialism—of pedantry, as it was currently called— which pervades much of the literature of the time, is directly expressed in the Memoirs of Martinus Scriblerus, in parts of Gulliver's Travels, and in many passages in The Dunciad; the other side of it is illustrated in such attempts at the popular treatment of things hitherto handled scholastically as will be found in Pope's Essay on Criticism, Essay on Man, and 'drawing-room' version of Homer. The general effect of all this on prose style will be evident.

its varied phases, and with the many streams of influence by which
this was fed. Much, of course, might be added to this point. But
enough has, I think, been said to make good my contention that
the historic study of style, thus broadly conceived, like the personal
study of it, has plenty to interest the reader for whom the ordinary
study of rhetoric would be barren of attraction.

VI

In the foregoing pages I have tried to indicate some of the main
lines of literary study, taking what seems to me the natural course,
by beginning with the primary interest of literature, which is the
personal interest, and working from that into the wider fields of
social and historical inquiry. But though we have followed our subject
as it branches out in various directions, our business has thus far
been expressly limited to the content and interpretative power of
literature—to the thought and feeling embodied in it, and to its
many-sided relationship with life; and even when we have paused
to deal with questions of style, it has been with style in its general,
and not in its technical, aspects. It remains for us now to touch
upon the interest which literature possesses when approached from
an entirely different point of view.

One essential characteristic of any piece of literature is, as we said
at the outset, that, whatever its theme, it yields æsthetic pleasure by
the manner in which such theme is handled. Beyond its intellectual
and emotional content, therefore, and beyond its fundamental quality
of life, it appeals to us by reason of its form. This means that literature
is a fine art, and that, like all fine arts, it has its own laws and
conditions of workmanship. And as these laws and conditions, like
the laws and conditions of all arts, may be analysed and formulated,
one other phase of literary study is obviously the study of literary
technique.

It is of course no part of our purpose here to attempt the task
of analysis and formulation. All that falls within the proper limits of
our plan is to suggest some lines of investigation in this new and

vast region of inquiry.

Our point of departure is the broad fact that whatever connects itself with workmanship—with method and treatment, form and style—will now, in the technical study of literature, become of interest for its own sake; as all such details become of interest for their own sakes in the study of other arts.

If, for example, we are studying the plays of Shakespeare, or Spenser's *Faery Queene*, or Tennyson's *Idylls of the King*, or a novel of Dickens or Thackeray, we may for a long while be quite contented to take these works as they stand, and to enjoy them for their human qualities, their power, beauty, and meaning. But there will presently come a time when we shall feel prompted to follow the dramatist, or the poet, or the novelist into his workshop, and to study his work in the making—to watch the processes and examine the methods by which the results we have been enjoying in the completed piece of art were achieved. Every stage in the history of play, poem, or novel, from raw material to finished product, will now come in for scrutiny; we shall observe the conditions under which the given work was wrought; the technical difficulties which the artist had to encounter; the way in which these difficulties were met and the extent to which they were overcome; the effects which he designed to obtain and the measure of his success in obtaining them; and from the consideration of these and other such points we shall pass naturally to a critical judgment upon the qualities of his work as a piece of literature—upon its merits and defects, its power and limitations, when regarded simply as drama, or poem, or novel. We shall thus be led further to inquire into the principles of the arts of drama, poetry, and prose fiction, and to an investigation of the sources, significance, and value of the standards by which these arts have been tried.

Many things, moreover, in any piece of literature which to the ordinary reader may seem of quite secondary importance or which he may even ignore altogether, will now be found to press for attention. Among the first questions, for instance, that will be likely to arise in connection with any work we may take up for technical study is that of its literary genealogy and antecedents. It is open to everyone to enjoy to the full the earlier plays of Shakespeare without troubling himself to consider the condition of the stage at the time they were produced or the dependence of their author upon the guidance of those who had brought the English drama to the point of development which it had reached at the beginning of his career. But Shakespeare's plays are not isolated phenomena, nor was Shakespeare himself (as, owing to our habit of detaching him from his surroundings, we are too apt to assume) a great initiator in dramatic forms and methods. He began to write under the powerful influence of Lyly in comedy and of Marlowe in both tragedy and chronicle drama; and the study of his earlier work thus necessarily involves an inquiry into the extent of his indebtedness to those two writers who, however much he may have bettered their instruction, may without exaggeration be described as his masters in the art of dramatic composition. Again, if we are taking up the study of *Paradise Lost*, we may begin by reading it as the expression of Milton's personality and philosophy of life, and, viewed historically, as the poetic masterpiece of English puritanism. Having so read it, we may next go on to consider its general qualities as a poem—its imaginative power, descriptive power, dramatic power, its merits and defects as a narrative, the splendour and range of its imagery, the majesty, beauty, and variety of its versification; and so on. But instead of finding that these matters exhaust its critical interest, we shall rather discover, sooner or later, that they lead us on to a different class of questions. Milton's poem belongs in plan and structure to a particular and well-defined kind of poetry—to the kind which we call 'epic' poetry; it was written by a man of enormous scholarship who sought to make his own work accord with the technical principles of the great epics of classical antiquity, and who not only adopted these as his models, but also drew continually upon them for various details—incidents, metaphors, similes, turns of speech. *Paradise Lost* has there- fore to be studied as an example of the epic; its plan and composition have to be examined from the standpoint of epic art; it has in particular to be compared with its acknowledged models. Milton's indebtedness to literature in a wider sense has also to be considered—to the Bible, the Greek dramatists, Ariosto, Tasso, Spenser; and while his countless borrowings are duly noted, special attention will have to be paid to the use to which these borrowings are put by 'the greatest of plagiarists,' and to the skill with which he adapts them and so makes them his own. In much the same way we may study with almost equal advantage the genealogy and literary antecedents of such poems as *The Faery Queene* and the *Idylls of the King*.

Of this more technical kind of literary inquiry, the aspects and bearings of which are manifestly too numerous and varied for anything like exhaustive treatment in so brief a survey as ours, one further illustration may be taken from the plays of Shakespeare.

If we are dealing with *King John, Macbeth, Julius Cæsar, Othello, As You Like It*, our first business will of course be with these dramas themselves and as they stand—with the finished products of the master's genius and skill; and if we choose, we may continue to regard them in their completed state only, and to set at nought all questions which would carry us beyond the finished product into considerations of genesis, external history, matter, technique. But when we have once become deeply interested in Shakespeare and his art, we shall certainly find ourselves tempted to give such questions at least a share of our attention. Even in the smallest details of his method—in such recondite problems, for example, as those of his management of the element of dramatic time, and the significance of the alternations of verse and prose in the dialogue of most of his plays—we shall discover something which will repay exploration; while a specially attractive and fertile field of study will be opened up in the comparison of the dramas as we have them with the raw material out of which they were made. Shakespeare, as everyone knows, rarely troubled himself to devise a plot outright, but commonly helped himself freely to such themes and incidents, wherever found, as he felt he could turn to good service. Thus *King John* is a *rifacimento* of an older play, *Macbeth* is based on the narrative of Holinshed's *Chronicles, Julius Cæsar* on Plutarch's lives of Brutus, Cæsar, and Antony, Othello on an Italian novella, *As You Like It* on a prose romance. As in each of these cases Shakespeare worked on the main themes and characters which he had taken over from others, the question of his manipulation of his borrowed subjects is one which it is scarcely possible to avoid. Here and there a reader may perhaps be inclined to object that this question has really nothing to do with the study of Shakespeare himself, and that our real business should be with the plays, with what we have termed the finished products, and not with the details of their composition. But to this objection a twofold answer may be returned. In the first place, the study of Shakespeare's use of his sources—the consideration of what he did with the stories he chose for dramatic treatment, how he adapted them to his own purposes, where he changed, what he omitted, what he added—must be in itself extremely interesting and suggestive, for so we may get very close indeed to the principles which governed his workmanship and the self-imposed laws which he obeyed. And secondly, such a study must, of necessity, throw a flood of fresh light on the plays themselves and therefore increase greatly our intelligent enjoyment of them. To follow Shakespeare in his transformation—often little less than miraculous—of the rough material on which he worked, to note the results of his humanising touch upon it, to be led in this way to appreciate his psychological insight and his technical skill; all this is not merely to gratify our curiosity in regard to questions which might just as well be left alone, and it is certainly not to be misled from the true highway of literary study into narrow bypaths of pedantic investigation. It is one of the best of all possible helps to the real comprehension of Shakespeare's greatness, and therefore one of the best of all possible ways to get into vital contact with the essential principles of his art.

Twice already we have spoken of the study of style, dealing with its interest first on the personal side and then on the historical side. We have now to add that there is a third way in which style may be studied and to which we are brought round by the view of literature as an art, which we are now emphasising—the technical or rhetorical way. That this way will have much attraction for the general student of literature in contradistinction to the rhetorical specialist, I do not suggest. Yet even for the general student it should not be without its value. Experts, leaving out of the discussion all question of that purely personal quality which, as we conceive it, is fundamental, have drawn up for us various lists of the elements which should combine in the making of a good style. There are the intellectual elements—the precision which arises from the right use of the right words; the lucidity which results from the proper disposition of such proper words in the formation of sentences; propriety, or the harmony which should exist between the thing said and the phrasing of it; and so on. There are the emotional, elements of force, energy, suggestiveness, or the elements by which a writer conveys not only his thought but his feeling, stimulating in his reader sentiments and passions akin to his own, and calling up vivid pictures of things he wishes his reader to see with him. There are the æsthetic elements of music, grace, beauty, charm, which make a style a pleasure in itself apart from the thought and feeling of which it may be the vehicle. This kind of analysis might of course be carried to almost any extent, but to pursue it further would be to overpass the line of demarcation which, wherever it is drawn, has to be drawn somewhere between the study of literature and the study of rhetoric. How far in our own study of literature we may find it profit- able to apply to the style of any great writer the abstract standards which the rhetorician proposes, is a question which must be left to each individual student to decide for himself. But it should be evident that if the rhetorician, looking at style simply as style, undertakes to analyse its elements and to estimate its merits and shortcomings without reference to the personality behind it, we, as students of literature, are not called upon, nor are we in the least likely, to do so. For us, the intellectual, emotional, and æsthetic qualities of any man's writings will relate themselves at bottom to all the personal qualities of his genius and character; and thus the technical study of his style will become an aid in our more systematic study of the individuality embodied in his work.

This remark suggests the important general principle that though the study of literary technique is in the hands of scholastic critics too often divorced from the study of literature in its personal and historical aspects, it need not and should not be so divorced. If the art of literature may be taken by itself as subject matter for analysis and discussion, it can also be connected directly with the substance and human meaning of literature, and indeed treated as supplementary to these. In this way, while, as we have said, everything connected with workmanship—method, treatment, form, style—may be considered for the interest they possess for their own sakes, it is not for their own sakes only that we shall be content to consider them. In fact, the further we go with our own study the more keenly we shall be likely to feel that any attempt to separate the art of literature from the life of literature must, both from the side of the art and from the side of the life, be unsatisfactory.

To this consideration, another of even greater importance has to be added. The art of the artist is to hide the art, and the business of the critic is to find it again. But we must be on our guard lest in our search for the art the true results of the art may be lost for us. Analysis must not be allowed to outrun its proper purpose and to become an end in itself; if we are right in considering how a great piece of literature has come to be what it is, it is still with the work as it is that we have mainly to do. To stand before a picture and to forget its totality of quality and effect as a picture in the interest which the method and technique of the painter may arouse, is to confuse the means of artistic study with the end which should always be kept in view. So it is with the study of a piece of literary art; for here too the ultimate secret of its power over us must be sought in our own personal apprehension, not of the artist's methods in the creation of its life and beauty, but in the life and beauty themselves. And thus we come round to emphasise once again one of the elementary principles with which we started. Good reading is better than all scholarship, and the cultivation of the art of good reading infinitely more important than all the acquisitions of scholastic learning. The study of literature in all its phases and details may be so planned and conducted as to render our enjoyment of literature ampler and richer. If it does this, its justification is incontestible. If it fails to do this, then, whatever else it accomplishes, it misses its true purpose.

3

The Study of Poetry

Were we challenged to answer offhand the question, What is poetry? most of us would probably be inclined to evade it with the words which St. Augustine once used in reference to other matters—'If not asked, I know; if you ask me, I know not.' A certain instinctive sense of what constitutes poetry we all have; but to translate this into exact language seems difficult, if not impossible. Nor, I imagine, should we be likely to find much practical help in even the most careful consideration of the innumerable definitions which from time to time have been offered by critics of poetry and by poets themselves. A few of these may be quoted by way of illustration.

Poetry, says Johnson, is 'metrical composition';[16] it is 'the art of uniting pleasure with truth by calling imagination to the help of reason';[17] and its 'essence' is 'invention.'[18] 'What is poetry,' asks Mill, 'but the thought and words in which emotion spontaneously embodies itself?'[19] 'By poetry,' says Macaulay, 'we mean the art of employing words in such a manner as to produce an illusion on the imagination, the art of doing by means of words what the painter does by means of colours.'[20] Poetry, declares Carlyle, 'we will call *Musical Thought*.'[21] Poetry, says Shelley, 'in a general sense may be defined as the expression of the imagination';[22] 'it is', says Hazlitt, the language of the imagination and the passions';[23] says Leigh Hunt, 'the utterance of a passion for truth, beauty, and power, embodying and illustrating its conceptions by imagination and fancy, and modulating its language on the principle of variety in unity.'[24] In Coleridge's view, poetry is the anti-thesis of science, having for its immediate object pleasure, not truth;[25] in Wordsworth's phrase, it 'is the breath and finer spirit of all knowledge,' and 'the impassioned expression which is in the

---

[16] *Dictionary.*

[17] *Life of Milton.*

[18] *Life of Waller.*

[19] *Thoughts on Poetry and its Varieties, in Dissertations and Discussions*, vol. i.

[20] *Essay on Milton.*

[21] *Heroes and Hero-Worship*, Lecture iii.

[22] *Defence of Poetry.*

[23] *Lectures on the English Poets*, i.

[24] *Imagination and Fancy*, i.

[25] *Lectures and Notes on Shakespeare and other English Poets, and Biographia Literaria*, chapter xiv.

countenance of all science.'[26] According to Matthew Arnold, it 'is simply the most delightful and perfect form of utterance that human words can reach';[27] it is 'nothing less than the most perfect speech of man, that in which he comes nearest to being able to utter the truth';[28] it is 'a criticism of life under the conditions fixed for such a criticism by the laws of poetic truth and poetic beauty.'[29]

According to Edgar Allan Poe, it is 'the rhythmic creation of beauty';[30] according to Keble, 'a vent for overcharged feeling or a full imagination.'[31] It expresses, says Doyle, our 'dissatisfaction with what is present and close at hand.'[32] Ruskin defines it as 'the suggestion, by the imagination, of noble grounds for the noble emotions';[33] Prof. Courthope, as 'the art of producing pleasure by the just expression of imaginative thought and feeling in metrical language';[34] Mr Watts-Dunton, as 'the concrete and artistic expression of the human mind in emotional and rhythmical language.'[35]

This list of definitions might be extended through many pages; but the above examples will suffice to indicate the enormous difficulties which beset every attempt to imprison the protean fife of poetry in the cast-iron terms of a logical formula, and the measure of success which has been reached. How far they help us, separately or in combination, to answer the question, what is poetry? is a matter which each reader must decide for himself. Suggestive, one and all, they doubtless are. Yet when we look at them critically, and compare them with one another, certain disturbing facts about them become clear. They are almost distracting in their variety because the subject

---

[26] *Preface* to second edition of *Lyrical Ballads.*
[27] *The French Play in London*, in *Mixed Essays.*
[28] *Wordsworth*, in *Essays in Criticism*, second series.
[29] *The Study of Poetry*, in *Essays in Criticism*, second series.
[30] *The Poetic Principle.*
[31] *Lectures on Poetry.*
[32] *Lectures on Poetry.*
[33] *Modern Painters*, Vol. III. Part IV, chapter i.
[34] *The Liberal Movement in English Literature.*
[35] Art. *Poetry*, in *Encyclopedia Britannica*, ninth edition. c

is approached from many different points of view. Some, strictly speaking, fail to define, because they express rather what is poetical in general, wherever it may be found, than what is specifically poetry. Some, on the other hand, are too narrow and exclusive, because they recognise only the particular kind of poetry in which the writer happened to be personally interested. And all are necessarily so abstract in statement that, whatever may be their philosophic value, they leave us in a region very remote from that world of concrete reality in which we move when we are reading poetry itself.

It is fortunate for us, then, as students, not of æsthetic theory, but of poetry, that we need not concern ourselves greatly to begin with about formulas and definitions, and the controversies about the ideal aims of poetry which these will often be found to involve. At the same time, some preliminary inquiry into the commoner qualities of poetry is manifestly necessary, since otherwise we should start on our work without any principles to guide us. Our initial task must therefore be, not to seek a formula of definition, but—a very different, and happily a much simpler thing—to mark out some of the characteristics of poetry which, when we take it as we find it, seem on the whole to be fairly general and constant.

We have said that literature is an interpretation of life as life shapes itself in the mind of the interpreter. What, then, it has to be asked, is the essential element in that interpretation of life which we describe as poetical? We have only to think carefully of the connotations of the word poetical, and an answer will at once suggest itself. By poetical we understand the emotional and the imaginative. In this sense, we use the word in current conversation to describe a person, a book (whatever its subject or form), a picture, an idea thrown out in talk. By the poetical interpretation of life, therefore, we mean a treatment of its facts, experiences, problems, in which the emotional and imaginative elements predominate. It is one chief characteristic of poetry, then, that whatever it touches in life, it relates to our feelings and passions, while at the same time by the exercise of imaginative power it both transfigures existing realities and 'gives to airy nothing a local habitation and a name.' Hence the emphasis thrown in sundry of the definitions we have quoted upon the emotional and imaginative attributes of poetry; and hence Bacon's conception of poetry as the idealistic handling of life which lends 'some shadow of satisfaction to the mind of man in those points wherein the nature of things doth deny it.'[36]

The full significance of poetry as an interpretation of life through imagination and feeling will be made apparent when we come presently to deal with the relations of poetry and science, and with the properties of poetic truth. Another aspect of the matter has first to be considered.

When we speak of imagination and feeling as predominating in poetry, we mean to distinguish these as general and constant characteristics of the poetic treatment of life; but we do not mean to say that their presence, even in the highest degree, is itself sufficient to constitute poetry. We may regard them as essential qualities of all true poetry, and we may insist that without them even that which offers itself as poetry, and is commonly accepted as such, must, as

---

[36]*Advancement of Learning*, II. iv. It may be worth while to remark that nearly all interpretations of poetry may be classed roughly as Baconian or Aristotelian in their fundamentals according as they approximate to the idealistic view above mentioned, or to Aristotle's antithetical conception of it as in its essence one of the imitative arts. The Greek philosopher's theory really breaks down in his own hands, since, as he himself admits, the poet's business (he is thinking of the narrative poet) is to relate, not what actually happens, but what may happen; for which reason, as he very justly argues, poetry is more 'philosophical' than history. That this admission yields much to the idealistic theory is evident. On the other hand, it is equally evident from Bacon's discussion of the subject, that in his view of poetry as 'feigned history,' and as an effort of the imagination to submit 'the shows of things to the desires of the mind,' he practically ignores the principle of poetic truth, and regards poetry as an untrammelled exercise of the imaginative power. Thus, for him it becomes a mere 'theatre' of the mind, to which we may repair for relaxation and pleasure, but in which it is 'not good to stay too long,' because it only 'feigneth,' while science is concerned with reality and truth. As we shall see later, his view cannot therefore be accepted without qualification; but the root of the matter is in it.

lacking these differentia, be pronounced unworthy of the name. But they are not the only essential qualities, because they may exist in what we should agree to call poetic prose, which is not the less to be denominated prose because it possesses these poetic attributes. The common way of looking at this matter seems to me perfectly sound. There is much 'poetry' which is purely 'prosaic'; there is much 'prose' which is markedly 'poetical'; but a dividing line between prose and poetry still exists. What does this imply? It implies that poetry, specifically so termed, is a particular kind of art; that it arises only when the poetic qualities of imagination and feeling are embodied in a certain form of expression. That form is, of course, regularly rhythmical language, or metre. Without this, we may have the spirit of poetry without its externals. With this, we may have the externals of poetry without its spirit. In its fullest and completest sense, poetry presupposes the union of the two.

Here, indeed, as must be frankly said, we touch upon a question concerning which there has been much controversy; for many critics have categorically denied that poetry has anything to do with form. Thus Sir Philip Sidney, while he acknowledges that 'the greatest part of Poets have apparelled their poeticall inventions in that numbrous kinde of writing which is called verse,' maintains that verse is 'apparell' only, 'being but an ornament and no cause to poetry; sith there hath beene many most excellent Poets, that have never versified, and now swarme many versifiers that neede never aunswere to the name of Poets.'[37] Bacon took the same ground when he stated that the 'feigning,' which was for him the peculiar function of poetry, may be 'as well in prose as in verse.'[38] Coleridge, too, emphatically declares that 'poetry of the highest kind may exist without metre,' and cites the writings of Plato and Jeremy Taylor, and even Burnet's *Theory of the Earth*, as 'undeniable proofs' of his assertion.[39] In these and in

---

[37] *An Apologie for Poetrie.*

[38] *Advancement of Learning*, II. iv. 2.

[39] *Biographia Literaria*, chapter xiv.

other similar cases, as in some of the definitions which have been quoted, the poetical qualities of thought and manner are emphasised to the exclusion of all consideration of poetry as a specific kind of art. But from the other side the reply has come that, whatever else poetry may or may not involve, the employment of a systematically rhythmical language is one of its necessary conditions. 'It has been contended by some,' writes Leigh Hunt, 'that poetry need not be written in verse at all; that prose is as good a medium, provided poetry be conveyed through it; and that to think otherwise is to confound letter with spirit, or form with essence. But the opinion is a prosaical mistake. Fitness or unfitness for *song*, or metrical excitement, make all the difference between a poetical and prosaical subject; and the reason why verse is necessary to the form of poetry is that the perfection of the poetical spirit demands it—that the circle of its enthusiasm, beauty, and power, is incomplete without it.'[40] This undoubtedly over-states the case for form, since the writer appears to ignore the fact that the truest spirit of poetry has often been expressed, and very adequately expressed, without recourse to the medium of verse. The difference in question, as I understand it, is not necessarily between a 'poetical' and a 'prosaical' subject, but between the forms in which perhaps the same subject may be handled. Treated in prose, it may be made richly poetical; but only when treated in metre is it fashioned into actual poetry. If poetry, then, as regards its substance and spirit, is the antithesis of science, or matter of fact, as Wordsworth and Coleridge rightly insisted, it is none the less to be distinguished from prose, as regards its form, by the systematically rhythmical character of its language.

This view receives important support from one great critic who, on general principles, might rather have been expected to oppose it. Carlyle thought of the poet always as the seer, and many of his own pages might be adduced as splendid examples of poetry in prose. Yet he distinctly says:—'For my own part, I find considerable

---

[40]*Imagination and Fancy.*

meaning in the old vulgar distinction of poetry being metrical, having music in it'; though he characteristically adds that there is much in the form of poetry which was under no 'inward necessity' to be in that form at all, and had far better therefore have been in plain prose.[41] Thus also, Matthew Arnold, despite his preoccupation with the idea of poetry as a 'criticism of life,' lays stress upon 'the essential difference between imaginative production in verse, and imaginative production in prose.' The 'rhythm and measure' of poetry, he maintains, 'elevated to a regularity, certainty, and force very different from that of the rhythm and measure which can pervade prose, are a part of its perfection.'[42]

That in thus asserting metre to be one of the general and constant characteristics of poetry and in making it the chief point of distinction between poetry and prose, we involve ourselves in various critical difficulties, is not to be denied. Whateley's declaration that 'any composition in verse, and none that is not, is always called, whether good or bad, a poem, by all who have no favourite hypothesis to maintain,'[43] is obviously correct. Yet it seems a hard saying, for to accept it means that we are bound to admit under the head of poetry much that we should be tempted to exclude, and to exclude much that we should like to admit. To call Garth's *Dispensary* poetry, and to deny the name to some of the magnificent imaginative and emotional passages in *Sartor Resartus*, seems at first a strange abuse of the word. Nothing but 'poetry,' Mr Frederic Harrison urges, can properly express what we find in portions of the *Morte d'Arthur* and in some of the chapters of *Job* and *Isaiah*.[44] Mr Bagehot goes farther, confessing that he cannot 'draw with any confidence' the 'exact line which separates grave novels in verse, like *Aylmer's Field* or *Enoch Arden* from grave novels not in verse, like *Silas Marner* or

---

[41] *Heroes and Hero-Worship*, Lecture iii.
[42] *The French Play in London*, in *Mixed Essays*.
[43] *Elements of Rhetoric*, III. iii. 3.
[44] *The Choice of Books*.

Adam Bede;[45] and such uncertainty as to precise boundaries becomes greater if we substitute for the narrative poems named such works as *The Inn Album, Aurora Leigh, Lucile,* and *Faithful For Ever,* in which the resemblance to prose fiction is much more marked. Other questions start up on every side. What, for example, it may be asked, are we to say about the hundreds of lines in *The Excursion* which have often been described as 'prose cut into lines of equal length,' and in which, as even the most devoted Words-worthian will admit, of all poetical qualities that of metrical form alone is retained? Does a poem cease to be a poem when it is turned into the prose of another language? Are the *Psalms* no longer poems when we read them in our ordinary English version? Is the *Odyssey* only a prose tale in Butcher and Lang's admirable translation, while it remains a poem in Pope's immeasurably less poetical as well as less accurate rendering? And how are we to deal with the many experiments which from time to time have been made in productions which are intended to be read and judged as poetry, but in which regularity of rhythm is abandoned, and the language used may be said to hover between verse and prose; such as Macpherson's *Ossian,* the rhapsodies of Blake, Gessner's *Death of Abel,* imitated by Rousseau in his *Lévite d'Ephraim* and by Coleridge in his fragmentary *Wanderings of Cain,* Fénelon's *Télémaque,* Chateaubriand's *Les Martyrs,* the *Prose Poems* of Turgenev, and (most important of all in recent discussions as to form) Walt Whitman's *Leaves of Grass?* These questions show the futility of attempting to enforce hard and fast distinctions in matters in which the border lines are often undefined and the territories overlap, and in which, therefore, the widest differences in point of view must always be allowed for; and they should be borne in mind as a warning against dogmatism. Yet on the whole, we may safely adhere to the 'old vulgar distinction' referred to by Carlyle. Without discussing the abstract problem whether regularity of rhythm is essential to a complete definition of poetry, and without considering

---

[45] *Essay on Wordsworth.*

whether we may not have to recognise, here and there, exceptions to our rule, we may lay it down as a principle that metre always has been and still is the most general and constant feature of poetry on the side of form. This is it, therefore, which we have to accept as the fundamental quality of poetry conceived as a distinct kind of literary art. Only in fact by an extension of its meaning and by a certain license of speech is the word poetry to be applied to any composition, no matter how high may be its poetical energy of thought and expression, which is not in verse.

Of the significance of rhythm in poetry much might be said, but the subject is too large and too intricately entangled with questions of psychology, to be dealt with in detail here. A few points only may be touched upon in passing.

In the first place, even if the relation between rhythmical form and poetical substance and feeling were only an accidental one, the ordered measure of verse would still hold its ground as an important accessory of poetry, because it adds greatly to the æsthetic pleasure which it is a chief function of poetry to afford. So familiar is this fact that to mention it is enough. A few theorists may argue in favour of the 'liberation' of poetry from the formal restraints of metre; a few practical exponents of the creed of enfranchisement may cast these restraints aside; but the vast majority of those who love poetry will acknowledge that the definitely regulated music of its language is one peculiar element in the satisfaction yielded by it. It is indeed by the use of this wonderful instrument that, as a means of producing æsthetic pleasure, poetry maintains an advantage over 'the other harmony'—the loose and unregulated rhythm—of prose. Metre, then, we may rightly call, with Arnold, is a 'part of its perfection.'

It is, however, in the second place, a part of the perfection of poetry in a much more important sense than is implied if we rest in the assumption that it is nothing but a mere accessory. A mere accessory in fact it is not. It is rather the form which the poetic spirit seeks spontaneously to fashion for itself, and as such, it 'perfects' poetry by providing it with its most natural and adequate means of expression. 'Ever since man has been man,' says Mill, 'all deep and sustained feeling has tended to express itself in rhythmical language, and the deeper the feeling the more characteristic and decided the rhythm.'[46] It is this psychological truth which lies at the root of the almost universal connection—which is therefore a causal, and not simply an accidental connection—between poetic feeling and metrical diction. It has often been noted as a striking proof of the closeness of the relationship that what is known as impassioned, or oratorical prose—prose which is fraught with strong imagination and emotion—commonly exhibits, as in many passages in the poetic books of our English Bible, a rhythmical emphasis which distinctly approaches, though it does not actually reach, the regulated cadences of verse.[47]

Nor is this all. It was noted by Hegel that the use of verse in a given piece of literature serves in itself to lift us into a world quite different from that of prose or everyday life. The German philosopher was thinking only of the influence of verse upon the reader. But that his remark has wider bearings is strikingly shown by the testimony furnished by a great German poet to the effect produced upon the poet himself by the substitution of the medium of verse for that of prose. 'I have never before,' writes Schiller to Goethe, 'been so palpably convinced as in my present occupation'—which was that of turning a prose composition into verse—'how closely in poetry Substance and Form are connected. Since I have begun to transform my prosaic language into a poetic rhythmical one, I find myself

---

[46] *Thoughts on Poetry and its Varieties.*

[47] There are cases indeed in which the rhythm becomes so marked and uniform that the dividing line between prose and verse is practically obliterated. Dickens occasionally fell into this bastard style; notably in the description of the death and burial of Little Nell, which, as R. H. Horne was the first to point out, though printed as prose, is really 'written in blank verse of irregular metres and rhythms.' Horne would find few critics now to echo his praise of it, for such metrical prose must, as prose, be pronounced a grave artistic mistake.

under a totally different jurisdiction; even many motives which in the prosaic execution seemed to me to be perfectly in place, I can no longer use; they were merely good for the common domestic understanding, whose organ prose seems to be; but verse absolutely demands reference to the imagination: and thus I was obliged to become poetical in many of my motives.'[48] The interest of this passage, as will be seen, lies in the fact that in it the relation between poetic substance and metrical form is regarded from an unusual point of view. Commonly we think of poetic feeling as fashioning metrical form for its expression. Schiller helps us to realise the intimacy of the connection between them by emphasising the influence of poetic form in stimulating the poetic spirit. We may conclude, therefore, that while verse is of course often used as the vehicle of purely prosaic thought, it ought not to be so used; and that conversely, while an exalted mood of passion and imaginative ecstacy may often find utterance in prose, prose is not its most appropriate or even its most natural medium. The offices of prose and verse are, in fact, distinct; and their distinction is neither fortuitous nor arbitrary, but vital. Thus it is that in all true poetry that union of substance and form, of which Schiller speaks, is so organic and complete that it impresses us with a conviction of its absolute inevitability. For this reason we may acquiesce in Herbert Spencer's grim remark that 'no one should write verse if he can help it.'[49]

This, however, is only one side of the matter. There is another side which, from the standpoint of the reader, is even more important.

Metre, like music, makes in itself a profound appeal to the feelings.

---

[48]Letter to Goethe, quoted in Lewes's *Life of Goethe*, Book V. chapter i. The quotation is made with reference to the original prose version of Goethe's *Iphigenie auf Tauris*, which, as Lewes suggestively notes, is 'saturated with verses.' Goethe 'meant to write prose,' because at the time he was much influenced by the current mania for prose-tragedy, 'but his thoughts instinctively expressed themselves in verse.'

[49]*Autobiography*, i. 264. Compare Carlyle's dictum about 'inward necessity,' already quoted.

Merely to arrange words in a definitely rhythmical order is to endow
them, as by some secret magic, with a new and subtle emotional
power—to touch them with a peculiar suggestiveness which in
themselves, simply as words conveying such and such meanings,
they do not possess. Why this is, the student of literature must leave
it to the psychologist to explain. For him it is a fact, and a fact of
the utmost interest and significance. He knows that the recurrent
beats and pauses, the rapid march or the languid movement, of verses
read to him in a language he does not understand, will often stir
him, as he is stirred by sonata or symphony, to moods of martial
excitement or pensive melancholy; and from this he learns—what
otherwise, indeed, his whole experience should have taught him—that
metre is a powerful aid in the emotionalisation of thought, and that
the various metrical forms in which the poet most naturally and
appropriately embodies his feeling, are also, of all possible forms, the
most potent to excite the reader's feeling to a sympathetic response.
'How much the power of poetry depends upon the nice inflections
of rhythm alone, may be proved,' as James Montgomery pointed
out, 'by taking the finest passages of Milton and Shakespeare, and
merely putting them into prose, with the least possible variation
of the words themselves. The attempt would be like gathering up
dew- drops, which appear jewels and pearls on the grass, but run
into water in the hand; the essence and the elements remain, but
the grace, the sparkle, and the form are gone.'[50]

More than ever, then, it is evident that metre is no mere accessory
or conventional ornament of poetry, but a vital product of the poetic
spirit, and that the common sense of the world is right in regarding
it—whatever occasional exceptions may have to be made—as a
distinctive and fundamental characteristic of poetry as a form of art.

II

We may now inquire a little more particularly into the purport of

---

[50]*Lectures on Poetry*, iii.

the statement that poetry is an interpretation of life through the imagination and the feelings. We can best approach this subject by noting the fundamental difference between poetry and science.

The world with which science deals is what we commonly call the world of fact; by which we properly mean the world of physical actuality objectively considered. The business of the scientist, as the current phrase has it, is with things as they are in themselves. He studies their forms and organisations, their qualities, characteristics, and connections; he collates and classifies them; he investigates the conditions and processes under and by which they have come to be what they are. Each science treats some one aspect of the external world in this purely objective way; while science in the larger sense advances from fact to generalisation, and from generalisation to still more and more comprehensive generalisations, thus seeking to reduce the multiplicity and apparent confusion of the universe to unity and order. Science, therefore, aims to afford a systematic and rational explanation of things—an explanation which shall include their natures, genesis, and history—in terms of cause, effect, and physical law. With what remains after such explanation has been given, science as science has nothing to do.

Yet no fact of experience can be more familiar or more patent than this—that with what remains after such explanation has been given, we ourselves have a great deal to do. In our daily converse with the world we are indeed chiefly interested, not in things as they are in themselves, but with the aspect which they bear and the appeal which they make to our emotional natures. While we are actually engaged in scientific study we may, it is true, think of the universe merely as a vast aggregation of phenomena to be examined, catalogued, accounted for; but in our common human dealings with it, we do not so think of it. When science has provided us with its completest rationale of things, we are still primarily impressed by their mystery and beauty. No explanation can ever destroy this impression; rather, we may say that every explanation will serve only to intensify it. In this simple fact we have to seek both the foundation and the

permanent significance of poetry. Though the mystery and beauty
of the world are habitually recognised by us, they are recognised for
the most part only in a vague and sluggish way. There are, however,
moods of heightened feeling in which they come home to us with
special vividness and power. It is then that we are deeply stirred to
delight or wonder, to gratitude or reverent awe. Out of such moods
poetry springs; to such moods it addresses itself. It reports to us
of things from their emotional and spiritual sides. It expresses and
interprets their appeal to us, and our response to them. It is thus at
once the antithesis and the complement of science.

'Poetry,' says Leigh Hunt, 'begins where matter of fact or of
science ceases to be merely such, and to exhibit a further truth,
the connection it has with the world of emotion, and its power to
produce imaginative pleasure. Inquiring of a gardener, for instance,
what flower it is we see yonder, he answers 'a lily.' This is matter
of fact. The botanist pronounces it to be of the order of *Hexandria
monogynia.* This is matter of science. It is the 'lady' of the garden, says
Spenser; and here we begin to have a poetical sense of its fairness
and grace. It is 'the plant and flower of *light,*' says Ben Jonson; and
poetry then shows us the beauty of the flower in all its mystery
and splendour.'[51]

In one sense, of course, this passage is unsatisfactory. It gives a
wholly inadequate idea of the work of science. For science is not
merely nomenclature and classification, and it has a great deal more
to tell us about the lily than that, according to the Linnæan system,
it is 'of the order of *Hexandria monogynia.*' Yet, allowance made for
this superficiality, the relation of poetic description to scientific fact
is quite felicitously indicated. The botanist may dissect the 'flower in
the crannied wall,' and, with its tiny members laid out before him,
may discourse to us of its bracts and petals, its stamens and pistils.
That everything he has to tell us will prove profoundly interesting
and wonderful, I need not pause to insist. Yet, after all, the botanist's

[51] *Imagination and Fancy*, i.

dissected flower is not our flower—is not the flower that we actually know and love; nor does his most elaborate analysis of it help us in the least to realise more keenly, what we often specially want to realise, the delight which we experience in its simple sweetness and beauty. For any vivid sense of such sweetness and beauty, for any translation into words of the pleasure they give us, we have rather to turn to the poet who, by his imaginative handling of his subject, catches the meaning that it has for us, and expresses, with absolute fidelity and stimulating power, the feelings to which it gives birth in ourselves. For this reason Matthew Arnold is perfectly right in maintaining that 'the grand power of poetry' is 'the power of so dealing with things as to awaken in us a wonderfully full, new, and intimate sense of them, and of our relations with them.' 'I will not now inquire,' Arnold continues, 'whether this sense is illusive, whether it can be proved not to be illusive, whether it does absolutely make us possess the real nature of things; all I say is, that poetry can awaken it in us, and that to awaken it is one of the highest powers of poetry. The interpretations of science do not give us this intimate sense of objects as the interpretations of poetry give it; they appeal to a limited faculty, and not to the whole man. It was not Linnæus or Cavendish or Cuvier who gives us the true sense of animals, or water, or plants, who seizes their secret, who makes us participate in their life; it is Shakespeare, with his

> 'daffodils
> That come before the swallow dares, and take
> The winds of March with beauty';

it is Wordsworth, with his

> 'voice...heard
> In spring-time from the cuckoo-bird, Breaking the silence of
> the seas Among the farthest Hebrides';

it is Keats, with his

> 'moving waters at their priest-like task

Of pure ablution round Earth's human shores';

it is Chateaubriand with his 'cime indéterminée des forêts'; it is Senancour, with his mountain birch tree: '*Cette écorce blanche,*

lisse et crevassée; cette tige agreste; ces branches qui s'inclinent vers la terre; la mobilité des feuilles, et tout cet abandon, simplicité de la nature, attitude des déserts.'[52]

The relations of poetic interpretation to scientific fact should now be sufficiently clear; but, as the subject is one of fundamental interests in the consideration of the place and functions of poetry, space may be found for one further illustration. This I take from the pages of Mr Edmund Clarence Stedman's book on *The Nature and Elements of Poetry*. 'The portrayal of things as they seem,' which is the special business of the artist, whatever his medium may be, 'conveys,' as Mr Stedman rightly argues, 'a truth just as important as that other truth which the man of analysis and demonstration imparts to the intellect' when he exhibits things as they are in themselves; and this doctrine he enforces by reference to the difference between the scientist's treatment and the poet's treatment of a storm on the Atlantic coast. 'The poet says:

> When descends on the Atlantic
> The gigantic
> Storm-wind of the Equinox, Landward in his wrath he scourges
> The toiling surges
> Laden with sea-weed from the rocks.

Or take this stanza by a later balladist:

> The East Wind gathered, all unknown, A thick sea-cloud his course before:
> He left by night the frozen zone, And smote the cliffs of Labrador;
> He lashed the coasts on either hand,

---

[52]*Essay on Maurice de Guérin, in Essays in Criticism*, first series.

And betwixt the Cape and Newfoundland
Into the bay his armies pour.

All this impersonification and fancy is translated by the Weather
Bureau into something like the following:

' 'An area of extreme low pressure is rapidly moving up the
Atlantic coast, with wind and rain. Storm-centre now off Charleston,
S.C. Wind N.E. Velocity, 54. Barometer, 29.6. The disturbance will
reach New York on Wednesday, and proceed eastward to the Banks
and Bay of St Lawrence. Danger-signals ordered for all North Atlantic
ports."

With these contrasted passages before us we have no difficulty in
realizing the weight of Mr Stedman's contention that the imaginative
rendering of fact is in its own way just as important as the plain
statement of it. But we may go even farther than this, and assert
that from one point of view the imaginative rendering contains a
quality of vital truth which is not to be found in the plain statement.
For which gives us the more genuine and vivid sense of a storm
as we ourselves actually feel it—the 'impersonification and fancy'
of the poet, or the colourless and unimpassioned language of the
Weather Bureau bulletin? The question can easily be decided by
a direct appeal to experience. Let anyone who has ever enjoyed a
great gale on some rocky sea-coast turn to the meteorologist's dry
catalogue of phenomena and ask himself if any suggestion of the
life and reality of what he then witnessed and felt be in it. For
the life and reality of the storm he will have to go to the poet's
imaginative version of it.

We are thus able to realise the essential quality of poetic truth.
By poetic truth we do not mean fidelity to facts in the ordinary
acceptation of the term. Such fidelity we look for in science. By
poetic truth we mean fidelity to our emotional apprehension of
facts, to the impression which they make upon us, to the feelings
of pleasure or pain, hope or fear, wonder or religious reverence,
which they arouse. Our first test of truth in poetry, therefore, is its

accuracy in expressing, not what things are in themselves, but their beauty and mystery, their interest and meaning for us.

Here, then, we reach the full significance of poetry as an interpretation of life—the life of nature and the life of humanity—through the imagination and the feelings. To prevent possible misapprehension, however, several points have now to be considered.

In the first place, it is not to be assumed that because a poet's principal concern is with the beauty and mystery, the human interest and meaning of the things with which he deals, he is under no restraint or obligation in respect of objective reality. Such assumption is, indeed, a not uncommon one; yet a moment's thought will convince us that it is utterly erroneous. The poet, it is true, gives us that intimate sense of things and of our relations with them, of which Arnold speaks, by touching them with imagination and feeling, and linking them with our own life. But we nonetheless demand of him that his vision of the world shall still be a clear and steady vision, and that absolute fidelity shall be his guiding principle in all his renderings of perceived facts. All poetry has to be tried by the criterion of this fidelity, for it belongs to the essential foundations of poetic greatness. When, for example, Oliver Wendell Holmes speaks of the crocus as the 'spenthrift crocus…with his cup of gold,' he does what the poet should do—he touches the flower with imagination and feeling, and links it with our own life; and by so doing, he doubtless gives the careless or ignorant reader a lively sense of its beauty and charm. But for the reader who really knows the crocus, and who has himself watched it closely, the magic of his description is spoilt by its inveracity; since, as Ruskin pointed out, the crocus cannot rightly be called 'spendthrift,' for it is a hardy plant, while its yellow is not gold but saffron.[53] Here, then, we have a case in which the imaginative handling of natural fact is unsatisfactory because it wants the basis of reality; the poetry is wrought, not out of, but at the expense of truth. The fidelity, and therefore, the poetic value of

---

[53] *Modern Painters*, Vol. III. Part IV. chapter xii.

some of Milton's natural imagery have similarly been impugned on the score of lack of substantial knowledge and accuracy of detail. 'A close observer of things around us would not speak'—as Milton does in *L'Allegro* and *Il Penseroso*—'of the eglantine as twisted, of the coswlip as wan, of the violet as glowing, or of the reed as balmy. Lycidas' laureate herse is to be strewn at once with primrose and woodbine, daffodil and jasmine,' which indicates a strange confusion as to the flora of the seasons in the poet's mind. 'The pine is not 'rooted deep as high' (P.R. 4416), but sends its roots along the surface. The elm, one of the thinnest foliaged trees of the forest, is inappropriately named starproof (*Arc.* 89). Lightning does not singe the tops of trees (*P.L.* i. 613), but either shivers them, or cuts a groove down the stem to the ground. These and other suchlike inaccuracies,' says Mr Mark Pattison, by whom they are collected, 'must be set down partly to conventional language used without meaning, the vice of Latin versification enforced as a task, but they are partly due to real defect of natural knowledge.'[54] To us the source of such infidelity does not for the moment matter. The point now to be insisted upon is simply this—that, despite all popular ideas to the contrary, the imaginative handling of nature does not properly include, and must certainly not be held to excuse, such lax treatment of natural facts.

As a contrast to Milton's occasional slips and conventionalisms we may note the detailed accuracy which almost invariably characterises Tennyson's treatment of nature. In such passages as

More black than ashbuds in the front of March;[55]

and

A crowd of hopes,
That sought to sow themselves like winged seeds;[56]

---

[54] *Milton*, in *English Men of Letters*, chapter ii.
[55] *The Gardener's Daughter.*
[56] *Thid.*

and

> Her hair,
> In gloss and hue the chestnut, when the shell
> Divides threefold to show the fruit within;[57]

and

> In the spring a fuller crimson comes upon the robin's breast;
> In the spring the wanton lapwing gets himself another crest;[58]

We know that the poet's eye has indeed been upon his object, that he has looked steadily at things for himself; that he records carefully what he has seen. Such firsthand knowledge of the aspects of nature dealt with, and such fidelity in the treatment of them, must be reckoned among the elements of poetic truth. We can now see in what ways Bacon's conception of poetry as mere 'feigning' has to be qualified before it can be accepted. The touch of imagination and feeling upon the outer world may often transfigure, but should never misrepresent or distort it. This principle holds good whether we consider the poet's rendering of particular natural phenomena, as in the instances cited, or his treatment of nature in general, or his interpretation of human life and experience.

It is often, it must be admitted, extremely difficult to distinguish between the poetic transfiguration of natural fact, which is entirely justifiable, because it gives us only another kind of truth, and that which is tantamount to misrepresentation, and should therefore be condemned. This question, though important, is one which is unfortunately too involved to be discussed fully within the narrow limits of the present section, and the briefest consideration of it must suffice. The reader will remember that it was definitely raised by Ruskin in his famous chapters on *The Pathetic Fallacy*

---

[57] *The Brook.*
[58] *Locksley Hall.*

and *Classical Landscape* in *Modern Painters*.[59] By 'pathetic fallacy'—an injudiciously chosen phrase, as a substitute for which Oliver Wendell Holmes proposed 'sympathetic illusion'[60]—Ruskin means our modern 'subjective' way of dealing with nature; that is, our habit of transferring our own mental and emotional states to the things which we contemplate. This Ruskin pronounces a defect. Yet it cannot properly be regarded as such; nor is he himself very clear or consistent in what he says in his criticism of it. He falls foul of Kingsley because in the ballad of *The Sands of Dee* he writes:

> They rowed her in across the rolling foam—
> The cruel, crawling foam;

'the foam is not cruel, neither does it crawl,' he protests, and to speak of it in these terms is to falsify it. But he presently acknowledges that, while the epithets used 'fallaciously describe foam,' they 'faithfully describe sorrow'; in other words, they truly reflect our feeling about the sea when in a mood of violent grief we think of it as a destructive agent. Again, he finds fault with the lines in which Keats depicts a wave breaking, out at sea:

> Down whose green back the short-lived foam, all hoar,
> Bursts gradual with a wayward indolence—

because salt water can be neither wayward nor indolent.

None the less he concedes that 'the idea of the peculiar action with which foam rolls down a long, large wave could not have been given by any other words so well as by this wayward indolence.' Surely, therefore, Keats's description furnishes us with an admirable example of poetic, as contra- distinguished from scientific, truth. I have said this much because the question of the subjective treatment of nature in modern poetry is one which perpetually arises, and cannot therefore be passed over in silence. Without pursuing the matter further we may, I think, lay it down as a rule for our guidance

---

[59]Vol. III. Part IV.
[60]*Life of Emerson*, chapter xiv.

that the translation of natural facts into terms of our own feelings is wrong only when those feelings are themselves morbid, or in the circumstances unreasonable or illegitimate, or when they are so violent as to render our vision of things untrustworthy and our transcript of them essentially untrue.[61]

This brings us to another consideration. While the poet will always, and of necessity, deal largely with such aspects of things as appeal directly to the senses and the feelings, there is nothing to prevent him from penetrating beneath their surface, or from taking as his subject-matter those more recondite truths of nature which are revealed by science. There is thus a poetic interpretation of nature

---

[61]Some remarks by the late Mr Roden Noel on Ruskin's criticism of Keats are here very much to the point, and should be read with close attention. 'Now, salt water cannot be either wayward or indolent; on this plain fact the charge of falsehood in the metaphor is grounded. Yet this expression is precisely the most exquisite bit in the picture. Can plain falsehood then be truly poetic and beautiful? Many people will reply 'certainly,' believing that poetry is essentially pleasing by the number of pretty falsehoods told or suggested. I believe with Mr Ruskin that poetry is only good in proportion to its truth. Now we must first inquire what the poet is here intending to describe. If a scientific man were to explain to us the nature of foam by telling us that it is a wayward and indolent thing, this would clearly be a falsehood. But does the poet profess to explain what the man of science would profess to explain, or something else? What are the physical laws according to which water becomes foam, and foam falls along the back of a wave—that is one question; and what impression does this condition of things produce upon a mind that observes closely, and feels with exquisite delicacy of sense the beauty of the movement of the foam, and its subtle relation to other material things, as well as to certain analogues in the sphere of spirit, to functions and states of the human spirit—this is a totally different question. I submit that the office of the poet in this connection is to answer the latter question, and that of the scientific man to answer the former. But observe that this is not granting license of scientific ignorance or wanton inaccuracy to the poet which some critics are disposed to grant' (*On the Poetic Interpretation of Nature*, in *Wordsworthiana*, ed. William Knight; reprinted in *Essays on Poetry and Poets*). The fault to be found with Holmes' description of the crocus as 'spendthrift,' therefore, is not that it imputes a human characteristic to the flower, but that it imputes the wrong characteristic, and thus through inaccuracy, arouses false feeling in regard to it.

based upon scientific knowledge and the emotions stirred by this, as there is a poetic interpretation which limits itself to appearances and the emotions stirred by them. When the hero of Tennyson's *Maud* Soliloquises over the tiny shell which he picks up on the Breton coast:

> See what a lovely shell
> Small and pure as a pearl,
> Lying close at my foot,
> Frail, but a work divine,
> Made so fairily well
> With delicate spire and whorl,
> How exquisitely minute,
> A miracle of design;

he gives us for the moment nothing beyond careful observation and appropriate feeling. But when his imagination begins to play about it and its history, and he continues:

> The tiny shell is forlorn,
> Void of the little living will
> That made it stir on the shore.
> Did he stand at the diamond door
> Of his house in a rainbow frill?
> Did he push, when he was uncurl'd,
> A golden foot or a fairy horn
> Thro' his dim water-world?—

we see that he is drawing in part upon knowledge furnished by science to complete that given by observation. Herbert Spencer, writing as a scientist, tells us how much more the geologist can find in a highland glen than can ever be found there by deer stalker or ordinary tourist. 'He, observing that the glacier-rounded rock he sits on has lost by weathering but half an inch of its surface since a time far more remote than the beginnings of human civilisation, and then trying to conceive the slow denudation which has cut out the whole valley, has thoughts of time, and power to which they are strangers—thoughts which, already utterly inadequate to their objects, he feels to be still more futile on noting the contorted beds of gneiss around, which tell him of a time immeasurably more remote, when far beneath the earth's surface they were in a half-melted state, and again tell him of a time, immensely exceeding this in remoteness, when their components were sand and mud on the shores of an ancient sea.'[62] Here in the mind of the scientist himself we have the mood of wonder arising from contemplation of the facts which science has brought to light—a mood, it is manifest, closely akin to the mood of poetry. It is by contemplation of the same facts that Tennyson is inspired to write:—

> There rolls the deep where grew the tree.
> O earth, what changes hast thou seen!
> There where the long street roars, hath been
> The stillness of the central sea.
>
> The hills are shadows, and they flow
> From form to form, and nothing stands;
> They melt like mist, the solid lands,
> Like clouds they shape themselves and go.[63]

In this case, it is evident, the poet is not thinking about the ordinary appearances of nature. He is thinking about what science has told him of the evolution of the world. His interpretation of nature is thus illuminated and transformed by science. Indeed, with a boldness possible only to one who has read the geologic record, he sets appearances at nought so completely that in his hands the hills become mere fleeting shadows—those everlasting hills which from time immemorial have been for men who judge by appearances alone the pillars of the universe and the very symbols of eternity.

Thus Wordsworth has the best of grounds for declaring that 'the objects of the poet's thoughts are everywhere,' and that 'though the

---

[62]*Ecclesiastical Institutions,* § 660.
[63]In Memoriam, § 121.

eyes and senses of man are, it is true, his favourite guides, yet he will follow wherever he can find an atmosphere of sensation in which to move his wings.'[64] It may indeed be said that, as a really great poet is, of necessity, a great thinker—a point we shall have to return to presently—he can hardly fail to be interested in and influenced by, if not the separate discoveries and controversies of science, at any rate the large movements in thought to which these give rise. The new knowledge of the time, with all the changes which it brings about in men's inherited beliefs and traditional views of the cosmic order and their relations with it, and all the fresh problems and speculations which it everywhere thrusts to the fore, must have an irresistible fascination for him on their emotional and spiritual sides. Their bearings for good or evil upon the cherished hopes and aspirations of the world will almost inevitably force themselves upon his attention; and even if he does not make them the subjects of direct consideration, they are certain in countless subtle ways to enter into and colour the texture of his verse, as they enter into and colour the current thought of his age. So far from its being true, therefore, that the poet has nothing to do with the scientific knowledge of things, it may rather be maintained that the wider issues of that knowledge can never be entirely ignored by him; while if he be a poet of the philosophic class, he will find himself specially tasked to challenge it in its relation with every question and interest belonging to the higher life of man.

In an era of rapidly accumulating scientific discoveries and vast and far-reaching intellectual change, like our own, we must expect to encounter a certain amount of antagonism between science and poetry, in the same way and for the same reason as we must expect to encounter a certain amount of antagonism between science and religion. In the development of thought the feelings can never quite keep pace with the intellect;[65] and, as a result of this, the poet

---

[64]*Preface* to second edition of *Lyrical Ballads*.
[65]See W. K. Clifford's essay on *Cosmic Emotion*.

is, in the average of cases, conservative; he clings by preference to what is old and familiar; he is commonly repelled by what is new and strange. Hence, the spiritual unrest, the uncertainties, the struggles and doubts and pessimism, which were so marked among the characteristics of our Victorian poetry. The emotionalisation of knowledge is inevitably a slow and gradual process; but meanwhile, one measure of a poet's greatness as a thinker is his ability to perceive the possibility of it, and by his insight into the spiritual meanings of scientific fact, to point forward and help in its accomplishment.

It is an important implication of the high conception of poetic truth which we have now reached, that the poet who is a philosopher no less than the philosopher who is not a poet must be held responsible in the fullest degree for the soundness of the foundations upon which he builds his arguments and rests his conclusions. The widest margin may be allowed to every poet for the play of his imagination so long as his purpose is only to delight by the creation of beauty. But the moment he enters upon the work of a teacher, we demand that his teachings shall satisfy the understanding as well as engage the fancy and touch the heart. The application of this principle may be made clear by a single illustration.

In his *Gebir*, Landor has a striking passage dealing with the old notion that the murmuring of a seashell held to the ear is the reverberation of the sea waves, still lingering in it:

> But I have sinuous shells of pearly hue
> . . . .
> Shake one and it awakens, then apply Its polished lips to your attentive ear, And it remembers its august abodes,
> And murmurs as the ocean murmurs there.

Wordsworth in turn takes up the same pretty notion (indeed, Landor complained that he stole his shell), and this is the use to which he puts it:

> I have seen
> A curious child, who dwelt upon a tract

Of inland ground, applying to his ear
The convolutions of a smooth-lipped shell;
To which, in silence hushed, his very soul
Listened intensely; and his countenance soon
Brightened with joy; for from within were heard
Murmurings, whereby the monitor expressed
Mysterious union with its native sea.
Even such a shell the 'universe itself
Is to the ear of Faith; and there are times,
I doubt not, when to you it doth impart
Authentic tidings of invisible things;
Of ebb and flow, and ever-during power:
And central peace, subsisting at the heart
Of endless agitation.[66]

Now it is evident that there is a very important difference between Landor's treatment of the seashell's murmur and Wordsworth's. Landor employs it only as what Arnold would call 'a play of fancy,'[67] and as such it is excellent. Wordsworth presses it into the service of a transcendental philosophy, and since, as everybody knows, the alleged fact is not a real fact, the use of it for such a purpose only serves to make the philosophy itself seem unreal. Then a third poet, Mr Eugene Lee-Hamilton, appears and, starting from Wordsworth's parallelism between the seashell and the universe, boldly turns the argument upon the transcendentalist himself by contending that what is demonstrably illusion in the one case is unquestionably illusion also in the other:

The hollow sea-shell which for years hath stood
On dusty shelves, when held against the ear Proclaims its stormy

---

[66] *The Excursion*, Book iv.

[67] Arnold describes the idea which forms the core of the *Ode on the Intimations of Immortality* as an idea 'of undeniable beauty as a play of fancy,' but as one which has not 'the character of poetic truth of the best kind; it has no real solidity' (*Essay on Wordsworth*). But on this special point, see Wordsworth's own introductory note to the poem.

parent; and we hear
The faint far murmur of the breaking flood. We hear the sea.
The sea? It is the blood
In our own veins, impetuous and near,
And pulses keeping pace with hope and fear
And with our feelings' ever-shifting mood.

Lo! in my heart I hear, as in a shell,
The murmur of a world beyond the grave, Distinct, distinct,
though faint and far it be.
Thou fool! this echo is a cheat as well,—
The hum of earthly instincts; and we crave
A world unreal as the shell-heard sea.

We are not now called upon to inquire into the general value
of Wordsworth's transcendentalism, or of Lee-Hamilton's reply. We
have only to insist that, so far as this particular case of the seashell
is concerned, Lee Hamilton is right, because he deals with the
known fact of the matter, and Wordsworth wrong, because he gives
us merely a bit of pleasing fancy. And the poet who assumes the
role of teacher of philosophic truth must not invoke fancy to do
the work of fact.

We need not here enter into any further discussion of poetic
truth. Its general nature is now clear. In some curiously wild and
whirling words, Macaulay once spoke of the truth that 'is essential
to poetry' as the 'truth of madness,' and went on to declare that in
poetry, though 'the reasonings are just,' the 'premises are false,' and that
their acceptance 'requires a degree of credulity which almost amounts
to a partial derangement of the intellect.'[68] No more glaringly absurd
a conception of poetry has ever been suggested by a critic of any
pretensions; Mr Gradgrind himself could hardly have improved upon
it as an expression of utter Philistinism. Poetic truth is emphatically
not the 'truth of madness.' It has, on the contrary, and in the fullest
sense of the term, the essential quality of sanity. It is the truth of

---

[68] *Essay on Milton.*

things as seen, indeed, from a point of view different from that of science; and it is this fact which misled Macaulay into his strange vagaries concerning it. But as we can never learn the whole truth of things until this other point of view has been taken—as to know things in their entirety means to know them in their poetic as well as in their scientific aspects and meanings—the truth of poetry while antithetical to that of science, is at the same time, as I have shown, complementary to it; and it has at least an equal importance.

Thus as Leigh Hunt says, to the poet 'truth of every kind belongs…provided it can bud into any kind of beauty, or is capable of being illustrated and impressed by the poetic faculty.'[69] Or, as Principal Shairp put it: 'There is no truth cognisable by man which may not shape itself into poetry. It matters not whether it be a vision of nature's on-goings, or a conception of the understanding, or some human incident, or some truth of the affections, or some moral sentiment, or some glimpse of the spiritual world; any one of these may be so realised as to become fit subjects for poetic utterance. Only in order that it should be so, it is necessary that the object, whatever it is, should cease to be a merely sensible object, or a mere notion of the understanding, and pass inward,—pass out of the coldness of the merely notional region into the warm atmosphere of the life-giving imagination. Vitalised there, the truth shapes itself into living images which kindle the passion and affections, and stimulate the whole man. This is what has been called the real apprehension of truths, as opposed to the merely notional assent to them.'[70] And this shows that poetic truth has a human value to which scientific truth cannot possibly lay claim.

III

We are now in a position to appreciate the relations of poetry to life, and the large part that it has to play in that comprehensive

---

[69] *Imagination and Fancy.*
[70] *On Poetic Interpretation of Nature*, pp. 19, 20.

cultivation of all our faculties by which alone we can ever get out of life all that it has to afford. One chief element of poetry is its revealing power. It opens our eyes to sensuous beauties and spiritual meanings in the worlds of human experience and of nature to which otherwise we should remain blind. There are few of us who have not some endowment of poetic insight and feeling, some measure of 'the vision and the faculty divine.' But in the large majority of cases such poetic capacity as we possess, slight as it probably is at the best, is cramped by the ordinary conditions of existence, crippled by the mere material interests which fill so vast a place in our daily routine, and sometimes even consciously or unconsciously repressed. The true poet, whatever his range and quality, is one in whom the power of seeing and feeling the sensuous beauty and spiritual meaning of things exists in a pre-eminent degree, and to whom, moreover, another special power has been granted—the power of so expressing and interpreting what he sees and feels as to quicken our own imaginations and sympathies, and to make us see and feel with him. Thus one great service that the poet renders to us is that of 'awakening the mind's attention to the lethargy of custom, and directing it to the loveliness and wonders of the world before us; an inexhaustible treasure, but for which, in consequence of the film of familiarity and selfish solicitude, we have eyes, yet see not, ears that hear not, and hearts that neither feel nor understand.'[71] This is why Browning calls poets the 'makers-see,' and why Carlyle writes of them as 'gifted to discern the god-like mysteries of God's universe'; and this is why we may describe every true poet, as Arnold once described Wordsworth, as 'a priest to us all of the wonder and bloom of the world.' How much we need the poet's help, how greatly we are benefited by it, a moment's thought will show. For, as Browning puts it, speaking through the mouth of his Fra Lippo Lippi:

> For, don't you mark? we're made so that we love
> First when we see them painted, things we have pass'd

---

[71]Coleridge, *Biographia Literaria*, chapter xiv.

Perhaps a hundred times, nor cared to see;
And so they are better, painted—better to us,
Which is the same thing. Art was given for that.

This is a painter's noble apologia for his own art. Manifestly, the poet might quite as justly say as much for his. Poetry, too, was given for that; and in carrying out this great purpose, let us never forget, while it helps us directly by revealing fresh beauty and unsuspected significance in the actual things with which it deals, it does at the same time something more than this. It educates us to look at life for ourselves with more of a poet's insight and power of comprehension; it strengthens our own vision and sympathies; and thus it develops within us the latent faculty of poetic interpretation.

Poetry, therefore, covers our relations with life at almost every point, appeals to nearly all our moods and finds its subject matter in whatever, rightly treated, will yield poetic beauty and meaning. Thus every kind of poetry—even the poetry which touches things intrinsically trivial with the charm which is its special function to give—has its efficacy and justification. Yet, if poetry be an interpretation of life through the imagination and the feelings, its essential greatness must ultimately be judged by the greatness of the power with which it handles life's greatest and most abiding things—the things which belong to our highest experiences and interests. Since poetry is an art, it must, it is true, be estimated also with respect to its purely artistic or technical features. But this consideration must not blind us to the fact that poetic art is after all an embodiment of spirit and a vehicle of thought and feeling, and that it is from the character of the spirit, thought, and feeling which it expresses that it derives its substantial value. This does not involve any denial of the proposition that the immediate object of poetry, as of all other forms of art, is to give pleasure. It simply means that the quality of the pleasure itself must depend upon the nature of the subject-matter and the manner in which it is presented. From time to time we hear more than enough of 'art for art's sake.' But this vague and shadowy doctrine is, so far as the art of poetry is concerned, brought into contempt by the rank and standing of those who inculcate it; for it is for the most part associated with minor poets and dilettante critics. The really great poets of the world have never taken any account of it.[72] One and all, they have been substantial men. They have always recognised that poetry is made out of life, belongs to life, exists for life. On this primary principle they have done their work; and it is by their grasp of life and power of interpreting it that their greatness may in large measure be explained. We can thus go every step with Matthew Arnold when he writes: 'It is important, therefore, to hold fast to this: that poetry is at bottom a criticism of life; that the greatness of a poet lies in his powerful and beautiful application of ideas to life—to the question: How to five. Morals are often treated in a narrow and false fashion; they are bound up with systems of thought and belief which have had their day; they are fallen into the hands of pedants and professional dealers; they grow tiresome to some of us. We find attraction, at times, even in a poetry of revolt against them; in a poetry which might take for its motto Omar Khayyam's words: 'Let us make up in the tavern for the time we have wasted in the mosque.' Or we find attractions in a poetry indifferent to them; in a poetry where the contents may be what they will, but where the form is studied and exquisite. We delude ourselves in either case; and the best cure for our delusion is to let our minds rest upon the great and inexhaustible word *life*, until we learn to enter into its meaning. A poetry of revolt against moral ideas is a poetry of revolt against *life*; a poetry of indifference towards moral ideas is a poetry of indifference towards *life*.'[73]

We need not, therefore, be afraid of laying the utmost stress upon the nature of a poet's subject matter, his powers of thought, his moral strength and influence. 'No man was ever yet a great

---

[72]Save, indeed, when, like Tennyson, they have distinctly repudiated it. See *Memoir*, ii. 92.

[73]*Essay on Wordsworth, in Essays in Criticism*, second series.

poet,' says Coleridge, 'without being at the same time a profound philosopher.'[74] 'The great poets,' says Emerson, in one of his penetrating apophthegms, 'are judged by the frame of mind they induce.'[75] 'We may', says Landor, 'write little things well, and accumulate one upon another, but never will any be justly called a great poet unless he has treated a great subject worthily. He may be the poet of the lover and the idler, he may be the poet of green fields or gay society; but whoever is this can be no more. A throne is not built of birds' nests, nor do a thousand reeds make a trumpet.'[76] And again: 'A pretty sonnet may be written on a lambkin or on a parsnip, there being room enough for truth and tenderness on the edge of a leaf or the tip of an ear; but a great poet must clasp the higher passions breast high, and compel them in an authoritative tone to answer his interrogatories.'[77]

I am not asserting that in order to fulfil the conditions of poetic greatness a poet must of necessity address himself to the direct communication of ideas, or even write with a conscious ethical aim. We are not to confuse the functions of the poet with those of the preacher or homilist; their business is to instruct and guide, his to stir and vivify, to inspire, energise, and delight. This vital distinction is indeed implied in everything that has been said about the specific characteristics of that interpretation of life which poetry affords; and too much weight can hardly be attached to it.

On the other hand, however, the horror which critics of the so-called æsthetic school continually express of any poetry which deals with ideas and is written with a conscious ethical aim, is entirely without warrant. With much that they urge against didacticism in art we may, it is true, cordially agree; but we must not be misled by them into an unqualified condemnation of it. When Browning

---

[74] *Biographia Literaria*, chapter xv.
[75] Preface to *Parnassus*.
[76] *The Pentameron*, iv.
[77] *Ibid.*, ii.

says—'Philosophy first, and poetry, which is its highest outcome, afterwards';[78] and when Lowell says, 'No poem ever makes me respect its author which does not in some way convey a truth of philosophy,'[79] we feel that in these utterances the scope and powers of poetry are unduly circumscribed. But there is no reason why poetry should not be the outcome of philosophy and the vehicle of philosophic truth without sacrificing anything of its essential poetic qualities and graces. The real objection to so much that passes as didactic poetry is not that it is didactic, but that it is not poetry. Nevertheless, there is no inevitable antagonism between the didactic and the poetical. It all depends upon the poet. Take, for example, the work of Wordsworth, who, as we remember, wished to be 'considered as a teacher or as nothing.' 'In deserts of preaching,' says Lord Morley, 'we find almost within sight of one another, delightful oases of the purest poetry.'[80] But examination shows that in his passages of 'purest poetry' Wordsworth is often quite as much occupied with ideas as in his passages of flat prosaic preaching. It is not, therefore, the presence or absence of ideas which makes all the difference; it is the difference in treatment which counts.[81] From this fact we learn that we have no just ground to take exception to a poet's didacticism; what alone really calls for adverse criticism is his inability to give to his ideas a poetic form and setting. We do not, therefore, quarrel with any poet who offers us philosophy in the fashion of poetry. We require only that his philosophy shall be transfigured by imagination and feeling; that it shall be shaped into a thing of beauty; that it shall be wrought into true poetic expression; and that thus in reading him we shall always be keenly

---

[78]In a letter to Professor William Knight.

[79]*Letters*, i. 73.

[80]Introduction to Globe edition of *Wordsworth's Poetical Works*, p. lxiii.

[81]The reader can test this for himself by comparing the passage cited by Arnold in his essay on Wordsworth, as an example of that poet's too frequent prosaic dullness, with the superb *Lines written above Tintern Abbey*, in which far more profound philosophic thought is embodied in poetry of the purest kind.

aware of the difference between his rendering of philosophic truth and any mere prose statement of it. These conditions fulfilled, we welcome the poet as teacher and moralist, because we know that in his hands the truths of life and conduct will acquire a higher potency and value.

In concluding this brief discussion of the relations of poetry and life, may, therefore, repeat that a poet's greatness must ultimately depend upon the greatness of his subject matter, the power of thought, which he brings to bear upon it, and his moral strength and influence. And if it should be objected that in putting the matter in this way I am over- stating the ethical side of poetry, I will reply by quoting the testimony of one who among our modern English critics stands out conspicuously as a supporter of the claims of art. 'It is', says Walter Pater, 'on the quality of the matter it informs or controls, its compass, its variety, its alliance to great ends, or the depth of the note of revolt, or the largeness of hope in it, that the greatness of literary art depends, as *The Divine Comedy, Paradise Lost, Les Misérables, The English Bible* are great art.'[82]

In the study of poetry, therefore, as in the study of all other kinds of literature, our attention must first be directed to the poet himself; to his personality and outlook upon the world; to the interpretation of life expressly given by or held in solution in his work; to the individual note in it. However deeply we may presently become interested in questions of art and form, origins and historical affiliations, these primary aspects of poetry must never be permitted to slip out of our sight.

IV

As a guide to the systematic study of our subject, we have next to pass under rapid review the principal kinds of poetry.

In a broad way, poetry may be divided into two classes. There is the poetry in which the poet goes down into himself and finds

---

[82]*Appreciations*, p. 36.

his inspiration and his subjects in his own experiences, thoughts, and feelings. There is the poetry in which the poet goes out of himself, mingles with the action and passion of the world without, and deals with what he discovers there with little reference to his own individuality. The former class we may call personal or subjective poetry, or the poetry of self-delineation and self-expression. The latter we may call impersonal or objective poetry, or the poetry of representation or creation. The boundary lines between these two divisions cannot, of course, be drawn with absolute precision, and in much poetry, especially in our extremely composite modern poetry, personal and impersonal elements continually combine. But the distinction none the less rests on a firm foundation of fact, and for purposes of classification it is undeniably useful.

We may begin with personal or subjective poetry, to which, rather loosely, the name lyrical is also often applied. Lyric poetry, in the original meaning of the term, was poetry composed to be sung to the accompaniment of lyre or harp. In this sense, much poetry belonging to the impersonal division—like the old ballads and even early epics—might strictly speaking be described as lyrical. But the use of 'lyrical' will be restricted here to the simpler forms of the poetry in which, in contradistinction to the epic and dramatic kinds, the poet is principally occupied with himself.

In such simpler forms this personal poetry is almost unlimited in range and variety, for it may touch nearly all aspects of experience, from those which are most narrowly individual to those which involve the broadest interests of our common humanity. Thus we have the convivial or bacchanalian lyric; the lyric which skims the lighter things of life, as in the so-called *vers de société*; the lyric of love in all its phases, and with all its attendant hopes and longings, joys and sorrows; the lyric of patriotism; the lyric of religious emotion; and countless other kinds which it is unnecessary to attempt to tabulate.

In our study of any lyric, certain elementary principles of valuation should always be kept in view. We must inquire into the character and quality of the emotion which inspires it and the manner in which that emotion is rendered; for a lyric, to be good of its kind, must satisfy us that it embodies a worthy feeling; it must impress us by the convincing sincerity of its utterance; while its language and imagery must be characterised not only by beauty and vividness, but also by propriety, or the harmony which in all art is required between the subject and its medium. It will also be found that the pure lyric, having for its purpose the expression of some single mood or feeling, commonly gains much in emotional power by brevity and condensation, and that over-elaboration is almost certain to entail loss in effectiveness.

Though the essence of lyrical poetry is personality, it must yet be remembered that the majority of the world's great lyrics owe their place in literature very largely to the fact that they embody what is typically human rather than what is merely individual and particular, and that thus every reader finds in them the expression of experiences and feelings in which he himself is fully able to share. In such cases we do not have to put ourselves in the poet's place because he has already put himself into ours. Moreover, there is much lyrical poetry which is communal rather than personal in character. Investigations into the beginnings of literature have shown that poetry originated in the desire to give outward form to the feelings not of the individual but of the clan or group.[83] Hebrew lyrical poetry was chiefly of this kind. 'The awakening of the individual consciousness in the western nations since the introduction of Christianity' had, as Canon Cheyne has said, 'no parallel in the Semitic East'; and though the old Hebrew was a magnificent egotist, his egotism was emphatically that of race. Thus the 'I' and 'me' of the Psalms, as modern scholars tell us, refer, not to David or any other individual singer, but to the community of Israel, with its common tribulations, hopes, contrition, trust. The immense development of individuality in the modern world has naturally been followed by an increase of the personal and a subsidence of the communal factor in poetry.

---

[83]See Gummere's *Beginnings of Poetry* and Posnett's *Comparative Literature*.

Yet group-consciousness still produces group-poetry; as in hymns and lyrics of patriotism. Of such group-poetry the chorus, which is so popular a feature of many songs, is also an interesting survival. A further fact of importance is that in periods when general feelings are deeply stirred, and men are lifted out of themselves and the concerns of their private lots, the communal element in poetry becomes specially conspicuous. Thus Byron, though one of the greatest egotists of our literature, and our fullest exponent of that extreme individualism which was one characteristic of the romantic movement, often poured into his verse the world-passions which shook all Europe in the revolutionary age.[84]

Personal poetry passes by insensible degrees from the simpler forms of 'lyric' into meditative and philosophic poetry, in which the element of thought becomes important. Here, of course, emotional qualities and the beauty, vividness, and propriety of language and imagery, have still to be considered; but in addition, as we have already shown in sufficient detail, the substantial value of the thought itself has also to be estimated, together with the poet's success in giving it a poetic rendering. Thus, if we pass adverse judgment on Pope's *Essay on Man*, it is not only because, while it contains many passages of brilliant rhetoric, it is on the whole rather a versified treatise than a poem, but also because its philosophy, as philosophy, is confused, inconsistent, and radically unsound. It should be observed that there is a good deal of poetry which is didactic in intention but narrative in form—poetry in which the truths to be conveyed are wrought into story, parable, or allegory. This poetry is of course commonly classed as narrative, and therefore falls into the objective division; but we mention it here on account of the purpose by which it is dominated. A poet will often choose such indirect method of inculcating his ideas because in this way he can obtain the immense advantage of translating abstract ideas into concrete forms. Tennyson's *Palace of Art and Vision of Sin* may be

---

[84]See Dowden's *The French Revolution and English Literature*.

referred to as popular illustrations.

It is here also that we may best find place for the Ode, which may be defined as 'a rimed (rarely unrimed) lyric, often in the form of an address; generally dignified or exalted in subject, feeling, and style';[85] or as 'any strain of enthusiastic or exalted lyrical verse, directed to a fixed purpose, and dealing progressively with a dignified theme.'[86] It will be seen from these definitions that the ode is not specifically differentiated by any one constant feature, or combination of features, from other kinds of lyric;[87] the term is, in fact, an elastic and most ambiguous one; and there has always been in consequence an extreme diversity of view among the critics as to what poems shall and what shall not be included under it. In addition to dignity or exaltation of matter and manner and a logical evolution of thought, which may be accepted among its more habitual characteristics, it is generally, though it would seem not necessarily, marked by a certain amount of complexity and elaboration; it has often something of the quality of a poetical oration; while often, again, it is inspired, like Lowell's *Memorial Poems*, by some great public occasion. In structure, it may be regular, like Spenser's *Epithalamion*, Collins's *Ode to Evening*, Shelley's *West Wind*, and Keats's Odes *To a Nightingale* and *On a Grecian Urn*; or irregular, like Dryden's *Alexander's Feast, Collins's The Passions*, Wordsworth's *Ode on the Intimations of Immortality*, and Tennyson's *Ode on the Death of the Duke of Wellington*. In some cases a classic form is taken as model; and we have imitations, more or less close, of the 'Horatian' ode, so-called; as in Jonson's *Ode to Himself* and Marvell's *Upon Cromwell's Return* from Ireland; or of the choric odes of Pindar, with their systematic disposition of parts into strophe, anti-strophe, and epode, or, in Jonson's language, turn,

---

[85] *New English Dictionary*.

[86] Gosse, *English Odes*, Introduction, p. xiii.

[87] Among the Greeks, Ode was used, generally, for any kind of lyrical composition, from the drinking songs of Anacreon to the love songs of Sappho, and from these again to the lofty 'occasional' poems of Pindar.

counter-turn, and stand.[88] Gray's Pindaric odes are probably the most successful examples in English of the latter type.[89] But such poems follow their model in appearance only, and as the original choric significance of the divisions no longer exists, they are, like all such attempts to reproduce 'an ancient form through which the spirit breathes no more,' essentially artificial productions.

We come next to one of the most important divisions of personal poetry, the Elegy. In its simplest form, as in David's *Lament for Saul and Jonathan*, Landor's *Rose Aylmer*, and Tennyson's 'Break, break, break,' this is a brief lyric of mourning, or direct utterance of personal bereavement and sorrow. Its basis is manifestly, therefore, absolute sincerity of emotion and expression, since on the slightest hint of simulation or artifice we are prompted to turn on the poet with the warning words of Guiderius to Arviragus:

Prithee, have done,
And do not play in wench-like words with that
Which is so serious.[90]

In the evolution of literature, however, the elegy has undergone great elaboration, and has expanded in many directions. It has sometimes become the medium of communal feeling; as in the five poems of the Book of Lamentations which, while fashioned on tie professional mourning-songs of the Hebrew 'cunning women,' are dirges, not for an individual, but over the fall of a city 'that was full of people.' It has grown into a memorial or encomiastic poem, containing the poet's tribute to some great man (not

---

[88]See his *Ode to the Immortal Memory and Friendship of that Noble Pair, Sir Lucius Cory and Sir Harry Morison*.

[89]The *Pindarique* Odes of Cowley were written in stanzas of unequal lengths and great variety of metre under the then prevalent, though quite mistaken idea, that this was the true Pindaric style. Only much later was it discovered that the Odes of Pindar are not metrically 'licentious,' but are, on the contrary, based upon a very rigid though exceedingly complicated system.

[90]*Cymbeline*, iv. 2.

necessarily relative or personal friend), and often a study of his life and character, with reminiscences and thoughts suggested by them; as in Spenser's *Astrophel*, Ben Jonson's celebrated verses *To the Memory of my Beloved…Mr William Shakespeare*, Milton's *Lycidas*, Arnold's *Rugby Chapel* and *Thyrsis*, Whittier's *In Remembrance of Joseph Sturge*. Often, too, the philosophic and speculative elements become predominant in it, sometimes even to the total subordination of the purely personal interest; the poet, brooding upon his subject, being moved to meditations over questions immediately raised by it, or over the deepest problems of life and destiny; as in Shelley's *Adonais* and Browning's *La Saisiaz*. In many cases, of course, all these characteristics are combined; as in some of the examples just cited, and even more notably in *In Memoriam*, which is at once one of the most frankly personal of elegies, a long tribute to the dead friend, a spiritual autobiography extending over some three years of intellectual struggle, and a philosophic poem of immense reach and significance.

Moreover, under the powerful influences of a bookish age, the elegy in modern literature has often been used as a vehicle for literary criticism; as by Arnold in *Heine's Grave*, the two 'Obermann' poems, and *Memorial Verses*, 1850; and by Sir William Watson in *Wordsworth's Grave*—unquestionably the finest poem of the kind in our language. The fact that these poems have an intrinsic value as appreciations of the authors dealt with, no less than for their beauty as poems, will serve to remind us that in our study of the critical elegy, as in our study of all other classes of poetry in which the thought-element is in the ascendant, the criteria already indicated have still to be applied.

One particular type of elegy calls for separate mention—the pastoral type, in which the poet expresses his sorrow under the similitude of a shepherd mourning for a companion, or otherwise through conventional bucolic machinery. This form arose among the Sicilian Greeks; it passed into modern European literatures at the time of the Renaissance; and it has often been employed by

English poets from Spenser to Matthew Arnold.

Thus far we have considered the elegy in its various developments as a memorial poem only. It remains to add that the word has long been more broadly uséd for any poem distinctively reflective in character, and of a markedly melancholy strain. One of the most famous of English poems—Gray's *Elegy in a Country Churchyard*—shows this extension of meaning.[91]

Under the general head of subjective poetry we may also include the descriptive poem, the Epistle, and the Satire. Finally, it may be mentioned that there are certain kinds of lyrical poetry which are classified wholly on the basis of form.[92] The only one

---

[91]It was in an even broader sense that elegy was understood among the Greeks. Greek elegy, says Jebb, 'deals with the greatest variety of subjects,—the wars which the poet's city is waging, the political feuds among the citizens, the laws or principles which the poet wishes them to adopt, his own opinions on the manners and morals of the day, his views as to the best way of enjoying life, festive pleasure, lamentation for the dead—everything that the poet and his friends are wont to think or talk of ' (*Primer of Greek Literature*, pp. 50, 51) An elegy was, in fact, any poem written on the 'elegiac' measure, which was a distich composed of a dactylic hexameter followed by a dactylic pentameter. This measure is admirably described and exemplified by Long fellow:

> Peradventure of old some bard in Ionian Islands,
> Walking alone by the sea, hearing the wash of the waves, Learn'd the
> secret from them of the beautiful verse elegiac, Breathing into his
> song motions and sounds of the sea;

> For as the wave of the sea, upheaving in long undulations,
> Plunges loud on the sands, pauses and turns and retreats,
> So the Hexameter rising and surging with cadence sonorous
> Falls; and in refluent rhythm back the Pentameter flows,

Goethe's *Roman Elegies* are among the most famous examples in modern literature of this classic form. The English reader may study the measure to perfection in Watson's noble *Hymn to the Sea*.

[92]Among these, the intricate verse-forms of old French poetry, Northern and Provencal, may be referred to in passing, on account of the vogue they enjoyed for a time in our nineteenth century literature. See the collection of *Ballades and Rondeaus*, edited by Gleeson White in *The Canterbury Poets*.

of these which has any real importance for English readers is the Sonnet, a poem of fourteen lines, governed by certain prescribed rules in general structure and in the disposition of the rimes. These rules have indeed been often ignored by English sonnet writers from Shakespeare downward, and thus a distinction has grown up between the regular (or Italian) and the irregular (frequently called the Shakespearian) types. The theoretical system of the sonnet should, however, be carefully analysed and mastered by every student of poetic technique.[93]

We now pass from subjective or personal to objective or impersonal poetry. The fundamental characteristic of this poetry is, as I have already said, that it deals directly, not with the thoughts and feelings of the poet, but with the outer world of passion and action. While, therefore, in subjective poetry, which is the poetry of introspection, the poet looks into his heart to write, and even draws the outer world down into himself and steeps it in its own emotions, in objective poetry he projects himself into the life without, and, seeking there his motives and subjects, handles these with the least possible admixture of his own individuality.[94]

---

[93]See, e.g., Mr Watts-Dunton's article in *Chambers's Encyclopædia* and William Sharp's Introduction to *Sonnets of this Century*, in *The Canterbury Poets*.

[94]I say 'with the least possible admixture of his own individuality,' because, despite much loose talk about 'dramatic self-obliteration,' no poet can ever completely eliminate himself from his work. Everything that we have said about personality as the foundation of literature holds good of even the most objective of poetry. But here, for the most part, the poet reveals himself indirectly through what he represents and creates, while in subjective poetry he expressed himself immediately. It may further be added, that only in a few rare cases (and among these the Shakespearean drama cannot be included) is no trace of even direct self-intrusion to be found. Something more will be said on this point when we come to the drama. Passing reference may meanwhile be made to the rather academic controversy concerning the alleged natural and essential superiority of objective poetry as a class to subjective poetry as a class. Brunètiere, for instance, drew up a 'hierarchy of *genres*,' and argued that the relative value of each was to be found in an inverse ratio to the degree to which it involved or permitted the direct expression of personality. On this basis he ranked the

Such impersonal poetry falls naturally into two groups—the narrative and the dramatic. As these must manifestly have much in common with the prose-story and the regular play, the reader will find a great deal which bears directly upon them in our succeeding chapters on the novel and the drama. A rapid survey of their principal subdivisions and of the more salient characteristics of these, is all that we have now to undertake.

In our study of narrative poetry we naturally begin with the popular ballad, or short story in verse; a form which appears to have arisen spontaneously in almost all literatures, and represents one of the earliest stages in the evolution of the poetic art. Our own literature is particularly rich in ballads of the true traditional kind, of which the authorship has long since been forgotten, and which alike in form and spirit bear evident traces of the unlettered but vigorous times out of which they sprang, and of the tastes of the popular audiences for which they were originally made.[95] Their themes are commonly furnished by the more elementary aspects of life; large space is given in them to tales of adventure, fighting, deeds of prowess and valour; they have frequently a strong infusion of supernaturalism; while love, hatred, pity, and the simpler interests of the domestic lot, receive a full share of attention. In method and style they are characterised by straightforwardness and

---

drama, as a form of art, higher than the novel. Among English critics, Arnold may in particular be mentioned as a stout upholder of the objective doctrine (see Preface to Poems, 1854, reprinted in *Mixed Essays*). It was in accordance with the principles there enunciated that his own most ambitious poems—his narrative and dramatic poems—were written. But by temper and natural bias of genius, Arnold was emphatically subjective; and his most characteristic verse belongs to the personal class.

[95]Percy's *Reliques of Ancient English Poetry*—the first important collection of our old ballads—has been already referred to as an epoch-making book. It is a work which, notwithstanding its many imperfections, every lover of poetry and every student of the history of literature should possess. But a number of much more comprehensive and more scholarly anthologies have been published since Percy's time; notably, the monumental work of Prof. F. J. Child.

rapidity of narration, and a certain childlike naiveté; often crude, they are often, too, astonishingly energetic; and while habitually garrulous in matters of detail, they seldom linger over description or concern themselves about motives and passions, save as these translate themselves immediately into action. Many of these ballads have immense dramatic power and wonderful metrical beauty, and for this reason they must be assigned to a distinct place among the great imperishable things of our literature. But apart from their intrinsic merits, they are specially deserving of study at a time like our own when, in literature as in music, the current runs so strong in the direction of ever-increasing complexity that our tastes are becoming sophisticated and we are in danger of losing all healthy appreciation of what is simple, broad, and elemental.[96]

The modern ballad may be defined as a literary development of the traditional form. To this form it often keeps very close; as in such admirable examples of the simpler narrative in verse as Scott's *Eve of St John*, Kingsley's *The Sands of Dee*, Longfellow's *The Wreck of the Hesperus*, Rossetti's *Stratton Water*, and William Morris's *Shameful Death*. More often, on the other hand, while it clearly owes much to the inspiration of early poetry, and preserves its best traditions, it shows the powerful influences of a later age in its tendency to greater elaboration, the enlargement of description and psychological interest, and a more finished style of art. The really characteristic modern ballad, therefore, represents the natural expansion, not the artificial reproduction, of the primitive type. It is not in laborious imitations of primitive models, with their attempts to recover the spontaneous simplicity of nature through the studied simplicity of art, their deliberate archaisms, and their consequent flavour of affectation and formalism, but in poems like Tennyson's *The Revenge*, Browning's *Hervé Riel*, Rossetti's *The King's Tragedy*, and Robert Buchanan's

---

[96]Mention has already been made of the fact that Percy's *Reliques* did much to help the reaction towards the end of the eighteenth century against the artificiality which had then long prevailed in our literature.

The Ballad of Judas Iscariot, that we are in the true line of literary evolution; for these, while they have all the sterling qualities of the old ballads, have nothing merely imitative about them, but are, on the contrary, essentially modern and original poems.

From the ballad, or story-poem, we pass to the longer narrative in verse. Of this large species a number of fairly well-marked varieties may be distinguished, the first place among which must be given to the Epic. For purposes of historical study, this again has to be subdivided into primitive epic and later epic. The former of these has also been called the 'epic of growth,' to mark the fact that, unlike the 'epic of art,' with which it is thus contrasted, it is not in its entirety the work of a single author, but to some extent the result of a process of evolution and consolidation, and that a large amount of pre-existing material, in the shape of floating legends and earlier folk poems and sagas, is gathered up into its composition. An epic of this kind may, therefore, be regarded as the final product of a long series of accretions and syntheses; scattered ballads gradually clustering together about a common character into ballad-cycles (like the English Robin Hood cycle), and these at length being reduced to approximate unity by the intervention of conscious art. Well-known examples are to be found in the Anglo-Saxon *Beowulf*, the old Germanic *Nibelungenlied*, and the Finnish *Kalevala*.[97] To the same general class we may also assign the *Iliad* and the *Odyssey*, though we must do this with some diffidence, since, as all but the most radical critics admit, whatever may have been their genesis and early history, the controlling power of a single supreme artistic

---

[97]The case of the *Kalevala* is indeed different from that of the other two poems mentioned, since it owes its epic form to the labours of a modern scholar, Dr Lönnrot, who, like Scott in his 'Border raids,' collected from the peasantry an immense number of ancient ballads and sagas, and then wove these together, with great skill, into a consecutive narrative, without, as he asserted, adding a line of his own. His work, therefore, provides an interesting object-lesson, for it shows the way in which, in early times, an epic may have been made out of masses of scattered legendary material.

genius is clearly evident in the poems as they stand. All primitive epics deal, broadly speaking, with the same kind of subject matter. Their themes are furnished, in Homeric phrase, by $\chi\lambda\acute{\epsilon}\alpha\ \acute{\alpha}\upsilon\delta\rho\varpi$—the 'deeds of heroes,'[98] generally the great legendary heroes of a race; and vast bodies of immemorial traditions provide the basis of their structure. As these traditions are almost invariably bound up with a people's mythology, the supernatural element is also more or less prominent; whether, as in the Homeric epics, it is distinctively religious in character and is everywhere interfused with the human interest of the action; or whether, as in the *Nibelungenlied*, it has become attenuated into the merely marvellous and appears only occasionally in the background. In the style of such poems there is much to remind us of the popular ballad; even the *Iliad* and the *Odyssey*, notwithstanding the individual greatness of their manner, being marked by the directness and simplicity, the naïveté and frequent garrulity, which, in all literatures, belong to the poetic art in the earlier stages of its development.

The relation of the 'epic of art' to the 'epic of growth' is much the same as that of the later ballad to the traditional form. It is the product of individual genius working in an age of scholarship and literary culture on lines already laid down. One great epic of art occupies a place of capital importance in literary history, not only on account of its own splendid qualities, but also because, itself fashioned closely on the Homeric poems, it became in its turn a chief model for other workers in the epic field—the *Æneid*. In *Paradise Lost*, English poetry possesses one of the supreme masterpieces of epic literature; while for other examples of the same class reference may be made to Tasso's *Gerusalemme Liberata*, the *Lusiadas* of Camoens, and on a much smaller scale, Arnold's 'episode,' or epic fragment, *Sohrab and Rustum*.

The literary epic naturally resembles the primitive epic, on which it is ultimately based, in various fundamental characteristics.

[98] *Iliad*, ix. 189; *Odyssey*, viii. 73.

Its subject matter is of the old heroic and mythical kind; it makes free use of the supernatural; it follows the same structural plan and reproduces many traditional details of composition; while, greatly as it necessarily differs in style, it often adopts the formulas, fixed epithets, and stereo-typed phrases and locutions, which are among the marked features of the early type. But examination discloses, beneath all superficial likenesses, a radical dissimilarity. The heroic and legendary material is no longer living material; it is invented by the poet or disinterred by scholarly research; and it is handled with laborious care in accordance with abstract rules and principles which have become part of an accepted literary tradition. Where, therefore, the epic of growth is fresh, spontaneous, racy, the epic of art is learned, antiquarian, bookish, imitative. Its specifically 'literary' qualities—its skilful reproduction and adaptation of epic matter and methods, its erudition, its echoes, reminiscences, and borrowings—are indeed, as the *Æneid* and *Paradise Lost* will suffice to prove, among its most interesting characteristics for a cultured reader.[99] A minor form of the epic of art may just be mentioned—the Mock Epic, in which the machinery and conventions of the regular epic are employed in connection with trivial themes, and thus turned to the purposes of parody or burlesque. The earliest specimen of this form is the fragmentary *Batrachomyomachia*, or *Battle of the Frogs and Mice*, once ascribed to Homer, while the finest example of it in English is Pope's *The Rape of the Lock*. It will be observed that thus far I have spoken of one particular kind of literary epic only—the classic kind. In rare instances, however, a non-classic form may be taken as model. Thus Longfellow's *Song of Hiawatha* was in part at least inspired by and fashioned upon the *Kalevala*, the rhythm and style of which are adopted in it.[100]

---

[99]See *ante*. pp. 58. 59.

[100]To prevent possible confusion I ought perhaps to call special attention to the fact that while epic is often employed as a synonym for a long narrative poem of any description, I have taken the word here, as will be seen, in a much more restricted sense. This limitation of its meaning is amply justified, I think, by the

Another division of narrative poetry which, with many resemblances to the epic, is yet distinguished from it in source, matter, and method, is the Metrical Romance. As, however, in the evolution of literature this term has undergone considerable enlargement of meaning, various different classes of composition have to be included under it. There are, first, those poems which fall under the strictest definition of romance, which originally signified a story told in one of the romance languages, and dealing, as all such stories did, with chivalry, knighterrantry, fighting, adventure, enchantments, love: like the *chansons de gestes* which were popular in France during the Middle Ages, and flourished in England in Anglo-Norman times. Then there are the English narratives of the same general type which, as the word had already come to denote a certain kind of matter and treatment, were called romances though not written in a romance tongue. In part developed from these earlier forms, though in part touched by the classic culture of Italy, Chaucer's splendid idealised picture of the fast-vanishing world of chivalry, *The Knightës Tale*, next deserves special mention on our list. Thence we pass to such poems as Ariosto's *Orlando Furioso* and Spenser's *Faery Queene*, in which the familiar characters and machinery of the old romances— wandering knights, distressed damsels, battles, tournaments, giants, dwarfs, wizards, enchanted castles—are remanipulated for different purposes by poets for whom such things have become as much matters of literary tradition as are heroic and mythical subjects for writers of epics of art. In yet another subdivision of the verse-romance we may place the numerous narrative poems of more recent literature which were inspired by that imaginative revival of the past which, as we have seen, was one conspicuous feature of

---

needs of classification. The attempt to bring all kinds of narrative poetry under one head is a result of the academic assumption that the divisions of poetic forms adopted by the Greeks, and satisfactorily enough in respect of their own poetry, had, as Arnold held, a 'natural propriety,' and are therefore to be accepted as final. Such assumption ignores the enormous evolution of literature since Greek rimes, with the consequent continual differentiation of literary types.

the romantic movement; for example, Scott's *Lay of the Last Minstrel* and *Marmion*, and later, Tennyson's *Idylls of the King*, Swinburne's *Tristram of Lyonesse*, Arnold's *Tristram and Iseult*, Hawker's *Quest of the Sangreal*, and the tales in Morris's *Earthly Paradise*. These last are specially interesting as showing the purely romantic handling even of subjects taken from Greek mythology. The *Idylls of the King*, on the other hand, are equally suggestive, because they exhibit the combination, natural in an age of literary eclecticism, of the romantic with the classic, since, while their theme is mediæval, their art owes so much to their author's long and loving study of Homer that with almost as much propriety we might define them as epic. It may further be remarked that, like the *Faery Queene*, they exemplify on a large scale the use of narrative for allegorical purposes, of which I have already spoken. Finally, the word romance has been still further extended to cover poems like Moore's *Lalla Rookh*, and the verse tales of Byron and his imitators, which are products of the romantic movement in literature, and are romantic in matter and spirit in that secondary, though now current, sense in which the term has now come to mean anything that is remote, passionate, fantastic, wild.

One other class of narrative poetry remains to be mentioned, but for this, unfortunately, it seems impossible to find any name which could be accepted as entirely satisfactory. It may be best described, perhaps, by saying that in contrast with both the epic and the romance it represents the tendency towards realism in poetic art. It is the distinguishing feature of such poetry, therefore, that in its subjects it keeps relatively close to the ordinary world of experience and action, though it may treat this world in very different ways; as we may see by comparing the hard and uncompromising literalness of Grabbe, who set out to 'paint the cot as Truth will paint it and as bards will not,'[101] with Tennyson's so-called 'idealistic realism,' or habit (as in the *English Idylls*), of transfiguring homely detail by

---

[101] *The Village*, Book i.

the subtle touch of poetic magic. Naturally, this land of narrative poetry often finds its themes and characters in the present; and even when it goes back into the past for them, it seeks them still, as in Longfellow's *Evangeline*, amid commonplace people and surroundings, and not in heroic legend, or romantic achievements, or among the great movements and figures of history. Sometimes it may take the form of a humorous transcript from contemporary manners, especially the manners of 'low' life, as in several of Chaucer's *Canterbury Tales*, and in the delightful character studies loosely set in the economic argument of Goldsmith's *Deserted Village*.

But the greatest interest belongs to two subdivisions of it, both of comparatively recent growth. The first of these comprises such poems as derive their material from 'the short and simple annals of the poor,' or from the lives of the humble and obscure; like Wordsworth's *Michael* and Tennyson's *Enoch Arden* and *Dora*. To the second we may assign all such poetic narratives as, like Mrs Browning's *Aurora Leigh*, Owen Meredith's Lucile, Coventry Patmore's *The Angel in the House*, and Robert Browning's *Red-Cotton Night-Cap Country*, are to all intents and purposes novels in verse. The former class has a special historical significance as marking the influx into narrative poetry of that ever-broadening sympathy with 'all sorts and conditions of men,' which is one aspect of the modern democratic movement. The latter is manifestly the result of that same complex of forces, social and literary, which produced the modern novel. It is particularly worthy of critical consideration, both because it exhibits the effort of poetry to follow prose fiction into the field of contemporary social life, and because it thereby raises the difficult problem as to how far, and under what conditions of treatment, modern facts and problems can be successfully handled in verse.[102]

---

[102]*Aurora Leigh*, which Leigh Hunt called 'kaleidoscopic presentment of modern life,' was, according to the author's own statement, intended to show that poetry could 'meet the age face to face.' See Book v., lines 139–221, for a vigorous assertion of the claims of modernity in poetic art; and contrast Arnold's contention (*Preface to First Edition of Poems, in Mixed Essays*), that, while modern subjects

The last division of objective poetry is the Dramatic. By this I do not here mean the regular acted drama which, as a specific form of literary art, is reserved for separate treatment. I mean simply poetry which, though intended not for the stage but to be read, is essentially dramatic in principle; poetry, that is, in which the poet merges himself in his character or characters, and does not, as in subjective poetry or ordinary narrative, describe or relate in his own person and from the outside. In all varieties of narrative poetry the dramatic element commonly appears more or less prominently in the shape of dialogue; while more rarely it fills considerable space as incorporated autobiographical material, as in the long tales told about themselves by Odysseus in the *Odyssey* and Æneas in the *Æneid*. In many cases it is not necessary to distinguish what should strictly be called dramatic narrative from ordinary narrative. Thus, to be entirely consistent, we ought to class *Aurora Leigh* under the former head; but nothing would be gained by doing this, and it seems more natural, therefore, to describe it as a narrative in verse in the autobiographical, or first personal form.[103] The use of the epithet 'dramatic' should rather, I think, be confined to poems in which the poet's assumption of character has a real importance in the working out of his theme. So understood, dramatic poetry may be subdivided into several groups. There is first the Dramatic Lyric. This is in spirit and method a subjective poem; but the subjective element pertains, not to the poet himself, but to some other person, into whose moods and experiences he enters, and to whose thoughts and feelings he gives vicarious expression. Browning's works furnish many familiar examples of this type,[104] and to these, such widely

---

may serve 'the comic poet' and 'the lighter kinds of poetry,' an 'action of present times' is 'too near,' and 'too much mixed, up with what' is 'accidental and passing; to form a sufficiently grand, detached, and self-sufficient object for a tragic poem.'

[103]On the general significance of this form, see chapter iv, pp. 187–189.

[104]Browning uses *Dramatic Lyrics* as a general title for one division of his works; but some of the poems contained in it are really dramatic stories.

differing productions as Macaulay's *Ivry*, Hood's *Song of the Shirt*, and Stevenson's *Child's Garden of Verses*, may be added by way of further illustration.

There is, secondly, the Dramatic Story, including the ballad, or short story in verse, like Tennyson's *The First Quarrel* and *The Revenge*, Browning's *How they brought the Good News from Ghent and Muléykeh*, and Arnold's *Forsaken Merman*; and the more extended narrative, like Browning's *A Forgiveness*, Rossetti's *A Last Confession*, and Tennyson's 'monodrama,' *Maud*. Sometimes the story is told entirely in dialogue, as in Rossetti's *Sister Helen*; and sometimes, while the bulk of the story is in direct narration, the dialogue element plays an important part in the scheme, as in *The Holy Grail*, in which Sir Percival's tale is interrupted from time to time, and its moral significance punctuated, by the questions and comments of his auditor, the old monk Ambrosius. This poem also shows that in a dramatic story there may be a certain amount of non-dramatic description and 'setting'; a point which is again illustrated by *The Ancient Mariner*. Another plan, adopted by Coventry Patmore in *Faithful for Ever*, is to unfold the incidents and characters in letters.[105]

A third species of dramatic poetry comprises the Dramatic Monologue or Soliloquy.[106] It is often difficult to distinguish this from the dramatic lyric on the one hand, and, on the other hand, from the dramatic narrative; from the former, because it too is vicariously subjective; from the latter, on account of the amount of story which frequently enters into its composition. Speaking generally, however, it differs from the dramatic lyric as the more elaborate forms of personal

---

[105]Another kind of dramatic narrative may just be mentioned, though it does not properly enter into our present analysis. It is the kind represented by the *Canterbury Tales*, in which the story is told in the third-personal form, but by a character created by the poet, and not by the poet himself.

[106]Though the two words are habitually employed interchangeably, Soliloquy really means a poem in which the speaker talks to himself, as in Browning's *Caliban upon Setebos*; monologue, a poem in which he addresses some listener or listeners, as in the same writer's *Andrea del Sarto* and *Fra Lippo Lippi*.

poetry differ from the simple lyric proper; while, however closely it may approximate to the narrative by its free use of incident, the fact that it treats all outward things as subordinate to those inner forces and problems upon which its interest is concentrated, is sufficient to put it into a class by itself. It is essentially a study of character, of mental states, of moral crises, made from the inside. Thus it is predominantly psychological, analytical, meditative, argumentative. Of this form, though it has been used with success by other modern poets, Browning is, of course, our greatest master, and in his work may be found examples of almost every variety of it, from brief and subtle self-delineation, as in My Last Duchess, to long and profound exploration of spiritual depths and moral complexities, as in *The Bishop orders his Tomb at St Praxed's, Bishop Blougram's Apology*, and *Prince Hohensliel-Sehwangau.*

One problem involved in the study of the dramatic monologue is too important to be passed over without a word. In theory, it is clear, dramatic poetry is the most entirely objective form of poetry, that in which the poet most completely loses himself. The ideal aim of a dramatic monologue may, therefore, be defined as the faithful self-portrayal, without ulterior purpose, of the personality of the supposed speaker. In practice, however, it is often used by the poet as a medium for his own philosophy. He may so use it to present his philosophy directly, as when the supposed speaker is to all intents and purposes his mouthpiece and representative; or he may so use it to present his philosophy indirectly, as when he makes the supposed speaker give expression to ideas antagonistic to his own in such manner as to convey or suggest adverse judgment upon them. The direct method is exemplified by Browning's *Rabbi Ben Ezra*; the indirect, by the same poet's *Clean*, and by Tennyson's *St Simeon Stylites*. Despite Browning's rather too emphatic claim for the absolute objectivity of his dramatic writing, his own religious and ethical teachings continually appear in it, in either positive or negative statement and the problem in his case, and in all other similar cases, therefore, is to disentangle the personal from the impersonal elements, and to determine how far, and in what ways, poetry which is dramatic in form and spirit is none the less to be taken as a contribution to the poet's interpretation of life.

The foregoing are varieties of the poetry which rests upon the dramatic principle, though it does not employ the actual structure and machinery of the regular stage-play. There is, however, another class of dramatic poetry in which such structure and machinery are adopted. Browning's *Paracelsus*, Longfellow's *Golden Legend*, Arnold's *Empedocles on Etna*, Ibsen's *Brand* and *Peer Gynt*, will indicate some of the shapes which this 'closet drama' may assume.

In closing this analysis, I must ask the reader to remember that it is not intended to be either rigorously logical or exhaustively complete. I have sought only so to arrange the principal genera and species of poetry according to a natural scheme of classification, as to provide thereby a useful basis for systematic study.

V

Thus far our attention has been directed mainly to the content of poetry and to its general importance as an interpretation of life. A few pages must now be devoted to its formal and technical aspects.

From what has already been said about the vital connection between poetic feeling and rhythmical expression, it is evident that careful consideration must be given, in the first place, to the facts and problems of metre.

By metre we understand that ordered rhythm which results from a regulated alternation of syllables of different characters or values. In the Greek and Latin languages, this difference in character or value depended upon what is called *quantity*, or the length of time taken in pronunciation; and the metrical 'foot,' or group of syllables forming the basis of the line or verse, was composed of short and long syllables arranged according to certain schemes. Thus the iambic foot was made up of a short syllable followed by a long one (♩♩ or ˘ ˉ); the dactylic, of a long syllable followed by two short ones (♩♩♩ or ˘ ˘ ˘); the spondaic, of two long syllables (♩ ♩ or ˉ ˉ);

and so on. In English, the basis of metre is not quantity but accent, and ordered rhythm arises from a regulated alternation of syllables which are stressed, or heavy, and unstressed, or light.[107] Now a stressed syllable may be combined in a foot with one unstressed or with two (never, in English verse, with more than two); and thus we may have feet of two syllables or of three, the character in each case being determined by the relative position of the accent. The five chief measures of English verse—two dissyllabic and three trisyllable—are thus reached:—

I. Feet of two syllables:—

---

(1) The **iambic**, in which the unaccented syllable precedes the accented (˘ ′), as in *begín*. Thus—

" Awáke | my sóul, | and wíth | the sún | ."

(2) The **trochaic**, in which this order is reversed, and the unaccented syllable follows the accented (′ ˘), as in *mércy*. Thus—

" Cómrades, | leáve me | hére a | líttle | while as | yet 'tis | eárly | mórn."

II. Feet of three syllables :

(1) The **anapæstic**, in which the two unaccented syllables precede the accented (˘ ˘ ′), as in *colonnáde*. Thus—

" And the sheén | of their speárs | was like stárs | on the séa | ."

(2) The **dactylic**, in which the accented syllable precedes the two unaccented (′ ˘ ˘), as in *mérciful*. Thus—

" Táke her úp | ténderly | ."

---

(3) The **amphibrachic**, in which the accented syllable comes between the two unaccented (˘ ′ ˘), as in *etérnal*. Thus—

---

[107]The question whether quantity does or does not also exist in English verse, and if so, to what extent it reinforces or interferes with accent, is one of the great problems of metrical specialists, and it has long been hotly debated. It is, however, of too technical a character to be discussed within the limits of a mere introductory sketch.

" Ŏ hush thee, | my babĭe | thy sĭre wăs | a knĭght."

Other feet are also recognised by some English metrists, and even of the five principal forms given, here there are numerous intricate variations and combinations. But limitations of space compel me to confine myself to the most elementary facts of a subject which is so vast and involved that for its adequate treatment a volume, not a section, would be required. As a matter of convenience I adopt, without discussion, the descriptive names which, though strictly applicable only to classic metres, have been, and are still, employed by the great majority of writers on English verse, though not without protest from those who advocate their abandonment in favour of a new nomenclature. It will of course be understood that in using them we take accented and unaccented as equivalent to long and short.

These feet form the foundation of lines or verses, which may be called iambic, trochaic, anapæstic, dactylic, and amphibrachic, as the dominating movement is one or another of these. Such lines or verses may then further be described as dimeter, trimeter, tetrameter, pentameter, heptameter, and octameter, according to the number of feet of which they are composed. Thus, the measure of *In Memoriam* is iambic tetrameter; of *Locksley Hall*, trochaic octameter; of *The Bridge of Sighs*, dactylic dimeter; our English blank verse is unrimed iambic pentameter; the closing line of the Spenserian stanza (generally called an 'alexandrine') is iambic hexameter; the measure of *Evangeline*, dactylic hexameter; and so on.

It must not be forgotten, however, nor is the attentive student ever likely to forget, that these theoretic systems are in actual practice subject to continual variation, and that much of our English poetry, and especially of modern English poetry, is characterised by great metrical irregularity. One of the simplest and most frequently occurring of all metrical phenomena, even in verse-structures marked by sustained uniformity, is the substitution of another kind of foot for that which constitutes the basic principle of the verse. Take these two lines from Akenside's delightful little poem, For a Grotto, which is written in iambic pentameter:

> To me, whom in their lays the shepherds call,

and

> Lulled by the murmur of my rising fount;

and, though in an ordinary way we read them with no suspicion of anything aberrant in them, examination at once shows that in the second foot of the former and in the first foot of the latter, the accent is so changed that a trochee takes the place of the normal iambus. This kind of substitution is, in fact, so common as to pass unnoticed.[108]

Often the accent is so evenly distributed between two syllables in reading that what may be analysed as an iambic foot becomes practically a spondee ($\bar{\ }\ \bar{\ }$), as in Milton's line (cited by Johnson):

> Thus at | their sha | dy lodge | arriv'd, | both stood | ,

and in one recurrent line of Newman's well-known hymn—

> The night | is dark, | and I | am far | from home | —
> Lead Thou | me on | .[109]

Frequently the entire character of an iambic line may be changed by an additional number of unaccented, or light syllables, which in such examples as—

> Myriads of | rivulets | hurry | ing through | the lawns |

and

> Of some | precip | itous riv | ulet to | the wave,

---

[108]Dr Johnson, though of course a great stickler for regularity, held that a certain amount of variation was justified by the fact that in a long com- position 'we are soon wearied with the perpetual recurrence of the same cadence.' He was therefore willing to admit deviation from 'the rigour of exactness' in the first foot of a verse, though its introduction elsewhere he regarded as savouring of 'licentiousness.' See *The Rambler*, No. 86, in which he points out that Milton's blank verse 'seldom has two pure'— that is, absolutely regular— 'lines together.'
[109]With such a line as this before us, we may fairly question whether the spondee ought not to be added to the list of English feet.

serve to give to the verse, in the one case a dactylic, in the other an anapæstic movement. As an addition of extra light syllables will thus turn an iambic or trochaic foot into an anapæst or dactyl, so the omission of a light syllable will turn an anapæst or dactyl into an iambus or trochee. The facility with which such changes may be made is therefore evident. To refer to a single example, Tennyson's *Vastness* is dactylic:—

> Peace, let it | be ! for I | loved him, and | love him for | ever - the | dead are not | dead but a | live | .

But there are in fact very few of such completely dactylic lines, and throughout trochees are frequently interspersed, as in—

> Lies upon | this side, | lies upon | that side, | truthless | violence | mourn'd by the | Wise,

and

> Household | happiness, | gracious | children, | debtless | competence, | golden | mean.

The frequent intermixture of iambic and anapaestic feet has been, since Coleridge introduced it in *Christabel*,[110] and Scott gave it vogue

---

[110]'I have only to add,' Coleridge explains in his preface to the poem, 'that the metre of *Christabel* is not, properly speaking, irregular, though it may seem so from its being founded on a new principle, namely, that of counting in each line the accents, not the syllables. Though the latter may vary from seven to twelve, yet in each line the accents will be found to be only four. Nevertheless this occasional variation in number of syllables is not introduced wantonly, or for the mere ends of convenience, but in correspondence with some transition in the nature of the imagery or passion.' Scott heard portions of the then unpublished *Christabel* recited by a friend, and was so enchanted by 'the singularly irregular structure of the stanza, and the liberty which it allowed the author to adapt the sound to the sense,' that he at once borrowed it for his *Lay*, afterwards making 'the acknowledgment due from the pupil to his master.' The principle in question was not, however, so entirely novel as Coleridge fancied. For Mr Watts-Dunton's theory that it was discovered by Chatter- ton, see his introduction to selections from 'the marvellous boy' in Ward's *English Poets*, vol. iii.

by *The Lay of the Last Minstrel*, one of the most common characteristics of octosyllabic poetry, of the now familiar free movement of which the following passage may be taken as a type:—

> And Christ | abel saw | the la | dy's eye, |
> And noth | ing else | she saw | thereby, |
> Save the boss | on the shield | of Sir Li | onel tall, |
> Which hung | on a murk | y old niche | in the hall | .

Sometimes the unaccented syllable may be dropped even from a dissyllabic foot, and its place supplied in reading by a pause, or the dwelling of the voice upon the accented word; as in Tennyson's

> Break, break, break,
> On thy cold grey stones, O sea!

and

> Birds in the high Hall-garden
> When twilight was felling,
> Maud, Maud, Maud, Maud,
> They were crying and calling.

In much trisyllabic verse, moreover, the interchange of the three kinds of foot is so continual that one almost hesitates to describe the metre by any single term. Thus in the first four lines of Byron's *The Bride of Abydos*—

> Know ye the land where the cyprus and myrtle
> Are emblems of deeds that are done in their clime? Where
> the rage of the vulture, the love of the turtle,
> Now melt into sorrow, now madden to crime?—

the first line, as will be seen, is dactylic, the second and fourth, amphibrachic, the third, anapæstic.

These few examples will suffice to introduce the question of metrical variation, which, of all questions connected with the subject of versification, is at once perhaps the most fascinating and the most difficult.

It is commonly recognized that each of our five principal measures has its own distinctive quality, and therefore its special fitness for particular purposes. The triple metres, owing to their greater number of unstressed syllables, are undoubtedly lighter and more rapid in movement than the dissyllabic. This explains why the introduction of anapæstic or dactylic feet into iambic verse tends to render it more swift and graceful; which in turn shows the inner motive of the variation in metre in Tennyson's two lines about the rivulets, quoted above. It is possible still further to distinguish differences in æsthetic character and effect within the two groups; and thus we find critics describing the iambic measure as smooth, dignified, and stately, and the trochaic as energetic and abrupt; the anapæstic as swift and forcible, the dactylic as airy and graceful, and the amphibrachic as swinging and free. On these matters, it is true, it is rather hazardous to generalise, for we do not have to go far in our practical study of poetry before we discover that every form of metre has a much wider range of power than such abstract statements would suggest. Iambic measure, for instance—the standard verse of English poetry—has been used with complete success for all kinds of subjects 'from grave to gay, from lively to severe'; while examples are not wanting to prove that the lighter trisyllabic metres are often (as in Tennyson's *Vastness*, Arnold's *The Future*, and Cosmo Monkhouse's *A Dead March*) singularly effective as vehicles for solemn meditation and feelings of tenderness and sorrow. On the principle that the connection between matter and form in poetry is an organic one, the question of the propriety and æsthetic value of the verse employed in a given case is, therefore, of the utmost interest. Similarly, in our study of any poet it will always be worthwhile to consider the measures most frequently and most successfully used by him, and their relation to the characteristic qualities of his temper and genius.

While metre is an essential concomitant of poetry, rime[111] is to

---

[111]It is perhaps desirable that I should call attention to the fact that I have

be regarded as only an accessory; yet it is so common an accessory in English verse, and in most of its forms, indeed, so nearly constant a feature, that its importance can hardly be overstated. It adds much to the beauty of poetry as 'musical speech,' and therefore to the pleasure which poetry affords. It has also frequently been pointed out that, by marking distinctly the close of lines and stanzas, it helps to emphasise rhythm.

Rime is the correspondence in sound between syllable and syllable; the conditions being: identity in vowel sound, and, if the words end in a consonant or consonants, in these also; as in *see, me, ark, mark*; difference in the consonant or consonants, if any, preceding the vowel, as in *ray, stray*; similarity of accent, as in *ringing, singing, beautiful, dutiful*; identity in the syllable or syllables, if any, which follow the accent, as in the illustrations just given. Thus, *singer* and *ringing, dutiful* and *beautify*, are not rimes.

Rimes, as will be seen, may be single (or 'masculine,' as they are sometimes called), as *ring, sing*; or, double ('feminine'), as *ringing, singing*; or triple as *unfortunate, importunate*. These different kinds may be employed at the discretion of the poet in different ways. A poem may be entirely in single rimes, or in double, or in triple; or different kinds may be introduced in regular alternation; or the alternation may be occasional and arbitrary. A large proportion of double or triple rimes unquestionably adds lightness and rapidity to the verse, and on general principles, therefore, we should expect to find them sparingly used in poems of a markedly serious or melancholy character. Yet no hard and fast rule can be laid down. Mrs Browning's *Cowper's Grave*, for example, is entirely in double rimes; but every reader must feel that they serve here to deepen, not to interfere with, the subdued elegiac tone.[112] Double and triple

---

ventured to discard a long-standing error, and to spell this word in the only correct way.

[112]Though we are here confining our attention to English poetry, we may just note the fact that Dante's *Divine Comedy* is in double rimes, as are also the great Latin hymns (e.g., Dies Ira) of the Middle Ages.

rimes which are too obviously ingenious and far-fetched, always produce a grotesque effect, and are therefore admirably adapted to the purposes of burlesque, as in Butler's *Hudibras*. Browning's frequent recourse to them in the treatment of high and solemn themes was a perverse habit, often attended with disastrous results.

A stanza (commonly, though incorrectly, called a verse) is a group of lines forming within itself a unit of organisation. In many cases the stanzas composing a poem are quite irregular alike in length and structure, as in Wordsworth's *Ode on the Intimations of Immortality* and Tennyson's *Maud*. But as a rule (poems in blank verse being excepted), a poem is built up of sections strictly identical in form. Regular stanzas are commonly defined by the number of their lines and the disposition of the rimes which bind these lines together. The stanza-forms of English poetry are so numerous and varied that no complete tabulation of them could be attempted here; but the following may be mentioned as some of the best-known examples:—the couplet (riming *aa*), as in Pope's *Essay on Man* and Keats's *Endymion*; the triplet (*aaa*), as in Tennyson's *Two Voices*; the quatrain in various forms, as, *e.g.*, that of Keats's *La Belle Dame sans Merci* (*abcb*); that of Gray's *Elegy* (*abab*); that of *In Memoriam* (*abba*); that of Fitz Gerald's version of the *Rubáiyát* (*aaba*); the six-line stanza in various forms, as, *e.g.*, that of Byron's 'She walks in Beauty' (*ababab*); that of Browning's *Rabbi Ben Ezra* (*aabaab*); that of Southey's *The Scholar* (*ababcc*); and a form much used by Burns (*aaabab*); the eight-line stanza (*abababcc*), as in Byron's *Don Juan*; the nine-line stanza (*ababbcbcc*), first used in *The Faery Queene*, and hence commonly called the 'Spenserian.' For a proper classification of stanzas, the relative lengths of the lines would also of course have to be taken into consideration. Thus it is not only the rime scheme but also the peculiar arrangement of the metres (three tetrameters, a dimeter, a tetrameter, a dimeter), which gives its special character to the six-line 'Burns' stanza; while the closing alexandrine must be emphasised as a constituent feature of the Spenserian stanza. It will be remembered that in the language of our hymnals, the octosyllabic quatrain (or measure of 'eights') is called 'long measure'; the quatrain of alternate 'eights' and 'sixes,' 'common measure,'; the quatrain of three 'sixes' and one 'eight,' 'short measure.'

Apart altogether from any question of their special propriety, otherwise considered, stanzas may be used with a sense of their traditional significance, or significance of literary association. It is with such a sense of fitness that Byron takes Dante's interwoven triplets (*aba, bcb, cdc, ded*, etc.) for his *Prophecy of Dante*, and the 'Italian' stanza (*abababcc*) for his *Beppo*; that Keats chooses the same form for his *Isabella*, and the Spenserian stanza for his *Eve of St Agnes*; and that Wordsworth, Longfellow, and William Watson all employ the 'Burns' stanza for memorial poems on the great Scots poet. But in a more general way the problem of the æsthetic qualities of different stanzas, and their applicability to particular purposes, will always have to be investigated. In a poet's choice of metres and stanzas alike, we shall furthermore find a great deal of interesting food for thought. Rossetti's frequent use of intricate and curious structures, heavily weighted with rimes, is itself an index of the exotic character of his genius and the fastidious element in his art. Longfellow's wide reading, eclecticism, power of absorption, and lack of originality are all indicated by the fact that he experimented with marked success in an astonishing number of metrical forms, derived from nearly all the literatures of Europe, while he struck out none of any importance for himself.

The use of different stanzas at different periods has also a great historical significance. The publication of some fifty poems, small and large, in the Spenserian form, and often on subjects for which that form was not in the least appropriate, in the half century between 1725 and 1775, is itself a sign of awakening interest during those years in Spenser and his work. The history of the iambic pentameter (or 'heroic') couplet, from the Augustan to the Romantic age, is familiar to every student of English poetry. In its 'classic' form, as perfected by Pope—the form in which the sense ended with almost absolute regularity at the end of every second line—it favoured epigrammatic terseness and force, and was thus an admirable instrument in the hands of writers of satire and gnomic verse. The rise of the 'romantic' form, reintroduced by Leigh Hunt and Keats—the form in which the sense was allowed to flow on uninterrupted from one couplet to another indefinitely, while the rhetorical pause could occur in any part of a line—was simply one more indication of that general quest for greater freedom and more variety in the harmonies of versification which had already given popularity to blank verse and the Spenserian stanza.

We have said that rime, though an important accessory of English poetry, is not essential to it. This is shown by the large amount of poetry, including much of the most important poetry in the language, which is without rime. The principal form of unrimed verse is the iambic pentameter, popularly called 'blank verse.' But other kinds exist; such as the trochaic tetrameter of *The Song of Hiawatha*; the dactylic hexameter (often loosely called 'hexameter' simply) of Longfellow's *Evangeline*, Kingsley's *Andromeda*, and Clough's *Bothie of Tober-na-Vuolich*; the irregular measures of Southey's *Thalaba the Destroyer*, Shelley's *Queen Mab*, and some of Arnold's poems, like *The Strayed Reveller* and *The Future*. These, however, have no established place in English poetry, unless, indeed, an exception be made in favour of the dactylic hexameter, which I personally hold to have justified itself completely, though many fierce critical attacks have been made upon it.[113]

The study of versification does not, of course, exhaust the interest of poetry on the technical side. There are innumerable other matters which are equally deserving of attention. There is, for instance, the whole vast problem of poetic diction; of the qualities which make

---

[113]For some interesting remarks on the English hexameter, see Arnold's *On Translating Homer*. For the study of English versification in general, the reader may be referred to E. Guest's *History of English Rhythms* (2nd ed., revised by Skeat); J. B. Mayor's *Chapters on English Metre*; F. B. Gunmere's *Handbook of Poetics*; H. Corson's *Primer of English Verse*; R. Bridges' *Milton's Prosody*; J. A. Symonds's *Blank Verse*; Sehipper's *Englische Metrik*.

it peculiarly strong or tender, passionate or beautiful; of the specific differences between it and the diction of prose; of the mysterious power of certain words and combinations of words, whether through association or through sound, to stir the imagination and go home to the heart; of the 'natural magic' of expression which belongs to the rare moments of highest inspiration, and that final felicity of phrasing by which language is steeped in meanings beyond the formal definitions of the lexicographer. Since the diction of poetry is inevitably figurative and allusive, those figures of speech and subtle suggestions and innuendoes which are so important an element in its texture, have also to be considered from the point of view alike of their sources and of their æsthetic value. And as further illustrations of the manifold interest of the lines of inquiry which I am now seeking just to open up, mention may be made of such details of poetic style as the varied use of consonants and vowels in the production of special effects, and of the service which, in the hands of an accomplished master, may be rendered by 'apt alliteration's artful aid.'

VI

Regarding the systematic study of poetry, enough has already been said, either statedly or by implication, in our chapters on the study of literature in general. All that is necessary, therefore, is to point out how, on the principles laid down for guidance, various plans may be suggested for definite courses of reading.

We may, for example, take up the work of a single poet, and our business will then be to analyse the content of his writings and investigate the salient qualities of his art; to examine his literary ancestry and affiliations; to trace to their sources the derivative elements in this thought and style; and to consider his relations with the spirit and movements of his time. After this, we may pass from him to the other poets of his age, taking his work, point by point, as a foundation for comparison and contrast. Or we may make an historical study of some great body of poetry, like our English poetry, following its ebb and flow from epoch to epoch, and the rise and decline of schools, methods, and traditions; noting every significant change in subject matter, spirit, and style; and seeking its explanation in the initiative power of particular men, in the circumstances which helped to give them popularity and influence, and in the larger tendencies of life and thought in the world outside. Or, limiting our field of inquiry on one side while broadening it on another, we may devote our attention to the history of some one great poetic form, such as the epic or the elegy, through the whole course of its evolution and transformation in different literatures and at different times. Or, again, we may select some special theme—the treatment of nature in poetry, for example—and make this the basis of a study which, as we shall soon discover, will branch out in various directions, and connect itself at many points with the consideration of the development of literature at large.

These are some of the ways in which our reading of poetry may be systematised, and thus made at once more interesting and more profitable than it would otherwise be. A warning, already given, should none the less be repeated here. However far afield we may pursue our researches, however wide and accurate our knowledge of the development and technique of poetry may become, however engrossing we may find the special problems of the historian and the critic, we must never forget that our chief purpose, after all, should be the enjoyment of poetry as poetry—of poetry for its own sake, as a thing of beauty fraught with infinite meanings for those who have the capacity to feel and the heart to understand. More important, then, than all the acquisitions of scholarship is the cultivation of the faculty of poetic appreciation. On this matter, indeed, it is of little use to discourse in the abstract; for though the lover of poetry may, by personal contact, transmit something of his enthusiasm to others, rules and counsels will prove of slight service to those who need them most, and in the end each reader must be left, very largely, to himself.

Perhaps the most valuable of all suggestions that may be thrown out in the way of help is one so simple and obvious that, but for the fact that its practical bearings are seldom realised, it would hardly call for formal statement. In our reading of poetry we should always remember that the poet appeals directly to the poet in ourselves, and that our real enjoyment of poetry therefore depends upon our own keenness of imaginative apprehension and emotional response. This means that the true secret and virtue of a poem are to be seized and appropriated by us only through the exercise on our parts of powers similar in kind to those which gave the poem life, however far they may fall short of these in strength and vitality. To those who are born without any poetic sense at all, it is, of course, as futile to talk about the beauty and meaning of poetry as it is to talk about the beauty and meaning of music to those who are born without a musical ear. But wherever the poetic sense exists, in however rudimentary a form—and it is at least latent in the majority of normally constituted men and women—it is capable of cultivation; and for its cultivation no better course can be proposed than its daily exercise in sympathetic contact with great poetry. Thus we learn to appreciate through appreciation and to enjoy through enjoyment. In this case the end and the means are one.

A word of practical advice on a matter of detail may be added. 'The art of printing,' as Prof. Butcher has pointed out, 'has done much to dull our literary perceptions. Words have a double virtue— that which resides in the sense and that which resides in the sound. We miss much of the charm if the eye is made to do duty also for the ear. The words, bereft of their vocal force, are but half alive on the printed page. The music of verse, when repeated only to the inward ear, comes as a faint echo.'[114] The moral of this is

---

[114]*Harvard Lectures*, pp. 229, 230. 'It is a fact but little known,' the writer continues, 'that throughout the Greek period, and far into the days of the Roman Empire— to the third and fourth century of our era—the custom survived of reading both prose and verse, not silently, but aloud and in company. There is a curious passage in Augustine's *Confessions*—one of the few in ancient literature where silent reading is mentioned. He there tells of the difficulty he had in getting

clear. If poetry is 'musical speech,' if it owes much of its beauty, its magic, its peculiar power of stirring the feelings and arousing the imagination, to its verbal felicity and its varied melodies of metre and rime, then its full significance as poetry can be appreciated only when it addresses us through the ear. The silent perusal of the printed page will leave one of its principal secrets unsurprised. As much as possible, therefore, we should make it a practice to read our poetry aloud.

---

access to his master, Ambrose, whose rare hours of leisure were spent in reading, and who was one day observed to run his eye silently over the page while 'his voice and tongue were still.' Various reasons are then suggested to account for so strange a departure from the common practice.' The reference is to the *Confessions*, VI. iii., where we read: 'His eyes scanned the pages, but his voice and tongue were silent....Whatever the reason, no doubt it was a good one in such a man.'

4

The Study of Prose Fiction

I. *The Novel and the Drama*. The Elements of Fiction. II. *Plot in the Novel*. Subject matter in Fiction—The Importance of Fidelity—Plot—The Gift of Storytelling—Loose Plot and Organic Plot—Simple and Compound Plots— Methods of Narration. III. *Characterisation*. Its Elementary Condition—The Mystery of the Creative Process—The Power of Graphic Description—The Analytical and Dramatic Methods of Characterisation—The Character in the Making—The Question of Range in Characterisation—Characterisation and Knowledge of Life. IV. *The Relations of Plot and Character*. Their Combination—'Motivation.' V. *Dialogue*. Tests to be applied to it. VI. *Humour, Pathos, and Tragedy*. The Quality of the Emotional Element in Fiction—Humour—The Painful Emotions. VII. *Social and Material Setting in Fiction*. Setting in the Novel—Specialisation in Modern Fiction— Special Social Settings—Setting in Historical Fiction—The Question of Anachronism—Material Setting—The Use of Nature. VIII. *The Novelist's Criticism of Life*. Its Place—The Novelist's Point of View—Ways of presenting a Criticism of Life in the Novel—The Dramatic, or Indirect Way—The Direct Way—Tests of a Novelist's Philosophy of Life—Truth in Fiction—Realism—Realism and Romance—Morality in Fiction—The Moral Responsibilities of Fiction.

In any historical study of literary forms, the drama, as the earlier to evolve, should of course take precedence of the novel. As a matter of convenience, however, we will here reverse the chronological order and deal with the novel first. Manifestly, the drama and prose fiction are compounded of the same raw materials. In this chapter, though our immediate business is with the novel, we shall therefore of necessity have much to say about characteristics which are common to both of them, and to some extent it will thus serve as an introduction also to the study of the drama. But quite as manifestly, owing to differences in conditions, the raw materials in drama and prose fiction are treated in very different ways. In the chapter which follows we shall therefore have to take up our subject at the point where they part company and consider the drama as a specific form of literary art.

We have already seen that the novel owes its existence to the interest which men and women everywhere and at all times have taken in men and women and in the great panorama of human passion and action. This interest, as we have noted, has always been one of the most general and most powerful of the impulses behind literature, and it has thus given rise, according to changing social and artistic circumstances, to various modes of expression—here to epic and there to drama, now to ballad and now to romance.

Latest to develop of all these modes, the novel is also the largest and fullest of them. This statement may perhaps be challenged by reference to the drama. But apart from many other considerations, which we need not now discuss, it must be remembered that the drama is not pure literature. It is a compound art, in which the literary element is organically bound up with the elements of stage setting and histrionic interpretation. The novel is independent of these secondary arts; it is, as Marion Crawford once happily phrased it, a 'pocket theatre,' containing within itself not only plot and actors, but also costume, scenery, and all the other accessories of a dramatic representation. This point has important bearings upon the comparative study of the novel and the drama. Evidently such complete immunity from those conditions of the stage to which the drama is bound by the very law of its being, and by which it is everywhere hampered, gives to the novel a freedom of movement, a breadth, and a flexibility to which, even in its most romantic developments, the drama cannot possibly attain. What the novel loses in actuality and vividness by its substitution of narrative for representation it thus amply makes up for in other ways. This is, of course, one reason why the novel has largely displaced the drama, as it has displaced other vehicles for the expression of our common interest in human life, and has established itself as the principal literary form of our complex and many-sided modern world. It is equally evident that we can thus explain one essential difference between the novel and the drama which it is necessary for the student of either to keep well in mind. The drama is the most rigorous form of literary art; prose fiction is the loosest. It is a familiar fact that for the writing of a play a long preliminary discipline in technique and a thorough knowledge of the stage are requisite, while anyone who has pens, ink, and paper at command, and a certain amount of leisure and patience can write a novel. The moral of this on the critical side is that while it is relatively easy to draw out and formulate the laws of the drama and the standards by which it is to be judged, it is extremely difficult to do this in the case of the novel. Yet some laws and standards there are, nonetheless, even for this most elastic and irregular of all the great forms of literary expression, and it must now be our business to seek out and illustrate the more general and important of these.

Though it is necessary to do so only in the way of a reminder, we will begin with a brief statement of the principal elements which enter into the composition of a novel. In this analysis, as will be seen, we are also tabulating the principal elements which enter into the composition of the drama.

In the first place, the novel deals with events and actions, with things which are suffered and done; and these constitute what we commonly call the plot. Secondly, such things happen to people and are suffered or done by people; and the men and women who thus carry on the action form its *dramatis personæ,* or characters. The conversation of these characters introduces a third element—that of dialogue, often so closely connected with characterisation as to be an integral part of it. Fourthly, the action must take place, and the characters must do and suffer, somewhere and at some time; and thus we have a scene and a time of action. The element of style may be put next on our list; and with this it might seem that for practical purposes our analysis is complete. But there still remains a sixth component to which too much importance can hardly be attached. Directly or indirectly, and whether the writer himself is conscious of it or not, every novel must necessarily present a certain view of life and of some of the problems of life; that is, it must so exhibit incidents, characters, passions, motives, as to reveal more or less distinctly the way in which the author looks out upon the world and his general attitude towards it. It is difficult to find a name for this sixth element which is altogether satisfactory, for whatever may be suggested, we are in danger of implying too little or too much. But postponing any discussion of this till we reach it in our proper course, we will for the present call this the novelist's criticism, or interpretation, or philosophy of life.

Plot, characters, dialogue, time and place of action, style, and a stated or implied philosophy of life, then, are the chief elements entering into the composition of any work of prose fiction, small or great, good or bad. Omitting the element of style, which, as commom to all kinds of literature, need not detain us here we will take the other components one by one and consider some of the questions which naturally arise in connection with each of them in any novel we may select for our study.

II

In dealing with the element of plot our first business will always be with the nature of the raw material out of which it is made and with the quality of such material when judged by the standards furnished by life itself. Take, for example, the works of four of the greatest novelists who wrote in English during the last century— Dickens, Thackeray, George Eliot, and Nathaniel Hawthorne. It is immediately evident that these four writers drew their subjects from widely different aspects of life and classes of incident; and as we turn from *David Copperfield to Vanity Fair*, and from these again to *Adam Bede* and *The Scarlet Letter*, we feel that with each transition we are passing, not only from one kind of plot-interest to another, but even from one kind of world to another. Yet, with all their differences in matter and method, Dickens and Thackeray, George Eliot and Hawthorne are at one in this—their themes possess in themselves a substantial value and a genuine human meaning because they are concerned, not with the mere trivialities which lie upon the surface of existence, but with passions, conflicts and problems which, however their forms may change, belong to the essential texture of life. Deduced from the fundamental conception of literature as an interpretation of life, the elementary test thus suggested is of universal applicability, for it is the certain mark of a great novel, as of all great literature, that, wide as may be the range of its accessory topics, it is primarily engaged with the things which make life strenuous, intense, and morally significant. This does not, of course, mean that greatness in fiction depends in the least upon the external importance of its incidents and characters. Life may be as strenuous, intense, and morally significant in the simplest story of the humblest people as in the largest movements of history or the most thrilling situations of the heroic stage; and in the agony of Arthur Dimmesdale and the pitiful story of Hetty Sorrel's downfall we are quite as closely in touch with some of the most powerful motive forces of life as in the fate of Macbeth or Agamemnon. Nor does it mean that it is to the tragic phases of experience only that a great novel must be confined, for the comedy of life is often as full of large and permanent human interest as its tragedy. The question is one of essential ethical value, and the principle proposed is simply this—that a novel is really great only when it lays its foundations broad and deep in the things which most constantly and seriously appeal to us in the struggle and fortunes of our common humanity.

To prevent possible misapprehension it should perhaps be further stated explicitly that to employ this test and to abide by its results does not imply any censorious denial of the claims to a warm place in our affections of many novels which would fail to meet it. One function of fiction is to provide amusement for the leisure hour and a welcome relief from the strain of practical affairs; and any novel which serves its purpose in this way may, on the sole condition that the pleasure it affords is wholesome and tonic, be held to have fully justified itself. Moreover, the excellence of its technique, or its dramatic power, or its exceptional cleverness in characterisation, or its abundant humour, or some other outstanding quality of its workmanship, may suffice to lift an otherwise insignificant story to a high rank in fictitious literature. These considerations must be duly recognised, and a narrow and pedantic view of the matter avoided. None the less, all qualifications admitted, our principle remains, unimpugned. Matthew Arnold's emphasis upon the need of sound subject matter in literature is here very much to the point. The basis of true greatness in a novel is to be sought in the greatness, or substantial value, of its raw materials.

It is, however, clear that though this is the basis, greatness of subject matter will not of itself ensure the greatness of a novel. Mastery of handling is now requisite in order that all the varied possibilities of a given theme may be brought out to the full. Here, of course, we approach the whole question of the making of a novel, including the two contributory elements of individual power and technical skill. But before we come to this, there is a preliminary problem to be touched upon, since individual power would be wasted and technical skill exercised to little effect unless they are both supported by an ample knowledge of life.

We are thus brought back to the cardinal principle, already often emphasised, of fidelity to oneself and one's experiences as the condition of all good work in literature. Because fiction is fiction and not fact, it is sometimes carelessly assumed that it has nothing to do with fact. No mistake could be more serious. Of the relations of fiction to truth we shall, however, speak presently. For the moment we have merely to insist that no novel can be pronounced, I will not say great, but even excellent in its degree, whatever that may be, if it lacks the quality of 'authenticity.' Whatever aspects of life the novelist may choose to write about, he should write of them with the grasp and thoroughness which can be secured only by familiarity with his material. What he is not familiar with he should leave alone.

This general principle has been rigorously interpreted to mean that the novelist should confine himself within the field, however small, of his own personal first-hand intercourse with the world, and never allow himself to stray beyond it. Thus we have George Eliot's well-timed attack upon the work of the ordinary women novelists of her day; they tried, she complained, to write like men and from the man's point of view, instead of taking their stand on the fundamental difference of sex, with all that this implies, and endeavouring to portray life frankly and sincerely as a woman knows and feels it.[115] One of the writers whom, for contrast, she singles out for special praise may indeed be taken as our supreme example of unfailing conscientiousness in this particular—that exquisite artist who was content to work upon 'two or three inches of ivory' because her knowledge of life was too limited to provide material for larger treatment, but whose novels may be regarded as perfect in their kind though they do not fulfil our first condition of real greatness in fiction.[116] Alike in theory and practice Jane Austen adhered strictly to this principle of absolute fidelity. When a niece asked

---

[115]See her essays on *Lady Novelists* and *Silly Novels by Lady Novelists*.

[116]Comparing Jane Austen and George Sand, and giving full praise to both, George Eliot indicated what she deemed the essential defect is each: the former never penetrated into the deeper experiences, the powerful emotional and spiritual things of life; the latter, while she had abundance of passion, lacked moral poise and clear ethical vision. It is interesting at this point to consider the purely feminine elements in George Eliot herself. Most of her early readers, misled by her masculine pseudonym, took her for a man; but others of keener perception, like Dickens, were not slow in discovering the womanly characteristics of her work.

her judgment on a manuscript story, she gave her the characteristic advice: 'Let the Portmans go to Ireland; but as you know nothing of the manner there, you had better not go with them. You will be in danger of giving false representations.' Equally instructive was her own example. Save in two brief passages in The Watsons, there is, I believe, no scene in all her novels in which men only are described as talking together and their dialogue reported. Her women converse with other women, and with men; but as she had no immediate knowledge of the behaviour of men among themselves in wholly masculine company, she simply left the subject alone. Such willingness to accept her limitations of knowledge, combined as it was with equal willingness to accept her limitations of power, goes far to explain the uniform excellence of Jane Austen's work.

How little this principle of fidelity is commonly recognised is repeatedly shown in the writings of our minor novelists, who frequently build their plots out of materials lying far beyond their own observation, and are seldom deterred even by the profoundest ignorance from following their story whithersoever it leads. They will boldly challenge comparison with Anthony Trollope in descriptions of the hunting field; with Halévy in pictures of theatrical life; with Bret Harte in scenes from the California gold diggings; with Stevenson and Clarke Russell in the romance of the sea; though they themselves have never ridden with the hounds, or entered a green room, or lived in the far west, or known more of salt water than may be gathered from a summer passage from Folke-stone to Boulogne.[117] It is often said that every man might produce at least one interesting

---

[117]Lapses in detail, due to ignorance, are sometimes very amusing. I have a recollection of a scene in one of Ouida's novels (though I could not give chapter and verse) in which her hero, rowing in a boat-race, is eulogised for his strength and prowess in pulling twice as fast as any other man in his crew! Dickens, as is well known, came to grief over the game of cricket (Pickwick Papers, chap. vii), which it is very evident he had neither played nor watched attentively. Practical yachtsmen have been much puzzled over the nautical manœuvres described in the storm in Stevenson's Treasure Island.

novel if he would only write faithfully of what he has known and felt for himself; but it is a curious fact that in the vast majority of cases this is the last thing that the would-be novelist ever thinks of doing. On the contrary, inspired rather by the work of some favourite writer, whom he seeks to imitate, than by life itself, he commits the fatal blunder of drawing upon second-hand information for the groundwork of his plot.

It is not, however, necessary to push the doctrine of authenticity to the extreme represented by the precept and practice of Jane Austen and, indeed, we should be warranted in doing so only on the supposition that a novel must be realistic in the narrowest acceptation of that word—a supposition which, as we shall see presently, we are not in the least called upon to accept. Knowledge of life may be obtained in various ways besides direct personal experience; it may, in particular, be obtained through books and through conversation with other people who have touched the world at points where we have not touched it ourselves. A writer or a real creative genius, with that power of absorbing and utilising all kinds of material derived form all kinds of sources, and that sheer power of realistic imagination which habitually goes with this, may thus attain substantial fidelity even when he is handling scenes and incidents which have never come within the range of his own experience and observation. Little fault has been found with *Robinson Crusoe* on the score of inaccuracy even in details, while in the quality of carrying conviction it stands in the front rank of fictitious narratives; yet it must not be forgotten that the man who wrote it had not only never lived on a desert island, but had never even seen the sea. The historical novelist is evidently compelled to rely upon indirect information for the specific characteristics of any period he undertakes to describe; and what the historical novelist does in dealing with the past, the novelist of contemporary life may do with equal assurance when the exigencies of his plot carry him beyond his individual field. The doctrine of fidelity must therefore be stated with due qualifications. What is required in all cases is a large many-sided experience of men and things and a resulting general knowledge of life both ample and thorough, the application of which to specific details may vitalise and humanise materials wheresoever gained; this, and what I have called that sheer power of realistic imagination which will often enable a writer to see more clearly and depict more convincingly a scene he has only heard or read of than could an ordinary person who had himself witnessed such a scene or even taken part in it.

The more technical side of the substance of a novel, which we designate in the word plot, has next to be considered. A novel, whatever else it is or is not, is at any rate a story. Two questions, therefore, suggest themselves which, though it is almost superfluous to do so, we must still state in definite form. Is the story, as story, fresh, interesting, and worth the telling? And, this being settled, is it well and artistically told? In other words, we demand, with the most uncritical reader, that the story shall in its own particular way be a good one; and also—a consideration to which the uncritical reader is for the most part curiously indifferent— that it shall be skilfully put together. By this we mean that, on careful examination of all its details, it shall reveal no gaps or inconsistencies; that its parts shall be arranged with a due sense of balance and proportion;[118] that its incidents shall appear to evolve spontaneously from its data and from one another; that commonplace things shall be made significant by the writer's touch upon them; that the march of events, however unusual1, shall be so managed as to impress us as orderly and natural in the circumstances; and that the catastrophe, whether foreseen or not, shall satisfy us as the logical product and summing up of all that has gone before.[119]

---

[118]The law of balance and proportion is often broken even by our greatest novelists. Thus, for instance, Scott (as I have elsewhere pointed out) 'is capable of writing pages of description about an occurrence that leads nowhither, or a character who forthwith drops into a second or third place' (*Life of Scott*, p. 278).
[119]It will be noted that many otherwise admirable storytellers have great difficulty in getting started and sometimes fumble painfully over their initial scenes. This

Mere power of narrative is also in itself a feature which will always repay attention. The gift of telling a story to the best possible advantage is, as anyone may soon discover for himself by listening critically to the anecdotes which are exchanged over a dinner table, much rarer than is commonly supposed; while, as the same experiment will further prove, it is also a gift by itself, having, like the histrionic faculty, little or nothing to do with a person's general intellectual ability. Among English poets, Chaucer, Dryden, Scott, and William Morris, dissimilar as were otherwise their qualities of genius, had this gift in a marked degree, while on the other hand, Spenser, great as he was in pure description, was here singularly weak; among our historians Carlyle and Macaulay in particular had it; and we must recognise this fact in our estimate of these writers apart from any other questions concerning Chaucer, Dryden, Scott and Morris as poets, and Carlyle and Macaulay as historians. So with prose fiction there are novelists whose books have little weight or

---

was conspicuously the case with Scott, whose cumbrous and heavy introductory chapters (as in the classical example of *Waverley*) are almost enough to deter the reader on the very threshold of his narrative. His conclusions are generally quite as unsatisfactory. 'Sometimes' (if I may again use my own words), 'as in *The Heart of Midlothian*, he dawdles over unimportant matters after the main interest has come to a close; but more often he is guilty, as Lady Louisa Stuart put it, of 'huddling up a conclusion anyhow, and so kicking the book out of his way." *Ivanhoe* and *Kenilworth* have exceptionally effective catastrophes, but 'any tyro in criticism could pick holes in the *dénouements* of the *Antiquary* or *Woodstock*.' Dickens's conclusions are commonly married by his desire to get all his characters together into a series of grand final scenes in which rewards and punishments may be distributed according to the strict demands of poetic justice; and to achieve this he is obliged to have recourse to means that are too patently forced and artificial to be in the least convincing. The contrast between the well-rounded and completely explanatory *dénouements* of most of our older novelists and the abrupt endings, which are often no endings at all, so popular in much of our later fiction opens up an interesting line of study in the changes which have come over the art of fiction since the days of the Victorian masters. The logic of the catastrophe will be dealt with in our chapter on the drama.

permanent value, who can at least tell a story naturally, easily, and in a way to bring out at each stage its maximum amount of interest; there are others of immeasurably greater intellectual power in whom this faculty is poorly developed, or in whose work its exercise is impeded by the pressure of other things. Thus in reading Dumas, for example, who is one of the world's very best storytellers, we cannot fail to admire the free and vigorous movement of the narrative, which sweeps us on from point to point with no apparent effort or strain, while a certain sense of effort and strain is almost always with us when we are reading George Eliot, or Balzac, or Tolstoi.[120] Nor is it only at the evolution of the action as a whole that we have to look. We must consider also the writer's power of managing his separate parts—of handling his situations and working up his effects. Much of the dramatic value of scenes of great potential interest is often allowed to escape under inadequate treatment; but a novelist who knows his business will make every incident tell with its proper proportion of effect in relation to the whole. Of course here as elsewhere, methods vary. We may have, for instance, the marvellous brevity and restraint of Thackeray's account of George Osborne's death at Waterloo; we may have, in a totally different manner, the elaborately-wrought detail with which Dickens describes the death of old Krook, and Hawthorne the death of Judge Pyncheon. Hence it will always be a matter of interest not only to observe results, but also to examine the means by which the results are obtained by different writers or by the same writer in different circumstances or at different stages of his career.[121]

---

[120]I am thinking here of Tolstoi's longer works of fiction only. Many of his shorter tales are almost perfect examples of the storyteller's art. They seem, indeed, not so much to be told as to tell themselves—the highest praise that can be given to a work of this description.

[121]Thus the student of Thackeray will note that while the satire of his later books is less pungent and their general atmosphere more kindly, the writer had also lost some of his earlier horror of dwelling, in Dickens's fashion, over sentimental or tragic situations. In *Vanity Fair*, in the account of Osborne's death, in the

In dealing with plot structure we may distinguish roughly between two kinds of novel—I say roughly, because the types, though clearly defined, shade into one another by imperceptible gradations. These are what we may call respectively the novel of loose plot and the novel of organic plot. In the former case the story is composed of a number of detached incidents, having little necessary or logical connection among themselves; the unity of the narrative depending not on the machinery of the action, but upon the person of the hero who, as the central figure or nucleus, binds the otherwise scattered elements together. Such a novel is, in fact, 'rather a history of the miscellaneous adventures which befall an individual in the course of life than the plot of a regular and connected epopœia, where every step brings us a point nearer to the final catastrophe.'[122] Thus while it may be overflowing with interesting separate episodes, it has little in the nature of a comprehensive general design, in the evolution of which each detail plays a distinct and vital part.

Robinson Crusoe and *Gil Blas, Joseph Andrews* and *Roderick Random, Vanity Fair* and *Pendennis, The Pickwick Papers* and *Nicholas Nickleby,* may be cited as familiar examples of this 'loose and incoherent' type of novel, as Scott called it; in them one scene leads to another, the characters cross and recross; but the books as a whole have little structural backbone or organic unity. In no one of these cases, it is evident, was it necessary that the author should have thought out beforehand the details of his drama; it was enough that he should

---

narrative of the struggles of his widow, in the great scene in which Rawdon Crawley surprises his wife with Lord Steyne, we have no suspicion that the matter is being specially worked up for effect; Indeed, Thackeray more than once openly checks himself for fear of becoming theatrical or mawkish. On the other hand, there is much elaboration in the description of the last years and death of the Colonel in *The Newcomes*, and of the death of the Baroness de Bernstein in *The Virginians*, Dickens, on the contrary, whose earlier pathos and melodrama were terribly over-wrought, showed a distinct tendency in later works towards increasing restraint.

[122]Scott, *Introductory Epistle* to *The Fortunes of Nigel.*

have in mind a broad general notion of the course the story was to take; it could then be left—as Thackeray confessedly left his stories—to unfold itself as it went along.[123] Just as manifestly, the case is entirely different with novels of the organic type—with such novels as *Tom Jones, Bleak House, Our Mutual Friend,* or *The Woman in White.* Here the separate incidents are no longer treated episodically; they are dovetailed together as integral components of a definite plot-pattern. In these cases, it is clear, something more than a general idea of the course of the story was necessary before the author began his work. The entire plan had to be considered in detail; the characters and events arranged to occupy their proper places in it; and the various lines laid down which were to converge in bringing about the catastrophe.

This distinction, however, as I have said, is a rough one only. I have instanced the above-mentioned books precisely because they represent well-defined types. Several qualifying remarks must now be made. In the first place, even in novels of the organic kind there is often a great deal of purely episodical material. Thus in *Tom Jones, Bleak House,* and *Our Mutual Friend* there are many incidents and characters which lie outside the general design and are not really connected with it. Secondly, all degrees of plot organisation are, of course, possible between the elaborate compactness of these books and the extreme looseness of *The Pickwick Papers* or *Pendennis.* Among Dickens's novels, for example, *David Copperfield* and *Martin Chuzzlewit* exhibit intermediate stages of plot unification. Again,

---

[123]Scott acknowledged that 'the tale of *Waverley* was put together with so little care that I cannot boast of having sketched any distinct plan of the work.' Thackeray said that his method of composition was to create in advance two or three of his chief characters, and then go on from chapter to chapter with only a general notion of the course he would be taking a few chapters later on. Even when he was actually at work on the episode of Pen and Fanny Bolton in *Pendennis*, he was by no means certain how it would turn out. 'When I sit down to write a novel,' said Anthony Trollope in his *Autobiography*, 'I do not at all know, and I do not very much care, how it is to end.'

there are innumerable novels in which (as in those of Jane Austen and Turgenev) the matter of the plot is so simple that no regular development of a dramatic scheme is to be looked for. Nor, finally, is it for a moment to be assumed that the organic novel, as such, is on a higher artistic plane than the loose novel, though Scott thought it necessary to apologise because his stories belonged to the latter class. Indeed, for reasons which will appear presently, a really great novel is likely, as a rule, to approximate rather to the loose than to the organic type. At the same time, compactness and symmetry—a good plot well worked out—undoubtedly give æsthetic pleasure, and we rightly admire the technical skill to which they testify; while no consideration of their excellence in other respects should tempt us to palliate the total want of structural unity and coherence in such works as *Vanity Fair* and *The Newcomes*.

The two drawbacks to which a highly organised plot is specially liable may here just be noted. It may be so mechanically put together that its very cleverness may impress us with an uneasy sense of laborious artifice. This is commonly the case with the novels of our most deft manipulator of mere plot, Wilkie Collins. Or it may lack plausibility in details. Here a frequent error is the abuse of coincidence. Thus in *Tom Jones* (the plot of which, perhaps because it was the first great effort of the kind in English fiction, has been absurdly overpraised) all sorts of unexpected things are perpetually happening in the very nick of time, while people turn up again and again at the right moment, and in the place where they are wanted only because they chance to be wanted then and there. Even Mr Austin Dobson is compelled to admit, though he does so reluctantly, the strain which the narrative for this reason frequently inflicts upon our sense of probability. The defence which is sometimes offered for the free use of coincidence—that coincidences do happen in real life—is scarcely to the point; for the obverse of the dictum that truth is stranger than fiction is, that fiction should not be so strange as truth. Two tests of any plot are thus suggested. It should seem to move naturally, and be free from any appearance of artifice; and the means used in working it out should be such as we are willing to accept, in the circumstances, as at least credible.

A special aspect of the principle of unity in plot structure has next to be considered. The plot of a novel may be simple or compound; that is, it may be composed of one story only, or of two or more stories in combination; and the law of unity requires that in a compound plot the parts should be wrought together into a single whole. Our criticism of *Vanity Fair*, on the structural side, bears chiefly on this point; the narrative is made up of two stories—the story of Amelia Sedley and the story of Becky Sharp; and these two stories are not properly amalgamated. In precisely the same way *Middlemarch, Daniel Deronda*, and *Anna Karenina* are alike open to criticism. In *Bleak House*, on the contrary, the three threads of Esther Summerson's story, the story of Lady Dedlock's sin, and the story of the great Chancery suit of Jarndyce *v.* Jarndyce, are very cleverly interwoven, and thus we have an admirable example on an immense scale of the unification of complex materials. It should also be noted that where several independent elements enter into a plot, it is often the practice of novelists to make them balance or illustrate one another. It was Dickens's habitual method to offset his melodrama by broad comedy, according to the plan of the romantic dramatists. Even in *Vanity Fair*, while there is little effort to fuse the two stories, the significance of the moral and dramatic contrast between them throughout is kept clearly in view; and some such moral and dramatic contrast will be found underlying the two stories in *Anna Karenina*. About this matter of balance among the different parts of a plot, however, we shall have more to say when we come to speak of the technique of the drama, when the various stages in the movement of a plot will also be considered.

One other point in the study of plot has still to be indicated. While the dramatist is, of course, confined to a single way of telling his story—by representation combined with narrative put into the mouths of his characters—the novelist has his choice among three methods—the direct, or epic; the autobiographical;

and the documentary. In the first and most usual way, the novelist is an historian narrating from the outside; in the second, he writes in the first person, identifying himself with one of his characters (generally, though not always, the hero or heroine), and thus produces an imaginary autobiography; as in *Robinson Crusoe, The Vicar of Wakefield, David Copperfield, Esmond, Jane Eyre*; in the third, the action is unfolded by means of letters, as in the 'epistolary' novels of Richardson, Smollett's *Humphrey Clinker*, Fanny Burney's *Evelina*, and Goethe's *Sorrows of Werther*; or—a favourite device of Wilkie Collins—by diaries, contributed narratives, and miscellaneous documents. Occasionally, the methods may be blended, as in *Bleak House*, where Esther Summerson's story is told by herself, while the rest of the book takes the direct historic form.

It is evident that each of these three ways has its special advantages; for while the direct method always gives the greatest scope and freedom of movement, a keener and more intimate interest may sometimes be attained by the use of either the first-personal or the documentary plan. Yet it will be observed that both these last-named methods involve difficulties of their own, and that on the whole it is best to avoid them save where the compensating gain is considerable. In adopting the autobiographic form, a novelist may frequently fail to bring all his material naturally within the compass of the supposed narrator's knowledge and power; and he may sometimes miss the true personal tone; as in the case of Esther Summerson, who (as the least critical reader must be aware) writes altogether too much like Dickens himself and with too marked an admixture of Dickens's insight and humour. And whatever may be urged in theory on behalf of the documentary method,[124] in practice

---

[124]The principal advantage of the epistolary method is to be found in the fact that full personal expression can be given to the feelings of all the important actors at the time of the events described, and before their issue is known to them. In this one respect the novel-by-letters is superior both to the ordinary epic novel, in which such feelings are in the main analysed by an outsider, and to the autobiographical novel, in which we have only the retrospective

it is very apt to become, even in the hands of a skilful artist, both clumsy and unconvincing.[125]

In our study of any novel in which either of these two plans is followed, we must always ask why the author has chosen to depart from the more ordinary narrative method, and to what extent, and in what ways, his work has gained or lost by the change.

III

In passing from plot to characterisation in fiction we are met at the outset by one of those elementary questions of which even the most uncritical reader is certain to feel the force. Does the novelist succeed in making his men and women real to our imaginations?

---

interpretation of a single character written after the incidents described are things of the past. This was perceived by Richardson, who, defending the epistolary form, writes in his preface to *Clarissa*: 'Much more lively and affecting must be the style of those who write in the height of the present distress, the mind tortured by the pangs of uncertainty (the events then hidden in the womb of time), than the dry narrative, unanimated style of a person relating difficulties and dangers surmounted, the relater perfectly at ease; and if himself unmoved by his own story, then not likely greatly to affect the reader.'

[125]It has been noted by various critics of Richardson that all his characters seem to have a perfect mania for correspondence, and, however busy otherwise, unlimited leisure for it; and that the world in which they live resembles nothing so much as a well-ordered office where everything is transcribed, docketed, and filed away for future reference. Richardson himself thought it desirable to explain Pamela's extraordinary devotion to letter-writing. Miss Byron's facility and industry (in *Sir Charles Grandison*) were specially dealt with by Sir Leslie Stephen. On March 22, he points out, she writes a letter filling fourteen pages of print, and two others of six and twelve pages respectively; the next day, two more letters of eighteen and ten pages; on the 24th, two more, making together thirty pages. At the end of the last of these she remarks that she is forced to lay down the pen; notwithstanding which, she adds six pages of postscript! In three days she thus produces ninety-six pages of print! Macaulay calculated that the interest of her small capital must have been wholly consumed in postage. Scott tried the epistolary method in *Redgauntlet*, but found it necessary to abandon it. Of course letters are often introduced with excellent effect in novels in other forms; like, e.g., those of Mr Micawber in *David Copperfield*.

Do they, in Trollope's phrase, 'stand upright on the ground'? That the great creations of our great novelists fulfil this initial condition is a fact too familiar to need particular illustration. They lay hold of us by virtue of their substantial quality of life; we know and believe in them as thoroughly, we sympathise with them as deeply, we love and hate them as cordially, as though they belonged to the world of flesh and blood. And the first thing that we require of any novelist in his handling of character is that, whether he keeps close to common experience or boldly experiments with the fantastic and the abnormal, his men and women shall move through his pages like living beings and like living beings remain in our memory after his book is laid aside and its details perhaps forgotten.

It is unnecessary to enter here into any discussion of the psychology of that dramatic genius by which life is thus given to the figments of fancy and the illusion of reality produced. Intensity of conception and what I have called realistic imagination are doubtless at the bottom of it. But it is well to remember that the processes of creation are confessedly as mysterious to those who possess such creative power as they are to other people. Thus Thackeray spoke of this power as 'occult'—as a power which seemed at times to take the pen from his fingers and move it in spite of himself. 'I don't control my characters,' he once protested; 'I am in their hands, and they take me where they please.' He had, as it were, endowed them with independent volition, and by so doing had to a large extent placed them beyond the range of his calculations; they spoke and acted on their own impulse; and so unexpected and surprising were occasionally the results that when, as he tells us, one or another of them had said or done something altogether unlooked for, he would be driven to ask in bewilderment, 'How the dickens did he come to think of that?' Such testimony is exceedingly instructive, for it touches upon an experience which, so far from being unique, has been, I am convinced, the experience of every writer of real creative genius from the delineator of Shylock and Hamlet downward. Herein, indeed, lies the ultimate distinction between creative genius and mere talent, however brilliant and well-trained. The latter simply manufactures, and its effects are always within the field of conscious and deliberate effort. The former really creates, and for this reason its outworkings are often as strange and inexplicable to the author himself at the time as to those who afterwards pick his characters to pieces in the hope of plucking the heart out of their mystery.

Putting on one side, however, this whole problem of power, and confining ourselves to the question of method, we may note that a novelist's success in characterisation necessarily depends in part upon his faculty for graphic description. In the representation of a play those secondary arts of which I have spoken are of immense service in the definition of personality, and the makeup of the actor and his interpretation of his part give us the dress and bearing, the looks and gestures, of the character portrayed by him. In the reading of a novel (save where occasional assistance is furnished by accompanying illustrations—a device seldom satisfactory enough to merit serious attention), all these things are of the imagination only; and thus it is an important part of the business of the novelist to help us by description to a vivid realisation of the appearance and behaviour of his people. Whatever is individual and characteristic in their physical aspect in general, whatever is of importance in their expression or demeanour at any critical moment, must be so indicated as to stand out clearly in the reader's mind. But how is this to be accomplished? This is a question which will always repay careful consideration. It will be found that as a rule a set and formal description, given item by item, is (as Lessing showed)[126] one of the least successful ways of making a character live before us, and that a skilled artist is specially known by his power of selecting and accumulating significant detail and of stimulating the imagination of the reader by slight occasional touches.

In regard to what is more specifically understood as characterisation—that is, the psychological side of it—the principal

---

[126]Laokoon, § 20.

thing to remember is, that the conditions of the novel commonly permit the use of two opposed methods—the direct or analytical, and the indirect or dramatic. In the one case the novelist portrays his characters from the outside, dissects their passions, motives, thoughts and feelings, explains, comments, and often pronounces authoritative judgment upon them. In the other case, he stands apart, allows his characters to reveal themselves through speech and action, and reinforces their self-delineation by the comments and judgments of other characters in the story. I say the conditions of the novel commonly permit the use of these two methods; they do not always do so, because in fiction in which the autobiographical or documentary plan is strictly adhered to, in fact as well as in theory, and the intrusion of the novelist in person is thus prevented, the presentation of character is confined within the limits of dramatic objectivity. Speaking generally, however, the very form of the novel as a compound of narrative and dialogue, practically involves a combination of the non-dramatic and the dramatic in the handling of character. In the examination of a novelist's technique, therefore, his habitual way of using these two methods, and the proportions in which he combines them, will evidently prove an interesting question. Often we may observe a distinct bias towards one or the other. Thus Thackeray, though he makes admirable use of the indirect method, supports its results by an enormous amount of personal interpretation and criticism; while direct analysis is seriously overdone by George Eliot and the so-called psychological novelists in general. In Jane Austen's works, on the other hand, the dramatic element predominates; her men and women for the most part portray themselves through dialogue, while she herself continually throws cross- lights upon them in the conversation of the different people by whom they are discussed. We shall naturally find that the largest place is given to direct analysis in novels which deal mainly with the inner life and with complexities of motive and passion; yet even here it may be abused, and the abuse of it must always be regarded as a grave artistic mistake.

Modern criticism rightly favours the fullest possible development of the dramatic method. The principle that it is always better that a character should be made to reveal itself than that it should be dissected from the outside, is thoroughly sound; and it is easy to perceive that where dissection is perpetually substituted for self-revelation, it is often because the novelist is deficient in true dramatic sense and power. But it is not therefore necessary to go with some extremists, who, on the supposition that the excellence of a novel is in the measure of its approximation to the drama, condemn entirely the employment of analysis and commentary. It is one advantage which prose fiction possesses in comparison with the drama that the author himself may from, time to time appear in the capacity of expositor and critic; and when he avails himself of this privilege he may justly maintain that as he is writing a novel and not a drama, it is by the laws of the novel and not by those of the drama that he is bound.

Further comparison of these two cognate forms of art suggests another important point. The immense scope of the novel, its freedom of movement, and its indifference to considerations of time and place, combine with the advantage just mentioned to give it a special power of dealing with character in the making. Even our earlier novelists were quick to seize the opportunity thus afforded, as we may see in the writings of Defoe and Richardson; while the whole tendency of literary evolution during the past century has been to force the dynamics of personality more and more to the front. So far as modern fiction is concerned, therefore, there is little exaggeration in the statement of Lotze that 'the slow shaping of character is the problem of the novel'; for it would be difficult to name any really great modern novel in which that problem does not occupy a conspicuous place, even if it does not furnish the kernel or centre of interest. A common practice with the novelist who writes as a serious student of character is thus to present at the outset some leading figure with certain potentialities of good and evil, and then to follow his movement upward or downward under the influence of other people, surrounding conditions, personal experiences and his reaction to them, and whatever else enters as a formative factor into his life. The problem may of course be worked out in many ways; in particular, the changes in question may be exhibited as the results either of some exceptional crisis by which an entire revulsion of feeling is brought about, or (as Lotze's view indicates), of a gradual unfolding or atrophy of the moral nature. In either case, our attention should be directed to the means by which the changes are produced, to the question of the adequacy of the assigned causes to account for the supposed effects, and to the psychological power and truth of the delineation as a whole. It is here that, however otherwise we may judge her work, George Eliot holds her special place among our English writers of fiction. Some problem in the dynamics of character (usually conceived on the tragic side) lies at the heart of every one of her novels, and their real greatness is ultimately to be sought in the wonderful insight and skill with which she handles her theme. Where so many illustrations might be given, choice is difficult; but it may, I think, be said without hesitation that as an elaborate study of moral deterioration under repeated shocks of temptation Tito Melema is the finest thing of the kind in English literature.

It may finally be noted that in our general estimate of any novelist's characterisation, the question of his range and limitations must not be left out of consideration. Catholicity of course counts greatly in our judgment of his work in the mass; for while we admire those who, like Jane Austen, are content to do a few things and to do them well, we naturally assign a higher place to those whose accomplishment is broader and more varied. But every novelist who writes much and covers a considerable field is certain to have his points of special strength and special weakness, and the strength and the weakness alike will always throw much light upon the essential qualities of his genius and art. There is, for example, no better way of getting to know the real powers, sympathies, and affiliations of Scott than by a careful analysis of the many different classes of character which make up the *dramatis personæ* of the *Waverley Novels*. His nominal heroes possess little life, and are generally, as he confessed, 'very amiable and very insipid young men.' 'I am,' he writes with his customary candour, 'a bad hand at depicting a hero properly so-called, and have an unfortunate propensity for the dubious characters of borderers, buccaneers, highland robbers, and all others of a Robin Hood description.' His heroines, though they often possess genuine charm, are usually rather conventional. He has little power over the deeper passions, save, significantly enough, those of loyalty and patriotism. Under the influence of the romantic movement, he made frequent excursions into the domain of the abnormal and the fantastic; but he was too much a man of the eighteenth century to succeed in this direction, and his Madge Wildfire, Meg Merrilies, Dame Urfried, Norna of the *Fitful Head*, Fenella, and the rest, though highly praised by Coleridge, are in fact poor things, while the White Lady of The Monastery is decisive proof of his deficient sense of the supernatural. We have, therefore, a long list of failures, comparative or complete, to allow for, before we come at length to Scott's great and memorable successes in characterisation. And where are these to be sought? I pass over the historical studies because they involve complicating considerations of accuracy into which we cannot now enter, and reply, chiefly among his homely figures from Scottish life; in such characters as Jeanie Deans and Saunders Mucklebackit; among his lawyers, peasantfolk, farmers, innkeepers, old-fashioned retainers and serving-men; in his humorous eccentrics, such as the Baron of Bradwardine, Dominie Sampson, Jonathan Oldbuck, and Duguld Dalgetty. That the facts thus elicited help us to understand the foundations of Scott's genius and the real value of his work in the novel is, I believe, evident; and a similar inquiry into the successes and failures of other novelists would be equally fruitful of results.

What has previously been said about the need of fidelity to personal observation and experience in the plot and manners of a novel is of course no less applicable to its characterisation. In his 'essay to prove that an author will write the better for having some knowledge of the subject on which he writes,' Fielding properly urged that 'a true knowledge of the world is gained only by conversation; and the manners of every rank must be seen in order to be known.'[127] This may be accepted as thoroughly sound doctrine, disregard of which has been responsible from time to time for some conspicuous failures on the part of even the greatest novelists. Yet the general statement must be qualified in the ways already pointed out; special information, concerning the manners and speech of particular classes and callings is indeed a pre-requisite of their correct portraiture. But a broad and intimate knowledge of human nature at large, a keen insight into the workings of its common motives and passions, creative power and dramatic sympathy, will together often suffice to give substantial reality and the unmistakable touch of truth to characters for which scarcely a single suggestion can have been taken directly from life.

IV

Thus far we have dealt with plot and characterisation separately; but as in practice they are always united, something must be said about their relationships.

In common talk we distinguish roughly between two classes of novels—those in which the interest of character is uppermost, while action is used simply or mainly with reference to this; and those in which the interest of plot is upper-most, and characters are used simply or mainly to carry on the action. Quite inadequate as the distinction is, since, like all such haphazard groupings of literature, it takes cognizance only of the more extreme forms, it is none the less useful because, as indicating differences of emphasis, it suggests the question of the relative value of incident and character in fiction. To this question I do not hesitate to reply that of the two elements, characterisation is the more important; from which it follows that

---

[127] *Tom Jones*, Book adv., chapter 1.

novels which have the principal stress on character rank higher as a class than those which depend mainly on incident. The interest aroused by a story merely as a story may be very keen at the time of reading; but it is in itself a comparatively childish and transitory interest, while that aroused by characterisation is deep and lasting. Now, there is ample evidence to show, as indeed one might have anticipated, that a certain amount of opposition always exists between the claims of plot and those of character; where attention is paid primarily to plot, the characters have often to be forced into its service, even at the cost of some sacrifice to their consistency; where attention is paid primarily to character, the expansion of personality—often quite unforeseen at the outset—as the story runs its course, will frequently prove fatal to the regularity of the plot design.[128] We now see why the novels which hold the highest places in literature are, in nearly all cases, novels of character and not novels of plot. Our greatest novelists, indeed, have habitually shown a disregard of mere plot sometimes amounting to positive carelessness; a fact which explains the generalisation already mentioned, that a really great novel is likely as a rule to approximate rather to the loose than to the organic type of plot structure.

These considerations lead to a principle of great importance. While in every novel plot and characters must be combined, there is a right way and a wrong way of treating their relationship. The wrong way is to bring them together arbitrarily and without making each depend logically upon each; the right way is to conceive them throughout as forces vitally interacting in the movement of the story. In a merely sensational novel, where the writer's main concern is with his plot, the machinery of the action will commonly be found

---

[128]Scott may be cited as a witness on this point: 'Alas, my dear sir, you do not know the force of paternal affection. When I light on such a character as Bailie Jarvie or Dalgetty, my imagination brightens, and my conception becomes clearer with every step I take in his company although it leads me many a weary mile away from the regular road and forces me to leap hedge and ditch to get back into the route again' (*Introductory Epistle to The Fortunes of Nigel*).

to have little to do, save in the most general sense, with the personal qualities of the actors. The plot itself having been put together with little or no reference to them, they are simply puppets pulled this way or that, as the intrigue demands, by the showman's string. But it is in the personal qualities thus subordinated that in all really good fiction the mainsprings of the action must ultimately be sought. Simple or complex, the plot evolves as a natural consequence of the fact that a number of given people, of such and such dispositions and impelled by such and such motives and passions, are brought together in circumstances which give rise to an interplay of influence or clash of interests among them. The circumstances themselves may indeed count greatly as co-operating factors, and an impersonal element may thus combine with the personal in the development of the action. Yet even so, the personal reaction to circumstance will always remain a central consideration. Incident is thus rooted in character, and is to be explained in terms of it. One point to be kept in view, therefore, in the examination of a novel, is the degree of closeness with which plot and characters are interwoven.

This introduces the special question of 'motivation.' 'It is a part of the author's duty,' as Scott properly remarks, 'to afford satisfactory details upon the causes of the separate events he has recorded.' This means that in the evolution of plot out of character, the motives which prompt the characters of the story to act as they do must impress us as both in keeping with their natures and adequate to the resulting incidents. If for the sake of the plot, a character is made to take a line of action in contradiction to the whole bias of his disposition, or on motives which seem insufficient or fantastic, then the true relation of plot and character is ignored, and the art is faulty. We are thus brought round again to the problem of psychological truth, which, as will now be seen, is as essential in the management of plot as in the handling of character itself.[129]

---

[129] Thus the rule of the 'conservation of character' is broken, when, in order to bring a story to a close, some character is represented as undergoing a complete

V

By a natural transition we pass from the characters of fiction to their conversation.

Dialogue, well managed, is one of the most delightful elements of a novel; it is that part of it in which we seem to get most intimately into touch with people, and in which the written narrative most nearly approaches the vividness and actuality of the acted drama. The expansion of this element in modern fiction is, therefore, a fact of great significance. Anyone who watches an uncritical reader running over the pages of a novel for the purpose of judging in advance whether or not it will be to his taste, will notice that the proportion of dialogue to compact chronicle and description is almost always an important factor in the decision. Nor is the uncritical reader to be condemned on this account. His instinct is sound. Good dialogue greatly brightens a narrative, and its judicious and timely use is to be regarded as evidence of a writer's technical skill.

Investigation shows that while dialogue may frequently be employed in the evolution of the plot—the action moving (as often in the drama) beneath the conversation—its principal function is in direct connection with character. It has immense value in the exhibition of passions, motives, feelings; of the reaction of the speakers to the events in which they are taking part; and of their influence

---

and violent change of heart. Fielding complained of modern writers of comedy on this head: 'Their heroes generally are notorious rogues, and their heroines abandoned jades, during the first four. acts; but in the fifth, the former become very worthy gentlemen, the latter women of virtue and discretion. There is, indeed, no other reason to be assigned for it, than because the play is drawing to a conclusion' (*Tom Jones*, Book viii., chapter i.). A classic example of this fault is furnished by the first of our English novels, Pamela, in the facile conversion at the right moment of Mr B., who is transformed from a profligate into 'one of the best and most exemplary of men.' Illustrations of unsatisfactory motivation in the inception of a plot may often be found in Dickens; *e.g.*, in the origin of the long-sustained deceptions practised by Old Martin in *Martin Chuzzlewit* and by the Golden Dustman in *Our Mutual Friend*.

upon one another. In the hands of a novelist who leans strongly towards the dramatic method, it may thus often be made to fill the place and perform the work of analysis and commentary. Where this can be done naturally and effectively, the gain, as I have already pointed out, is considerable. Even where the analytical method is freely used, dialogue will prove of constant service as a vivifying supplement to it.

The chief requirements which dialogue should fulfil may be briefly formulated.

In the first place, it should always constitute an organic element in the story; that is, it should really contribute, directly or indirectly, either to the movement of the plot or to the elucidation of the characters in their relations with it. Extraneous conversation, however clever or amusing in itself, is therefore to be condemned for precisely the same reason as we condemn any interjected discourse on miscellaneous topics by the author himself; namely, that having no connection with the matter in hand, it breaks the fundamental law of unity. Examples of such infraction will be found in plenty in the discussions on politics, society, literature and art, which fill so many pages in the novels of Bulwer Lytton. Conversation extended beyond the actual needs of the plot is to be justified only when it has a distinct significance in the exposition of character.

Beyond having this organic connection with the action, dialogue should be natural, appropriate, and dramatic; which means that it should be in keeping with the personality of the speakers; suitable to the situation in which it occurs; and easy, fresh, vivid, and interesting. It is evident that these are elementary conditions of good dialogue. Yet it must be noted that the last named of them is to a certain degree in antagonism to the other two, and that to fulfil them all in combination is possible only by a delicate compromise which is one of the most difficult parts of the novelist's art to attain. The actual talk of ordinary people, and even the talk of brilliant people in exceptional situations, would, if realistically reproduced, seem hopelessly slipshod, discursive, and ineffective; while on the other hand there is a constant danger lest, in his effort to escape from the flat and common-place, the writer should become just as hopelessly stilted, bookish and unconvincing. 'In a quarrel that takes place in real life,' says Mr Henry Arthur Jones, 'you will find a great many undramatic repetitions and anti-climaxes, and sometimes a vast amount of unnecessary language. On the stage all this has to be avoided.'[130] In the novel, too, all this has to be avoided; but in the one case as in the other, while the periphrases and ineptitudes of an actual altercation must be eliminated and the entire matter recast with an eye to dramatic effect, theatrical declamation is not to be accepted as the proper substitute for racy and natural utterance. It was one of the besetting sins of Dickens that, master though he was of admirable dialogue, he habitually fell into melo-dramatic rant and bombast in scenes of tragic stress or passion. It will be admitted by all, but the most uncompromising realists, that to use the exact language which such a girl as Alice Marwood would have employed in her passionate outbursts of anger and hatred, would never do at all; but then the language which Dickens puts into her mouth, not one syllable of which rings true, will never do either.[131] To find the proper mean between such extremes, alike in ordinary conversations and in situations of emotional intensity, is the problem which the novelist has to solve. He has to edit and refashion his dialogue, but to do this without taking the genuine flavour out of it. His aim must therefore be, not to report the actual talk of everyday men and women, but to give such a conventionalised version of this as shall at once maintain the required dramatic rapidity and power, and leave the reader with a satisfying general sense of naturalness and reality.

VI

In speaking of plot, characterisation, and dialogue in prose fiction

---

[130] *On Playmaking, in The Renaseence of the English Drama.*
[131] *Dombey and Son*, chapter xxxiv. *Cf.* Gissing's *Dickens*, chapter V.

I have not, it will be remarked, made any overt reference, though reference has several times been implied, to the question of the novelist's powers of humour, pathos, and tragic effect. These special attributes are so conspicuous by their presence or absence, as the case may be, and they are so inevitably recognised or missed by even the most careless reader, that it is unnecessary to do more than make passing mention of them. It is no less evident that in our estimate of any novelist's work as a whole, there are two points which in particular will come up here for examination. There is first the question of the extent and limitations of his powers. In the comparative study of fiction this question has some interest, since one writer who is strong in pathos is weak in humour; with another the conditions are reversed; a third is most at home among the fiercer passions; while here and there we may find one who has something of Shakespeare's assured mastery of many moods, and can touch us with equal certainty to mirth, to pity, to terror. Secondly, there is the more important question of the quality of his accomplishment in any of these directions; for humour may vary from broad farce to the subtlest innuendoes of high comedy; pathos from weak sentimentalism to the most delicate play of tender feeling; tragedy from a crude revelling in merely material horrors to the most soul-moving calamities of the moral and spiritual life. Without further discussion it may be taken for granted that in the study of any novel or author both these questions of range and quality of emotional effect will be considered as a matter of course.

It must however be added that, simple as it may at first seem, the question of quality involves the large, and in some respects, difficult problem of the use and abuse of the emotional elements in fiction. This problem has many sides, only one or two of which can be indicated here.

That humour, one of the greatest endowments of genius and the one which beyond all others should help to keep a novelist's work sane and wholesome, may yet be misemployed in various ways, will readily be perceived. It is misemployed, for example, when it is enlisted in the service of indecency or used to turn to ridicule what should arouse sympathy or the sense of revulsion rather than mirth. To lay down an abstract rule is impossible, for many things which are intrinsically pitiable or disgusting, like drunkenness, have still their comic aspect, and may therefore rightly be handled in the comic way. Often too such comic handling is morally most effective, and for this reason humour has always been a potent instrument for the correction of manners and the castigation of vice. Much depends upon spirit and treatment. But we are at least safe in saying that when our laughter is stirred it shall be by no unworthy subjects, that it shall not partake of cruelty, and that it shall leave no bad taste in the mouth.

A similar problem confronts us in connection with the painful emotions. Why we enjoy them at all when we experience them in the mimic world of art, is a question concerning which, since Aristotle stated it in a famous passage in the *Poetics*, much has been written and countless theories propounded. That we do enjoy them is at any rate a patent fact, while the place that they occupy in much of the world's greatest imaginative literature testifies eloquently to the depth and permanence of their appeal. Yet these painful emotions may easily be abused, and often have been abused. Sentiment may degenerate into sentimentalism and an unhealthy indulgence in the luxury of grief, and no one will deny the danger of this tendency who remembers how much fiction is written with the express purpose of satisfying a widespread craving for this particular kind of morbid excitement in weak or oversensitive natures. In the same way, the proper bounds of tragic feeling may be overstepped or its power perverted, as in the numerous instances in which descriptions of suffering are drawn out to a point at which they become positively agonising, or the reader is compelled to linger over scenes the whole effect of which depends upon their profusion of pathological detail. Once more it is impossible to formulate general principles for the guidance of taste, for healthy sentiment passes by insensible degrees into sickly sentimentalism, while the borderline between the tragic

horror which is justifiable and that which is unjustifiable is equally
shifting and vague. We can only suggest the importance of watching
carefully the after effect of fiction upon ourselves. If, the spell of
the moment being broken, we look back on a novel we have just
been reading and become conscious that we have been tricked into
strong feeling without sufficient or upon unworthy cause, that our
emotion has been merely factitious and will not stand the impartial
judgment of the next say, or that the interest aroused has been of
that gross and morbid kind which leaves a taint upon the mind,
then, no matter what may be its artistic merits, the book must stand
condemned. A rough test is thus provided, and though it is only a
rough one, in practice it should prove of some utility.

VII

We turn next to the question of setting in a novel, or what we
have called its time and place of action. In this term we include the
entire milieu of a story—the manners, customs, ways of life, which
enter into its composition, as well as its natural background or
environment. We may therefore distinguish two kinds of setting—the
social and the material.

One marked feature of modern fiction is its specialisation.
Fielding probably intended to give in *Tom Jones* a fairly complete
picture of the English life of his time. Balzac and Zola alike attempted,
not in one novel but in a series of novels, to embrace the whole
of French civilisation in all its phases and ramifications. How far
in these, and in other such cases, success has been achieved, it is
unnecessary now to inquire. We have only to note the fact that
few novelists have written with so comprehensive an aim. The
tendency of the modern novel to spread out in all directions until it
has become practically coextensive with the complex modern world,
has inevitably been accompanied by a parallel tendency towards the
subdivision of its subject matter. A certain largeness of design is
indeed often noticeable, as in the work of Dickens; yet, for the most
part, life is rather treated in sections, each novel concerning itself

chiefly with one or two aspects of the great social comedy. Thus we have novels of the sea and of military life; of the upper classes, the middle classes, the lower classes; of industrial life, commercial life, artistic life, clerical life; and so on.

Subdivision also follows topographical lines, as in the innumerable novels of different localities and of local types of character: Scotch novels, Irish novels, 'Wessex' novels; the 'sectional' stories which have long been popular in America; and many novels in French literature which, like Daudet's wonderful studies of the southern temperament, have a similar concentration of interest. Frequently, of course, the local type of character is presented amid its natural surroundings, but often its peculiarities are brought out by the device of transplanting it into another and contrasted environment. Whichever plan is adopted, it is evident that in all novels in which particular phases of life are kept to the fore, characterisation and social setting are vitally associated, and each element must therefore be considered in its connection with the other. But it must further be remembered that many novels owe much of their attractiveness and literary value to their skilful portrayal of the life and manners of special classes, social groups, or places. At this point the work of the novelist has again to be judged by the accuracy and power of his descriptions.

These principles hold good for the historical novel, which aims to combine the dramatic interest of plot and character with a more or less detailed picture of the varied features of the life of a particular age. Sometimes the historical setting has comparatively little to do with the essence of the narrative, the basis of which is provided rather by the permanent facts of experience than by the forms which these facts assume in special circumstances. George Eliot utilises in *Romola* the setting of the Italian Renaissance, and gives a laborious study not only of the outer life but also of the peculiar intellectual movements and spiritual struggles of that strange and brilliant period. Yet the central tragedy of Tito's downfall is largely independent of the historical surroundings—a fact which she herself indicates in advance by dwelling as she does in her introductory chapter on the broad uniformities of human life beneath all superficial variations of place and time. Sometimes, on the other hand, the permanent is so bound up with the temporary and interpenetrated by it, that the setting becomes an essential element in the human drama itself. This is illustrated in Hawthorne's *Scarlet Letter*. As a study of sin and the effects of sin upon the soul, this powerful romance transcends all conditions of time and place. But the actual tragedy is wrought out of the materials furnished by New England Puritanism, and permanent moral issues thus assume in it a local and temporary form. While therefore it is possible to think of Tito's story with little reference to the particular phases of life which constitute its background, to think in this way of the story of Arthur Dimmesdale and Hester Prynne is impossible. It will thus always be well to observe the connection between theme and setting and the extent to which the latter is essential to the former. In some cases we shall find that the plot and characters are used simply to focus the outstanding features of the period dealt with; as in Newman's *Callista* and Pater's *Gaston de Latour*.

In whatever way the setting may be treated, however, the interest of an historical novel will always inhere in part—for this in one sense is the very justification of its existence—in its vivid reproduction of the life of a bygone age. Here again the tests to be applied are those of descriptive power and substantial accuracy. It is the business of the historical novelist to bring creative imagination to bear upon the dry facts of the annalist and the antiquarian, and out of a mass of scattered material gleaned from a variety of sources, to evolve a picture having the fulness and unity of a work of art. It is this power of making real and picturesque some particular period of civilisation, and of doing this without any suggestion of the dry-as-dust and pedantic, that the ordinary reader values most in the writer of historical fiction. About the question of his scholarship and fidelity he probably troubles himself little.[132] That question must, however, ultimately enter into our estimate of any novel which purports to describe a past epoch, though it is far too large and complex to admit of consideration here. Two points only may just be mentioned In the first place, while of course an historical novel should adhere to truth in the narrative of such actual events as fall within its compass, it is far more important that it should represent faithfully the manners, tone, and temper of the age with which it deals. Thus we blame Scott because he is often guilty of anachronism in detail; as when he brings Prince Charlie back to Scotland after Gulloden, and makes Shakespeare the author of *A Midsummer Night's Dream* at a time when he could have been only some eleven years old; but still more we blame him because in *Ivanhoe*—which is from first to last one sustained anachronism—he gives us a totally false impression of the life and spirit of the Middle Ages. Secondly, though, despite his many defects as an interpreter of history, Scott still remains our greatest historical novelist, it must not be forgotten that the sense of the importance of truth in historical fiction has developed enormously since his time. The historical novel was in part a product of the romantic movement, and in the hands of a writer like Dumas, it was almost pure romance. But the scientific spirit has now invaded it, and the writer who undertakes to rehabilitate the past has in a measure to accept the responsibilities of the chronicler. He has thus to satisfy at once the claims of history and the claims of art.

---

[132]Occasionally the novelist provides some record of his sources and thus throws light upon his preparation and equipment for his task. Scott does this to some extent in his prefaces and notes. A full display of authorities will be found in Becker's *Gallus* and *Charicles*. These works, however, can scarcely be classed among historical novels, as the slight story is avowedly contrived only as the vehicle for a study in the one case of Roman, in the other of Greek antiquities, and the human interest is wholly sub- ordinated to this scholarly purpose. A similar remark may be made of Strutt's unfinished *Queenhoo Hall*, concerning which see Scott's *General Introduction to The Waverley Novels*.

On the other kind of setting in fiction—the material—little needs to be said. Every reader will perforce note for himself the difference between novelists who, like Jane Austen, pay slight attention to the milieu of their scenes, and those who, like Balzac and Dickens, specially delight in minute descriptions of streets, houses, and interiors; while the question of skill, vividness, method, and general artistic value will just as inevitably come up for consideration.

There is, however, one special problem connected with material setting which should perhaps be emphasised. In our examination of a novelist's use of nature, our first concern will be with his power as a landscape painter. But it must be remembered that, like the narrative poet, he may treat the natural background and accessories of his action in various ways. He may introduce them for picturesque purposes only and without relating them to his human drama; or he may associate them directly with his drama either through contrast or through sympathy. There is, for instance, a touch of contrast suggested by the fact, though it is not mentioned in the scene itself, that little Paul Dombey's death occurs on a fine Sunday in June; there is, on the other hand, a hint of sympathy when Barkis dies at the hour of the outgoing tide. Hawthorne makes effective use of contrast when he shows the 'fresh, transparent, cloudless morning' peeping through the windows of the silent chamber in which Judge Pyncheon sits dead; Daudet employs the opposed principle of sympathy when in *Le Nabab* he describes the pitiless deluge of rain at the close of the day which had witnessed the absolute collapse of Jansoulet's great fête. Of these two methods, that of making external conditions harmonise with the action or the mood of the characters is the more common one. The use of nature in sympathy with man is indeed one of the most familiar of all dramatic devices; and the connection is often accentuated to the full and most elaborately worked out; as in the many storms which, as every novel reader will remember, synchronise with and intensify situations of tragic power. The effect of contrast, of course, depends upon the sense of nature's ironical indifference to human joys and sorrows, which are thus thrown into greater relief. In the sympathetic use of natural background nature often becomes almost symbolical.

VIII

It remains for us now to consider that sixth element in the novel, which we have described as the writer's criticism, interpretation, or philosophy of life.

I put the matter first in its simplest form. Like the drama, the novel is concerned directly with life—with men and women, and their relationships, with the thoughts and feelings, the passions and motives by which they are governed and impelled, with their joys and sorrows, their struggles, successes, failures. Since, then, the novelist's theme is life, in one or several of its innumerable aspects, it is impossible for him not to give, expressly or by implication, some suggestion at least, if nothing more than a suggestion, of the impression which life makes upon him. Little as he may dream of using his narrative as the vehicle of any special theories or ideas, certain theories or ideas will none the less be found embodied in it, and even the slightest story will yield under analysis a more or less distinct underlying conception of the moral values of the characters and incidents of which it is composed. To this extent, therefore, if no further, every novel, no matter how trivial, may be said to rest upon a certain view of the world, to incorporate or connote various general principles, and thus to present a rough general philosophy of life.

To this statement the reply may be made that it would manifestly be absurd to talk about a philosophy of life in connection with the ordinary run of our ephemeral works of fiction, which have no depth of interest, and are written with no purpose beyond that of providing amusement for the idle hour. Undoubtedly. But this is not because some kind of philosophy is not there; it is only because it is not fresh and serious enough and is not expressed with sufficient truth and power, to be worthy of consideration. But the great novelists have been thinkers about life as well as observers of it; and their knowledge of character, their insight into motive and passion, their illuminative treatment of the enduring facts and problems of experience, to say nothing of the ripe wisdom which they often bring to bear upon their task, combine to give to their view of the world a moral significance which no thoughtful reader is likely to overlook. How important this philosophical element in their work really is, is strikingly shown by the fact that in discussing any great novel we soon find ourselves involved in the discussion of life itself.[133]

It is not to be understood by this that we are to think of a novelist as starting out to expound a set body of ethical doctrines, or as contriving his story as an embodiment of certain ideas about life. This would be to misconceive grossly the attitude and method of the true creative artist. Of the question of purpose in the novel something will be said presently. For the moment we have only to insist that philosophical significance does not necessarily imply any preliminary philosophic aim. What a novelist thinks about life will inevitably guide him, consciously or unconsciously, in the arrangement of his plot and the treatment of his characters. But his primary concern is not with abstract questions but with the concrete facts of life, and he may—I do not say that he generally does, but that he may—handle these concrete facts without any effort or desire to suggest their moral meanings. It is certainly safe to assume—to take the example of the greatest creative power in literature—that Shakespeare's interest throughout was in concrete facts—in action and character as such. There is therefore a sense in which it would be quite unwarrantable to speak of Shakespeare as a moralist at all. Yet, even if we waive the question whether he himself cared in the least about the ethical problems involved in his

---

[133]Thus Prof. Moulton properly notes that, of what passes currently as commentary on Shakespeare, 'the vast proportion is comment upon human life itself, touched as life is at myriad points by the creations of the Shakespearean Drama' (*The Moral System of Shakespeare*, p. 5).

plays, there is another sense in which he may be regarded as one of the greatest of moralists. Thus Prof. Moulton is entirely justified in discussing the 'moral system of Shakespeare'; by which phrase he does not mean that Shakespeare wrote his dramas to prove any thesis or convey any lesson, or that he had any thesis or lesson in mind while composing them; but simply that, as they stand, they actually present 'a vast body' of 'creative observations in human life,' which 'invite arrangement and disposition into general truths.' In precisely the same way, if in no other, we may speak of the moral system of any great novelist, and regard his works as bodies of 'creative observations' capable and worthy of being formulated into general truths.

Such moral system, or philosophy of life, may be given, and commonly is given, in the novel in two ways. In the first place, like the dramatist, the novelist interprets life by his mere representation of it. He selects certain materials out of the mass which life offers to him; by his arrangement of these he brings certain facts and forces into relief; he exhibits character and motive under certain lights; and in the conduct of his plot indicates his view of the moral balance among the things which make up our human experience. As Prof. Moulton puts it, 'every play of Shakespeare,' critically examined, turns out to be 'a microcosm, of which the author is the creator, and the plot its providential scheme.' Similarly, every novel is a microcosm, of which the author is the creator and the plot the providential scheme. Merely by selection and organisation of material, emphasis, presentation of character and development of story, the novelist shows us in a general way what he thinks about life; and it is one business of criticism to reduce this scattered and implied philosophy to a systematic statement of fundamental principles.

Thus far the novelist's course is the same as the dramatist's: they both interpret life by representation. But while the dramatist is confined to this indirect method, the novelist is able, if he chooses, to supplement it by direct personal commentary and explanation. He can, as it were, step before the curtain, elucidate the action, discuss the characters and their motives, and generalise on the moral questions suggested by them. Where he avails himself of the privilege afforded by the free form of the novel to do this, he becomes himself the interpreter of the mimic world he has called into existence, and therefore of life at large; thus anticipating the critic in the task of systematising and formulating his thought.

In estimating the philosophy of life contained in any novel, we have to test it from two points of view—that of its truth and that of its morality. But in applying these tests, we must be on our guard against some rather serious misconceptions which are current in respect of them.

The truth we demand in fiction is not identical with the truth we demand from science. Plato made the mistake of confusing them, holding that all imaginative literature is 'false' because it does not reproduce the actual facts of existence; that Homer's poetry, for instance, is full of 'lies.' Even today we may meet with people who are more or less troubled by this difficulty, and who, failing to perceive any difference between fiction and falsehoood, look askance at all kinds of fictitious writing in consequence. But with the penetrative insight which carried him to the heart of so many questions, Aristotle pointed out the fallacy of Plato's view, rightly maintaining the existence in all great works of the imagination of a 'poetic truth' which is really deeper and more comprehensive than the mere literal fidelity to fact which we expect in the work of the historian. For while the historian is bound down to things which, in Charles Reade's witty phrase, have gone through the formality of taking place, the creative artist is limited only by what Aristotle called 'ideal probability.' In the one case, truth means fidelity to what was or is; in the other, fidelity to what may be. Already the great Greek philosopher detected the distinction, for a clear statement of which we are indebted to De Quincey, between the literature of knowledge and the literature of power. The literature of knowledge must be judged by its accuracy in matters of fact; and with every step forward taken by science, it necessarily becomes anti-quated.

Thus it is that our textbooks of biology and physics have perpetually to be rewritten, and that even our histories have continually to be revised. But the truth of the literature of power is fidelity to the great essential motives and impulses, passions and principles, which shape the lives of men and women; and because these change so little amid all the vast upheavals of the ages, the books which have in them this supreme element of essential truth remain, however old in years, as fresh and vital in their human interest as in the days when they were written. Aristotle's own science has now only a curious significance for the special student of thought, but when are we likely to outgrow the *Odyssey, Agamemnon, Antigone*?

A wit has said: 'In fiction everything is true except names and dates; in history nothing is true except names and dates.' I am not at the moment concerned to defend history against this cynical assault. I quote the paradox only because it describes so sharply the kind of truth upon which all greatness in fiction ultimately depends. The novelist may take innumerable liberties with his subject; he may rearrange his materials in fresh and startling combinations; he may invent outright; but we insist that he shall still be true to ideal probability and the great elemental facts and forces of life. If at this point his work proves to be faulty, without hesitation we adjudge it unsound.

It will be seen that this does not in the least tend to check the free play of the imagination in fiction. We have heard more than enough in recent years of realism in the novel, and advocates of this realism have told us with wearisome iteration that the one and only business of the novelist who takes his art seriously is to go direct to actual life and reproduce what he finds there with photographic fidelity. Now, in common practice this doctrine of realism is often shamefully abused. Sometimes it is made to justify detailed pictures of the sordid, base, and ugly—pictures which, while they may be painfully accurate in their presentation of selected particulars, are so completely out of perspective that they are anything but true, to life at large. Sometimes it is employed to dignify the much-ado-about-nothing of a certain class of writers whose chief concern seems to be the elaboration of the trivial and the commonplace, and who offer us little but cross-sections of life as seen through a powerful microscope. But even when not so abused in one or other of these two ways, the theory of realism as generally understood—that the novelist should never venture beyond actual fact—is to be rejected because it involves in another form the old confusion between scientific and poetic truth. Art cannot without self-destruction adopt the aims and borrow the methods of science. 'The artist's work,' as Goethe admirably says, 'is real' in so far as it is always true; ideal, in that it is never actual.'

Bearing this principle in mind, we shall cease to be greatly disturbed by the loud quarrel of the rival schools of novelists and critics over realism and romance. We shall see that, properly understood, both are justified, since both spring from fundamental instincts: the source of the one being our delight in seeing the near and familiar artistically rendered; of the other, our pleasure in the remote and unfamiliar. We shall see too that while each has its justification, each has likewise its conditions. Realism must be kept within the sphere of art by the presence of the ideal element. Romance must be saved from extravagance by the presence of poetic truth.[134]

In dealing with the question of truth in fiction I have, to some extent, anticipated the consideration of the closely-allied question of morality. The ethical element too has to be interpreted broadly; but so interpreted, it has to be emphasised to the full. The common distrust of so-called 'novels with a purpose'—by which is properly meant novels written specifically to make out a case or to prove a set thesis—is well grounded; for, though there are exceptions, the

---

[134]Compare Coleridge's statement of the twofold aim of the *Lyrical Ballads*:—on the one hand, 'to give the charm of novelty to things of ever day,' by touching them with the 'modifying colours of imagination'; on the other hand, to give substantial interest to supernatural incidents and agents 'by the dramatic truth of Such emotions, as would naturally accompany such situations, supposing them real' (*Biographia Literaria*, chapter xiv.).

attempt to do two things at once—to write a good story and at the same time to produce a sermon on a stated text, an essay in philosophy, or a political pamphlet—has seldom ended in anything but failure. But to confuse specific purpose with general purpose—direct didacticism with large moral meaning—is to make a serious mistake. I have said that a novelist's chief concern must always be with the concrete facts of life, and in doing this, I assumed that he may deal with concrete facts without troubling himself in the least about their moral bearings. Such assumption was made for the sake of the argument.

It has now to be added that, while theorists of a certain school may say what they like about the moral indifference of fiction, it remains none the less true that nearly all the really great novelists of the world have been declared moralists, and have troubled themselves a great deal about the moral bearings of the concrete facts presented by them. A general moral philosophy is, therefore, almost always embodied in their work as a more or less distinctly avowed part of their plan. But the conditions of success in the carrying out of such moral purpose under the forms of fiction and with due regard to the demands of art, must be clearly recognised. The ethics must be wrought into the texture of the story; the philosophy must be held in solution; the novelist must never for a moment be lost in the propagandist or preacher. It is therefore less in its directly inculcated lessons than in its whole interpretation of life, thought, character, and action, and its occasional illuminative commentary upon these, that the fundamental morality of a novel has habitually to be sought. Even its plot, with its perhaps quite arbitrary scheme of poetic justice, may have little to do with its true philosophy. For example, at the end of *The Vicar of Wakefield*, Goldsmith restores his long-suffering hero to earthly prosperity and happiness, and thus exhibits 'virtue rewarded' in the most orthodox fashion. He does this, however, by means so desperate that, it is sometimes urged, the moral value of the book is destroyed. But on further consideration it will be found that the happy ending is only a weak concession to the taste of the average novel reader of the time; it was not an essential part of Goldsmith's ethical design. Where then is the real moral of the tale? As the author himself suggests in the heading of the twenty-eighth chapter, it lies in the beautiful and sympathetic portrayal of simple courage, piety, and faith in God under stress of accumulated afflictions. This, and not the conventional and hopelessly unconvincing conclusion, 'shows Goldsmith,' as Prof. Waiter Raleigh has well remarked, 'high among the moralists of the century.' In our estimate of the moral philosophy given or implied in any novel, we have therefore to consider chiefly the impression made upon us by the spirit and temper of the work as a whole.

That we have a perfect right to include the problem of moral value in our final judgment upon any work of fiction— that, until this problem is settled, our judgment remains in fact incomplete— is a proposition concerning which I personally do not entertain the slightest doubt. Discussing poetry as a criticism of life, John Addington Symonds wrote: 'If one thing is proved with certainty by the whole history of literature down to our own time, it is that the self-preservative instinct of humanity rejects such art as does not contribute to its intellectual nutrition and moral sustenance. It cannot afford to continue long in contact with ideas that run counter to the principles of its own progress. All art to be truly great, must be moralised—must be in harmony with those principles of conduct, that tone of feeling, which it is the self-preservative instinct of civilised humanity to strengthen. This does not mean that the artist should be consciously didactic or obtrusively ethical. The objects of ethics and art are distinct. The one analyses and instructs; the other embodies and delights. But since all the arts give form to thought and feeling, it follows that the greatest art is that which includes in its synthesis the fullest complex of thoughts and feelings. The more complete the poet's grasp of human nature as a whole, the more complete his presentation of life in organised complexity, the greater he will be. Now, the whole struggle of the human race from barbarism to civilisation is one continuous effort to maintain and extent its moral dignity. It is by the conservation and alimentation of moral qualities that we advance. The organisation of all our faculties into a perfect whole is moral harmony. Therefore artists who aspire to greatness can neither be adverse nor indifferent to ethics.'

The application of these admirable remarks to the special question of prose fiction will be evident. In respect of the novel, as of other kinds of imaginative literature, it is often said that art as art has nothing to do with morality. The reply is, that in the sense in which morality is understood by Mr Symonds—in the sense in which the word has been employed throughout the present discussion—art is vitally connected with morality. Art grows out of life; it is fed by life; it re acts upon life. This being so, it cannot disregard its responsibilities to life. It is therefore to the last degree absurd to talk of the artist, whatever his line of work, as if he stood without the field of ethics. Certainly, we cannot thus speak of the novelist. As he deals with life, he must deal with the moral facts and issues everywhere involved in life; and it is upon his moral power and insight and upon the whole spirit and tendency of his philosophy, that the real greatness of his work very largely depends.

5

The Study of the Drama

I. *Dependence of the Drama upon conditions of Stage-Representation.* The Drama and the Novel—The Drama as 'Stage-play'—Dependence of the Drama on Stage Conditions—Illustration: Greek Tragedy—Another Illustration: The Shakespearean Drama. II. *Plot in the Drama.* III. *Characterisation in the Drama.* Its Conditions: Brevity of Treatment—Impersonality—Methods of Characterisation—Action—Dialogue—The Soliloquy and 'Aside'—Shakespeare's Use of Soliloquy. IV. *The Natural Divisions of a Dramatic Plot.* Exposition—Initial Incident or Exciting Force—Rising Action—Crisis—Falling Action or Dénouement—Catastrophe or Conclusion—Some General Considerations. V. *Some Features of Dramatic Design. Parallelism*—Contrast—In Plot—In Characterisation—Ethical Use of Contrast—Dramatic Irony—Concealment and Surprise. VI. *The Different Types of Drama.* Greek Drama—The Chorus—Latin Drama—Early History of Modern Drama—Triumph of the Romantic Type in England—The Spanish Drama—Comparison of the Neo-Classic and Romantic Types—Themes and Styles—Unity and Variety of Tone—The Three Unities—The Unities of Time and Place—Unity of Action—Narrative and Action—Narrative and Action in Shakespeare—The Contemporary Drama. VII. *The Drama as Criticism of Life.*

At the opening of the last chapter it was premised that, as the novel and the drama are compounded of the same elements, a great deal of what would be said about the former would be found equally applicable to the latter. We are now in a position to realise the force of this statement. The general principles of criticism which we have laid down for the study of plot, characterisation, dialogue, local and temporal setting, and interpretation of life, in prose fiction, hold good, for the most part, as will be seen, in respect, of the same constituents in a play. In taking up the study of the drama, therefore, we shall discover that the ground is already broken, and that many questions, especially questions of valuation, have been answered by anticipation. But it was further pointed out that, though their elements are identical the novelist and the dramatist work under very dissimilar conditions, and for this reason have to manipulate their material in dissimilar ways. Hence the immense difference between novel and play in everything that pertains to technique. This difference is the starting point of our present inquiry. Other matters will be dealt with later, which, though involved in the analysis of the novel no less than in that of the play, have been held over till now because they can be more easily considered in this part of our study. But our first business will be with some of the elementary characteristics of the drama, as—in the phrase already used—a specific form of literary art.

It is important at the outset to understand that what we call the principles of dramatic construction and the laws of dramatic technique arise out of and are imposed by the requirements, which, owing to the very circumstances of its existence, the drama is compelled to meet. The ancient epic was composed for recitation; the modern novel is written to be read; the drama is designed for representation by actors who impersonate the characters of its story, and among whom the narrative and the dialogue are distributed. While, then, the epic and the novel relate and report, the drama imitates by action and speech; and it is by reference to the fundamental necessities entailed by such imitation that the structural features of the drama have to be examined and explained. Because it helps us to keep this point clearly in view—because it serves to remind us that the literary art of the drama is organically bound up with its histrionic conditions—there is much to be said in favour of the good old name for drama—stage-play.

It may of course be assumed that the essential difference in technique between the novel and the drama is commonly recognised in theory by every reader of the one or the other. But its practical bearings for the student of literature are, I believe, very seldom appreciated to the full, and to these, therefore, some attention should be given.

The novel is self-contained; that is, it provides within its own compass everything that the writer deemed necessary for the comprehension and enjoyment of his work. The drama, on the other hand, when it reaches us in the form of print, and when we read it as literature, in the same way as we read a novel, is not in this sense self-contained. It implies everywhere the co-operation of elements outside itself, and for the moment these elements are lacking. What we read is, in fact, little more than a bare outline which the play- wright intended to be filled in by the art of the actor and the 'business' of the boards—a literary basis for that stage-representation upon which he calculated for the full execution of his design. In the mere perusal of a play, therefore, we labour under certain drawbacks and difficulties, for much of its effect is likely to be lost upon us for want of those continual appeals to the imagination, those descriptions, explanations, and personal commentaries, which in a novel help us to visualise scenes, understand people, estimate motives, grasp the ethical import of actions. For this reason, the comprehension and enjoyment of a play as a piece of literature must always make immeasurably greater demands upon us than the comprehension and enjoyment of a novel. We have to supply for ourselves the external conditions from which it derives much of its life, and the whole machinery of actual performance; in countless cases of detail, where, had we been spectators, we should have relied upon the 'reading' of the actor, we must as students have recourse to our own powers of apprehension and interpretation; our imagination must be so alert that every scene may be conceived as if it were passing before us in action. In ordinary practice—and particularly in our study of Shakespeare, whose works we persist in treating as 'pure' literature, and rarely regard in their primary qualities as plays written expressly for the stage—we are too apt to neglect these simple but far-reaching considerations. It is worthwhile, therefore, to insist that in our study of any drama we should do our utmost to recreate its proper theatrical circumstances and surroundings, and thus to make our private reading of it so far as possible an adequate substitute for public performance.[135]

Nor is it only the general conditions of stage-representation which thus demand attention. We have also to investigate the special conditions which at different times have affected the methods of the dramatist, and given a certain form and tendency to his art.

Thus, it is impossible either to understand the structural peculiarities or to appreciate the æsthetic effect of Greek tragedy without some knowledge of the economy of the Attic theatre. Take, for instance, the enormous size of the audiences which commonly numbered upward of 20,000;[136] the shallowness of the platform,

---

[135]In the printing of modern plays, provision is now frequently made for the needs of the mere reader by the introduction of a great deal of explanatory material. In Ibsen's dramas, for example, the setting of each scene is almost invariably given in detail; often the appearance, bearings, tones, gestures, by-play of the characters are described; and much of the stage 'business' is indicated. With such 'extra-dramatic' aids we may read a play very much as we read a novel, to which, indeed, as a piece of literature, it is thus made to approximate. Had such aids been furnished by the editors of the First Folio, our appreciation of the dramatic life and movement of many of Shakespeare's scenes would have been much more vivid than it commonly is. If the student will turn from himself to the interpretative notes which the great American actor, Edwin Booth, contributed to Furness's Variorum edition of *Othello*, he will realise at once the extent to which in our ordinary reading of Shakespeare we miss the wealth of detail which gives significance to character and situation when one of his plays is put on the stage.

[136]According to recent calculations, the great theatre of Dionysius at Athens accommodated about 17,000 spectators. Plato, in his *Symposium*, speaks of more than 30,000 being present on one occasion; but this is now regarded as an

or 'speaking place,' to which the regular dialogue and action were confined; and the heavy conventional costume of the actors, who were 'made up' with padding and the thick-soled, high-heeled cothurnus, or buskin, to appear of heroic proportions, and who always wore masks representing 'a set of features much larger than those of any ordinary man.'[137] Now these three facts, taken together, go far to explain various outstanding principles of the ancient drama, and especially its want of anything approaching the free and rapid action, the well-marked individuality of character, and the realistic quality, with which we are familiar in modern plays. The shallowness of the 'speaking place' prevented mass-scenes and elaborate stage pictures requiring depth and perspective; the arrangement of the chief persons and their retinues being that of a processional bas-relief. The distance of the performers from the spectators made by-play and detailed gesture impossible. As rapid utterance, low tones, and changing inflections would have been lost in an immense open-air theatre, the language employed was of the rhetorical, not of the conversational, kind—of the kind adapted to recitative or declamation, which accounts for 'the extreme stiffness and formality which distinguishes the tragic dialogue of the Greeks from that dexterous and varied play of verbal interchange which delights us so much in Shakespeare and other masters of English tragedy.'[138] The costume of the actors compelled them to move with a measured and stately gait, to adopt 'abrupt and angular' gesticulations,[139] and to avoid all vigorous activity; while the use of the mask not only 'precluded all attempts at varied expression,'[140] but necessarily tended also to stereotype the passions portrayed, to prevent any rapid changes of emotion, and to give to the persons represented a generic or typical

---

exaggeration. See Haigh's *Attic Theatre*, p. 100.

[137]J.W. Donaldson, *The Theatre of the Greeks*, p. 248.

[138]J. S. Blackie, *Introduction to the Lyrical Dramas of Æschylus*, I. p. xlvi.

[139]Donaldson, *op. cit.*, p. 269.

[140]*Ibid.*, p. 270.

rather than an individual character.[141] 'The effect produced by the unchangeable expression of the actor's countenance,' writes Müller, 'unnatural as it seems to us, was of less consequence in the ancient tragedy, because the principal characters appeared throughout the piece under the influence of the same feelings by which they were actuated at the commencement. Thus we may easily imagine an Orestes in Æschylus, an Ajax in Sophocles, or a Medea in Euripides, retaining the same expression from the beginning to the end of a play, although it may be impossible to conceive this of a Hamlet or a Tasso.'[142] All these facts suffice to show why the conditions of representation in the Greek theatre were particularly suitable 'for the exhibition of processions, plastic situations and groups, and for solemn measured declamation, rather than deeds of passion and violence'; why 'single combats, battles, murders, and similar scenes, would have produced a strange, we may almost say a ludicrous, effect on the Athenian stage'; and why, therefore, 'such events were invariably related, instead of being enacted in presence of the audience.'[143] Some other points of interest have been admirably dealt with by Prof. Moulton: 'The influence on Ancient Tragedy of the Theatre and theatrical representation rests mainly on the fact that Tragedy never ceased to be a solemn religious and national festival, celebrated in a building which was regarded as the temple of Dionysus, whose altar was the most prominent object in the orchestra, and in the presence of what may fairly be described as the whole 'public' of Athens and Attica.... One effect flowing from the religious associations of Tragedy was limitation of subject matter, which was confined to the sacred Myths, progress towards real life being slow. Surprise as a dramatic effect was eliminated where all knew the end of the story. On the other hand, great scope was given for irony—ignorance of

---

[141]The mask could indeed be changed during the progress of the play, but not of course while the actor was on the stage.

[142]*History of Greek Literature.*

[143]Witzchel, *The Athenian Stage*, trans. Paul, p. 119.

the sequel on the part of the personages represented clashing with knowledge of it on the part of the audience....[144] But the general influence of representation in Ancient Tragedy may be best summed up in the word 'conventionality.' This and the antithetical term, 'realism,' are the two poles of dramatic effect, all acting having reference to both and varying between the two: the latter aims directly at the imitation of life, conventionality is for ever falling into recognised positions of beauty. Not only did the ancient drama lean to the conventional, but the conception of beauty underlying it was different from the spirited movement and picturesque situations of the modern stage, and approached nearer to the foremost art of antiquity—statuary. The acting of an ancient scene is best regarded as a passage from one piece of statuesque grouping to another, in which motion is reduced to a minimum and positions of rest expanded to a maximum—a view which accounts for the great length of speeches in Greek drama. The episodes of Ancient Tragedy were displays of animated statuary, just as the choral odes were feats of expressive dancing.'[145]

Apart from any consideration of the abstract æsthetic principles by which the Greek poets were guided in their work, and with which we are not for the moment concerned, we can now understand that many of the most marked peculiarities of Attic tragedy—its ideal quality, its large simplicity of manner, the rhetorical nature of its dialogue, its broadly typical handling of character, its want of movement and action—were direct and necessary results of those special conditions of public performance which the evolution of dramatic art in Greece had brought in its train.

One other matter may just be mentioned. To the modern reader no single feature of the classic drama is more curious than the Chorus. Into the question of the origin and function of this essential element of Attic tragedy, this is not the occasion to enter;

---

[144]On this point, see further, post, § v.
[145]The Ancient Classical Drama, pp. 127–129.

reference is made to it now only that we may note its influence in two ways upon dramatic form and method. In the first place, it was the prominence of the Chorus, with its elaborate odes and solemn dancing, which gave to Greek tragedy its pre-eminently lyrical and operatic character.[146] Secondly, since 'the action of the drama was carried on from beginning to end in presence of the Chorus, a band of witnesses, always the same, and remaining in the same place, the poet...had scarcely any choice but to limit the scene to one spot, and the time to one day';[147] and thus the so-called unities of place and time became accepted principles of dramatic construction.[148]

Another illustration, and one of capital interest to the student of the English drama, will serve to make clear in a somewhat different way the immediate dependence of a playwright's technique upon the histrionic methods and resources of his time. When, ceasing to regard Shakespeare's plays merely as literature, we think of them in their connection with the principles and requirements of stage effect, it is the stage as we know it today that we almost invariably have in mind. Now a comparison of any modern acting version of one of these plays with the original text will reveal many points of difference; it will be found that numerous passages and even whole scenes are cut out entirely; that scenes which Shakespeare separated are brought together; that the order of events in the plot is sometimes changed. Often, of course, these alterations are arbitrarily made, and, except in so far as they throw a curious light upon the taste of this or that manager and the public for which he caters, they are therefore without significance. But often, on the other hand, as analysis will show, they carry us back directly to the fact that

---

[146]The 'proper designation' of Hellenic tragedy, says Prof. Blackie, 'is *sacred opera*, and not *tragedy* in the modern sense of the word,' *Op cit.*, I. p. xlvi.
[147]Witzchel, *op. cit.*, p. 43.
[148]The fact that a change of scene is occasionally found in extant tragedies (as in the *Eumenides of Æschylus and the Ajax* of Sophocles) seems to prove that the unity of place was adhered to rather as a matter of practical convenience than on account of any preconceived theory.

the stage for which Shakespeare wrote was in various fundamental particulars quite unlike our own, and that many characteristics of his dramas are thus to be understood only when they are studied in relation with theatrical conditions which have long since ceased to exist. We must not be beguiled by the fascination of the subject into any general discussion of the arrangements of the Elizabethan stage, our present task being merely to indicate the importance of these for the student of Shakespeare. Confining our attention to a couple of points only, let us therefore simply note the way in which his work was affected by the lack of movable scenery and the absence of a drop-curtain.

In connection with what follows, the reader is advised to study carefully the pen-and-ink sketch of the Swan Theatre reproduced on the next page. This was made by a Dutchman, one Johannes de Witt, in about the year 1596, and discovered in 1888 by a German scholar, Dr Gaedertz, in the Library of the University of Utrecht. It is, of course, very rough, and in sundry details it does not altogether correspond with what we otherwise know or infer about the Elizabethan stage. But it is of immense interest and value as our only contemporary picture of the interior of a playhouse in Shakespeare's time.

As movable scenery was then unknown, the dramatist was under no necessity to give, scene by scene, a definite locality to his action. The stage on which his plays were performed—a narrow platform running out into the auditorium—was divided into three parts; of which the first, or 'front stage,' was conventionally employed for any kind of open space—street, or square, or field; the second, or 'back stage' (the portion behind the columns of De Witt's drawing), with its few common articles of furniture, was similarly accepted as representing a room in a palace, a council chamber or any other interior; while the third, or 'upper stage,' a gallery behind this inner stage and above the actors' 'tiring house' (mimorum ædes), was used for any elevated spot—the walls of a castle or town, for

example, or Brabantio's window, or Juliet's gallery.[149] Evidently, this simplicity of stage setting permitted and encouraged a freedom and rapidity in the movement of the action which are rendered practically impossible by the elaborate and cumbersome scenic devices of the modern theatre. Just because there was, in our sense of the term, 'no change of scene' to be made, it could be made without difficulty, and as frequently as might be desired; for as soon as one group of characters went off, another group could enter, and a fresh scene begin, even though the spectators were supposed to be transported in imagination to a different place.[150]

---

[149]In our sketch, however, this balcony seems to be occupied by spectators.
[150]Occasionally the scene would change while people remained on the stage. There is a good example of this in Act II. scene iii. of Marlowe's *Jew of Malta*.

Thus the lack of movable scenery on the Elizabethan boards helps us at once to explain various structural features in which Shakespearean drama differs conspicuously from the drama of recent times. Its complete indifference to all considerations of locality and the unity of place; its numerous minor scenes, which break up the plot and are a source of so much perplexity to modern managers; its frequent recourse to a series of such minor scenes, which follow one another in quick succession, and over which the interest of the action is scattered in a way which seems singularly unsatisfactory to us who are accustomed to more concentrated effects:[151]— these, and various other peculiarities (such, for example, as the wealth of natural description often to be found in the dialogue) are to be largely accounted for by reference to this one fact that the Elizabethan stage was a stage without scenery.

The second of the two facts above mentioned—that the Elizabethan stage was likewise a stage without a drop-curtain[152]—

Barabas announces his intention of going to the market-place to buy a slave. Lodowick says: 'And Barabas, I'll bear thee company.' Barabas replies: 'Come then—here's the market-place. What's the price of this slave? 'In the interval represented by the dash in the text, the Jew and his young companion took a walk round the stage, and this brought them to the market. The Jew's words sufficed to indicate their arrival.

[151]A striking example of the use of a series of short scenes where a modern playwright would naturally have massed his incidents together, will be found in the alternate appearances of groups of Roman and Volscian boldiers in the first act of *Coriolanus*. The dispersion of interest over a number of minor scenes in the crisis of *Antony and Cleopatra* has often been noted as a grave defect in the construction of that play. Yet it must be remembered that owing to the rapidity with which they could be represented, these scenes were far more effective on Shakespeare's stage than they can ever be on our own. Every student should seize the first opportunity of witnessing the performance of one of Shakespeare's dramas as given from time to time, with a careful reproduction of the original conditions, by the Elizabethan Stage Society. From such a performance he may learn more about Shakespeare's technique than from the study of many volumes of criticism.

[152]There was a 'traverse,' or draw-curtain which (though there is no sign of it in

had also a marked, though perhaps a less obvious, influence on Shakespeare's dramatic methods. As in the absence of such curtain there was no way of closing a scene except by taking all the characters off in full view of the spectators, provision for a general clearance had always to be made; and it had to be made in the case not only of the living but also of the dead. This explains the specific commands which are frequently given among the scanty stage directions of the original text, for the carrying away of the bodies of those who had been slain, such as 'Exit Hamlet tugging in Polonius';[153] and the orders which are often incorporated in the dialogue, such as the Prince of Verona's 'Bear hence this body,'[154] and Cornwall's 'throw this slave upon the dunghill.'[155] But this, though an interesting, is a comparatively trivial, matter. 'A far more important result of the absence of the drop-curtain, and one which shows that this deficiency profoundly affected Shakespeare's entire structural plan, will be brought to light by a careful examination of the manner in which he rounds off his scenes and acts. It is not too much to say that the skill of a modern playwright is largely exercised in the contrivance of a thoroughly effective 'curtain'; a scene is worked up to its most thrilling situation, and upon this it closes abruptly, the incident being left incomplete. Shakespeare knows nothing of this device. He is obliged by the very necessities of the case to carry each scene to its natural conclusion; and the consequence is that he often passes beyond the note of highest dramatic interest in a situation into what from a modern playwright's point of view would be pronounced an anti-climax. His general method is, therefore, as one writer on the subject has well said, 'peculiarly unsuited to the

---

our sketch) could on occasion be employed to separate the backstage from the front. This had many uses, which in various ways affected dramatic construction. But into these details we cannot now enter.

[153] *Hamlet*, III. iv.

[154] *Romeo and Juliet*, III. r.

[155] *King Lear*, III. vii. Compare the dying king's request in *Henry IV*, IV. iv.: 'Bear me hence into some other chamber.'

act-drop. Upon one of Shakespeare's plays the curtain falls like the knife of a guillotine.'[156]

We thus see, without going further, that Shakespeare's work is not only essentially theatrical, in the sense that it was written with an eye to the conditions of performance in a public theatre, but also that it possesses a special kind of theatrical quality which can be appreciated only when it is examined from the historic side. Produced to meet certain conditions, it was everywhere moulded by these conditions. The study of Shakespeare's plays must therefore include a study of the theatrical methods in vogue at his time.

II

The foregoing remarks will perhaps suffice to open up a fruitful line of investigation for the student who is specially interested in the changing technique of the drama at different periods of its development. But as considerations of space prevent us from pursuing this large subject into further details here, we will at once pass on to note how, with little reference to local and temporary influences, and therefore in ways that are fairly uniform, the dramatist's practice is directly affected by the necessities of stage representation in regard, first, to the constitution and management of his plot, and, secondly, to the treatment of his characters.

In the constitution of his plot, it is obvious, he labours under one elementary disadvantage as compared with his fellow craftsman in the field of prose fiction. The novelist enjoys almost absolute freedom as to the length of his work, and therefore as to the amount of material that may go to its composition. At both points the dramatist is subject to severe restrictions. A novel is not designed to be read through in a single sitting. It can be put down and taken up again at the pleasure or convenience of the reader; its perusal may extend over days and weeks; and the only requirement it

---

[156]Lawrence, *Some Characteristics of the Elizabethan-Stuart Stage, in Englische Studien,* *xxxii.* 36–51.

has to meet is, that its interest shall be so sustained as to prompt a return to it when occasion offers.[157] A play, on the other hand, is intended, in Aristotle's phrase, for 'a single hearing'; and as the physical endurance of the spectator is limited, and as, when the limit is once reached, even the most engrossing scenes will fail to arrest the flagging of attention, relative brevity is a first practical law of dramatic being.[158] A dramatist then, to begin with, is compelled to work within a much more confined space than the novelist. He

---

[157]It may, however, be justly contended that the principle of limitation should be applied even to the novel, which should never be so long that we cannot easily grasp it as a whole, or, as Aristotle said in regard to the epic, comprehend the beginning and end in a single view. Such enormous and complex works as *Clarissa, Monte Cristo, The Mysteries of Paris, Les Misérables, War and Peace,* and most of the novels of Dickens and Thackeray, may thus be criticised as so far exceeding the due length that all sense of wholeness and artistic unity is destroyed in the mind of the reader. It is clear that, with all his admiration of Homer, Aristotle felt that the Iliad and the Odyssey were really too long.

[158]Even the spectator's power of maintaining interest seems, however, to have varied considerably at different times. As Freytag remarks, 'we read with astonishment of the capacity of the Athenians'—on whose stage a number of dramas were enacted in succession—'to endure for almost an entire day the greatest and most thrilling tragic effects' (*Technique of the Drama*, chapter vi.). Shakespeare speaks of 'the two hours' traffic of our stage' (*Prologue* to *Romeo and Juliet*; cp. the 'two short hours' of the *Prologue to Henry VIII*); but it is very clear that if his plays were produced as they stand in our texts, they must have been allowing for the great rapidity with which they were performed) have often exceeded, and in some cases very much exceeded, the limit assigned, Freytag lays it down as a general rule that 'a five-act play which, after its arrangement for the stage, contains an average of five hundred lines to the act, exceeds the allotted time,' and that 'not more than two thousand lines should be considered the regular length of a stage piece.' Shakespeare's *Macbeth* has 2108 lines, but this is one of the shortest of his plays. *Othello* has 3317 lines, *King Lear*, 3332; while *Hamlet* with 3931 and *Antony and Cleopatra* with 3991, run to twice the proposed bulk. It is a well-known, and in our present context a suggestive fact, that plays written by dramatists who have little or no expert training in theatrical technique have nearly always to be abridged for stage representation. Freytag notes that it was notoriously difficult for Schiller to complete a play within the required stage time.

has therefore to compress his materials; to eliminate everything not absolutely essential to his purpose; to select the most important incidents and situations, and concentrate his attention upon these. Hence the significance of Aristotle's warning to the playwright that he should not attempt to 'construct a tragedy upon an epic plan'; meaning by 'epic plan' a 'fable composed of many fables; as if anyone, for instance, should take the entire fable of the Iliad for the subject of a tragedy.'[159]

In the same way, it is easy to appreciate the difference between the expansive plan permitted by the conditions of prose fiction, and the condensed plan demanded by the drama, and to understand how much excision and compression are required in dramatising in a novel of any length and complexity. In securing brevity, the dramatist is greatly helped, it is true, by the secondary arts of the stage; since much that the novelist has to explain he may leave to histrionic interpretation, while stage setting practically relieves him from the necessity of verbal description. Yet the problem of the clear and effective disposition of his material within the narrow limits he is forced to accept, is one which will always tax his constructive skill; and it is to this aspect of his plot, therefore, that attention may first be directed. Analysis will show that, unlike the novelist, who generally tells his tale in a comprehensive narrative, incorporating all the necessary details as they arise, the dramatist commonly reserves for full treatment a number of important scenes, providing within these scenes the links of the story which are required to bind them together. Yet even here allowance must be made for the differences of technique which have resulted from differences in the conditions of stage representation. There is far more massing of incident and

---

[159] *Poetics*, II. xx. But Aristotle elsewhere contends that the structural superiority of the Homeric poems to other epics lies in their unity; for which reason, as he points out, the *Iliad* and the *Odyssey* would not furnish material for more than one, or at most two tragedies each, while 'more than eight' dramas had been made out of a chronicle poem called *The Little Iliad*. It is evident that several plays might be made, *e.g.*, out of *Bleak House*.

concentration of interest upon a few outstanding points in the works of a skilled modern playwright than in our romantic drama. Compared with the method of Sardou, or Ibsen, or Sudermann, Shakespeare's is much more nearly allied to the method of the epic poet or romance writer, since, like them, he habitually follows his plot through a succession of minor scenes in which he directly exhibits transitional movements which the modern playwright would give in the form of explanatory narrative. The peculiar freedom of the stage for which he wrote, as we have already observed, largely accounts for this practice. Thus, when Shakespeare appropriates some story in prose or verse (like Brooke's *Romeus and Juliet*, Lodge's *Rosalynde*, or Greene's *Pandosto*), and turns it into a play, he does so without undertaking that entire recasting of its materials which would now be deemed necessary. In one conspicuous case—that of *The Winter's Tale*—he produces indeed what is rather a dramatised romance than a drama. One striking illustration of the general looseness of texture which was permitted by the conditions of the Elizabethan stage and encouraged by the spirit of the time, is provided by the chronicle play, which the criticism of our own day is bound to regard, so far as formal structure is concerned, as an unsatisfactory compromise between the claims of history and those of dramatic art.

The points which have been here touched upon belong, of course, to the mere rudiments of dramatic theory, and it is quite unnecessary to consume space in their elaboration. Some important questions connected with the laws and principles of dramatic construction will be considered later.

III

Great, however, as are the structural differences between drama and novel in the management of plot, they are even greater in the exposition of character.

It is sometimes carelessly assumed that, since the business of the stage is so largely and so necessarily with action, characterisation in a play is really of minor importance. On this assumption, indeed, many plays are still written. It is none the less so far a mistake that everything that has been said about the supremacy of the character element in prose fiction is equally applicable to the drama. 'I suppose,' says Mr Henry Arthur Jones, 'that the first demand of an average theatrical audience to its author will always be the same as the child's—Tell me a story.' And then, after explaining that he has no desire to belittle the value of a story as such, Mr Jones continues: 'Story and incident and situation in theatrical work are, unless related to character, comparatively childish and unintellectual. They should indeed be only another phase of the development of character.... A mere story, a mere succession of incidents, if these do not embody and display character and human nature, only give you something in raw melodrama pretty much equivalent to the adventures of our old friend, Mr Richard Turpin.'[160] This is sound doctrine. Characterisation is the really fundamental and lasting element in the greatness of any dramatic work. We have only to turn to Shakespeare to find a telling illustration. No one would contend that his plays owe their permanent place in literature to the quality of his plots. The interest which keeps them alive is the interest of the men and women in them. As I have elsewhere said, 'it is only because the core of *Macbeth* is not the murders which Macbeth commits, but the character of Macbeth himself, that *Macbeth* is a stupendous tragedy and not a mere farrago of sensational horrors. It is only because the core of *The Merchant of Venice* is not the things which are done, but the people who do them, that our play is a great comedy, and not a mere tissue of childish absurdities.'[161] Considered simply on the side of its plot, *Hamlet* has to be classed with those numerous 'tragedies of blood,' or 'revenge plays,' which, with their crude violence and monstrous passions, made a stirring appeal to the strong nerves of the Elizabethan public. But out of this unpromising material, Shakespeare has made a drama of inexhaustible interest;

---

[160] *The Renascence of the English Drama*, p. 232.
[161] Introduction to *The Merchant of Venice*, in *The Elizabethan Shakespeare*, p. xxiii.

and he has done this by the development of what in the language of our time we call the psychological element. And it is, in the last analysis, upon this psychological element that the permanent vitality of any play depends.

As in the handling of plot, so again in characterization, a first condition of dramatic art is brevity. In defence of an over-long novel it is sometimes urged that the exposition of motive and the full portrayal of character demand and justify prolixity. But the dramatist has to deal with motive and character within the narrowly circumscribed area of a comparatively few scenes, in which at the same time (since the drama affords little scope for characterisation divorced from action) he has to be more or less concerned with the progress of his story. Until their attention has been specially directed to it, few readers realise the full meaning of this fact. It may be well, therefore, to emphasise its significance by taking a single illustration. *Macbeth* is often referred to as a wonderful example of the condensed treatment of action. It is even more remarkable as an example of the condensed treatment of character. It is trite to say that Macbeth and his wife are among the most vital and permanently interesting figures in literature; the endless critical discussions which have gone on about them testify to the fact that Shakespeare has endowed them with the reality and the mystery of life. We may well be surprised, therefore, to discover by direct investigation how little there is of them, and how few are the master strokes with which they are drawn. If we examine the first act, we find in it a marvellously complete exhibition of the potentialities of both of them for good and ill—Macbeth's physical courage, his prowess on the battlefield, the confidence of others in him, the evil already fermenting in his mind, his imaginative and superstitious temperament; Lady Macbeth's strength and moral courage, her singleness of purpose, the power and direction of her influence over her husband's more sensitive and less resolute nature—all these things are made clear to us in broad outline; we feel that we have been brought into the closest contact with the motive forces of these two mighty personalities. Yet this

192 ❖ WILLIAM HENRY HUDSON

act contains, all told, only some twenty-five pages of ordinary print, or fewer than five hundred lines; and in it Lady Macbeth speaks only fourteen times, uttering 864 words, and Macbeth only twenty-six times, uttering 878 words. In the whole play Lady Macbeth has something less than 60 speeches, Macbeth barely 150, and in each case some of the speeches are very short.[162] Perhaps it is only when we put it in this way that we are quite able to appreciate the extraordinary range and resources of Shakespeare's art, which, once appreciated, must remain, as Prof. Barrett Wendell says, 'a matter for constant admiration.' *Macbeth* is indeed an exceptional example of condensation, but any other of Shakespeare's greater plays would, on analysis, reveal results only a little less surprising. Hamlet's, for instance, is the longest single part in the Shakespearean drama; yet when we think of the enormous complexity of the character and of the place which it holds among the great imaginative creations of all literature, it is not the length of the part, but its brevity which should impress us.

Concentration as a necessary condition of dramatic characterisation, of course, implies the most carefully considered emphasis upon the qualities which have to be brought into relief. More even than in the novel, therefore, every word of dialogue must be made to tell, each feature must be elaborated in strict relevancy to the whole, and all mere supererogatory talk must be avoided. The rule being that every character should be so presented as to appear absolutely adequate to all the demands which the plot makes upon it, 'dramatic criticism is inclined to insist,' as Prof. Tolman says, 'that only those characteristics of the hero'—or indeed of any important personage—'should be made prominent which really influence the course of the action; and that these characteristics should be unmistakable.'[163] The principles of dramatic economy may justly be appealed to in support of this opinion. Yet it is interesting

---

[162]Barrett Wendell's *William Shakespeare*, p. 308.
[163]*The Views about Hamlet and other Essays*, p. 44.

to note that the great creators of character in the drama seem sometimes to become absorbed in the development of character for its own sake, with a resulting occasional tendency to what we may call 'over-characterisation'—that is, characterisation in excess of the real needs of the action. Shakespeare not infrequently exhibits this tendency. There is undoubtedly more in the character of Hamlet, for example, than is actually required to account for his part in the plot.[164]

An even more important condition of characterisation in the drama than that of mere brevity is its necessary impersonality. The novelist can himself mingle freely with the men and women of his story, take them to pieces from the outside, lay their thoughts and feelings bare before us, pass judgment upon them. The dramatist cannot do this; he is compelled to stand apart. Here again, and most obviously, the advantage is on the side of the novelist, especially where complexities of character and the subtler shadings of motive and passion are concerned. When, remembering this, we join with such advantage his practically unrestricted freedom in respect alike of movement and of space, we can see that the peculiarities which critics sometimes regard as the artistic imperfections of the novel—its wide range, its looseness of structure, its eminently personal quality— really give it an enormous superiority to the drama in the field of characterisation. Here we have one among several reasons which go far to explain the displacement of the drama by prose fiction in an age greatly occupied with the problems of the inner life.

---

[164]Coleridge was evidently inclined to regard Dogberry and his companions as instances of over-characterisation—'any other less ingeniously absurd watchmen and night-constables would,' he declares, 'have answered the mere necessities of the action' (*Lectures and Notes on Shakespeare*, p. 139). But Coleridge, who had such a marvellous power of dis- covering things which Shakespeare did not put into his plays, often failed to see what he did put there. Dogberry and his fellows provide, in fact, an admirable example of the vital dependence of action upon character. Their interview with Leonato in Act III., scene v., suffices to prove this.

It is clear that we have now reached the point of fundamental distinction between characterisation in the novel and characterisation in the drama. There arises, therefore, the question of the methods of dramatic characterisation. Debarred as he is from adopting the novelist's simple plan of constituting himself the official interpreter of his men and women, and telling us himself all that we need to know about them, how does the playwright disclose their personalities to us? How does he make us realise what manner of men and women they are? He has, of course, to do so wholly through the medium of the plot and the utterances of his characters.[165] It is possible that, drawing as we often do an arbitrary line of demarcation between them, we commonly overlook the significance of plot as a means of characterisation. Yet action connotes character and implies it. Through the very movement of a story, and particularly through its great crises and situations, the larger intellectual and moral qualities of the persons who take part in it are necessarily impressed upon us. We know them by what they do, as the tree is known by its fruit.

The importance of this point will become more manifest if we recall what has been said about the proper interrelations of plot and character in a well-constructed story.[166] In a good play, as in a good novel, plot really rests upon character; it evolves, as I have said, 'as a natural consequence of the fact that a number of given people, of such and such dispositions and impelled by such and such motives and passions, are brought together in circumstances

---

[165]It is scarcely necessary to point out, though it may perhaps be desirable to do so, that the novelist, too, makes continual use of plot and the utterances of his characters; the contrast lies in the fact that he is at liberty also, whenever he deems it requisite for clearness in characterisation, to reinforce the results so obtained by personal explanation and commentary. As shown in the last chapter, there are novelists who lean towards the 'analytical' or non-dramatic method, and novelists who lean towards the dramatic method (see *ante*, pp. 146–148). In the works of the former, the intrusion of the writer is frequent; in those of the latter, personal explanation and commentary are introduced as sparingly as possible.

[166]See *ante*, pp. 152, 153.

which give rise to an interplay of influence or clash of interests among them.' This being so, the evolution of the story inevitably reveals their dispositions, motives, and passions, which are indeed the actual forces behind the events of which the story is composed. This is a corollary from the remark of Mr Jones which I have quoted, that in theatrical work, story, incident, and situation 'should be only another phase of the development of character.' It was a curious practice of Diderot, when he went to the theatre, to stop his ears to the dialogue and to watch the play as mere pantomine. He did so for the purpose of isolating the acting and studying this by itself. But such an experiment might be made for the isolation of the action and the study of the exposition of character through this and the histrionic interpretation which would be required to make it effective. Were *Agamemnon* or *Œdipus the King*, *Hamlet*, *Macbeth*, or *Othello*, represented in dumb show only, we should still be left in little doubt as to the broad characteristics of their principal personalities. We should at least have certain outstanding features to rely upon, and from these much else might be safely inferred.

Plot, however, since it can show us nothing more than the man in action, discloses such broad characteristics only; and that it may do even this at all clearly, it is necessary that it should be bold in outlines and full of movement, that its critical situations should be so well defined that to mistake their meaning is impossible, and that the characters themselves should be of the massive and relatively simple kind. All these conditions, we may just note in passing, are fulfilled in our English romantic drama. For all details of characterisation, and for the exhibition of passions, motives, feelings in their growth, entanglements, and conflicts, we must in every case refer from the action itself to the dialogue which accompanies it; and evidently this must be particularly true where the interest of a drama is predominantly psychological and the plot concerns itself rather with the play of the forces behind action than in the external events in which these discharge themselves. Dialogue then becomes an essential adjunct to action, or even an integral part of it: the story moving beneath the talk, and being, stage by stage, elucidated by it. Yet the principal function of dialogue in the drama as in the novel is, as I have said, in direct connection with characterisation.[167] Even in the hands of the novelist, as we have already seen, dialogue will often be used to fill the place and do the work of analysis and commentary. In the drama (save for the exception presently to be mentioned) it is not simply an aid to analysis and commentary; it is, in fact, a substitute for them.

We may regard dramatic dialogue as a means of characterisation under two heads; taking, first, the utterances of a given person in his conversation with others, and then the remarks made about him by other persons in the play. Of the former aspect of dialogue there is little to be said. Speaking broadly, the utterances of any person in a play will furnish a continual running commentary upon his conduct and character; and when, for any reason, such commentary is particularly necessary, we may expect to find scenes in which the action practically stands still while thoughts, feelings, and motives are brought to the front. 'Mere talk'—as it is sometimes called by those who are impatient of any delay in the movement of a story—talk in which we are directly concerned with character and only indirectly with incident—the kind of talk of which there is so much, for instance, in the greater plays of Molière, and in the works of modern psychological playwrights like Ibsen—is thus amply justified on the one condition that it really serves the end for which it is intended. Of course, in the critical examination of dialogue the demands of natural reticence, and occasionally of deliberate disguise, may have to be allowed for. Much that a person tells us about himself may have to be told, as it were, unconsciously and by implication. Alceste in Molière's *Le Misanthrope* will very properly make a full statement of his feelings to his friend and confidant Philante; but just as properly the arch-hypocrite in the same writer's *Le Tartuffe* will do his utmost to hide his real nature from those about him. In this case, indeed, we already know him too well to be deceived. But now and then it may be necessary that some character should at first throw us more or less completely off our guard as to his aims and motives, and reveal these only gradually, or, as is far more likely to happen, in some sudden turn of the action, like Euphrasia in Beaumont and Fletcher's *Philaster*. When this occurs, we shall then have to go back over the whole play and consider all the utterances of the person in question under the fresh light which this final revelation throws upon them. A skilful playwright, unless he has some special motive for concealment or delay, will take pains to indicate the fundamental qualities of his principal characters—the qualities on which the plot is to hinge—as soon and as clearly as possible. This is Shakespeare's general method. 'The later a new characteristic trait enters the action, the more carefully,' as Freytag says, 'must the motive for it be laid in the beginning, in order that the spectator may enjoy to the full extent the pleasure of the surprise, and perceive that it corresponds exactly to the constitution of the character.'[168]

While, however, this direct self-portrayal through a person's own speech must always constitute the principal means of characterisation by dialogue, it may be greatly reinforced by what other people say about him either to his face or among themselves. In this way we may often obtain a number of cross-lights which, taken together, may prove of utmost value. In considering this indirect evidence we must, it is obvious, keep steadily in mind its essentially dramatic quality. Every utterance must therefore be tested by reference to the character of the particular speaker, his own situation and relation to the action, the possible bias given by his interests, his sympathy, his antipathy. To catch at a phrase here and there, and, without thought of its context, to treat it as an impartial and authoritative expression of opinion, is in the last degree uncritical. There are commentators who have thus caught at the words 'ambitious Constance,' in the opening scene of Shakespeare's *King John*, and have hastily assumed,

---

[168] *Technique of the Drama*, chapter IV. iii.

on the strength of them, that Shakespeare intended us to understand that ambition was the keynote of Constance's character. The question whether or not this view of Constance is in fact just, is not one which we now have to discuss. The point is, that the words cited do not in themselves warrant the interpretation which is thus rashly put upon them. For the phrase is used by Elinor in a private speech to her son; and a moment's consideration will suffice to show how greatly its significance must therefore be discounted; since Elinor, in using it, is manifestly inspired by a powerful personal animus against Constance, and by a desire to influence the king against her. The expression thus tells us how Constance appeared to Elinor, or how Elinor wished her to appear to the king; but before we conclude that it also tells us how Shakespeare would have Constance appear to us, the whole play must be passed under careful examination. In considering the language employed by any character about any other, then, we have always to note who it is that is speaking, what motive such a person may in the circumstances have for speaking as he does, how his utterances may be coloured by his own feelings. Only then shall we be able to determine how far we are justified in taking his words as a factor in the formation of our own opinion.

While, however, occasional phrases must thus be carefully scrutinised before they are accepted as aids in the analysis of the character to whom they refer, we cannot go far wrong when we find that various utterances scattered through the dialogue of a play, all converge towards the same point. In this case we have a body of cumulative evidence, each item of which gains in value by its correspondence with all the rest. A dramatist who is anxious to throw some particular figure into clear relief is likely to avail himself freely of this method of cross-lighting. Shakespeare often employs it with great effect. He employs it, for example, with Antonio in *The Merchant of Venice*. To deepen our feeling of horror at Shylock's nefarious scheme against his life, his nobility and purity of nature are repeatedly impressed upon us by the attitude of the other characters towards him. Bassanio's praise of him in III, ii, 287–291, is cunningly introduced for emphasis at a critical moment; and we feel that this is no mere heated expression of friendship and agitation, because nearly everybody else in the play catches the same tone of admiration and affection:—Salanio calls him 'the good Antonio'; Lorenzo refers to him as a 'true...gentleman'; Gratiano 'loves' him; the chief men in Venice respect him; the gaoler, as Shylock complains, grants him unusual privileges;[169] while even Shylock's own sneer at his 'low simplicity' is only another bit of testimony—and it is not the less significant because it is oblique—to the merchant's goodness of heart. In the case of Brutus in *Julius Cæsar*, again, the measure of the man is continually suggested by his associates, both friends and foes; the cynical Casca is bound to acknowledge his probity; Cassius lays stress upon his nobility and influence; Ligarius shows blind faith in him; Portia's devotion brings out the tender side of his nature; and, as a final stroke, his enemy Mark Antony, in the last important passage in the play, pronounces an eloquent eulogy upon him as 'the noblest Roman of them all.' It is unnecessary to add further examples to show the value of this indirect method of characterisation.

In considering this method we shall occasionally find that a certain character in a play seems to stand a little apart from the rest and to speak, as it were, with somewhat greater authority. Such a character is sometimes described as the 'Chorus' of the drama in which he appears, because to a limited extent he fulfils the interpretative function of the Chorus in Greek tragedy.[170] Of his role as commentator I shall speak later. Here we have only to note that where it seems safe to conclude that any character is thus used to point the dramatist's own judgment, his utterances must, of course, be accepted as having a special weight. Enobarbus, for instance, is commonly regarded as a kind of 'Chorus' in *Antony and*

---

[169]See *Introduction* to *The Merchant of Venice*, in *The Elizabethan Shakespeare*, p. xxxviii.
[170]See *post*, § vi.

Cleopatra; among those who come into personal contact with the queen, he alone remains untouched by the spell of her marvellous fascination; he sees her as others do not; and his pungent criticisms thus help very greatly to set her under the proper light.

I have said that there is one exception to be made to the general statement that dialogue is the dramatist's only substitute for the direct analysis and commentary of the novel. This exception is furnished by the device known as the Soliloquy, under which term we include not only the Soliloquy proper, but also that minor subdivision of the same form which we call the 'aside.'

The purpose of this piece of pure convention is, of course, clear. It is the dramatist's means of taking us down into the hidden recesses of a person's nature, and of revealing those springs of conduct which ordinary dialogue provides him with no adequate opportunity to disclose. It may be necessary for our complete comprehension of his action that we should know certain of his characters from the inside. He cannot himself dissect them, as the novelist does.[171] He therefore allows them to do the work of dissection on their own account. They think aloud to themselves, and we overhear what they say.

A very fair account of the rationale and functions of Soliloquy in characterisation will be found in the following remarks by Congreve. His *Double Dealer* had been criticised because, among other things, of the place given in it to Soliloquy. As this criticism did 'not relate in particular to this play, but to all or most that were ever written,' Congreve undertakes to answer it 'not only for my own sake, but to save others the trouble, to whom it may hereafter be objected,' and he proceeds:—

'I grant that for a man to talk to himself appears absurd and unnatural; and indeed it is so in most cases; but the circumstances

---

[171]The Soliloquy was much used (probably under the influence of the drama) in early prose fiction, and it occasionally appears in novels of quite recent date. In fiction, however, it is more objectionable because it is so manifestly unnecessary.

which may attend the occasion make great alteration. It oftentimes happens to a man to have designs which require him to himself [*sic*], and in their nature cannot admit of a confidant. Such, for certain, is all villainy;[172] and other less mischievous intentions may be very improper to be communicated to a second person. In such a case, therefore, the audience must observe, whether the person upon the stage takes any notice of them at all, or no. For if he supposes any one to be by when he talks to himself, it is monstrous and ridiculous to the last degree. Nay, not only in this case, but in any part of a play, if there is expressed any knowledge of an audience, it is insufferable.[173] But otherwise, when a man in Soliloquy reasons with himself, and pros and cons, and weighs all his designs, we ought not to imagine that this man either talks to us or to himself; he is only thinking, and thinking such matter as were inexcusable folly in him to speak. But because we are concealed spectators of the plot in agitation, and the poet finds it necessary to let us know the whole mystery of his contrivance, he is willing to inform us of this person's thoughts; and to that end is forced to make use of the expedient of speech, no other better way being yet invented for the communication of thought.'[174]

Apart from its interest as a playwright's statement of the case for the Soliloquy, this passage is noteworthy because it serves to remind us that the convention in question was a common feature of our early

---

[172]This particular statement, as I need scarcely say, is wholly without warrant.

[173]Congreve's point is not very clearly put, but the reference is to a device occasionally used on the stage—that of allowing a speaker to take the audience themselves into his confidence. In the lighter French drama of the last century (as in the farces of Labiche) Soliloquies were frequently addressed to the audience. Sometimes the appeal has been carried farther; as when the slave girl, Halisca, in the *Castellaria* of Plautus, begs any one in the audience who may have picked up the casket she has lost to restore it to her and so save her from a whipping; and when Euclio, in *Aulularia* of the same writer, seeks among the spectators for the robber of his gold; a trick imitated by Molière in a famous scene in *L'Avare* (IV, vii.).

[174]*Epistle Dedicatory to The Double Dealer.*

English drama. Despite such adverse opinion as is here referred to, a common feature it remained down to quite recent times, as a glance at the standard English plays of the Victorian period will at once prove. The criticism of our own day is, however, distinctly against its use, at any rate in realistic drama; it is now held to be not only a convention, but a clumsy convention, and one, strictly speaking, non-dramatic; a chief aim of the dramatist, it is asserted, should be to avoid it; whilst its appearance is deemed sufficient to stamp any new play as 'old-fashioned' in its style of workmanship. Even Mr Jones, who has valiantly undertaken its defence, admits that it is 'childish,' that it should be employed as sparingly as possible, and that 'it is never permissible to do by Soliloquy what can be adequately done by dialogue.'[175] The practical disappearance of both formal Soliloquy and incidental aside from our greater contemporary drama, notwithstanding the fact that this drama is so largely psychological in its interest, is thus a most significant index of a general change in our ideas of dramatic technique.

In our study of the older drama, however, we must accept the Soliloquy without protest as an established convention, and, setting aside all question as to its theoretical justification, must concern ourselves only with the use to which it is put. That Shakespeare systematically has recourse to it is a fact familiar to even the most casual reader of his plays. Again and again his leading persons, through their direct and confidential utterances, make us participants of their intimate thoughts and desires, exhibit the motives by which their conduct is governed, and define their true relations (which are often very different from their apparent relations) to the progress of events about them. He adopts this course in particular with his more complex characters, with characters who are engaged in internal conflict, and, generally, in all cases in which, but for the illumination thus given, we should find it difficult or impossible to explain the words and doings of the people who talk and act before us. In the

<hr>

[175] *On Playmaking, in The Renascence of The English Drama*, pp. 246–249.

Soliloquies of Shakespeare's characters we shall therefore naturally expect to find the real basis for our interpretation of them. But while every passage of self-delineation must thus be carefully examined, special importance must be attached to the first Soliloquy or aside. It has been noted that it was Shakespeare's practice to reveal very early in a play and very clearly those qualities of character in any principal personage on which the plot is to turn. It will be found that he often provides us with the necessary clue in the first words when this personage has an opportunity—thinking aloud—to utter to himself.

To complete this part of our subject it should be added that the Soliloquy is often more or less successfully disguised by being turned into a speech addressed to some listener who is brought forward for the purpose. The so-called confidant originated in the Chorus of Greek tragedy, and passed thence through Seneca into the drama of the Renaissance under the form of the intimate friend, or nurse, or duenna, or some such person to whom the speaker, without restraint, could unburden his soul. Modern criticism accepts the confidant, but only on condition that he shall cease to be a mere lay-figure, and shall himself be provided with an essential part in the action.

IV

We cannot go far in our study of any play without some knowledge of the general principles of dramatic design. To these, therefore, we will now direct our attention.

Every dramatic story arises out of some conflict—some clash of opposed individuals, or passions, or interests. In the most elementary, and still most popular type of story, such conflict takes a purely personal form; the collision is between good and evil as embodied respectively in the hero and the villain of the piece. But it may of course assume various other shapes; the struggle may, for example, be waged by the hero against fate or circumstance, as in *Œdipus the King*; or against the code or conventions of society, as in *Antigone, Le Misanthrope, An Enemy of the People*; or the collision of the hero with outer antagonistic forces may be involved with and even largely subordinated to the inward struggle which goes on in the nature of the man himself, who is, like Brutus, 'with himself at war,' as in the case of Orestes in *The Libation Bearers*, of Hamlet, of Macbeth, of Nora in *A Doll's House*. Some kind of conflict is, however, the datum and very backbone of a dramatic story.[176] With the opening of this conflict the real plot begins; with its conclusion the real plot ends; and since, between these two terms, the essential interest of the story will be composed of the development and fluctuations of the struggle, the movement of the plot will necessarily follow a fairly well-defined and uniform course. The complications which arise from the initial clash of opposed forces will, as a rule, continue to increase until a point is reached at which a decisive turn is taken in favour of one side or the other; after which, the progress of events will be inevitably, though often with many minor interruptions, towards the final triumph of good over evil or of evil over good. Through every plot we may thus trace more or less clearly what is sometimes called 'the dramatic line.' We have, to begin with, some Initial Incident or Incidents in which the conflict originates; secondly, the Rising Action, Growth, or Complication, comprising that part of the play in which the conflict continues to increase in intensity while the outcome remains uncertain; thirdly, the Climax, Crisis, or Turning Point, at which one of the contending forces obtains such controlling power that henceforth its ultimate success is assured; fourthly, the Falling Action, Resolution, or Dénouement, comprising that part of the play in which the stages in the movement of events towards this success are marked out; and fifthly, the Conclusion or Catastrophe, in which the conflict is brought to a close.[177]

---

[176]A play in which the element of conflict is slight will always be found defective as a play, however great its other merits may be. Two of Shakespeare's dramas are thus defective, because owing to the overtowering predominance of a single character, who from first to last practically controls the action, the interest of struggle is almost entirely wanting. These are *Henry V* and *The Tempest*.

[177]In the above epitome I have given the principal alternative terms which are

It is probable that this natural five-fold structure of a dramatic story may account for the common, indeed at one time universal, division of a play into five acts.[178] It must be remembered, however, that in a Shakespearean or other five-act drama, the mechanical divisions do not actually correspond with the natural divisions, since, as the most casual examination of any such play will show, the complication commonly arises in the first act and runs on into the third; the third act generally contains, along with a portion of the complication, both the crisis and the beginning of the resolution; while the resolution continues through the fourth act into the fifth. Moreover, the natural divisions, inasmuch as they are natural, are of course independent of any artificial disposition of the materials of a story into a given number of acts. In the four-act dramas of our modern stage, and in a brief one-act play, we shall still find the dramatic line.

Our analysis of dramatic structure, however, is not yet complete. Though the real plot of a play begins with the beginning of a conflict, such conflict arises out of and therefore presupposes a certain existing

---

in common use to designate the different divisions of a plot. The word Climax, as a synonym for Crisis or Turning Point, though currently accepted, is really unsatisfactory, because it means ladder, and should therefore refer to the rise of the action towards its turning point, and not to the turning-point itself. Dénouement is sometimes carelessly made to do duty for Catastrophe. Catastrophe itself is frequently restricted, particularly in ordinary speech, to the calamitous close of tragedy, but it may properly be used for the happy issue of comedy as well. I may add that Greek words are occasionally substituted for those here given; *Protasis* for Exposition (for which, see later); *Epitasis*, for Growth; *Peripeteia*, for Turning Point; *Caiabasis*, for Falling Action; but their employment in English criticism savours of pedantry, and is not to be recommended.

[178]This division reached the modern stage through the Latin tragedies of Seneca, which exercised an enormous influence over the drama of the Renaissance in England as well as in Italy and France. It was doubtless based directly upon the normal (though by no means uniform) division of a Greek tragedy into a Prologue, three Episodes, and an Exodus—five parts in all. Latin comedies appear to have been first broken up into acts, also five in number, by the editors of the sixteenth century.

condition of things and certain relations among the characters who are to come into collision. These conditions and relations have to be explained to us, since otherwise the story will be unintelligible. We have therefore to distinguish another division of a drama—the Introduction or Exposition, comprising that part of it which leads up to and prepares for the initial incident.

Since Freytag first pointed out that the plot of a play may be symbolised as a 'pyramidal structure,' it has been a common practice with writers on dramatic theory to represent the dramatic line in the form of a diagram. Different versions have been adopted; the one I should select would be this:

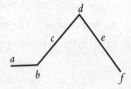

In this diagram, *a* stands for the exposition; *b,* for the initial incident; *c,* for the growth of the action to its crisis; *d,* for the crisis, or turning point; *e,* for the resolution; and *f,* for the catastrophe. This particular figure, however, will evidently serve only to represent a play in which, as, *e.g.,* in *Julius Cæsar,* the crisis comes almost exactly in the middle of the plot, which is thus divided into two practically equal parts. It would of course have to be varied to meet cases in which this extreme symmetry is not found. Thus, in *King Lear* the real crisis of the main plot is in the very first scene; in *Othello* it does not occur till the first scene of the fourth act. In order to indicate approximately the plot movement in these two instances, we should have to use for the one some such form as—

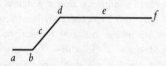

and for the other, some such form as—

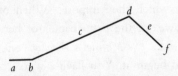

The use of this pyramidal diagram in the study of dramatic technique is now so popular that I could not possibly pass it over here without some reference. Its principal claim upon our attention undoubtedly lies in the fact that it helps to bring the great divisions of a dramatic story vividly before our minds. On the whole, however, I am inclined to deprecate the employment of such diagrams in the study of literature in general, as tending to make it too mechanical and formal. I will, therefore, without further discussion, leave this 'dramatic pyramid' with the reader for his own consideration.

Having now learned what are the great divisions of a dramatic story, we have next to examine these one by one, and to inquire under each head what constitute some of the chief demands of good dramatic workmanship.

The purpose of the introduction or exposition is to put the spectator in possession of all such information as is necessary for the proper understanding of the play he is about to witness. At the outset, he finds himself in the presence of a number of people in whose fortunes he hopes soon to be interested, but of whom and of whose circumstances he for the moment knows nothing; and as it is essential that he should learn as quickly as possible who and what they are, and what the relations in which they stand to one another before the action begins, the opening scene or scenes of any drama must be largely occupied with explanatory matter. It is a commonplace of dramatic criticism that the management of this explanatory matter is one of the severest tests of a playwright's skill; be his story ever so simple, difficulties will be involved in it; and these difficulties of course increase with the complexity of his subject and the number of his characters. Even the novelist is often greatly taxed by his preliminaries, and sometimes staggers awkwardly beneath the heavy burden which they impose. 'When one has a story to tell,' says Mrs Stowe, in the first chapter of her best, though not her best-known book, *The Minister's Wooing*, 'one is always puzzled which end of it to begin at. You have a whole corps of people to introduce that you know and your reader doesn't; and one thing so presupposes another that, whichever way you turn your patchwork, the figures still seem ill-arranged.'[179] If such be the experience of the novelist, who can always, when necessary, have recourse to direct narrative and explanation, the difficulty of exposition in the drama must be apparent.

Among the expedients which have been adopted to overcome this difficulty, the least dramatic is the set speech of some particular character, to whom, more or less appropriately, the task of elucidation is thus assigned. The crudest form of this is the detached explanatory prologue, or 'versified programme,'[180] habitually used by Euripides and Seneca. This has never had an established place on the modern stage; yet some of Shakespeare's introductory Soliloquies—notably that of Gloucester in *Richard III*—may almost be regarded as attenuated survivals of it. But the set speech, though now indeed embedded in dialogue and occasionally broken by it, may still be recognised in those lengthy passages of retrospect and description which are so clumsy a feature of the opening scenes in many Elizabethan and Stuart plays. Dryden may have been guilty of some little exaggeration when he said that such passages 'are seldom listened to by the audience':[181] but it is certain that only a very perfunctory attention is commonly accorded to them, and unless they are marked by real dramatic power, they are sure to drag. The tedious narrative of Prospero in the second scene of *The Tempest* is a case in point; another is furnished by Horatio's long

---

[179]*Cp. ante*, p. 137, note ii.
[180]L. D. Barnett, *The Greek Drama*, p. 18.
[181]*Essay of Dramatic Poesie*.

account of the political relations of Denmark and Norway, which greatly mars the exposition in *Hamlet*, otherwise an admirable piece of work. Evidently, then, the dramatist will always be well advised when he breaks up his introductory narratives as much as possible, and relieves them of their formal quality by giving them the tone of conversation. Thus we pass, though of course by insensible degrees, to exposition through dialogue, and here it is easy for the veriest tyro in criticism to distinguish between what is really excellent in dramatic workmanship and what is slovenly or poor. Every playgoer is familiar with the servants who, while busy dusting furniture or laying the breakfast table, discourse freely of their master's concerns; with the person just returned from abroad, who hungers for all the local news, and opportunely meets an old acquaintance who is able and eager to satisfy his curiosity; with the 'First Gentleman' and 'Second Gentleman' whom Shakespeare employed when he was in a hurry, and whom Tennyson artlessly borrowed from him. In all such cases the artifice is so obvious and so 'stagey' that, while we listen to the talk because we know that from it we must glean all the particulars that are necessary if the coming action is to be intelligible to us, we do so with an irritating sense that it has all been arranged for nothing but our own edification. This maladroit kind of exposition was happily satirised by Sheridan in *The Critic*. Sir Walter Raleigh is introduced in conversation with Sir Christopher Hatton, and proceeds to give his friend a great deal of manifestly gratuitous information. Dangle interrupts the rehearsal with the remark: 'Mr Puff, as he *knows* all this, why does Sir Walter go on telling him?' Puff 's reply is: 'But the audience are not supposed to know anything of the matter, are they?' 'True,' says Sneer, 'but I think you manage ill; for there is no reason why Sir Walter should be so communicative.' Whereupon Puff retorts: 'Foregad now, that is one of the most ungrateful observations I have ever heard; for the less inducement he has to tell all this, the more I think you ought to be obliged to him; for I am sure you'd know nothing of the matter without it.' The art of a dramatist is nowhere shown to greater advantage than in his power so to conduct his exposition as to relieve it of all such appearance of effort and artifice. Good exposition will therefore take the form of dialogue which seems in the circumstances to be natural and appropriate, which is put into the mouths of characters who are made at once to interest us, and which is, moreover, so bound up with the beginning of the action as to be practically undistinguishable from it. In such fine dramatic openings as, for example, those of *Othello* and *The Alchemist*, the business of the play starts almost with the rise of the curtain; our attention is immediately arrested and our curiosity aroused by scenes and talk which are full of life and character; and in following these we unconsciously learn all that is for the moment requisite about the initial situation, the events which have led up to it, and the people whose fortunes are to provide the substance of the plot. It must, of course, be understood that it is often impossible for the dramatist to attain ideal perfection in this portion of his work. His introductory matter may prove so intractable that even under the most dexterous handling some signs of effort and artifice will remain; and since it is the first condition of exposition that, at whatever cost, it shall at least furnish us with the necessary clues to the coming action, the employment of purely conventional stage devices may have to be accepted as unavoidable. Yet the ideal should none the less be kept in view as a standard for judgment. Exposition should be clear; it should be as brief as the nature of the material will permit;[182] it should be dramatic; it should if possible be vitally connected with the first movements of the plot; and it should be so disguised that, while analysis will never fail to reveal its mechanism, the impression left upon the spectator shall be one of absolute naturalness and spontaneity. In our diagrammatic representation of plot in the drama,

---

[182]In the opening scenes only those details will commonly be given which are needed for the comprehension of the first stages of the action, other particulars being left for later introduction. We shall see presently that in a certain type of drama, exposition in one sense forms the very substance of the play.

it will be seen that exposition is marked off as a separate division, preparing for, but independent of, the action proper. From what has just been said, however, it will be evident that this is only an arbitrary way of conceiving the matter, since plot will commonly be found to begin before exposition is over. Somewhere in the early part of a play, possibly in the very first scene,[183] in any case before the end of the first act, we shall come upon the genesis of the action in some incident or incidents which, as giving birth to the conflict out of which the play is to be made, may be described, in Freytag's terminology, as 'the exciting force.' It is not necessary that this exciting force should stand out prominently at the time, or that we should be made to realise at any given moment that the action of the play has begun; though it was Shakespeare's general practice to mark distinctly the starting point of his dramatic conflict. It should perhaps be noted that the use of the word 'incident' to define this starting point, while very common in technical criticism, is open to objection on the ground that the real inception of the action is often to be found (as, *e.g.*, in *Richard III, Julius Cæsar*, and *Othello*) not in some particular occurrence, but in the purpose formed suddenly or gradually in the mind of one of the characters, whose subsequent efforts to carry out his designs will thus become the motive-principle of the plot.

'Incident' must therefore be interpreted broadly enough to cover mental processes as well as external events. In many cases we may distinguish two springs of action: as in *Romeo and Juliet*, where the conflict arises both from Romeo's determination to attend the Capulets' ball and from the resolve of Juliet's parents to marry her to the County Paris; and again in *Macbeth*, in which the motive of the drama is to be sought in the mind of Lady Macbeth no less than in that of her husband. Of course in a play composed of

---

[183]In *King Lear*, the business of the main plot really begins with the entrance of the king at line 33 of scene I, and with scarcely anything that we can call exposition.

two or more stories, each story will have its initial incident; and these initial incidents may or may not occur close together. In *The Merchant of Venice*, for example, the principal plots arise almost at the same time in the first act, while the minor imbroglio of the rings, which is to help to fill out the drama after its main interest has been completed, does not originate until the second scene of the third act. But such late introduction of new motives is not as a rule to be regarded as satisfactory.

With the initial incident we enter upon the real business of the play, the first portion of which comprises the complication, or rise of the action to its crisis. Here the instinct of every thoughtful reader will lead him, as a matter of course, to test the dramatist's workmanship by the elementary canons of clearness and logical consistency. Given the characters and their circumstances, then every event should appear to grow naturally out of what preceded it; while in the movement of the action as a whole, that which is essential should never be obscured by unimportant details, however interesting in themselves these may be. The play of motives should be distinctly shown, and should be obviously sufficient to account for what is said and done; and the proper relations, between character and action should be carefully maintained. Moreover, every scene should occupy a definite place in the evolution of the dramatic organism, either by marking a fresh stage in the development of the plot, or by adding to our knowledge of the characters, or in both of these ways. The rigorous application of this principle of dramatic economy to Shakespeare's plays will occasionally yield rather unexpected results. No one of course will require to be told that the scene in *The Merry Wives of Windsor* (IV. i.), in which Sir Hugh Evans cross-examines little William on the rudiments of Latin accidence, has really nothing whatever to do with the play: but it may perhaps give us a shock of surprise to discover that Hamlet's famous interview with the Grave-diggers (V, i, 1–240), while we should never now dream of sacrificing it to the demands of structural unity, has in fact no artistic justification.[184]

The playwright's treatment of his material is also a subject for careful consideration from the point of view of technique and dramatic effect. Swept along by the strong current of interest, the ordinary reader or spectator accepts a great scene—like the Trial Scene in *The Merchant of Venice*, or the Play Scene in *Hamlet*, or the scene in Ibsen's *Doll's House*, in which Nora dances a tarentella while Krogstad's incriminating letter lies close at hand in her husband's letterbox—as if it were a spontaneous growth, and all its details matters of mere happy chance. It is only when we place such a scene under searching analysis, and note every turn of the action and every phrase in the dialogue, that we begin to appreciate the consummate skill by the exercise of which the dramatist has made the very most of his opportunity. When once our attention has been directed to this side of his art, however, every particular relating to plan and structure will be found to have its significance. We shall instantly perceive—to take a single example—how greatly the effect of the central incident in *Much Ado about Nothing*, Act II, scene iii, is enhanced by Benedick's long Soliloquy which leads up to it. It must at the same time be remembered that as the aim of the dramatist must always be to achieve the appearance of naturalness and spontaneity even in his most cunningly devised effects, whatever obtrudes itself upon us as contrivance must be accounted an artistic mistake. Such obtrusion is one secret of the 'staginess' which offends us in many otherwise well-made dramas. Every student of Shakespeare knows that one difference between his experimental and his mature plays lies in the fact that in the former the devices employed to obtain effect are so obvious that they cannot escape even the least attentive reader, while in the latter they are so deftly managed that it needs critical examination to bring them to light.

---

[184]Critics of Shakespeare are indeed coming more and more to realize that *Hamlet* is throughout overloaded with matter which has little or no vital connection with the plot.

214 ♦ WILLIAM HENRY HUDSON

The foregoing considerations, though it has been convenient to deal with them in connection with the first stage of the dramatic action, will manifestly be found to apply to the management of the plot as a whole. One special feature of the complication must, however, be referred to. It may be laid down as a general rule that during the rising action those elements in the conflict will already be indicated which at the crisis are to come into prominence, for good or evil, as the chief agents in bringing about the catastrophe. If the conflict is mainly between persons, then the first part of the play should familiarise us with the characters who are to dominate the second part; if it lies mainly in the mind of the hero, then by the careful presentation of those qualities which are presently to gain control, the conduct should be foreshadowed which will lead him to happiness or disaster. In this way the foundations of the subsequent action will be firmly laid at the outset. To spring a fresh force upon us without warning or preparation—to introduce an entirely new character—to bring forward interests and motives of which hitherto no hint has been given—must, save in very exceptional circumstances, be pronounced extremely poor art.

Since the play of antagonistic forces cannot go on indefinitely, every dramatic story sooner or later reaches a stage in its development at which the balance begins to incline decisively to one or the other side. This we have called the turning point or crisis of the action.[185]

The great law of the crisis is that it shall be the natural and logical outcome of all that has gone before; which means that we shall be able to explain it completely by reference to the characters and to the condition of things existing at the time. An event which is to determine the whole course of the action to its catastrophe should thus arise out of the action itself; it should not, like the death of

---

[185]As the movement of any plot resolves itself under analysis into a series of crises, the real turning point should, strictly speaking, be described as the chief crisis. But no serious objection can be urged against the common use of the unqualified word.

the French king in *Love's Labour's Lost*, be a mere accident thrown into the plot from the outside. Provided that this law be obeyed, the treatment of the crisis may be allowed to vary according to circumstances. It may often be made emphatic by being condensed into a single incident or group of incidents, which, moreover, may perhaps be attended by accessories which will serve to accentuate the importance of what is occurring; as in the Capitol scene in *Julius Cæsar* and the Banquet scene in *Macbeth*. Such concentration and emphasis, however, are not by any means necessary. On the other hand, it is certainly requisite that the critical change in the movement of events shall be made so clear that no doubt shall be left in our minds as to its significance. This, as we have already noted, is the weakness of *Antony and Cleopatra*—it has no well-defined crisis; for Antony's relapse, instead of being exhibited in one powerful scene as a final choice of passion before honour, is spread over a number of minor scenes, which do not arrest our attention, and the essential point of which is lost amid masses of unessential detail.

Though the aim of many modern playwrights seems to be to postpone the crisis as long as possible, the practice of our older stage was to place it somewhere about the middle of the action, perhaps, generally, a little beyond this. In Shakespeare's plays it is commonly to be sought towards the close of the third act, or quite early in the fourth. Thus, as has already been pointed out, in *Macbeth* it occurs in III, i, where with the escape of Fleance and the appearance of Banquo's ghost begins the tragic reversal of Macbeth's fortunes; in *Othello*, in IV, i, where the Moor is finally convinced of his wife's infidelity; in *Julius Cæsar*, in III, i, the scene of Cæsar's death; whilst *King Lear*, a singular and perplexing exception to the 'Shakespearean rule, the crisis of the main-plot, 'instead of standing in the centre of the composition...stands almost at the beginning.'[186]

---

[186]Thomas R. Price, *King Lear: A Study of Shakespeare's Dramatic Method*, in *Publications of the Modern Language Association of America*, 1894. Mr Price says: 'There is a protasis of only 34 lines, followed at once by the opening of the

The crisis past, we enter upon that portion of the play in which the dramatic conflict is to be brought to its conclusion. The conduct of this dénouement will depend upon the answer to the question whether the play is to have a happy or an unhappy ending. In comedy it will take the form of the gradual withdrawal of the obstacles, the clearing away of the difficulties and misunderstandings, by which the wishes of the hero and heroine have been thwarted and their good fortune jeopardised. In tragedy, on the contrary, its essence will consist in the removal of those resisting elements which have held the power of evil in check, and in the consequent setting free of that power to work out its own will. In any case, what remains after the crisis is the development of the new movement which has arisen out of it; and to the extent to which we now foresee, more or less distinctly, the outcome of events, our interest will be different in kind from that which had been excited during the earlier stages of the action. Hitherto, we have watched the plot with growing uncertainty and suspense; now, uncertainty and suspense being largely set at rest, our interest will be due in part to that sympathy with the characters which makes us desirous of following their story to its very close, in part to the dramatist's skill in the treatment of the incidents by which the anticipated results are to be accomplished.

The special difficulty of the dénouement is now apparent. The problem of the dramatist will always be, how to keep the interest alive after the spectators have become aware that the resolution has begun, and that the current of events has definitely set in towards a certain

---

action in I, i, 35–81. This opening of action, contained in 47 lines, is in reality the only epitasis that the drama contains. Then comes, in 58 lines, the climax itself. Lear, misled by the false ardour of Goneril and Regan, and by the apparent coldness of Cordelia, gave his kingdom to them, and reserved for her only his curse. At this point, the 138th line of the first scene, the climax of the action is fully reached, and the fate of Lear determined. By this arrangement, unprecedented, as I believe, in dramatic art, all the remainder of the tragedy… is thrown together into one huge catabasis.'

catastrophe. We can now understand why Fielding anathematised 'the man who invented fifth acts,' and why, as we have already noted, the tendency with many modern playwrights is to extend the rising action and reduce the resolution to their utmost possible limits. Mere power in the handling of the necessary material is now the chief point to consider; as in the case of Shakespeare's great tragedies, in which, despite our clear premonition of the upshot of things, the interest continues to increase in intensity to the very last. An expedient frequently adopted to sustain interest in the second part of a play is worthy of particular attention. It is that of delaying the catastrophe by the interposition of events which interrupt the progress of the falling action and thus serve temporarily to revive uncertainty and suspense. In comedy this is often done by the employment of various unexpected obstacles which check the happy course of things; in tragedy, by suggestions that a way of escape for the hero and heroine may yet open up, and the fate that awaits them be averted. In *Much Ado about Nothing*, for example, the plot against Hero is discovered in time for its complete frustration, but a fresh difficulty arises through the failure of the watchmen to give Leonato information of it before he leaves for the wedding ceremony. In *Antigone* we are led for a moment to hope that Creon's order to release the maiden from her cave-prison may not be too late. Edmund's revocation of his command that Lear and Cordelia shall be put to death has something of the same effect. A great effect in the falling action of *Romeo and Juliet* is attained when it seems at least possible that success may yet crown the Friar's plans. This sudden flash of light amid the fast gathering gloom is not only poignantly dramatic in itself; it also intensifies the darkness which follows.

We now come to the ultimate stage of the plot, in which the dramatic conflict is brought to an issue on which the imagination is willing to rest with a sense of finality and completeness. In modern plays, as in modern novels, we have often indeed 'a conclusion in which nothing is concluded'—in which we are left, as Tennyson once complained, poised on the crest of a wave which does not break.

Critical advocates of extreme realism defend this inconclusiveness on the ground that the drama and fiction should be true to life, and in life there is no such thing as an 'end,' since every situation contains within itself the germ of fresh activities. In one sense, this view is of course correct; as a resting-place for the imagination nothing can be more purely conventional, for instance, than the marriage upon which the curtain falls in the vast majority of comedies. Yet against this doctrinaire contention it may surely be urged that while experience is undoubtedly continuous, any series of incidents selected out of it for dramatic treatment may be traced from a real beginning to a fairly definite, if only temporary, close; that imagination does in fact conceive any such series as a detached and self-existent whole; and that while in real life, as we are all well aware, no record is ever completed, and the last term of one series is only the starting point of the next; art, on the other hand, may justly claim as part of its privilege of selection and arrangement the right to adopt the convention of the 'end.' These matters belong, however, to theory only. It is certain that in practice all of us instinctively demand a catastrophe in which all the lines of the story are gathered together and no loose threads are left.

It is usual to distinguish between the two chief kinds of drama—comedy and tragedy—by reference to the nature of the catastrophe: the one having a happy, the other an unhappy, ending. There are many plays, however, in which, as in the tragicomedy of our older stage and in our modern melodramas, the interest of the plot is largely tragic, though at the last Fate smiles on most of the good characters. Moreover, whether the catastrophe be in the main unhappy or happy, it may be qualified in various ways. In tragedy the darkness may be somewhat broken by a suggestion that virtue has not suffered nor good been overcome in vain; while into the general rejoicing of a comedy-close an element of pathos may be introduced by the undeserved misfortune or unrequited affection of some one among the persons of the drama in whom our sympathetic interest has been specially aroused. Thus, for example, in *Romeo and Juliet* our sorrow is to some extent mitigated when we realise that the family hatred which has been the ruin of love is at length conquered by the love which it has destroyed; while in Beaumont and Fletcher's *Philaster* a tender touch is given to the final scene by the faithful and charming Euphrasia's hopeless passion for the hero.[187] It will also be understood that, though a happy close necessitates the discomfiture of evil, such discomfiture may be managed in accordance with one or the other of two opposed principles. Evil may be foiled and delivered over to the fate which it deserves, as in *The Merchant of Venice* and *Much Ado*; or it may be turned to good and caught up in the general harmony of forgiveness and reconciliation, as in *As You Like It* and *The Tempest*.

What has been said about the crisis must now be repeated with reference to the catastrophe—whatever form it takes, it must obey the great law of causality, and thus satisfy us as the natural and logical outcome of the forces which have been at work during the entire action. This law was explicitly stated by Aristotle when he wrote: 'It is therefore evident that the unravelling of the plot, no less than its complication, must arise out of the plot itself; it must not be brought about by the deus ex machina. Within the action there must be nothing irrational.'[188] Any ending which does not grow inevitably out of the characters and the action, but which is of the nature of an accident introduced from the outside, is therefore to be pronounced defective. To the large class of such merely arbitrary solutions belongs the device mentioned by Aristotle and so frequently employed by Euripides—that of the 'god out of the machine,' who, at the required moment, was brought upon the scene to secure that conclusion which, though really alien from the dramatist's treatment of his story, was none the less prescribed by tradition. Parallels to this may occasionally be found in modern drama when some powerful

---

[187]Compare the use which Dickens makes of Smike in *Nicholas Nickleby*, and, even more particularly, of Tom Pinch, in *Martin Chuzzlewit*.
[188]*Poetics*, XV.

external agency is invoked to cut the knot which the playwright is unable or too impatient to untie; as in the interposition of the king to accomplish the overthrow of the hypocrite in Molière's *Le Tartuffe*. In modern plays the fortuitous element assumes a number of forms; as when the villain is removed by a timely accident, or a lost will turns up, or an uncle, long reported dead, proves to be very much alive. But perhaps the commonest kind of arbitrary conclusion is that which depends upon a sudden and incredible change of heart in one of the persons of the drama.

Here we have to re-emphasise another great law, to which allusion was made in our chapter on prose fiction— the law of the conservation of character.[189] Conspicuous illustrations of the transgression of this law will be found in *The Two Gentlemen of Verona and As You Like It*.

It should, however, be added that in plays in which the handling of life is relatively light and superficial, it would be impertinent to insist too rigorously upon the application of the foregoing principles. The dramatist may be justified, therefore, when working in the mood of comedy, in devising a conclusion by contrivances which, in the mood of tragedy, he would never dream of employing. Considerable latitude may thus be granted to the writer of comedy even in the treatment of the logic of motive and passion. This qualification has also ethical bearings which it is important to keep well in mind, since the closing scenes in comedy are by no means bound to possess that moral weight and significance which of necessity belongs to the catastrophe in any serious drama. Thus, while the character of Claudio in *Much Ado* must, undoubtedly, always remain an ugly blot upon an otherwise delightful play, his marriage at the end to the girl he has so foully wronged must not be criticised in that strenuous spirit in which it is often discussed. After all, notwithstanding the pathetic interest of its central theme, *Much Ado* is only light comedy, and for the purposes of such a piece it is enough that each Jack shall have

---

[189]See *ante*, p. 153, note i.

his Jill, and that the curtain shall fall with a promise of wedding
bells. To enforce moral standards and to indulge in the refinements
of over-curious scholastic interpretation in such a case as this is,
therefore, more than a trifle absurd. We are, in fact, satisfied, and
we have a perfect right to be satisfied, in a play of this description,
with a certain laxity of moral treatment which we should at once
resent in a drama which purported to grapple seriously with life's
deeper realities. We can now understand why, as Canon Beeching
has well pointed out, roguery is dealt with by Shakespeare in one
way when it is found in the world of pure comedy, and in another
and quite different way when it is entangled with the moral issues of
actual life. 'In *The Merry Wives of Windsor*, Falstaff, notwithstanding
his enormities—and Shakespeare needs all the excuse of a Royal
Command for the way he has degraded him—meets no further
punishment than the jeers of his would-be victims; it is sufficient
in comedy that faults should be judged by laughter. Nobody wants
Sir Toby put on the black list as a tippler, or Autolycus sent to gaol
for filching linen from the hedges. But when the world of comedy
touches the real world, as in *Henry IV* and *Henry V*, social offences
have to meet social punishment, and so we have not only Falstaff
exiled from court and dying of a broken heart, but poor Nym and
Bardolph hanged for stealing in the wars.'[190]

In concluding this brief survey of the natural divisions of plot
in the drama, I would ask the reader to remember several things.
In the first place, so formal an analysis must necessarily give to the
principles of dramatic structure an appearance of simplicity which
is in fact rather delusive. In our study of any play, therefore, we
must never expect to find that the various points of the dramatic
line will be as distinctly marked and as easily detected as our abstract
statement might lead us to suppose. Secondly, there are types of
play which do not exactly correspond with the plan outlined. In
many comedies of intrigue, for example, as in Massinger's *A New*

---

[190] *William Shakespeare*, p. 101.

Way to Pay Old Debts, and works of the same general class, the main interest of the plot is provided by the efforts by which the intriguer gradually overcomes all difficulties and achieves complete success, and in such cases the diagrammatic representation would have to take the form, not of a pyramid, but of an irregularly ascending line. Moreover, there are modern dramatists, like Henry Becque and Gerhart Hauptmann, who, in their anxiety to escape convention and to exemplify the principles of naturalism, deliberately disregard the formulas of what the French critics used to call the 'well-made' play.

Finally, it is often quite possible to interpret the dramatic movement of any play in various different ways according to the particular point of view which we chose to adopt in regard to it. Thus, in *Macbeth*, it is usual to place the crisis, as we have said, in III, i, the scene which marks the turn in Macbeth's outward fortunes. But if we look rather at the spiritual significance of the tragedy than at its plot, we may with perfect justice contend that the real crisis is reached at the moment when Macbeth, yielding to the evil in his own nature and to the solicitations of the witches, definitely commits himself to a career of crime, and that the subsequent deterioration of his character from this point onward, and not his external ruin, constitutes the true falling action. Similarly with *King Lear*. Here we have accepted Mr Price's view that the crisis arises with the king's division of his kingdom. But it is much more usual to put it, says Freytag, in the hovel scene in the fourth act. These illustrations will suffice to show that our interpretation of a play is not to be governed by hard and fast mechanical rules.

V

A few outstanding features of structural design have still to be considered, which are too important to be omitted even from a mere introductory study of dramatic art.

Among these, the first place must be given to the principles of Parallelism and Contrast.

Parallelism is a familiar element in the composition of plot, especially in the form of the reduplication of motives. An excellent effect is often obtained when the central idea of one part of the action reappears in another part of it, and each is thus made to illustrate and reinforce the other. Shakespeare was much addicted to this practice of repetition. Sometimes he adopts it for the mere purpose of further complicating the dramatic interest of his story. Thus, e.g., in *The Comedy of Errors*, he adds to the confusion which he had found in the *Menaechmi* of Plautus by providing the two twin brothers with two slaves who are also twins and also indistinguishable in appearance; while in his version of the imbroglio of the rings in *The Merchant of Venice* he gives us two rings instead of the one which had figured in the original story in *Il Pecorone*.

Sometimes, however, the repetition is not used merely to complicate the action and so increase its theatrical effectiveness, but rather to draw its diverse materials together into an organic whole. In *Much Ado*, for example, Shakespeare set out to dramatise a borrowed story in which a pair of lovers were driven apart by an evil trick; with this story he finds it necessary to combine an under-plot; and he invents one in which there are also two lovers (at all events, potential lovers) who are brought together by a merry trick. The idea of trickery, in the one case for evil, in the other for good, is thus used to fuse two stories which otherwise stand in the sharpest contrast.

But the most extraordinary example of parallelism in the Shakespearean drama is that which is presented by *King Lear*, the two plots of which correspond in almost every detail. In this play, the dramatist worked upon two narratives derived from widely different sources. 'In the one story, there was the father deceived in the character of his daughters, and finding love only in that one whose love he had denied and spurned. In the other story, there was the father deceived in the character of his sons, and finding allegiance and affection only in him that he had sought to destroy as assassin and parricide. Thus, in the two stories, along with their antithetical difference, there was an almost artificial symmetry of plan and movement. And so, in the mind of the poet, at some happy moment of stimulated creative power, the two stories, coming from regions and times so different, and so completely independent, flashed together, as capable of so supplementing each other, as to merge in one great movement of tragical emotion.'[191]

In such cases of parallelism, in which we have, as it were, a series of variations upon a single theme, the repetition of motive provides the real bond of connection between the different parts of a play, and thus secures a kind of moral unity. This is exemplified again in *A Midsummer Might's Dream*. In this comedy, as the commentators have pointed out, a common motive seems to be furnished by the idea of love as a lawless power, by which friendship is broken, and girls are inspired to rebellion against their parents, and lovers are led into strange inconstancy, and even the Queen of the Fairies is made the victim of a monstrous infatuation. Many other illustrations of such unification through repetition will be found in the Shakespearean drama.

Occasionally parallelism is employed for the purposes of burlesque; in other words, the repetition of motive is introduced in the way of ridicule. Such burlesque parallelism was a singular feature of the Spanish drama of the seventeenth century, in which the *gracioso*, or valet—the recognized 'funny man' of the stage—was often specially entrusted with the task of parodying the high-flown sentiments, the flamboyant language, and the romantic actions, of his master. A ludicrous example may be cited from one of the best known of the Spanish plays—*El Mágico Prodigioso* (*The Wonder-working Magician*) of Calderon. The main plot of this curious drama shows how Cipriano, to obtain possession of Justina, sells himself to the Devil, to whom he gives a contract signed in the blood which he draws from his own arm. In all this he is aped by his servant Clarin, who, with much absurd mock-heroic talk, also sells himself to the

---

[191]Thomas R. Price, *loc. cit.*

Devil for the sake of the 'cruel Libia,' and that he too may sign the contract in his own blood, strikes his nose and makes it bleed. It would probably be difficult to discover any instances of so crude a sort of parody as this in our English drama, unless it be in the so-called 'comic' scenes in Marlowe's Doctor Faustus. But in subtler, forms, burlesque parallelism has from time to time been employed by our playwrights with telling results. It is occasionally employed by Shakespeare; as, for example, in the Silvius-Phœbe and Corin-Audrey episodes in *As You Like It*, and even more distinctly in Bottom's interlude in *A Midsummer Night's Dream*, which, travestying as it does the central motive of the main action, completes the series of variations contained in it upon the underlying theme—the lawless power of love.

Far more important, however, than parallelism as an element in dramatic design, is the principle of contrast. As this principle inheres indeed in the very nature of conflict—as it must be involved in any clash of opposed persons, or passions, or interests—it belongs of necessity to the very substance of every dramatic story. But contrast in the drama takes so many different forms, and is employed in such a large variety of ways, that a comprehensive discussion of it would require a separate treatise. Here we must confine ourselves to a few of its simpler and more common uses.

Of its primary manifestation as one of the constituents of every plot, little needs to be said; it is enough merely to recognise in passing that some antithesis will always be found between the good and evil, or the 'sympathetic' and 'unsympathetic' sides of the action; and, specifically, among the characters and groups of characters by whom these different sides are respectively represented. But one particular aspect of this elementary distinction perhaps calls for notice, and this is the contrast between the growth of the action and its final stages of resolution and catastrophe. Whether a play begins happily and ends in disaster, or begins with a struggle and ends in success, the difference in tone and spirit between the opening and closing parts is likely to be more or less clearly marked. This is perhaps especially true of tragedy, in which the gloom which gathers about us as the plot proceeds is intensified by the sunshine which we have only just left behind. So important indeed is this change as a factor in the heightening of tragic effect that a dramatist will often, in one way or another, throw stress upon it. Even Æschylus, who was hardly a playwright in the modern sense of the term, was alive to the value of this form of contrast, and carefully prepared for the fall of Agamemnon by a preliminary picture of his greatness and glory in the hour of his happy return from Troy. So, too, the pitiful fate of Sophocles' Œdipus is rendered more pitiful by the skill with which in the opening scenes we are impressed by the fine qualities of his character, the esteem in which he is held by his people, his kingly state and self-confidence. In our first acquaintance with Macbeth enough is told us of the nobler possibilities of his nature to enhance the significance of the ultimate triumph of evil and the spiritual ruin which this entails. The gay and sportive preliminaries in *Romeo and Juliet*, and the scenes of lyric passion which immediately follow, add immensely to the pathos of the heart-rending close, for the memory of them lingers with us as we gaze into the tomb where the young lovers lie clasped in death, and instinctively we look upon this picture and on that; while Othello's absolute confidence in Desdemona, and the utter happiness which each has found in each, constitutes an admirable prelude to the awful crash which is soon to come. Ibsen frequently utilises, and with wonderful effect, this principle of contrast, for he opens several of his plays (e.g., *An Enemy of the People* and *Rosmersholm*) at a moment of calm and peace just before the bursting of a great storm.

Contrast as an element of plot design is, however, by no means, confined to this difference between the rising and falling actions. It is often most clearly presented in the difference in character (other, I mean, than that between good and evil) between the different materials which enter into the composition of a play. We are all familiar with this kind of contrast in our romantic drama in the humorous relief, which indeed sometimes assumes the proportions of a regular comic under-plot, which is frequently introduced amid the serious or tragic interests of the main action. In the balancing of plots in a compound play, contrast frequently combines with parallelism, as in several of the examples of parallelism given above. In *Much Ado*, for instance, while the Hero-Claudio and Beatrice-Benedick actions correspond in motive, there is, as we have pointed out, the greatest difference between them in tone. In the same comedy, the successful use of contrasted parallelism is delightfully illustrated by the way in which the Beatrice-Benedick action and the Dogberry episodes are set off against each other, since the fun depends upon two opposite kinds of effect—in the one case, upon brilliant, daring, intellectual wit; in the other, upon blundering stupidity, muddle-headedness, and ignorant verbosity. Contrast, moreover, often appears in the evolution of the plot, and in the arrangement or articulation of the successive scenes. In the romantic drama, with its blend of the serious and the comic, it is often emphasised by rapid and sudden transitions from the one to the other.

Enough has now been said to indicate the many-sided interest of contrast in the structure of a dramatic plot. It must, however, be remembered that, like all other artistic principles, this too is liable to abuse; and that, just because its place and value are so obvious, it is in fact very frequently overdone or injudiciously employed. To lay down any abstract rule for guidance in such a matter is, indeed, impossible, for each case will have to be judged on its own merits. Keeping to general terms we can only say that when, under any of its aspects, contrast impresses us as forced or mechanical, when it suggests 'theatrical' over emphasis and a striving after sensational effect, or when it is of such a nature that the harmony of the plot design is destroyed, then, certainly, it must be condemned. The contrasts of the Elizabethan drama, while they strongly appealed to the 'groundlings' of the time, often seem to us crude and violent, and we frequently have the same feeling in regard to those of modern melodrama, which are devised to delight the gallery rather than to meet the demands of critical taste.

Contrast in plot, of course, implies contrast in characterisation, and this introduces us to another and extremely important phase of our subject. Merely noting that it is under this head that we have to include that inner struggle which often occurs between opposed passions and interests in a single complex and paradoxical nature, we have here chiefly to remark that the principle of contrast commonly underlies the scheme of characters in any well-organised play. When we first read or witness a certain drama, we are perhaps aware only of the fact that its story is carried on by a number of people who are interesting in themselves. But when we look a little more closely into the matter, we discover that the particular qualities of each individual are accentuated, and his motives and feelings thrown into sharper relief, through his relations with other individuals of unlike qualities, motives, and feelings, who thus act continually as foils to him. The character-scheme of any play, therefore, deserves careful study, not as a collection of individuals only, but as a scheme; while in following the working out of a plot we should always take special note of the way in which the principal figures are brought out by contrast with those among whom they move. With dramatists of all times and schools it has been a favourite practice to present the leading persons of a drama as companion studies. A very early instance of this is to be found in the two sisters in the Antigone of Sophocles. This method was much used by Shakespeare, who indeed hardly ever brings two characters into intimate connection without making each a foil to each. Such balanced pairs as Romeo and Juliet, Beatrice and Benedick, Prince Hal and Hotspur, Brutus and Cassius, Macbeth and his wife, Othello and Iago, Timon and Alcibiades, will at once occur to every reader as a few among the many cases in point. But this bilateral symmetry is only a first step in the arrangement of a character scheme, in which careful analysis will seldom fail to reveal a number of well-considered contrasts and resemblances. Here, again, the warning against abuse must be repeated. The balancing of characters, like the balancing of motives and incidents, to be artistically satisfactory, must never be so obvious or so mechanical as to appear unnatural. Thus it is because it is at once too obvious and too mechanical that we take exception to the contrast between Hermia and Helena in *A Midsummer Night's Dream*. The elaborate and artificial symmetry which governs the disposition of the characters in Shakespeare's early comedies is, moreover, clearly a mistake. One service to which the principle of contrast is often put must also be mentioned. It is often expressly used to illustrate and enforce the thesis or moral purpose of a play; the different aspects of the subject treated being thus presented from various different points of view. The balancing of the two sisters in Antigone, just referred to, has evidently something of this moral significance. The contrast between Alceste and Philinte in Molière's *Le Misanthrope*, and that between Léonor and Isabelle in the same writer's *L'Ecole des Maris*, are manifestly inspired by a direct ethical aim. Again, in Lessing's magnificent didactic drama (which, as a didactic drama, may safely be described as the greatest thing of its kind in all literature)—*Nathan der Weise*—the whole cast of characters, from the Patriarch of Jerusalem at one end of the scale to the Jew himself at the other, is most skilfully arranged in a delicately graded series of antitheses to bring out the author's teaching in regard to tolerance and the essential spirit of true religion. Shakespeare repeatedly uses contrast for moral as well as dramatic effect. The appearance of Orlando with old Adam at the close of the melancholy Jaques' cynical speech on the seven ages of man (*As You Like It*, Act II, scene vii) is evidently not an accident. If, to take another illustration, we are right in concluding that the underlying motive of *A Midsummer Night's Dream* is that of the lawless power of love, then we can see how this motive, which runs through the main story and the fairy scenes, and is burlesqued in the handicraftsmen's play, receives additional emphasis from the contrast provided by the framework of the action, with its dignified figures of Duke Theseus and his Amazonian bride, and its fine picture of their mature and noble love. When contrast is thus employed for ethical purposes, exaggeration is not only artistically unsatisfactory, but also morally disastrous. By over-charging his antithesis between the English and the French in *Henry V*, Shakespeare has really defeated the very object which he had in view—the glorification of the triumph of English arms at Agincourt.

One other kind of contrast remains to be mentioned— that to which the name Dramatic Irony is generally given. This we may define, in the broadest sense, as the contrast between two aspects of the same thing, whether such contrast is perceived at the time or becomes apparent later. In critical discussion, the term is most commonly used to express the effect produced when there is a marked and significant difference in the meaning of what is being done or said on the stage for the characters themselves on the one hand, and for the spectators on the other; and this difference necessarily arises whenever the characters act or speak in ignorance of important facts of which meanwhile the spectators are in possession. As the difference may turn in the main, either on action or on utterance, we may make a formal distinction between Irony of Situation or Incident and Verbal Irony, though in practice of course these are often found in combination. A wonderful example of the irony of situation is furnished by the scene at the close of the *Electra* of Sophocles, when Ægisthus stands beside the covered corpse which we know to be the corpse of Clytæmnestra, though he believes it to be that of Orestes, which Orestes himself, unrecognised by him, bids him withdraw the veil and disclose the face. As an illustration of the same kind of irony in the Shakespearean drama we may take the scene in *Henry V* (Act II, scene ii) in which the conspiracy against the king is brought to light. While the conspirators are firmly convinced that their plot is a secret, we on the contrary know already that the king himself is fully aware of their designs; and it is our knowledge of this fact which gives point and interest to every detail of the interview in which the guilty men, led on by Henry, step by step, to their complete self-condemnation, move blindly forward to the fate which we have foreseen from the outset.

Again, if we know that a certain character is actually trembling on the brink of terrible disaster; and if, at that critical moment, he none the less appears to himself to occupy a position of greatness and security, and proceeds accordingly to give expression to feelings of pride, or safety, or self- confidence (*e.g., Richard II*, Act III, scene ii; *Julius Cæsar*, Act III, scene i), a similar effect of irony is obtained. In these cases, in which the tragic suggestion inheres in the person's own unconsciousness of what we know to be his real situation, dialogue evidently plays an important part in accentuating the difference between his point of view and ours. But verbal irony, or equivoke, has an independent value when the language used by any character, though in its primary sense perfectly natural in the circumstances, possesses at the same time for the audience a secondary meaning and application which sometimes the speaker himself does not understand; and of which, at any rate, those whom he addresses are entirely ignorant. It thus arises when, in the words of Prof. Moulton previously quoted, 'ignorance of the sequel on the part of the personages represented' clashes 'with knowledge of it on the part of the audience.' This species of irony is specially characteristic of the Greek drama. As the plot of a Greek tragedy was not invented by the poet, but was drawn by him from some great common storehouse of tradition, local or pan-hellenic, its main outlines at least, and its general course and issue, must have been familiar to all who witnessed its representation,[192] and thus continual opportunity was afforded for effective contrast between

---

[192]It has indeed been questioned whether Greek audiences were always so familiar as is generally supposed with the legendary stories which formed the basis of the great Attic tragedies; but in respect of the vast majority of the audience, at all events, the statement in the text seems to me incontrovertible. It should, however, be remembered that considerable freedom was granted to the poet in the treatment of his material. It was open to him to select any one of the often numerous variants of a given story; and that, within limits, he was permitted to arrange and modify its details in ways which best accorded with his design, is proved not only by the practice of the dramatists themselves, but also by the precept of Aristotle that 'the poet must himself invent, or at least exercise much skill in using what has been handed down.'

the real significance of events as understood by the spectators, and their apparent significance as regarded by the persons taking part in them.[193] Of this opportunity Sophocles in particular availed himself to the full, as notably in *Œdipus the King*—one of the world's master- pieces of sustained irony—the dialogue of which is packed with skilfully devised ambiguous detail. When the dramatist himself deliberately informs us in advance of facts which are concealed from some, at least, of the leading actors in his story, such irony again becomes prominent. Thus the scenes in Shakespeare's comedies, in which (as in *Twelfth Night* and *As You Like It*) the heroine appears disguised as a young man, are often charged with equivoke, both the remarks of the masquerading girl and those with whom she is in conversation assuming a humorous complexion for us who know, as the characters on the stage do not, her sex and position.

Ironic effect, it should also be noted, does not necessarily depend upon elaboration. Sometimes a mere casual phrase or even a single word may become pregnant with double meaning. Thus, for instance, the simple epithet 'honest,' which Othello applies to the fiend in human shape who is already busy plotting his ruin, has a tragic suggestiveness for us, because we so well understand its hideous inapplicability.

In the forms thus far considered, irony is produced by the opposition between the point of view of the characters on the stage

---

[193] The following passage admirably defines the vital connection between the irony of Greek tragedy, and that spirit of fatalism by which it was often pervaded: 'The purpose of Greek tragedy, in its highest efforts, was inconsistent with the excitement caused by curiosity. The favourite and most impressive theme of the old tragic poets was the irony of destiny and the futility of human wisdom. To exhibit man as the unconscious victim of fate, boldly advancing on his own destruction, and more and more confident as he approaches his doom, was the object of most of their greatest dramas. But to unfold the full pathos of the situation, it was necessary to lift the veil from the eyes of the spectators, and to let them discern clearly the dark figure of destiny in the background, towards which the doomed man was being drawn with slow but certain steps' (Haigh's *Tragic Drama of the Greeks*, p. 346).

and that of the spectators, as this opposition is perceived by the spectators at the time of its occurrence. But, as we have already implied, the revelation of the contrast may be delayed; we may for the moment only suspect a double meaning; or perhaps the secondary significance of what we see and hear may be brought home to us by the subsequent course of the action. This subtle kind of verbal irony may be amply illustrated from the tragedy of *Macbeth*. The protagonist's first words—'So fair and foul a day I have not seen'—contain an obvious and direct reference to the state of the weather; but they so clearly echo the witches' 'fair is foul and foul is fair,' that they at once suggest to us a bond of sympathy between the speaker and those agents of evil who are to lure him to his doom, while later on we recall them as an index of the moral struggle between the foul and fair in Macbeth's own nature. When his Soliloquy—

> I have no spur
> To prick the sides of my intent, but only
> Vaulting ambition, which o'erleaps itself
> And falls on the other—

is interrupted by the entrance of his wife; her timely appearance just at that juncture emphasises the part which, as his spur, she is to play in the coming crime. In the same way, when Duncan in describing the traitor Cawdor, says—

> There's no art
> To find the mind's construction in the face;
> He was a gentleman on whom I built
> An absolute trust,

and at that moment Macbeth enters; we instinctively feel that the words are so placed that they apply to Macbeth as much as to Cawdor. There are other phrases in the play which distinctly point forward; and which, though not perhaps specially noted at the time, are remembered afterwards, when circumstances bring out their tragic significance. In these cases we have equivoke, but an equivoke the disclosure of which is postponed. Thus, Lady Macbeth's words in the murder scene—

> These deeds must not be thought
> After these ways; so, it will make us mad;

and—

> Go get some water
> And wash this filthy witness from your hand;

and—

> A little water clears us of this deed:
> How easy is it, then;

are full of terrible prognostications of the sleep-walking scene, and of the remorse which finds utterance in the conscience-stricken woman's despairing cry—

> Out, damned spot! out, I say!...What, will these hands ne'er
> be clean?—No more o' that, my lord, no more o' that: you
> will mar all with this starting. ... Here's the smell of the blood
> still: all the perfumes of Arabia will not sweeten this little hand.
> Oh, oh, oh!

Another aspect of this Prophetic Irony, as it may be called, is also exemplified in the same tragedy—the contrast between the course of events as anticipated, and what actually comes to pass. The predictions of the witches are indeed fulfilled to the very letter, but in a way quite different from that upon which Macbeth had been led to count; the irony being pointed by Macbeth's own words—

> And be these juggling fiends no more believed, That palter
> with us in a double sense;
> That keep the word of promise to our ear, And break it to
> our hope.[194]

---

[194]Prophetic anticipation is, on the other hand, often used, and with great effect,

A problem of some importance is suggested by the foregoing considerations—that of the artistic value of concealment and surprise as elements in sustaining interest. In the conduct of his plot, the dramatist may often have a choice between two methods. He may elect to hold back from his audience essential particulars relating to characters, motives, or incidents, which, while they will of course enter into his action, will do so as hidden agencies, to be inferred only, if at all, by their results: and he may calculate upon the production of a telling effect when the real facts are disclosed, and the causes of what has been happening made evident. Or he may, on the contrary, prefer to take his audience into his confidence, exhibit to them at the outset the nature of the chief forces which are involved in his plot, and then rely upon the interest with which they will follow the action and reaction of these forces in working out a certain issue.[195]

The question of the relative advantages of these two methods is, again, one which cannot be answered in general terms; it is only when all the circumstances of any given case are considered that it is possible for us to decide what the dramatist has lost, and what he

---

in the reverse way—that is, the prediction, utterly incredible as it may have seemed, is in the end fulfilled. The accomplishment of the oracle in Œdipus the King may be cited as a case in point. Sometimes we have veiled hints only, or vague foreshadowings of coming things. Compare Dickens's use of this device in Dombey and Son: 'Let him remember it in that room, years to come' (chapters xviii and lix), and the unconscious prophecies of which skilful use is made in Tennyson's Enoch Arden.

[195]In his preface to The Woman in White, Wilkie Collins speaks of 'the interest of curiosity and the excitement of surprise' as 'two main elements in the attraction of all stories.' In his preface to the later No Name, he writes: 'It will be seen that the narrative related in these pages has been constructed on a plan which differs from the plan followed in my last novel, and in some other of my works published at an earlier date. The only secret contained in this book is revealed midway in the first volume. From that point, all the main events of the story are purposely fore-shadowed before they take place—my present design being to rouse the reader's interest in following the train of circumstances by which these foreseen events are brought about.'

236 ❖ WILLIAM HENRY HUDSON

has gained, by adopting the one or the other. It should, however, be borne in mind that the effort to create excitement and maintain attention by means of mystery, secrecy, and the unexpected, though perfectly legitimate, is so common a characteristic of the merely sensational kind of novel and play that it comes under suspicion of belonging to the more rudimentary stages of art; and that the interest of the reader or spectator is generally quite as keen as well as more intelligent when, instead of having the motive forces of the plot withheld from him, and perhaps being misled as to their real meaning and direction, he is enabled by preliminary knowledge to follow, as it were, from the inside the play of passion and the evolution of events. Every student of his technique is aware that Shakespeare, though (as in the supposed death and final restoration of Hermione in *The Winter's Tale*) he occasionally has recourse to concealment and surprise, rarely depends much upon them;[196] even his great villains and intriguers betray themselves to us at the beginning, and it is with a full insight into their characters and purposes that we watch them working out their designs.

A suggestive fact comes to light when we examine his way of using the device of sex-ambiguity, already referred to. This he employs a number of times—in *The Two Gentlemen of Verona, The Merchant of Venice, As You Like It, Twelfth Night*, and *Cymbeline*; but in every instance we are taken into the secret, and thus no effect of surprise is sought through revelation of the truth that a character we had been led to take for a youth is really a girl. Now it happens that in the two best-known pieces in our romantic drama, after these, in which sex-ambiguity is introduced—Beaumont and

---

[196]If we compare the case of Hermione with that of Hero in *Much Ado*, we see that difference in method produces marked difference in effect. 'We know that Hero is not really dead…and thus, though the element of tragedy is used to heighten the effect of the comedy, the comedy-tone is not destroyed. In *The Winter's Tale* the truth is kept back. For all we know to the contrary, the grave of Mamilius has also closed over his wronged and patient mother. The result is that for a time the drama moves in the darkness of unrelieved tragedy' (*Introduction* to *The Winter's Tale*, in *Elizabethan Shakespeare*).

Fletcher's *Philaster* and Ben Jonson's *Epicœne or The Silent Women*—the opposite plan is adopted. In the former it is not till the end that we learn that the supposed page Bellario is the maiden Euphrasia; in the latter, we are kept in the dark to the very last of the fact that Epicœne is a youth in disguise. So far as this particular matter is concerned, we need, I think, have no hesitation in saying that Shakespeare's is the better way.

VI

Mention has already been made of the familiar fact that under the influence, in part of those different technical conditions of which we have spoken, but in part also of different artistic aims and ideals, the drama has assumed very different forms in different periods and countries. It is customary for the historian and critic to distinguish sharply between two antithetical types of drama—the classic and the romantic. This broad division is, however, insufficient. The classic type must be subdivided into the ancient, or true classic, and the neoclassic, or pseudo-classic, while a separate place must be made for the drama of our own time.

Greek tragedy and comedy, with which any systematic study of the drama must begin, alike originated in rustic festivals which in early Attica were periodically held in honour of the nature-god, Dionysus—the one from the serious, the other from the frolicsome side of such celebrations. Comedy in Athens passed through three stages: Old Comedy, or the comedy of political and personal satire; Middle Comedy, which marked the transition from this to the comedy of social life and manners; and New Comedy, in which this change was completed, and a kind of comedy evolved in many ways resembling our own. With the exception of eleven plays by one writer—the greatest master of Old Comedy, Aristophanes—all the productions of the comic writers of Athens have been lost; and though we have examples in two plays of Aristophanes—the *Ecclesiazusœ* (or *Women in Parliament*) and *Plutus*—of Middle Comedy, New Comedy we know only through the imitations of Latin playwrights. The Greek tragedy, fortunately, a larger and more representative body of work has come down to us, for we possess thirty-two plays of the three great tragic poets—Æschylus, Sophocles and Euripides.[197]

Some of the salient features of Greek tragedy have already been described.[198] A few words must, however, be added in regard to one point of primary importance—the Chorus. I have said, that to the modern reader no one characteristic of the Attic drama is more curious than this. When we first take up the study of Greek tragedy, indeed, it is with some astonishment that we find in every play such a chorus,[199] or body of persons, forming, as it were, a multiple individuality, moving, singing, and dancing together, and continually interrupting the dialogue and the progress of the action with their odes or interludes. This feature seems to us so strange and even so undramatic, it appears to be such a clog upon the movement of the play, that we are naturally impelled to ask when and why it was incorporated into Greek tragedy. The answer is, that it was never 'incorporated' into Greek tragedy—that it was not, in other words, an imported element or artistic invention. It was simply a necessary result of the conditions out of which Greek tragedy arose. The genesis of tragedy is to be found in the dithyramb, or choral hymn, which was chanted by the village worshippers around the altar of Dionysus; the individual actor and dialogue were later developments out of this. Thus the chorus belonged to Greek tragedy because it was the germ from which it sprang. It is true that from the very beginning

---

[197]Of these, seven are by Æschylus, seven by Sophocles, and eighteen by Euripides (or seventeen, if we exclude the *Rhæsus*, the authenticity of which is disputed). Our feeling of regret over the disappearance of the great mass of Greek tragic literature is deepened by our knowledge of the fact, noted by Prof. Jebb, that 'many of the best plays we have were vanquished [in the dramatic contests] by rivals the very names of which have been lost.'

[198]See *ante*, pp. 177, 178.

[199] E.g., the Chorus of Ocean Nymphs in Æschylus' *Prometheus Bound*, of Theban Elders in Sophocles' *Antigone*, of the companions of Odysseus and Neoptolemus in the same poet's *Philoctetes*, of captive Greek women in Euripides' *Iphigenia in Tauris*, and so on.

of real tragedy with Æschylus, the tendency of artistic evolution was consistently towards the subordination of the choral element to that of the individual actors, who were correspondingly brought to the front. This change in the centre of interest is strikingly shown by a comparison of the works of the first with those of the last of our three tragic poets. In Æschylus, roughly speaking, about one half of a play is occupied by choral odes; in Euripides, only from a quarter to a ninth part. Nor is this all. Along with this decrease in the prominence of the chorus went its gradual detachment from the action. In Æschylus, the connection between the chorus and the movement of the plot is very close and organic; it remains very close and organic in Sophocles; but in Euripides, the choral odes are generally little more than musical interludes, with only the slightest relevancy to the dramatic context.[200] Thus, as Mr Haigh has said, the history of the chorus in Greek tragedy is a history of gradual decay. Nonetheless, the chorus remained a formal feature of it till its end, and from it was taken over in turn by the Latin dramatists.

Yet, while from our point of view, this gradual subordination of the chorus seems a perfectly natural effort to eliminate a vestigial element which we cannot but regard as clumsy, the student must still remember that the exquisite tact of the Greeks was rarely more triumphantly shown than in the skill with which they turned this very element to the higher purposes of dramatic art. The lyrical portions

---

[200] Compare the remark of Aristotle: 'The chorus should be considered as one of the persons of the drama; it should be a part of the whole, and a sharer in the action; not as in Euripides, but as in Sophocles' (*Poetics*, c. xviii). Mr Haigh points out that, with increasing complexity of plot in the hands of Euripides, the chorus 'began to be felt as a positive encumbrance.... It was often impossible that the mystery on which the plot depended should be concealed from the knowledge of the chorus; and the various intrigues, stratagems, and misconceptions had to be carried out to their conclusion in the presence of fifteen witnesses who were acquainted with the facts, and could easily have prevented the catastrophe' (*Tragic Drama of the Greeks*, pp. 251, 252). This shows how great was the influence of the chorus in maintaining that simplicity of structure which was one characteristic of Greek tragedy as a whole.

of their tragedies were employed as channels for the expression of the emotions aroused by the action, and of such general moral reflections as would be likely to suggest themselves to a sympathetic spectator. It is in the plays of Sophocles—'the mellow glory of the Attic stage'—that this use of the chorus reaches perfection, and it is in these plays, therefore, that we can best study its functions as they are admirably explained in the following passage by Matthew Arnold:—

'The Chorus was, at each stage of the action, to collect and weigh the impressions which the action would at that stage naturally make on a pious thoughtful mind; and was at last, at the end of the tragedy, when the issue of the action appeared, to strike a final balance. If the feeling with which the actual spectator regarded the course of the tragedy could be deepened by reminding him of what was past, or by indicating to him what was to come, it was the province of the ideal spectator so to deepen it. To combine, to harmonise, to deepen for the spectator the feelings excited in him by the sight of what was passing on the stage—this is the one grand effect produced by the Chorus in Greek tragedy.'[201]

Following the movement of dramatic history, we pass from Greece to Rome, which at the time of its literary awakening under Hellenic impulses, began to fashion both comedies and tragedies on the lines which the Greeks had laid down. The great mass of Latin dramatic literature has perished. But in comedy we possess twenty plays of Plautus and six of Terence, while tragedy is represented by the ten dramas which have come down to us under the name of

---

[201]Preface to his *Merope*, pp. xlii, xliii. It should, however, be added that this theory of the chorus as an 'ideal spectator' requires a certain amount of qualification. The chorus in Sophocles is sometimes (as notably in the *Antigone*) the exponent, not so much of the impartial criticism of 'a thoughtful pious mind,' as of the opinions and feelings of the ordinary bystander, which are thus focussed and defined. See Lewis Campbell's *Sophocles*, p. 128.

Seneca.[202] Both the comedies and the tragedies have great historical importance; the comedies, in part because it is through them, as I have said, that we derive our knowledge of the Greek New Comedy, which they copied or adapted, and in part because of the influence which they exerted on modern drama; the tragedies, on account of the fact that it was these imitative productions, and not the works of the original Greek masters, which became the great incentives and models of the neo-classic dramatists of the sixteenth and seventeenth centuries.

Religion in origin, like that of the Greeks, the drama of modern Europe arose out of the rich symbolic liturgy of the mediæval church through the gradual dramatisation of important events commemorated in the chief services of the calendar. This liturgical drama in course of time evolved into a fully developed and widely popular religious play—the Mystery, or Miracle Play; the subject matter of which was derived mainly from the Bible, but in part also from tradition and the lives of the saints. Mr Symonds described the religious drama in England as the 'Dame School' of our dramatic genius. The phrase is not inapt. Very crude of course it was; but dramatic elements were not altogether wanting—elements of tragedy, as in the Crucifixion and Last Judgment; elements of pathos, as in the story of Abraham and Isaac; elements, even, of humour, as in the scenes between Cain and his boy, between Noah and his wife, and in the Shepherd plays of the Chester and Wakefield cycles.

A little later, another kind of didactic drama arose and flourished in the Morality, or allegorical play, in which the scholastic philosophy of the Middle Ages, and presently, the new learning and the theological ideas of a period of fierce controversy, found a vehicle of popular expression. Closer attention than is usually accorded to them should, I am convinced, be given by the student to these experimental forms, which counted more than is commonly supposed

---

[202]Whether this was the famous philosopher of this name is doubtful. It is not even certain that all the ten plays are by the same hand.

in the after-development of the drama in England.[203] At the same time, they were of course mere preliminaries.

The real beginnings of modern comedy and tragedy are closely connected with that particular phase of the Renaissance which we call the classic revival. Fired by enthusiasm for everything belonging to the newly discovered world of pagan antiquity, men turned back to that world for inspiration and example in the drama as in all other forms of literary art. In comedy, the native and popular elements were too strong in England to permit mere academic imitation; but the study of Plautus and Terence helped greatly to teach the rising school of dramatists the principles of structure and form. Evidence of this will be found in our first English comedy—Nicholas Udall's *Ralph Roister Doister* (about 1550)—in which characters and humours of ordinary contemporary life form the substance of a play which yet admittedly owes much to the influence of the Latin masters.[204]

Tragedy, on the other hand, was at the outset purely academic. It began with a deliberate attempt on the part of the humanists to produce the entire system of the tragic drama of classical antiquity. Here the historical importance of Seneca becomes manifest; since it was upon his plays, and not directly upon those of the Greek poets,

---

[203]Some representative specimens of the pre-Elizabethan drama will be found in *English Miracle Plays, Moralities, and Interludes*, edited, with an admirable introduction, by Alfred W. Pollard. That Shakespeare was familiar with the old religious plays, which were still popular when he was a boy, is evinced by such phrases as Hamlet's 'out-doing Termagant' and 'out-Heroding Herod,' Bottom's 'Cain-coloured beard,' and Celia's reference to Orlando's hair as 'something browner than Judas's' (*As You Like It*, Act III, scene iv). His recollection of the Vice—the comic personage of the moralities, and the forerunner of the Shakespearean clown—is shown in Feste's (the Clown's) song in *Twelfth Night*, Act IV, scene ii.

[204]Reference is made in the prologue to Plautus and Terence. The plot of the comedy is largely modelled on the *Milas Gloriosus*, or *Braggadocio*, of the former writer. Matthew Merrygreek, the mischief-maker of the piece, combines many of the characteristics of the Vice of the moralities and of the parasite of Latin comedy.

that, as I have said, the new serious drama was closely fashioned.[205] Now Senecan tragedy, while in matter it tended to a free use of the violent, the horrible, and the supernatural, presented the structural principles of the classis drama in an exaggerated form, action being entirely eliminated and long stately speeches, full of rhetoric and declamation, taking the place of dramatic dialogue. This was the pattern adopted for tragedy by the Italian and French dramatists of the sixteenth century; this was the pattern adopted also by the writers of our first regular English tragedy, Gorboduc, which was performed at the Inner Temple three years before Shakespeare was born. But here we reach the great point of rupture between the destinies of Italian and French tragedy on the one hand, and those of English tragedy on the other. In Italy and France, while the Senecan type was modified in various particulars, it was still taken as a foundation, and neoclassicism was firmly established; its ideals, backed by the enormous power of the Academy, ruling supreme in the latter country till the time of Dumas and Victor Hugo. In England, after a few abortive experiments, and despite the efforts and influence of humanists like Sidney, Seneca and neoclassicism were abandoned, and an independent type of drama—the romantic— triumphed instead.[206]

---

[205]Various translations of the separate plays appeared in England between 1559 and 1566, while a complete edition was published in 1581. Direct influence was at the same time powerfully reinforced by the vogue of the contemporary Italian drama in cultivated circles in England. Sidney in his *Apologie for Pocsie* uses Seneca as the standard of excellence in tragedy.

[206]This triumph was accomplished by Shakespeare's immediate predecessors, the 'scholar-playwrights,' and especially by Marlowe. Neo- classicism was represented among Shakespeare's contemporaries by Samuel Daniel and Ben Jonson, and its influence was later shown from time to time in such plays as (to mention only two which have a certain place in English literary history) Addison's *Cato* (praised by Voltaire as the first 'regular tragedy' of the English stage) and Johnson's *Irene*. Milton's *Samson Agonistes*, Shelley's *Prometheus Unbound*, Swinburne's *Atalanta in Calydon* and *Erechtheus*, and countless other examples of the 'closet drama,' do not of course belong to the history of the true stage- play. As a matter of

In one other country beside England, the national genius was too strong to accept the classic yoke, and a rich romantic drama arose in defiance of all the attempts of scholars and critics to regulate it by line and rule. This was Spain. The Spanish romantic drama of the seventeenth century—best known to us in the work of its two chief masters, Lope de Vega and Calderon—deserves the attention of the student for various reasons, and especially for its immense fertility and ingenuity in the matter of plot, and for the influence which it exerted on this side upon the Italian, French, and English dramas.[207] Yet the permanent literary value of this drama is, after all, very slight. Its very strength implies its radical weakness. It is essentially theatrical. Its interest depends almost entirely upon incident and intrigue—upon skilfully devised complications, telling situations, unexpected turns in the action, and surprises. In characterisation it is thin and poor; in psychology, crude and unconvincing. Tested by the criteria upon which we have repeatedly insisted, it must therefore be assigned a very subordinate rank among the great dramas of the world.[208]

---

detail, it must not be forgotten that neo-classicism gave blank verse to English poetry, and that this magnificent instrument of the higher drama was first used in English tragedy in *Gorboduc.*

[207]'It is not enough to say that the two Corneilles, Scarron, Molière, Quinault and Lesage translated and adapted the works and scenes of Spanish writers. It is not enough to say that our own writers pillaged them without scruple. To express the obligation truly, we must say that the European Drama is saturated with Spanish influence. Take from the French, and from Beaumont and Fletcher, and their contemporaries, from Dryden, Congreve, Wycherley, Shadwell, from Goldoni, Nota, Giraud, and others, all that they have borrowed directly or indirectly from Spain, and you beggar them in respect of situation' (Lewes's The *Spanish Drama*—a little volume which, though published as long ago as 1846, still remains for the English reader the best and most readable brief sketch of the subject)

[208]It is significant that, with reference to the question already raised as to the artistic value of concealment and surprise, Lope de Vega should explicitly recommend the employment of these as important dramatic devices. 'Do not,' he writes, 'allow the solution to be revealed till the last scene, because when

We will now make a brief comparison of the two great types of modern drama, the neoclassic and the romantic. While the latter is represented for us chiefly by the works of our Elizabethan and Stuart playwrights, with Shakespeare at their head, we must add to these two later products of the romantic spirit—the German drama of Lessing, Goethe, and Schiller, and the French drama of Dumas, Victor Hugo, and their contemporaries. The finest examples of the former type are furnished by the writings of the great French masters of the seventeenth and eighteenth centuries—Corneille, Racine, and Voltaire, though a place beside them may also be made for the tragedies of the Italian poet, Alfieri.

Two points at which the neoclassic tragedy departed from its Senecan model must first be mentioned. In the substance of its plots it gave great prominence, and generally indeed the principal place, to the interest of romantic love, a motive which had been conspicuous by its absence from the serious drama of pagan antiquity.[209] In structure it introduced a great change by dropping the chorus, though a survival of this is, as I have said, to be detected in that familiar figure in many neo-classic plays, the confidant, who has little or nothing to do with the action except as the alter ego of the hero or heroine, to listen to their confessions and reply with sympathy and advice.[210] These

---

the audience know the result, they turn their faces to the door' (*Arte Nuevo de hacer Comedias*, or *Art of Writing comedies*). This may be said to formulate the regular principle of the Spanish drama.

[209] The intrusion of this motive is destructive of the antique tone and spirit of many modern dramas dealing with classic themes. A most remarkable illustration is to be found in Goethe's *Iphigenie auf Tauris*, which was based on the *Iphigenia in Tauris* of Euripides. Here the barbarian king Thoas is turned into the romantic lover of Iphigenia. This is one of several new features introduced by Goethe, which are 'fatal to the essentially Greek character of the story.' The drama, though formerly much praised, is 'in fact an unfortunate mixture of Greek scenery and modern sentiment, and as such is rather a literary curiosity than a great play' (Mahaffy's *Euripides*, p. 57).

[210] Rare examples of the chorus will be encountered in regular French tragedy; as, *e.g.*, in Racine's *Athalie*—perhaps the most famous example.

points of difference between the neoclassic and the antique drama
are, however, of less importance for us than their broad resemblances.
As between the neoclassic and the romantic drama, on the contrary,
the interest of the comparison lies in their fundamental contrasts.
In the first place, neoclassic tragedy (notwithstanding its innovation
in the matter of romantic love) followed the classic model in the
general nature of its subjects, and in the way in which these subjects
were treated. Classic drama had dealt with the great legends of a
remote mythical age; its chief characters had been majestic heroes
who belonged to a world of tradition altogether apart from and far
above that of ordinary humanity and experience; and in its handling
of such themes and persons it had sought a purely poetic rendering
in harmony with them. Thus the dialogue was kept throughout at
the ideal tragic pitch of stateliness and nobility, and homely phrases
and realistic details were avoided as discordant notes. It is true that
this general statement is subject to some exceptions. There is even
in Æschylus an occasional approach to the tone of common life;
and in Euripides, the most modern of all the Greek poets in this
as in other respects, the homely phrase and the realistic detail are
often conspicuous.[211] Yet ideal treatment and undisturbed unity of
tone were the theoretical principles of Greek tragic art; while as
for the Senecan drama, it was uniformly elevated, stately, dignified,
and rhetorical. In neoclassic drama the same principles are studiously
maintained. The subjects are drawn from a great variety of sources,
but they are always aristocratic in quality. 'Kings, emperors, generals
of armies, principal chiefs of republics—it does not matter,' says
Voltaire, 'but tragedy always requires characters raised above the
common plane.'[212] This formulates the conception of tragedy which
was repeated again and again by Italian, French, and even English
critics of the period of the Renaissance, and during the seventeenth

---

[211]This was one of the points at which he was attacked by Aristophanes in
The Frogs.
[212]*Remarques sur le Second Discours de Corneille*.

and eighteenth centuries. Tragedy, in brief, had to confine itself to 'great' themes and 'illustrious' persons. In treatment, meanwhile, the neoclassics were more consistently classic than the Greeks themselves. No attempt to mirror ordinary life, or to reproduce common human nature, was ever permitted. All had to be on the grand, the heroic, scale. Unity of tone had to be preserved, as Voltaire distinctly says, by the banishment from the dialogue of everything savouring of colloquialism or suggestive of familiarity.

The contrast at this point between the neoclassic drama and the romantic is manifest. Romantic tragedy is indeed commonly aristocratic in character; as its very name implies, it too is generally concerned with matters remote from the interests of ordinary life, and with the struggles and misfortunes of more or less 'illustrious' people.[213] But in its treatment of its subjects, it repudiates entirely the neoclassic method. No attempt is made to preserve the ideal atmosphere or unity of tone. The tragic hero is often set in a world of commonplace men and things. The dialogue, though predominantly poetical, is often racy with colloquialism, and has many touches of familiarity. Realistic details—like Lear's famous 'Pray you, undo this button'—abound, which to neoclassic playwrights and critics would appear shockingly trivial and vulgar.[214] Thus, while the neoclassic

---

[213]Ordinary life furnished the material for a few Elizabethan tragedies, such as *Arden of Feversham, The London Prodigal,* and *The Yorkshire Tragedy,* the two last-named of which have occasionally, though without the slightest warrant, been ascribed to Shakspeare. These may be regarded as the forerunners of the 'Domestic Drama,' or *Tragédie Bourgeoise,* of the eighteenth century; a form initiated in England by George Lillo (*George Barnwell, Fatal Curiosity*), in France by Diderot (*Le Fits Naturel, Le Père de Famille*), and in Germany by Lessing (*Miss Sara Sampson, Emilia Galotti*). This Domestic Drama was one product of that democratic movement in literature which about the same time gave birth to the modern novel.

[214]It is amusing to remember that when the great battle between neoclassicism and romanticism began in France with Victor Hugo's Hernani, one of the principal grounds of conflict was the King's question 'Est-il minuit?'—and the reply—'Minuit bientôt.' To supporters of the old tradition, question and answer

tragedy is entirely ideal, the romantic tragedy combines the idealistic with the realistic.

The fundamental principle of unity of tone in the neoclassic drama leads, in the second place, to an important result in the complete separation in it, as in the ancient drama, of tragedy and comedy. Though comedy was, rather grudgingly, allowed to rise into seriousness, and even on occasion to become 'heroic,' as in Corneille's *Don Sanche d'Aragon* and Molière's *Don Garcie de Navarre*, no touch of humour was ever allowed to mar the sustained solemnity of a tragic scene. It is unnecessary to dwell at length upon the difference here presented between the two types of drama. The free use of tragedy and comedy in the same play is one of the most striking and familiar features in the work of Shakespeare and his contemporaries. Romantic drama revels in variety of effect, while tragi-comedy, or the 'mixed play'—according to Addison, 'one of the most monstrous inventions that ever entered into a poet's thought'[215]—has always been a particularly popular form on the romantic stage.

A third fundamental contrast between the two types of dramatic construction is to be found in their opposed attitudes towards the unities of Time, Place and Action. Neoclassicism adhered to these in tragedy, at least in theory. Romantic drama ignored the first two, and, while it adopted the third, put an interpretation upon it quite different from that maintained by disciples of the other school. As in the one case, the distinction is between acceptance and rejection, while in the other it is between diverse views of the same principle,

---

seemed positively indecorous—'a king asks what's o'clock, like a private citizen, and they tell him, as if he were a ploughboy, midnight' (Gautier's *Histoire du Romantisme*).

[215] *Spectator*, No. 40. Thus also Lisideius, the advocate of the French against the English drama in Dryden's *Essay of Dramatic Poesis*, says— 'There is no theatre in the world has anything so absurd as English tragi-comedy.' Compare Milton's scornful reference to the practice of 'interweaving comic stuff with tragic sadness and gravity' (*Of that Sort of Dramatic Poem called Tragedy*, prefixed to *Samson Agonistes*).

it will be convenient to deal with the two questions separately.

A definition of the neoclassic position is first required, and this is provided in the following couplet of the 'law-giver of Parnassus,' Boileau—

> Qu'en un lieu, qu'en un jour, un seul fait accompli
> Tienne jusqu'à la fin le théâtre rempli.[216]

'Let the stage be occupied to the end by a single completed action, which takes place in one spot, in one day.' Disregarding for the moment the question of singleness of action, we have here a clear and compact statement of the rule concerning time and place—the former must be confined to one day; the latter must never be changed. Into the history of the rise and formulation of these supposed laws of the drama, we cannot now enter, nor is it necessary, or indeed possible, to undertake any discussion of their artistic justification from the point of view of their supporters. It is important, however, to understand that they are, strictly speaking, neoclassic, and not classic; that is, that their real source and authority must be sought in the theories of modern critics, and not in the principles or practice of the Greek stage.[217] They took definite shape

---

[216]*L'Art Poétique*, Chant III.

[217]Aristotle's only reference to the unity of time is contained in the following passage: 'Epic poetry agrees so far with Tragic, as it is an imitation of serious actions; but in this it differs, that it makes use of a single metre, and is confined to narration. It also differs in length; for Tragedy endeavours, as far as possible, to confine its action within the limits of a single revolution of the sun, or nearly so; but the time of epic action is indefinite' (*Poetics*, c. V). Of unity of place, Aristotle makes no mention at all; an omission which led the French critic, D'Aubignac, to the amazing conclusion that he left it out because it was so well known at the time that it did not need his attention (*Practique du Théâtre*). At any rate, Aristotle's object was rather to formulate the practice of the great tragic poets than to lay down abstract rules for tragedy. As to that practice, we have already seen that a general adherence to the unities in Greek tragedy was largely the result of the presence of the Chorus (see *ante*, p. 177). Lessing, in his famous and brilliant attack upon French neo-classicism in his *Hamburgische Dramaturgie*, was probably the first critic to point out this fact. Infractions of

among the Italian humanists of the Renaissance, and passed thence into France, where they maintained a tyrannous sway till the time of the Romantic revolt. Yet their rule was not accepted without occasional protest, and even some attempts at compromise. Corneille, the first great master of French tragedy, but a Romantic by temper, clearly chafed under them. Against the rigorous reading of the unity of time, for example, he pleaded hard for 'quelque élargissement'— for thirty hours, where necessary, instead of the prescribed twenty-four. Moreover, many instances may be found in French tragedy in which, as Lessing said, even if the letter of the law is obeyed, its spirit is broken. Thus, in Corneille's *Le Cid* we have a quarrel, a couple of scenes in which the heroine has audience of the king, two agitating interviews between the heroine and her lover, two duels, and a great battle with the Moors. No wonder that Corneille himself admitted, as well he might, that for a single day's work the action was 'un peu précipitée'; or that the Academy, in passing judgment upon the play, should have declared that 'the poet in trying to observe the rules of art had chosen rather to sin against those of nature.' In more perfect examples of neoclassic drama we do not indeed encounter absurdities so glaring as these. Yet the impression often left is one of artificially contrived simplicity, and quite unnatural condensation.

That to these pedantic rules concerning time and place, romantic dramatists have always been supremely indifferent is a fact well known to every student of the English stage. Shakespeare cared nothing for them, moving his scene freely from town to town, and from country to country, as often as occasion required, 'jumping o'er times,' and 'turning the accomplishment of many years into an hour glass.'[218] In two cases, it is, true—in the *Comedy of Errors* and *The Tempest*—he confines his plot to one day and practically to

---

the unity of place have been noted. In several of the surviving Attic tragedies, as in the *Agamemnon* of Æschylus, the *Trachinian Maidens* of Sophocles, and the *Suppliants* of Euripides, the unity of time is ignored.

[218] *Prologue to Henry V.*

one spot; the latter play being specially remarkable because in it the ideal of time-unity is reached in the almost complete correspondence of stage-time with actual time. But these exceptions only prove that, like other romantic playwrights, Shakespeare felt himself at perfect liberty to accept as well as to reject academic convention, and to work in whatever form seemed most suitable to the matter in hand. To us who are bred in the Shakespearean tradition, this romantic freedom in the handling of time and place appears, of course, so natural and proper that it is difficult for us to give quite serious attention to the arguments of the neoclassic school. Yet we must never forget that romantic liberty may easily degenerate into licence, and that if liberty is to be defended, licence is still to be condemned. Shakespeare himself, with his too rapid and frequent changes of scene within an act, and his total carelessness as to the number of days, or months, or even years required by his action, provides many illustrations of the abuse of freedom. *The Winter's Tale* may be regarded as a classic example of romantic excess; and such excess is again almost equally conspicuous in the straggling and incoherent chronicle plays.

In turning from the unities of time and place to that of action or plot, we pass from mere arbitrary restraints imposed from the outside to what has been universally acknowledged as an inherent and essential principle of dramatic construction. The difference between the neoclassic and the romantic types of drama is, therefore, at this point, as I have said, one of interpretation only, and this difference can be very easily explained. Aristotle's canon—πράράά μάά άρ άάι ὁρά—an action one and complete (the 'seul fait accompli' of Boileau) was taken by the neoclassicists in its most rigorous acceptation to mean a single plot, undiversified by episodes and uncomplicated by subordinate incidents and characters. So severely was this rule enforced that adverse criticism was passed upon *Le Cid*, because Infanta's love for the hero, though not developed into a subplot, diverted attention from the real theme of the play by introducing an independent centre of interest. In the romantic reading of the law, on the other hand, the largest freedom has always been conceded in the use of episodes and subordinate incidents and characters. Unity, according to this view, is not incompatible with complexity; it does not mean singleness of action; it means merely organic connection and coherence. Minor actions or subplots are therefore admitted on the one condition, which is, however, indispensable, that all the elements of the plot are woven together and made interdependent as co-operating factors in the evolution of the plot as a whole. Here again it is evident that the difference between the two conceptions ultimately rests upon the difference between the assumptions from which the two schools of dramatic theory respectively start; that of the neoclassic being that the drama should aim at ideal simplicity; that of the romantic, that it should reflect the variety and complexity of actual life. Our romantic drama, then, is habitually a drama of compound plot. It is important, however, to hold fast to the principle that the variety and complexity which delight us in it must not be obtained at the sacrifice of that organic wholeness upon which I have just laid stress.[219] The law of dramatic structure requires that there shall be a well-marked central interest to which all other interests are duly subordinated; that as Dryden happily put it, the pawns on the chessboard shall be made of service to the 'greater persons';[220] that all the lines of action shall run together in a single catastrophe. Such unity through complexity is achieved, for example, in *Much Ado about Nothing*, in which the two principal plots, though for a time practically independent, coalesce in the church scene (IV, i), and in which the episodical watchmen have a vital part in working out the main intrigue. But Shakespeare is often guilty of violating the law of structural unity. His plots frequently hang very loosely together. *The Winter's Tale* is really two plays rolled into one. In *Julius Cæsar*, as in the English chronicle dramas, he fails to reduce the scattered events of history to artistic consistency. Many of his plays suffer from

---

[219]See *ante*, p. 142.
[220]*Essay of Dramatic Poesie.*

a plethora of matter. Marvellous as is the skill with which the two distinct stories in *King Lear* have been dovetailed into one another, there are critics who hold, with Freytag, that the tragedy loses more than it gains by its immense and almost bewildering intricacy. In numerous instances, secondary incidents and characters are allowed to expand until they occupy a wholly disproportionate place in the general scheme, the balance and symmetry of which are thus destroyed. While, for instance, we should be un-willing to suppress a single detail in the great Falstaffian comedy in *Henry IV*, criticism has still to insist that from the strictly artistic point of view there is in fact altogether too much of it; that it forms by itself a separate play within the play; that it is so brilliant and so fascinating that it not only splits the interest but even throws the main plot into the background; and that, finally, it is to be condemned also because it has no real connection with the business of the historic action.[221]

One other important point of contrast between our two types of drama has still to be noted. They differ fundamentally in their methods of conducting their plots.

Faithfully following in this respect the practice of the Greeks[222] and the precept of Horace[223]—'Let not Medea slay her children before the public'—the neoclassic drama depends almost entirely upon narrative; nearly everything that happens, especially everything of a violent character, happens, in technical phraseology, 'off,' and is simply reported to the audience. In the groundwork of its story, a neoclassic tragedy often contains as much sensational material as the most romantic of romantic plays, but we only hear of the incidents, we do not witness them. Take, for example, our first English tragedy, *Gorboduc*. The 'argument' prefixed to this drama runs

---

[221]It is probable that Shakespeare realised that he had allowed Falstaff to run away with him, and that this was the reason why he broke his promise and did not introduce the fat knight into *Henry V* in which his purpose clearly was to focus attention from first to last upon his heroic central figure.

[222]See *ante*, pp. 175, 176.

[223]*Ars Poetica*, I. 185.

thus: 'Gorboduc, king of Brittaine, divided his realme in his life-time to his sonnes, Ferrex and Porrex; the sonnes fell to discention; the yonger killed the elder; the mother, that more dearely loved the elder, for revenge killed the yonger; the people, moved with the crueltie of the fact, rose in rebellion and slew both father and mother; the nobilitie assembled and most terribly destroyed the rebels; and afterwardes, for want of issue of the prince, whereby the succession of the crowne became uncertaine, they fell to civill warre, in which both they and many of their issues were slaine, and the land for a long time almost desolate and miserably wasted.' It is evident that such a plot—which, like that of *Hamlet*, literally reeks with gore—provides abundant material for vigorous action and thrilling situations. But all the murder and bloodshed take place behind the scenes, and we are kept informed of what is occurring by descriptive speeches of enormous length. So again with *Le Cid*. Two duels and a big battle are amply sufficient to redeem this play from any charge of uneventfulness. But the duels are simply reported, while instead of a representation of the battle, such as Shakespeare would have given us, we have Rodrigue's vivid account of it in a magnificent oration of seventy-three lines. The only thing that we should commonly regard as an incident which occurs on the stage is at the very beginning, when Don Gomès strikes Don Diègue across the face with his glove; and even this was condemned by the Academy as a breach of dramatic decorum.

While the neoclassic drama is thus a drama of narrative, the romantic, on the contrary, is essentially a drama of action. Nearly everything that happens in it happens on the stage, and duels are fought, murders and suicides committed, outrages perpetrated, and battles waged, in full view of the spectators. The great public of the virile and full-blooded Elizabethan age, with their overflowing energies, their thirst for adventure, their love of stirring deeds, were too keenly interested in the immense and many-sided pageantry of actual life to tolerate rhetorical description as a substitute for movement and representation and spectacle. For dramatic decorum they cared nothing; in their craving for realistic display and delight in seeing things done, they accepted the crude inadequacy (ridiculed by Ben Jonson)[224] with which the battle scenes were perforce enacted; they did not even recoil from sights which seem to us too shocking for exhibition. The fact must never be overlooked that the plays of Shakespeare and his contemporaries were written to satisfy this enormous appetite for action.

We must not allow our familiarity with the romantic drama, and our general adherence to its principles, to betray us into the supposition that representation is always to be preferred to narrative, and that nothing is to be said in favour of the neoclassic method. While the greatest scope for action should undoubtedly be granted, and while its practical absence from neoclassic tragedy necessarily leaves us with a sense of baldness and unreality, the question of how much in any given case shall be exhibited and how much merely reported is still one that is open to discussion. Here indeed we touch upon an important and sometimes very difficult problem of dramatic technique. It may fairly be argued that Shakespeare's numerous battle scenes are really unfortunate concessions to the taste of the 'groundlings' of his time; that in many instances they are more than a trifle absurd, and that his plays would often have been vastly improved by their excision.

A similar judgment may safely be passed upon the great 'realistic' scenes—the fires, and floods, and railway accidents—of modern melodrama. The contention of Dryden's Lisideius,[225] that 'those actions which by reason of their cruelty will cause aversion in us,[226] or by reason of their impossibility, unbelief, ought either to be wholly avoided by the poet, or only delivered by narration,' is also, broadly

---

[224]*Prologue* to *Every Man in his Humour.*

[225]*Essay of Dramatic Poesie.*

[226]Such, for example, as that rare instance of actual barbarity in the Shakespearean drama—the plucking out of Gloucester's eyes on the stage (*King Lear*, III, vii), and the horrible exhibition of the mutilated Lavinia in the pseudo-Shakespearean *Titus Andronicus*, II, iv.

speaking, perfectly sound. Nor is the widely current notion, to which even Horace lent his authority—that 'things heard make a feebler impression than things seen'[227]—by any means universally true, for the impressiveness of representation may frequently be marred by imperfection of detail, as in many of the boasted sensational effects of the modern stage; while, as common experience teaches, there are countless cases in which an appeal to the imagination is much more powerful than one to actual sight. Shakespeare gives us many murders, but it is surely a significant fact that the most terrible of all—that of Duncan in *Macbeth*—takes place off the stage. We must also be on our guard against too narrow an interpretation of action and incident. This point is well emphasised in Dryden's *Essay*—"'Tis a great mistake in us,' says Lisideius, 'to believe the French present no part of the action on the stage: every alteration or crossing of a design, every new-sprung passion, and turn of it, is a part of the action, and much the noblest, except we conceive nothing to be action till the players come to blows.'

The reference just made to the murder of Duncan suggests one point to which the student of Shakespeare will do well to devote some attention. Like other romantic playwrights, Shakespeare leans strongly towards action. His usual practice is to put as much of his story as is possible on the stage. But every now and then we come upon marked exceptions to this general rule—upon scenes in which important events are thrown into narrative instead of being represented; and then the question naturally arises as to the reason which prompted him to depart from his customary plan. I need hardly say that there is no one answer to this question which will meet all cases. Sometimes, it is evident, he is governed by mere practical necessity. Sometimes we shall find that he has substituted narrative for action for the purpose of condensing a large amount of material which would otherwise have become unmanageable, or which would have occupied too much space. But sometimes,

---

[227] *Art Poetica*, 1. 180.

as the briefest investigation will show, neither of these superficial explanations will serve, and the cause will then have to be sought in considerations of artistic purpose and effect. *Macbeth* will suffice to illustrate all these phases of the subject. Though Macbeth's head is immediately afterwards brought on the stage, the actual decapitation takes place behind the scenes. This we can scarcely hesitate to ascribe to practical necessity. The flight of Malcolm and Donalbain to England and Ireland provides an example of narrative condensation. But two incidents of the utmost importance occur 'off'—the murder of Duncan, which has led to this discussion, and the death of Lady Macbeth. In neither of these instances can any considerations of necessity or condensation be alleged; both could have been represented perfectly well, and the play is so short that time could easily have been spared for them Why, then, is neither of these enacted? Here the question resolves itself into one of artistic purpose and effect, and the answer to it is not, I think, very far to seek. After the awful sleepwalking scene in which appropriate nemesis overtakes the guilty queen, the actual exhibition of her death would have been almost an anticlimax, while coming where it does, its significance for us is not so much in the incident itself, as in the revelation it is made to furnish of the condition of her husband's mind. In the great murder scene the real tragedy manifestly lies not in the murder as a physical fact, but in the emotional stress which accompanies it—not in the death of the king, but in the souls of his slayers. This essential tragedy is driven home upon us with infinitely greater force in the scene as its stands—heightened as it is with all the accessories of horror—than would have been the case had the murder been done before our eyes, because our attention is never for a moment distracted by the details of the crime as such. It is the concentration of all our interest upon the inner meaning of the situation that makes it so tremendous and overwhelming.

Such, then, are some of the fundamental differences in principle and method between the neoclassic and the romantic types of drama, each of which has, in its own particular way, triumphantly justified itself by a brilliant history and many masterpieces. The drama of our own time, while it must not be passed over in silence, may be much more briefly dismissed.

The product of an age of electicism and experiment in every department of art, the modern drama exhibits so many varieties that no summary statement of its characteristics would be possible. Keeping to generalities, however, we may say that, in the sense that it is quite indifferent to all academic rules and conventions, it carries on the romantic tradition. It habitually assumes an absolute freedom as to time and place of action; it consults its own convenience only in the use of subplots and subordinate interests; it has no scruple about the combination of the serious and the comic; action and narrative are employed in it without reference to precepts, and simply as the exigencies of the plot may dictate. Little trace, moreover, is anywhere to be found in it of the aristocratic limitations of older tragedy. Here even the pre- possessions of the romantic stage have been abandoned, and under the co-operating influences of the democratic spirit and of realism the Domestic Drama, the avowed aim of which is to hold the mirror up to ordinary human life, has definitely established itself as the most completely representative form of modern dramatic art—the form in which, with few exceptions, its most noteworthy work has been done.

Yet while always holding themselves at liberty to pursue their own course without regard to the theories of the older schools, it happens that some of our greatest recent dramatists tend in various ways towards the principles of the neoclassic play. This is pre-eminently the case with the chief masters of the Domestic Drama, in which mere convention of every kind is most openly defied. Referring to the three unities, a writer on practical stage technique has said: 'At the present time the terms no longer have any meaning, save in the historical sense, when speaking of plays written under the influence of the old rules of criticism. No one pretends to regard them at the present day.'[228] So far as any conscious recognition of these rules simply as rules is concerned, this is undoubtedly true. But if the unities are not obeyed as a matter of theory, they are often more or less closely observed in practice. If we turn, for example, to the work of the most skilful as well as most powerful of modern playwrights, Ibsen, we occasionally find a concentration of treatment even in excess of that required by the most rigorous upholders of the neoclassic view. The whole action of Ghosts, for instance, passes in one room, and occupies only a few hours of a single day. In *The Pillars of Society and Hedda Gabler*, the scene never changes; in *John Gabriel Borkman*, the correspondence of stage time with actual time is approximately complete. Such com- pactness and condensation are largely due to the nature of the dramatist's themes, his controlling psychological purpose, and his whole conception of structure and effect. But we must also remember that throughout the modern drama in general the elaborate methods of stage-representation now in vogue have tended to make frequent changes of scene both difficult and costly, and thus through mere stress of practical necessity the extreme laxity of the old romantic play has been for the most part abandoned. In realistic drama, the unities of time and place are now very commonly preserved within each act.

This leads us to touch upon one other feature in which Ibsen, and many modern playwrights whom we may roughly class as belonging to his school, often revert not only to neoclassic methods, but also to the principles of the pure Greek type of tragedy. Since it was entirely unchecked in respect of time and place, the romantic drama could represent the whole of a story, however long and intricate. Since it was severely limited in respect of time and place, Greek tragedy, on the other hand, was compelled to confine its action to the closing portions of its story, leaving all antecedent circumstances to be explained by dialogue and retrospective narrative.

The difference becomes clear, if, for example, we compare

---

[228]Hennequin, *The Art of Playwrighting*, p. 89.

Macbeth with *Œdipus the King*. In the one case, the action on the stage begins with the rise of the motive of ambition in Macbeth's mind. In the other case, it begins only at the moment when the predictions of the oracle are about to be fulfilled.[229] Thus a Greek tragedy may be regarded from the point of view of the matter which actually falls within the performance as equivalent to the dénouement—to the fourth and fifth acts, or sometimes even to the fifth act only—of a romantic play.[230] Ibsen's work provides some striking examples of the same structural plan. The roots of his actions often run far down into the past; but when the curtain rises on the first scene, we have already reached the beginning of the end, and the stage-representation is concerned only with the last term of a long series of events. Such is the case with *Ghosts* and *Rosmersholm*. In these plays, moreover, as in *Œdipus the King*, an immense amount of space is necessarily devoted to the elucidation of those antecedent circumstances which constitute the foundations of the tragedy which we are asked to witness. In dramas of this type, therefore, exposition often undergoes enormous expansion; it continues through the action, and belongs indeed to its very substance.

---

[229]In the Shakespearean drama the difference may be illustrated by a comparison of *The Winter's Tale* and *The Tempest*—the one ultra-romantic in design, the other quite classic. 'Had *The Tempest* been written on the plan of *The Winter's Tale*, the long story unfolded in Prospero's retrospective narrative would have occupied the earlier acts of the drama, and the dénouement would have been condensed into the closing two acts. Had *The Winter's Tale* been written on the plan of *The Tempest*, the matter of the first three acts would have been thrown into retrospective narrative, and the whole play devoted to the love story of Perdita and the restoration of Hermione' (*Introduction* to *The Winter's Tale*, in the *Elizabethan Shakespeare*, p. xxi, note).

[230]See Haigh's *The Tragic Drama of the Greeks*, pp. 337–342. This must be borne in mind in analysing the structure of a Greek tragedy according to the principles previously given. Prof. Moulton has made an ingenious attempt to emphasise the differences between Greek and Shakespearean tragedy in this and other respects by a reconstruction of *Macbeth* in the form of a classic play (see his *Ancient Classical Drama*, chapter vi).

VII

Thus far we have dealt almost wholly with the technical aspects of the study of the drama. But since, like all other kinds of literature, the drama has also to be judged on the broad basis of its moral power and value, something must be added about it as the vehicle of a criticism or philosophy of life.

It is unnecessary to go again over the ground which we have already traversed in the closing section of our chapter on prose fiction; the more so, as in our consideration of the novelist's criticism of life the dramatist was specifically included. Everything that was then said about the importance of the ethical element in any work of fiction, whether in the narrative or in the dramatic form, and about the moral standards which have to be applied to it, may, therefore, be taken for granted without repetition. Our only concern now is with the way in which the drama interprets life.

Here we are brought back again to that fundamental distinction between the novel and the drama upon which we have more than once had to dwell at length. In theory, the drama is entirely objective; the novel permits the continual intrusion of the personality of the writer. Thus, as we have shown, the novelist may interpret life both indirectly by his exhibition of it, and directly by his comments upon it. The dramatist is supposedly limited to the former in- direct method. 'A novel,' says Henry James, 'is, in the broadest definition, a personal impression of life.'[231] The drama, on the contrary, may be regarded, from the strictly theoretical standpoint, as an impersonal representation of life. Hence we shall always find it far more difficult in the case of a drama than in the case of a novel to reduce the writer's consciously given or unconsciously suggested philosophy to formal statement. The novelist, as I have said, often helps us greatly in this task by his own incidental interpretations. The whole burden of responsibility in reading his meaning, and making explicit what he gives only by implication, is, according to the commonly accepted

---

[231] *The Art of Fiction in Partial Portraits.*

view, thrown by the dramatist on our shoulders.

It will be observed, however, that in speaking of the impersonality of the drama, I have done so with qualifications. I have said that in theory the drama is entirely objective, and that the dramatist is supposedly limited to the indirect method of interpretation. The drama is indeed the most completely objective form of literary art; the novel combines the objective with the subjective. Dealing with the matter in a general way, therefore, we cannot well overemphasise the importance of the fact that, unlike the novelist, the dramatist can never appear in proper person in his action. But it has still to be remembered that in practice he has often contrived a way of escape from the cramping restraints imposed upon him by the conditions under which he has to work. If he cannot appear in proper person in his action, he may nonetheless make his presence felt there in the person of some accredited representative.

Such an accredited representative may undoubtedly be recognised in the Chorus of many Greek tragedies, the significance of whose interpretative functions has already been pointed out. To accept the Chorus as an 'ideal spectator' is tantamount to regarding its utterances as having special authority as an expression of the thoughts and feelings which the poet would wish that his plot should arouse in ourselves. The Chorus in Greek tragedy, then, is often, though not necessarily or always, the delegate of the poet, and the mouthpiece of his philosophy of life. On the modern stage this mediating element is no longer at the dramatist's disposal. But that its place is sometimes, and to a certain extent, taken by one of the characters in a drama is shown by the fact, already noted, that such a character is occasionally picked out by the commentators and described as the 'Chorus' of the action. We have previously spoken of Enobarbus as a kind of chorus in *Antony and Cleopatra*, because in his detachment from the queen he helps to put us at the right point of view in regard to her, while by his comments at critical moments in the action he brings out the meaning of Antony's degeneration under the spell of the 'serpent of old Nile.' I have elsewhere said of Berowne, in

Love's Labour's Lost, that though it is uncritical to see in him 'either a deliberate study in self-portraiture or an unconscious reflection of the personality of the author,' he 'does stand a little apart from the other characters,' is 'nearer to Shakespeare than any of them,' and is in fact from time to time 'pushed forward as the designed interpreter of the dramatist's own thought,' to whom is entrusted the business of underscoring the moral.[232] Even more distinctly is the Bastard, the chorus in *King John*; for though, like Berowne, he makes all his comments in his own proper character, there is no possibility of mistaking the significance of his Soliloquy on 'Commodity, the bias of the world,' or of that splendid outburst of fervid patriotism with which he closes the play, and in which indeed he strikes the keynote of all Shakespeare's chronicle dramas.

In modern 'thesis plays'—plays in which the main purpose of the dramatist is to open up moral problems or expound specific opinions—we often find some one character whose principal function in the plot (whether or not he has also any active part in it) is clearly to move through it as a philosophic spectator, and to formulate its meaning on the writer's behalf. So prominent has such an expositor become in this class of drama that French critics have adopted a special name for him; they call him the *'raisonneur.'* There are numerous examples of the *raisonneur* in the plays of the younger Dumas and other playwrights of the doctrinaire school. As, according to his own well-known declaration, Ibsen's mission was to ask questions and not to answer them, the real expositor is rare in his work. But we have, I think, a case in point in the cynical Dr Relling in that strangest and most puzzling of all his social dramas, *The Wild Duck*. 'Life might yet be quite tolerable,' says the doctor, 'if only we were left in peace by these blessed duns who are continually knocking at the doors of us poor folks with their 'ideal demand.'' Just as truly as the closing words of a Sophoclean chorus serve to strike 'the final balance' of the action, does this remark sum up the

---

[232]*Introduction* to *Love's Labour's Lost*, in the *Elizabethan Shakespeare*, pp. xxxiii, xxxiv.

pessimistic moral which Ibsen designs his play to enforce.

It is scarcely necessary to point out that great care must always be exercised in the search for a chorus or expositor. Because a certain character in a play talks a good deal and expresses his opinions more freely and more explicitly than any other person on the stage, it is not hastily to be assumed that what he says carries with it the authority of the dramatist himself. His utterances must be rigorously tested by the whole spirit and tendency of the action, and only when it is evident that they harmonise with these and help in their elucidation are we warranted in regarding them as possessing a general in contradistinction to a merely dramatic value.

Some commentators have chosen to discover in the melancholy Jaques in *As You Like It* the representative of Shakespeare and the interpreter of his view of life. But the entire plot is surely against this identification; as Canon Beeching has well said, 'We know that Shakespeare does not mean us to admire Jaques's melancholy, because he makes all the healthy-minded people in the play, one after another, laugh at it.'[233] In the same way, two distinguished German critics, Gervinus and Kreyssig, have found in the reflections of Friar Laurence in the philosophic text of *Romeo and Juliet*, and basing their reading upon these, have turned a young poet's superb glorification of youthful love into a sort of homily against unregulated passion. That the Friar's moralisings do give us one point of view from which the tragedy may be regarded is undeniable: but that this point of view, while most appropriate to the speaker, in the least represents Shakespeare's, the whole burden of the drama makes it impossible to believe.

The chorus or *raisonneur* is, however, an occasional figure only in the drama, and unless he is properly disguised by having a real part to play in the plot, criticism is justified in objecting to him entirely. We have therefore to ask whether, keeping more strictly within the bounds of impersonal art, and without having recourse to

---

[233] *William Shakespeare*, p. 89.

this device of direct representation, the dramatist may not still find an opportunity of conveying to the audience his own thoughts and feelings. The answer is that he may do this through the utterances of his various characters, who, while never ceasing to speak in accordance with their personalities and situations, may none the less be utilised by him as exponents of his ideas about men and things.

Here we have to be on our guard against what Prof. Moulton has called 'the Fallacy of Quotations.'[234] This fallacy is familiar to us all through the typical case of our own greatest dramatist, from whose plays maxims and judgments are continually cited as illustrations of what 'Shakespeare says,' without regard to the fact that every one of these passages was spoken in character, and must therefore be primarily accepted only at its dramatic value as an expression of the mind of the speaker. No mere miscellaneous collection of quotations or 'beauties' will serve to throw the slightest light for us upon the essential principles of Shakespeare's own thought; and Prof. Moulton does well to warn us against any attempt to penetrate into these principles by the wholly uncritical method of taking even the wisest and most pregnant sayings out of their context and referring them directly to the dramatist himself. But he is surely guilty of serious exaggeration when he writes: 'Dramatic differs from other literature in this, that quotations from a play can never reveal either the mind of the author or the spirit of the drama.... For every word in a play some imaginary speaker, and only he, is responsible; and thus in dramatic literature no amount of quotations can give us the mind of the poet or the meaning of the poem.'[235] I do not question that this is a perfectly correct statement of the abstract theory of the drama—of its ideal objectivity. But I contend that, as the above remarks on the chorus and *raisonneur* have shown, this abstract ideal is not always realised in practice, and that it was not always realised even by Shakespeare. Prof. Moulton's protest against the use of quotations

---

[234] *The Moral System of Shakespeare*, p. 1.
[235] *Ibid.*, p. 2.

in the interpretation of Shakespeare's thought must, therefore, be taken with much modification. Can we doubt that the dramatist does sometimes, wittingly or unwittingly, drop the mask, and give utterance to sentiments for which he, and not his imaginary character and spokesman, is responsible?—that, to take only one outstanding example, it is Shakespeare and not Hamlet who unpacks his heart in musings over 'the proud man's contumely, the pangs of despised love, the law's delay,' who discourses on the drunkenness of his fellow countrymen, who lectures the players on the art of acting, and complains of the popularity of the boy-actors of the Queen's Revels? In all these passages, curiously inappropriate as they are to character and situation, we are listening, it is obvious, not to Hamlet but to Shakespeare: even so conservative a critic as Prof. Boas admits that they put 'out of court all *a priori* theories of Shakespeare's pure objectivity.'[236] But Hamlet is an exceptional case. It is more important therefore to insist that even when he does not thus manifestly drop the mask—even when his characters speak entirely in accordance with their personalities and circumstances—Shakespeare again and again gives us through their lips a clear indication of his own ideas and judgments. But how are we to know when he does this? How are we to discriminate—as no mere miscellaneous collection of 'beauties' will enable us to dis- criminate—between the passages which are simply dramatic and those which, while still dramatic, may safely be read as representing Shakespeare's own mind? The answer is one which, I believe, every intelligent student who is not hampered by '*a priori* theories of Shakespeare's pure objectivity' must have discovered for himself. 'We can,' as Canon Beeching says, 'observe the sentiments put into the mouths of those characters with whom we are plainly meant to sympathise, and contrast them with those that are put into the mouths of other characters with whom we are meant not to sympathise. This,' Mr Beeching rightly adds, 'is a consideration sufficiently obvious, but it is too often neglected, although it is of

---

[236] *Shakspere and his Predecessors*, p. 389.

the utmost importance in the interpretation of the dramas.'[237] Nor is this quite all. Mr Beeching might also have remarked, though he has not done so, that even the characters with whom we are not meant to sympathise may very clearly at times be used to bear indirect and unwilling testimony to moral truths formerly defied by them, and expressed perhaps by characters with whom we are meant to sympathise. 'The gods are just,' says Edgar, at the end of *King Lear*, 'and of our pleasant vices make instruments to plague us.' And Edmund replies: 'Thou hast spoken right, 'tis true; the wheel has come full circle; I am here.' Edmund's villainy has brought about its own fitting nemesis, and even more than Edgar's generalisation does this final admission on his part of the reality of the moral law which he has broken provides the dramatist's commentary upon this part of his plot. In our attempt to interpret a dramatist's criticism of life, therefore, guidance may properly be sought in the systematic examination and collation of the sentiments distributed among the characters. But the principle already laid down in connection with the chorus must again be emphasised. Every utterance of every character must, as I have put it, be rigorously tested by the whole spirit and tendency of the action.

This brings us to our last point. It is in the whole spirit and tendency of the action that a dramatist's criticism of life is, after all, most fully embodied. In dealing with the ethical aspects of prose fiction, I quoted with approval Prof. Moulton's remark that 'every play of Shakespeare,' critically examined, turns out to be 'a microcosm, of which the author is the creator, and the plot is its providential scheme.' It can never be too often repeated that the world which the dramatist calls into being, with all its men and women, actions, passions, motives, struggles, successes, failures, is a world of his own creation—a world for which, when the last word about objectivity in art has been said, he alone is responsible. Now, because it is a world of his own creation, it must of necessity be

---

[237] *William Shakespeare*, pp. 91, 92.

the projection of his own personality; of necessity it must reveal the quality and temper of his mind, the atmosphere through which he looked out upon things, the direction of his thought, the lines of his interests, the general meaning which life had for him. It is quite true that to express the spirit and tendency of his work in any abstract statement which will satisfy us as comprehensive and final, is often very difficult, and sometimes impossible. But by carefully analysing the total impression, intellectual and moral, which that work makes upon us, we shall gain a broad sense at least of the dramatist's underlying philosophy of life.[238]

---

[238]Note to page 231.—In referring the genesis of Greek tragedy to the primitive Dionysiac Dithyramb, I adopted the theory which was still in almost undisputed possession of the field at the time when the present pages were written. This theory has now been challenged by Prof. Ridgeway in his *Origin of Tragedy, with Special Reference to the Greek Tragedians*, published in 1910. Prof. Ridgeway maintains with great learning and skill that tragedy in fact arose, not out of the rustic worship of Dionysus, but out of ancestor-worship or the cult of the dead. In my judgment he has made out a very strong case for this view, and his book is one which every student of Greek drama should read. At the same time, the substitution of the one theory for the other would make no difference to the general principles enunciated in the text. It is still conceded that Greek tragedy was choric in origin, and thus the statement is correct that 'the chorus belonged to Greek tragedy because it was the germ from which it sprang.'

6

The Study of Criticism and
the Valuation of Literature

I. *The General Nature of Criticism*. What is Criticism?—Common Objections to Criticism—Criticism as Literature—The Abuse of Criticism—The Use of Criticism. II. *The Two Functions of Criticism*. The Critic as Interpreter—'Inductive' Criticism—Older Methods of 'Judicial' Criticism—Illustrations: Addison—Johnson—Influence of the Modern Spirit on Criticism—The Need and Justification of Judicial Criticism. III. *The Study of Criticism as Literature*. Personal Aspects—Some Qualifications of the True Critic—His Equipment—Points for Study in a Critic's Work. IV. *Historic Aspects*. The Comparative Method in the Study of Criticism—The Historical Study of Criticism—Changes in Opinion about Representative Authors—How to be Explained?—The History of Criticism as a Supplement to the History of Literature—Criticism and Production. V. *The Problem of the Valuation of Literature*. Is all Judgment necessarily Personal?—Differences in Value in Personal Judgments—The Real Problem of Personal Enjoyment—Some Practical Aspects of this Problem—Is Criticism a 'self-cancelling Business?'—What does it mean when the Critics agree?—How greatness in Literature is Proved—What is a 'Classic'?—'Catholicity' in Literature—The Struggle for Existence, and Survival in Literature—Why Some Books Survive?—The Valuation of Contemporary Literature—The 'Classics' as Standards of Comparison.

In its strict sense the word criticism means judgment, and this sense commonly colours our use of it even when it is most broadly employed. The literary critic is therefore regarded primarily as an expert who brings a special faculty and training to bear upon a piece of literary art, or the work of a given author, examines its merits and defects, and pronounces a verdict upon it. Yet when we speak of the literature of criticism we evidently include under the term more than the literature which records judgment. We comprehend under it the whole mass of literature which is written about literature, whether the object be analysis, interpretation, or valuation, or all these combined. Poetry, the drama, the novel, deal directly with life. Criticism deals with poetry, the drama, the novel, even with criticism itself. If creative literature may be defined as an interpretation of life under the various forms of literary art, critical literature may be defined as an interpretation of that interpretation and of the forms of art through which it is given.

The prejudice often expressed against criticism is thus easily explained. Our first business with a great author is with the author himself. It is his work that we want to understand, and to understand for ourselves. What, then, it is frequently asked, is the use of so many intermediaries? Why should we consume time in reading what someone else has said about Dante or Shakespeare, which we might surely employ much more profitably in reading Dante and Shakespeare themselves? We have so many books about books that our libraries are being choked with them, and our attention distracted. Nor is this the worst. The enormous growth in recent times of the parasitic literature of explanation and commentary has in turn bred a fast-multiplying race of secondary parasites—of critics who write about critics, and undertake to interpret their interpretation of the interpretation of life presented in real literature. We have therefore an ever-increasing number, not only of books about books, but also of books about books about books. We have histories of criticism; we have analytical studies of the methods of this critic and that; we have magazine articles in which such studies are summarised and discussed. We are thus tempted to get our knowledge of much of the world's greatest literature at second hand, or even at third hand. Scherer examines *Paradise Lost*. Then Matthew Arnold examines Scherer's examination of *Paradise Lost*. We may be much interested in what Scherer thinks about Milton, and in what Arnold thinks of Scherer's view of Milton, and perhaps in some other person's view of Arnold's opinion of Scherer as a critic of Milton. But meanwhile there is a serious danger lest, our whole leisure being devoted to Scherer and Arnold, Milton's own work may remain unread. Is not the critic, therefore, a mere cumberer of the ground? At best, the study of criticism can be no substitute for the study of the literature criticised. At worst, it may stand in the way of such study by inducing us to rest content with that superficial sort of knowledge about books and their authors, which, as I have already insisted, is a vitally different thing from personal knowledge of the books and authors themselves.

These objections are quite intelligible, and in an age when creative literature is undoubtedly in peril of being overlaid by, and practically buried under, a growing mass of exposition and commentary, due weight must certainly be given to them. Against the abuse of criticism, as a marked feature in the intellectual life of our time, a protest may therefore be very justly made. But we are not for this reason to deny the utility of criticism. It has its legitimate place and function.

Let me emphasise in passing a point which is commonly lost sight of. The distinction between the literature which deals directly with life, and the literature which deals with literature, fundamental as it may at first seem, is after all an artificial one. Literature is made out of whatever interests us in life. But personality is manifestly one of the chief facts in life, and one of the most profoundly interesting. It follows, therefore, that the critic who undertakes the interpretation of the personality of a great writer as it is revealed in his work, and of that work in all its varied aspects as the expression of the man himself, is just as truly dealing with life as was the poet or dramatist whose writings form the subject of his study. A noble book is as living a thing as a noble deed, and the processes of art are just as vital as those which are involved in any other of life's many-sided activities. This view has been admirably expressed by Mr William Watson, who, to the objection that he has too often sought 'in singers' selves'—in the work of other poets—his 'theme of song,' replies that he has taken the great poets as his matter deliberately,

> Holding these also to be very part
> Of Nature's greatness, and accounting not
> Their descants least heroical of deeds.

So far as the current prejudice against criticism is based upon its supposed difference in kind from that creative literature which draws matter and inspiration directly from life, it has thus to be set aside. True criticism also draws its matter and inspiration from life, and in its own way it like- wise is creative.

It is important therefore to distinguish between the abuse and the use of criticism. This fortunately is a problem which presents no serious difficulty. We can easily learn from our own experiences when the reading of criticism becomes a snare, and when it is of help to us.

To put the matter broadly, it becomes a snare whenever we remain satisfied with what someone else has said about a great author, instead of going straight to that author, and trying to master his work for ourselves. Shortcuts to knowledge are now being rapidly multiplied in literature as well as in all other fields of study; and in the rush of life, and the stress of conflicting interests, we are sorely tempted to depend upon them for information about many writers of whom the world talks freely, and of whom we should like to be able to talk freely too, but with whom we have not the time, or perhaps not the patience, to become acquainted on our own account. To read the *Odyssey* through is a task from which many of us may recoil on the ground that it is very long, and that there are so many other things that we are equally anxious to read.

Such a handy little epitome of the contents of that wonderful old poem as is provided in the *Ancient Classics for English Readers* seems therefore exactly to suit our needs. Now it is not to be assumed, as it is in fact assumed too often by writers on the subject, that such dependence upon the literature of exposition is open to unqualified condemnation. The matter must be treated practically, and to say that we should try to read for ourselves every book in the world's literature that is worth reading at all, is, so far as the majority of us are concerned, to lay down a counsel of perfection. If the question takes the form, as it often must, as to whether the *Odyssey* is to remain an entirely sealed book for us, or whether we are to get some idea of its story and characters at second hand, then I for one should not hesitate to answer that it is far better to know something about the poem from the briefest sketch of it, than to know nothing about it at all. Life is short, our margin of leisure generally limited, the special line of our individual interests often of necessity narrowly defined; and thus out of the enormous mass of the world's really great literature that portion which we can ever hope to make a personal possession is small indeed. Our curiosity concerning many important writers who lie beyond our opportunities or our chosen field of study, our wish to understand something of their character, production, place and influence, are perfectly natural and justifiable, and it would be absurd to argue that we should not freely turn to service what others have written about them, using this, if needs be, as a substitute for our own reading of their work, or perhaps as a guide for subsequent use to what is most valuable for us in it.

Everyone will admit, for example, that Voltaire is one of the greatest men of letters of the eighteenth century. As such, he is interesting both in himself and on account of the enormous place which he fills in the literary history of his time. About such a man, and about his work, certain questions, sooner or later, are sure to arise. What did he really stand for? What were his aims? his methods? his achievements? How much of his work is important only from the historical point of view? How much of it has any permanent value, and why? To such questions we should be glad to obtain at least a general answer. But Voltaire's separate publications number upwards of 260; he wrote society verses and epic poems, dramas and dramatic criticism, history and biography, philosophical tales and philosophical treatises. For the ordinary English reader the mass of this immense and varied output must of necessity remain an unexplored territory. But meanwhile he will find in Lord Motley's admirable volume of under 400 pages a compact and luminous study of the man, his milieu, his work; and the careful perusal of this will give him a far better idea of Voltaire's genius, power, limitations and accomplishment than it would be possible for him to derive from hasty and undirected efforts to acquaint himself directly with Voltaire's own work. Again, among the countless minor writers in all literatures there are many who deserve some attention, because, as Matthew Arnold very justly says, being in their own way 'real men of genius,' and thus having 'a genuine gift for what is true and excellent,' they are 'capable of emitting a life-giving stimulus.' It is therefore 'salutary from time to time to come across a genius of this kind, and to extract his honey,' for 'often he has more of it for us...than greater men.'[239] But to read many of these writers in their entirety for ourselves is manifestly impossible, and we may thus be grateful to the intermediary who extracts the honey for us and sets it before us in available form. Modest such service may be; but it is of inestimable value, and we have every right to take advantage of it.

To say that we must never depend upon other people for our knowledge of authors and books is therefore to be guilty of gross exaggeration. But the general importance of the principle that our chief business is directly with literature, and not with even the best critical interpretation of literature, is none the less not to be impugned. 'Some books,' as Bacon says, 'may be read by deputy'; yet, as he rightly adds, 'distilled books are like common distilled

---

[239]Essay on *Joubert*, in *Essays in Criticism*, First Series.

waters, flashy things.' If the primary aim of literary study be the cultivation of intimate personal relations between student and writer, then our too frequent practice of contenting ourselves with books about books can scarcely be too strongly deprecated. The essential virtue of a great book, its individual power, its 'life-giving stimulus,' can be felt in their fullness only through immediate contact. They cannot be transmitted, save, in a very slight degree, by any agent or expositor. A well-known American professor once told me of a student of his who came to him with the question: What was the best book he could read on *Timon of Athens*, on which he was then writing an essay. My friend's reply was: 'The best book you can read on *Timon of Athens* is—*Timon of Athens*.' This was a view of the matter which apparently had not occurred to the inquirer, who went away a sadder and wiser man. It is a view which is too often neglected by most of us. No analysis or criticism of a book, let it therefore be repeated, can ever be an adequate substitute for our own personal mastery of the book itself. The labour which we bestow on a determined effort to gain such mastery is, as a means of literary culture, of infinitely greater value than any knowledge of the book which we obtain from the outside.

This suggests another danger inherent in our continual recourse to the literature of exposition and commentary. We are too apt to accept passively another person's interpretation of a book and his judgment upon it. This danger is the more to be emphasised because it increases with the power of the critic himself. If he is a really great critic—that is, if he is a man of exceptional learning, grasp, and vigour of personality—he is likely to impose himself upon us. Pain- fully aware by contrast of his strength and our own short-comings, we yield ourselves to him. He dominates our thought to such an extent that we take his verdict as final. Henceforth we look at the book, not with our own eyes, but through his. We find in it what he has found there, and nothing else. What he has missed, we miss too. Our reading runs only on the lines that he has laid down. Thus, in fact, he stands between us and his subject, not as an interpreter, but as an obstacle. Instead of leading us, he blocks the way. Personal intercourse with our author is prevented, and the free play of our mind upon his work is made impossible.

Yet serious as are the results which follow from the abuse of criticism, its real use in the study of literature is not for a moment to be called in question. To deny its service is tantamount to asserting either that no one else can ever be wiser than ourselves, or that we can never profit by another person's deeper experience or superior wisdom. The chief function of criticism is to enlighten and stimulate. If a great poet makes us partakers of his larger sense of the meaning of life, a great critic may make us partakers of his larger sense of the meaning of literature. The true critic is one who is equipped for his task by a knowledge of his subject which, in breadth and soundness, far exceeds our own, and who, moreover, is endowed with special faculties of insight, penetration, and comprehension. Surely, it would be the height of impertinence to assume that such a man will not see a great deal more than we do in a given masterpiece of literature, and the extreme of folly to imagine that with his aid we may not discover in it qualities of power and beauty, a wealth of interest and a depth of significance, to which, but for that aid, we should in all probability have remained blind. The critic often gives us an entirely fresh point of view; often, too, renders particular assistance by translating into definite form impressions of our own, dimly recognised indeed, but still too vague to be of practical value. He is sometimes a pathfinder, breaking new ground; sometimes a friendly companion, indicating hitherto unperceived aspects of even the most familiar things we pass together by the way. Thus he teaches us to re-read for ourselves with quickened intelligence and keener appreciation. Nor is this all. He frequently helps us most when he challenges our own judgments, cuts across our preconceived opinions, and gives us, in Emerson's phrase, not instruction, but provocation. If we read him, as we should read the literature of which he discourses, with a mind ever vigilant and alert, it will matter little whether we agree with or dissent from what he has to tell us. In either case we shall gain by contact with him in insight and power.

II

As already implied, criticism may be regarded as having two different functions—that of interpretation and that of judgment. It is indeed true that in practice these two functions have until our own time been generally combined, since the majority of critics, while conceiving judgment to be the real end of all criticism, have freely employed interpretation as a means to that end. Within recent years, however, the distinction has been forced into prominence by various students of literature, who, setting the two functions in opposition, have more or less consistently maintained the thesis that the critic's chief duty is exposition, even if (and this, as we shall see, has been denied) he is ever warranted in venturing beyond exposition into questions of taste and valuation.

Accepting for the moment this view of the scope and limitations of criticism, we have to ask, what is it that the critic as interpreter should set out to accomplish? The answer will show that, even as thus defined, his task is both large and difficult. His purpose will be to penetrate to the heart of the book before him; to disengage its essential qualities of power and beauty; to distinguish between what is temporary and what is permanent in it; to analyse and formulate its meaning; to elucidate by direct examination the artistic and moral principles which, whether the writer himself was conscious of them or not, have actually guided and controlled his labours. What is merely implicit in his author's work he will make explicit. He will exhibit the interrelations of its parts and the connection of each with the whole which they compose. He will gather up and epitomise its scattered elements, and account for its characteristics by tracing them to their sources. Thus, explaining, unfolding, illuminating, he will show us what the book really is—its content, its spirit, its art; and this done, he will leave it to justify and appraise itself. 'To feel the virtue of the poet or the painter, to disengage it, to set it forth—

these,' says Walter Pater, 'are the three stages of the critic's duty.'

In the execution of his task such a critic will, of course, follow his own particular line of exposition. He may confine himself strictly to the book in hand, and fix his attention wholly upon what he finds there. He may elucidate it by systematic reference to other works of the same author. He may throw light upon it from the outside by adopting the method of comparison and contrast. He may go further afield and seek his clue in the principles of historical interpretation. But whatever his plan, his one aim is to know, and to help us to know, the book in itself. He will pass no definite verdict upon it from the point of view of his own taste, or of any organized body of critical opinion.

An elaborate statement of the aims and methods of the critic as interpreter will be found in the long plea for a purely scientific kind of literary criticism with which Prof. Moulton prefaces his study of *Shakespeare as a Dramatic Artist*. 'The prevailing notions of criticism,' Mr Moulton points out, 'are dominated by the idea of *assaying*, as if its function were to test the soundness, and estimate the comparative value of literary work. Lord Macaulay, than whom no one has a better right to be heard on the subject' (this, I may say in passing, seems to me a much exaggerated view of Macaulay's importance as a critic), 'compares his office of reviewer to that of a king-at-arms, versed in the laws of literary procedure, marshalling authors to the exact seats to which they are entitled. And, as a matter of fact, the bulk of literary criticism, whether in popular conversation or in discussions of professed critics, occupies itself with the merits of authors and works; founding its estimates and arguments on canons of taste, which are assumed as having met with general acceptance, or deduced from speculations as to fundamental conceptions of literary beauty.'

In opposition to these ideas, Mr Moulton advocates the principles of what he calls 'inductive' criticism. The name itself betrays the origin of the proposed method in the powerful influence of modern science; and Mr Moulton distinctly says that its avowed object is 'to bring the treatment of literature into the circle of the inductive sciences.' Such criticism is, indeed, as he insists, to be regarded, not as a branch of literature, but as a branch of science. As such, it seeks scientific accuracy and scientific impartiality. 'The treatment aimed at is one independent of praise or blame, one that has nothing to do with merit, relative or absolute.' The inductive critic, like the investigator in any other field of scientific research, with whom he boldly claims comradeship, therefore 'reviews the phenomena of literature as they actually stand, inquiring into and endeavouring to systematise the laws and principles by which they are moulded and produce their effects,' and recognising 'no court of appeal except the appeal to the literary works themselves.'

Three important points of contrast may thus be indicated—we still follow Mr Moulton—between the older judicial and the new inductive methods. In the first place, judicial criticism is largely concerned with the question of the order of merit among literary works. This question lies outside of science. 'A geologist is not heard extolling old red sandstone as a model rock-formation, or making sarcastic comments on the glacial epoch.' As a scientist, the inductive critic knows nothing about differences in degree; he knows only differences in kind. Contrasted literary methods—as, *e.g.*, the method of Shakespeare and the method of Ben Jonson in the drama—are considered by him, not as higher and lower, but simply as distinct, 'in the way in which a fern is distinct from a flower.' Such distinction allows 'no room for preference because there is no common ground on which to compare.' The differences between author and author are therefore to be marked and formulated, but no attempt is to be made to estimate their respective values.

Secondly, judicial criticism rests on the idea that the so-called laws of literature are like the laws of morality or the laws of the state—that is, that they are imposed by an external authority, and are binding on the artist as the laws of morality and of the state are binding on the man. For the inductive critic such laws do not exist. For him the laws of literature are precisely what the laws of nature are for the natural scientist—not conditions superimposed from without, but 'facts reduced to formulæ.' The laws of nature are merely a generalised statement of the order actually observed among phenomena. The laws of literature are to be taken in a precisely similar sense. They express what is, not what conceivably ought to be. Thus 'the laws of the Shakespearean Drama are not laws imposed by some external authority upon Shakespeare,' and for obedience to which he has to be held responsible, 'but laws of dramatic practice derived from the analysis of his actual works.' It is only in the language of metaphor, therefore, that we can properly say that Shakespeare 'obeys' such or such 'laws' of the drama, as it is only in the language of metaphor that we can properly say that the stars 'obey' the law of gravitation. The critic's business is thus not to test Shakespeare's practice by its conformity, or want of conformity, to certain abstract ideas of the drama or to rules independently drawn up, but simply to discover by direct examination of his plays the principles upon which they were written, and then to reduce the results of such examination to a generalised statement.

This leads to the third point of contrast between the judicial and the inductive methods. Judicial criticism proceeds upon the hypothesis that there are 'fixed standards' by which literature may be tried and adjudged. These standards have varied greatly with different critics and in different ages, and this fact furnishes us with one reason why criticism in general has so frequently fallen into disrepute; yet the existence of some such standards has none the less been assumed. In ductive criticism recognises no fixed standards, and indeed denies their possibility. Like all other phenomena dealt with by the sciences, literature is a product of evolution; its history is a history of unceasing transformations; and thus the quest for permanent criteria is foredoomed to inevitable failure, since it postulates finality where in the very nature of things no finality will ever be found.[240]

---

[240]Contrast the following emphatic statement in an early number of the *Edinburgh Review*: 'Poetry has this much in common with religion, that its canons were fixed long ago by certain inspired writers, whose authority it is no longer

Thus, to sum up, 'inductive criticism will examine literature in the spirit of pure investigation; looking for the laws of art in the practice of artists, and treating art like the rest of nature as a thing of continuous development, which may thus be expected to fall, with each author and school, into varieties distinct in kind from one another, and each of which can be fully grasped only when examined with an attitude of mind adapted to the special variety without interference from without.'

According to this view of its functions, then, criticism has nothing whatever to do with the supposed or possible value of a piece of literary art, or with our personal feelings concerning it. Ignoring all considerations of individual taste and all questions of absolute or comparative merit, the critic, as scientist, addresses himself wholly to the labour of investigation. He is, as Taine once phrased it, a kind of botanist whose subject matter, however, is not the phenomena of plant-life, but those of literature.

We have here, it will be seen, a theory of inductive criticism which carries us no further than this—that the law of each author's work must be sought within that work itself: the implication being that the law so found can never be applied to the work of any other author, and therefore can never be used as a standard of judgment or even as a guide. This conclusion raises a problem which we shall have to deal with presently. In the meantime we must not fail to note that a conception of criticism is possible which, while denying the validity of the older judicial practice, does not necessarily entail the repudiation of the critic's right to estimate and judge. The key to this conception is provided by the principle of the relativity of literature and the historical method of interpretation.

For a succinct account of it we may turn to a great French critic already named—M. Edmond Scherer. Taking up the study of *Paradise Lost*, Scherer was struck by the diametrically opposed opinions of it of two such men as Voltaire and Macaulay, of whom the one indulged

---

lawful to call in question.'

in unmeasured disparagement, the other in unqualified laudation. Is either the disparagement or the laudation, he asked, to be taken as a real verdict upon the poem? Does either give us any true account of its greatness, its shortcomings, its place among the masterpieces of literature? Certainly not. These are not unbiassed judgments at all; they are merely expressions of personal idiosyncracies in the critics. They lack entirely that quality which beyond all others we should demand in one who sets up as a judge of literature—the quality of detachment and impartiality. They tell us what a brilliant Frenchman of the eighteenth century and what a clever Englishman of the nineteenth century respectively thought about Milton's monumental work; but they do not help us to form for ourselves a disinterested judgment upon it. As they stand, they simply cancel one another; our own pre- possessions may impel us towards Voltaire's view, or towards Macaulay's; but in themselves they leave us unconvinced and unenlightened. How then shall we ourselves proceed in the hope of establishing a point of view beyond personal feeling—a point of view from which, irrespective of any question whether we ourselves enjoy or do not enjoy the poem, we may see *Paradise Lost* as it really is? By adopting, Scherer replies, the modern historical method. This method, he argues, is 'at once more conclusive and more equitable' than that of the older schools of criticism, because it 'sets itself to understand things rather than to class them, to explain them rather than to judge them.' Its aim is 'to account for a work from the genius of its author, and from the turn this genius has taken from the circumstances amidst which it was developed.' Our first business in approaching the study of *Paradise Lost*, therefore, will be to eliminate as far as possible all personal bias, arising either from individual temperament and predilections or from the literary habits and tastes of our own time and circle, and to 'account for' the poem—to explain it as it is, in all its varied characteristics of matter and style—by an exhaustive analysis of Milton's genius and environment—of the man himself and the sum total of the influences, intellectual, artistic, political, which, whether we deem it to have

been for good or evil, actually left their impress upon him.[241] Up
to this point the critic is still regarded as an investigator, though
the elements of personality and milieu—factors which do not enter
into Mr Moulton's scheme—are now brought forward for special
emphasis. But here Scherer parts company with those who, like
Mr Moulton, decline to advance from interpretation to judgment.
'Our of these two things,' he maintains—'the analysis of the writer's
character and the study of his age—there spontaneously issues the
right understanding of his work:' and this right understanding, in turn,
furnishes us with a criterion by which to estimate its position and
value. 'In place of an appreciation thrown off by some chancecomer,
we have the work passing judgment, so to speak, upon itself, and
assuming the rank which belongs to it among the productions of
the human mind.'[242]

As it is manifestly no part of our present plan to undertake
any comprehensive discussion of modern theories concerning the
purposes and methods of criticism, these two writers must suffice to
illustrate the marked tendency of our time to regard interpretation
as the chief, if not the only, end of the critic's task. While Mr
Moulton rejects judicial criticism entirely, M. Scherer endeavours
to find foundations for such criticism deeper and more stable than
can ever be provided by *a priori* formulas or individual tastes. But
the English critic and the French critic are at one in their desire to
escape from the narrow, inflexible, haphazard methods of the older
schools, and in their attempt to carry into the study of literature

---

[241]To underline the moral of Scherer's advice, we may recall the case of William
Morris, who, making no attempt to escape from himself and his age, openly
expressed his dislike of Milton on the ground that he was at once a puritan
and classicist. But for the historical student the fact that Milton uses the forms
of the classic epic and the humanistic learning of the Renaissance as a vehicle
for his puritan philosophy, is of the utmost value in helping him to 'account for'
Paradise Lost, and therefore in the deepest sense to understand and appreciate it.
[242]In these citations from Scherer I have adopted Arnold's translations as given
in his essay, *A French Critic on Milton*, in *Mixed Essays*.

the larger, more flexible and more systematic methods of science.

It would not be easy to exaggerate the importance of the fresh leads thus indicated. We may follow them with an exhilarating sense that they will assure us of substantial results in a real and living knowledge of the things which concern us most in whatever work or author we may take up for our study.

Lord Morley has rightly protested that it is nothing short of a disgrace to human intelligence that, generation after generation, learned men should have continued to dispute about the meaning of Aristotle's famous dictum about tragedy, instead of going straight to the phenomena of tragedy and inquiring into their significance for themselves.[243] But literary criticism, throughout its entire range, was long crushed in this way beneath the dead weight of authority and the tyranny of preconceived notions. The only way of escape possible from the fluctuations of individual tastes was supposed to lie in recourse to some established code.

Every author had therefore to be judged by canons applied to his work from the outside, while the quality of any new departure in literature was to be estimated only by reference to models—to what had already been accomplished by other writers at other times. The superstitious veneration of the classics, which began with the Renaissance and lingers in scholastic circles even today, inspired a general belief in the value of the Greek and Latin writers as permanent standards of excellence; and even when this particular theory broke down, the critic's practice was still to appeal to some author or school of authors by whom the true laws of literature were assumed to have been exemplified once and for all.

Thus criticism too often degenerated into pedantic disquisitions on matters of little real importance, and sterile efforts to keep production within certain prescribed bounds. It became conventional, dogmatic, arbitrary. It condemned all deviation from the lines it had chosen to lay down in advance; as in the familiar case of Shakespeare

---

[243] *Diderot and the Encyclopedists.*

who, for a long time in France, and by a number of critics even in England, was pronounced barbarous and inartistic because his work did not conform to the laws of that 'classic' drama which had been postulated as the ideal type. Seeing its guidance mainly in the past, such criticism practically denied the principle of development and the right of the new spirit in literature to strike out into fresh paths for itself. It ignored the great fact emphasised by Wordsworth, and illustrated again and again in literary history, that 'every author, as far as he is great and at the same time original, has had the task of creating the taste by which he is to be enjoyed' and therefore, it may be added, of establishing the standards by which his work has to be adjudged.

The methods and results of this older kind of criticism may be studied to advantage in the writings of two of its best-known practitioners—Addison and Johnson.

Addison undertakes a systematic criticism of *Paradise Lost*. But he proceeds upon a plan very different from that advocated by Scherer. He does not seek a 'right understanding' of Milton's poem in 'an analysis of the writer's character and the study of his age.' His method is to 'examine it by the rules of epic poetry, and see whether it falls short of the *Iliad* and the *Æneid* in the beauties which are essential to that kind of poetry.'[244] How are we to discover these 'rules' of epic poetry? How are we to learn in what 'the beauties which are essential' to it actually consist? By the careful study of Homer, Virgil, and Aristotle. By the tests which they furnish our English poet must stand or fall. Now, it must not, of course, be forgotten that, in this particular instance, a certain justification for the critic's procedure may be found in the fact that Milton avowedly fashioned his work upon the structural principles of the classic epic, and that the canons applied by Addison were such, therefore, as, in the main, he himself would have been willing to accept.[245] There

---

[244]*Spectator*, No. 267.
[245]See ante, pp. 58, 59, and contrast Addison's papers on the ballads of *Chevy*

is thus a vital difference between the trial of Milton by 'the rules of epic poetry' and the trial of Shakespeare by the canons of the classic drama. The dogmatic narrowness of the method is none the less apparent in many places; as when the critic finds fault with Milton's 'fable'—as Dryden had done before him[246]—because 'the event is unhappy,' while Aristotle had laid it down as a general rule that an epic poem should end happily; and when he complains of Milton's allegories that they 'rather savour of the spirit of Spenser and Ariosto, than of Homer and Virgil.'

It is therefore the more curious to notice that in one case Addison recognises in passing the principle of development in literature and the consequent impossibility of taking even Aristotle's dicta as definitive: 'in this, and some other very few instances,' he writes, in concluding his survey of Milton's characters, 'Aristotle's rules for epic poetry, which he had drawn from his reflections upon Homer, cannot be supposed to square exactly with the heroic poems which have been made since his time, since it is evident to every impartial judge his rules would still have been more perfect could he have perused the Æneid, which was made some hundred years after his death.' This incidental admission, prompting as it does the further question—would not Aristotle's rules have been even more perfect still could he have perused not only the Æneid but also Paradise Lost—is manifestly fatal to the whole conception of finality in literature, and therefore to the fundamental assumptions on which Addison's criticism rests.[247]

Chace (Spectator, Nos. 70 and 74), and The Babes in the Wood (No. 80), in which the constant appeal to the authority of Horace and Virgil is to us so inopportune as to seem absolutely ludicrous.

[246]Discourse on Satire.

[247]Addison, it will be seen, acknowledges that the Father of Criticism drew his rules for epic poetry 'from his reflections upon Homer'—that is, that he proceeded by the method of induction. He took the writings of the poets he knew and sought to discover by the examination of them the true laws of epic and tragedy. But these laws are only generalised statements of the poets'

Johnson's criticism is equally instructive. As Macaulay says, he 'took it for granted that the kind of poetry which flourished in his own time, which he had been accustomed to hear praised from his childhood, and which he had himself written with success, was the best kind of poetry.'[248] So far as he depended at all upon criteria or precedents for his judgments, it was in this poetry that he sought them. Tacitly, if not expressly, it was to this poetry that he always appealed. The result was that he could see little meaning or merit in any poetry belonging to a different class. He thus failed to rise to the greatness of Shakespeare and Milton, was grossly unjust to Gray, and almost consistently opposed and ridiculed every movement in literature in which—as in the ballad revival of the later eighteenth century—he detected any signs of revolt against what was for him the orthodox literary creed.

If now we turn from Addison and Johnson, whom I have taken as popular exponents of the kind of criticism which prevailed in England down to comparatively recent times, to the writings of any representative critic of the Victorian age, we at once become conscious of an enormous change. The older view of the purposes of criticism is greatly modified even where it is not entirely abandoned; the older methods are practically obsolete. It is not, of course, to be supposed that our critics have ceased to regard themselves, and to be regarded by others, as in a sense at once law-givers and judges, or that they no longer express personal preferences, which on occasion they support by reference to canons and models. It is only here and there that we find the new scientific conception carried out so rigorously that the legislative and judicial functions are

---

practice. In this sense, therefore, Aristotle may be regarded as a forerunner of Mr Moulton. It was not his fault that the *Poetics* subsequently became an obstruction rather than a guide. The great blunder of generations of modern critics was that, instead of following and developing his method, they seized upon his generalisations and made them into a creed, which they proclaimed as having absolute authority and universal applicability.

[248]Essay on Boswell's *Johnson*.

288 WILLIAM HENRY HUDSON

288 WILLIAM HENRY HUDSON

288 ◊ WILLIAM HENRY HUDSON

altogether repudiated. Elsewhere, criticism continues to appraise, and, in appraising, to make free use of æsthetic principles and of standards of comparison. Thus even Matthew Arnold, with all his dread of abstract ideas and of system-making, was still pre-occupied with questions of the 'grand style,' which alone is to be pronounced truly 'classic,'[249] and with the establishment of 'touchstones' of poetry;[250] while in his horror of the vagaries of English thought he even went so far as to eulogise the French Academy as a 'sovereign organ of the highest literary opinion, a recognised authority in matters of intellectual tone and taste'.[251] Nonetheless, the general transformation is unmistakable. The modern critic—and Arnold himself may be taken as a type—is for the most part more anxious to understand and interpret than to 'distribute praise and blame; while that spirit of eclecticism, which is one of the salient features of our age, and the evolutionary methods which are fast invading every department of thought, have combined to give him a breadth of outlook, a catholicity of comprehension and sympathy, a sense of change and growth, of personality and historic relationships, all of which were conspicuously lacking in the criticism of the older schools.

With most of what Mr Moulton says so forcibly about the ineptitude and futility of the criticism of the past, we of the present generation, bred in the new ways of thinking, must therefore cordially agree. At the same time it is, I believe, impossible to follow him to one of his principal conclusions. I do not for the moment discuss the general question whether, as he maintains, literary criticism can ever be reduced to a science in the same way as botany and geology have been reduced to sciences.[252] My point of dissent is his

---

[249] *On Translating Homer.*

[250] *The Study of Poetry* (*Essays*, Second Series).

[251] *Literary Influence of Academies* (*Essays*, First Series).

[252] A consideration which Mr Moulton appears to have overlooked may here just be touched on. As Herbert Spencer showed, the work of science in any given field of phenomena is never completed until the generalisations established by induction have been explained by reference to principles, and thus restated in deductive form. Science, therefore, seeks to answer the question *Why*, as well

total condemnation of judicial criticism as such. However valuable may be the results achieved by the inductive method, they are results with which the student of literature cannot, after all, be permanently satisfied. While this method may thus be welcomed as a most important instrument of criticism, it cannot be accepted as a complete substitute for all other methods.

The scientific critic of literature, let us remember, has, according to Mr Moulton's emphatic statement, 'nothing to do with merit, relative or absolute.' Differences in kind he knows; differences in degree he does not know. He seeks 'the laws and principles' of a given body of literature, like the Shakespearean drama, within the work itself; having found them, he formulates them; but he has no opinion to pass upon them. The questions whether the criticism of life contained in the Shakespearean drama is sound or unsound, and whether the artistic principles underlying its practice are good or bad, are questions which lie outside his field as a scientific investigator of the phenomena as they stand.

These questions, and all other questions of the same general character, are, however, both inevitable and legitimate. They force themselves upon our attention; we cannot evade them; if for no other reason than that we need guidance in our reading, we have a right to demand an answer to them. For here, as it must be evident, the parallel between literature and a natural science, like geology, collapses. Geology deals with phenomena which involve no elements of personality, truth and falsehood, emotional power, artistic effects. Such elements are of the essence of literature, which exists to interpret life under the forms of art, and which, therefore, must be estimated by the quality both of the interpretation and of the art. In studying geology we inquire only what a given thing is and how it came to be what it is. We explain it; and with the

---

as the question *How.* Thus the problem arises as to the way in which the critic is to proceed in any attempt to present, for example, not merely a generalised statement of the 'laws' of the Shakespearean drama, but a rationale of those laws in the form of a series of deductions from the first principles of dramatic effect.

explanation our interest ends. In studying literature, these inquiries lead straight to the further problem of the significance of the thing explained to us and to other people—to the problem, that is, of its human and technical merits and defects. It is useless, indeed, to insist that even for one who approaches the subject matter of literature as he would approach that of geology, in the spirit of 'pure investigation,' merits and defects do not exist. They are assumed by the scientist himself; Mr Moulton assumes them; for if he devotes a bulky and most stimulating volume to the inductive exposition of Shakespeare's art, it is clear that he holds it worthwhile to do so because, like the rest of us, guided to begin with by some 'canons of taste,' he is convinced of Shakespeare's supremacy as a dramatic artist, and thus believes that his artistic methods are interesting not only as Shakespeare's methods, but also as methods which we may consider on the whole excellent in their kind. Otherwise, precisely as the geologist is indifferent to any considerations of 'value' in the rocks he studies, he might just as well have written at large on the dramatic art of Sheridan Knowles or even the author of *Box and Cox*. Mr Moulton, however, picks out Shakespeare because he is admittedly 'great,' and his work is in fact designed to exhibit, not only his methods, but his greatness. A certain estimate of Shakespeare is thus postulated to start with. Merit, relative or absolute, is recognised.

This is only what we might expect. However much we may talk about a science of criticism, judgment in literature is universal. The schoolboy judges, in his own simple fashion, when he pronounces a book 'jolly' or 'slow'; his sister judges when she speaks of a story as 'pretty' or the reverse. No one can read intelligently without forming some opinion as to the value of what he reads; and one of the first questions that we put to a friend who brings a new book to our notice is the question what he thinks of it. As we go further in our study of literature, the problem of valuation necessarily becomes increasingly complex and difficult; more and more we find ourselves bound to reserve judgment where once we pronounced a dogmatic opinion; to reconsider where formerly we had assumed a view as final. The failure of the critics themselves to come to any agreement upon matters which seem fundamental often induces a mood of scepticism, sometimes a mood of disgust. But not for these reasons shall we ever be tempted to abandon the problem, or to adopt the wholly impartial and non-committal attitude of the scientific investigator. What the inductive critic gives us we shall always accept with gratitude; but we shall none the less turn to the judicial critic in the hope that he may complete the work of induction by helping us, on the basis of the results obtained, to distinguish between what is excellent in literature and what is not. Differences in degree do exist, and "tis to mistake them, costs the time and pain.' Unless we take up the position that, as to the geologist all kinds of rock-formation are of equal importance, so to us as 'scientific' students all kinds of literature are of equal importance—in which case it can hardly matter whether we spend our lives over masterpieces or trash—the great problem of literary values remains as urgent as ever. This being so, judicial criticism—the criticism which seeks to solve this problem— however numerous its past errors may have been, however certain the failures which in the future will continue to testify to the countless difficulties which beset its path—will thus have a place to fill and a duty to perform.

III

Thus far we have dealt with the literature of exposition and judgment from the point of view only of its connection with the literature which forms its theme. Another aspect of our subject has now to be introduced.

While in the first instance we shall probably have recourse to a given piece of criticism because of our interest in the book or author discussed in it, we shall soon be led to realise that it has at the same time another claim upon our attention. Arnold's *Essays in Criticism*, for example, may appeal to us, to begin with, only as aids to the fuller appreciation of Wordsworth or Byron, of Shelley or Keats. But apart from the help they may give us in this way, apart therefore from their subordinate significance as means to an end, they have a substantial value of their own as an expression of the critic himself—of his personality, thought, methods, aims. Even if we should find Arnold's utterances on this or that poet unsatisfying, even if they prove of little or no service to us as means to an end, they will still remain interesting as *his* utterances; and what is true in regard to Arnold is equally true, of course, in regard to all great critics. This implies that criticism, though it may be conceived primarily as an instrument in the study of literature, is not to be conceived as an instrument only. It is itself a form of literature, and as such it deserves to be considered for its own sake. In the study of the literature of criticism we shall naturally follow the lines already indicated for the study of literature in general.

Personality being the elemental fact in all literature we start, of course, with the critic himself. Our chief occupation will now be with his fitness for the post of interpreter and judge. It is evident that his report upon a book or author can have no real interest for us unless we have some assurance that he speaks as one having in respect of the particular matter in hand a special right to be heard. Various questions regarding his qualifications will, therefore, have to be considered, upon the more important of which only it will be necessary here to touch.

In the first place, how far does he approximate in intellectual composition and temper to what we may define as the perfect critical ideal? And, since approximation only is humanly possible, to what extent and at what points is it requisite that we should make allowance for his deficiencies? The true critic must be mentally alert and flexible, keen in insight, quick in response to all impressions, strong in grasp of essentials; he must, moreover, as Matthew Arnold will tell us, be able to see a thing as it really is, and not distorted through a mist of his own idiosyncracies and prepossessions; which means that he must be entirely disinterested and free from bias of all kinds—bias of individual tastes, bias of education, bias of creed, sect, party, class, nation. Now since, as we say, we can never expect to have these conditions completely fulfilled—since, in fact, even the greatest critics, even a critic like Lessing, fail only too conspicuously to fulfil them—it will be needful for us to watch carefully for every sign of disturbance in the free play of the critic's mind upon his subject, to trace it if we can to its sources, to 'account for' it, as Scherer would seek to account for the qualities and limitations of Milton's genius, and to estimate the range of its influence and the bearings of its results. A critic's attitude to his author—the attitude, for example, of Arnold to Wordsworth and Shelley respectively—will often lead us to question whether this attitude is not to be explained by some peculiarity in the critic himself. We shall find that in many instances criticism which, within certain limits, is marked by vigour of understanding and sound sense is, outside those limits, sadly marred and sometimes rendered wholly untrustworthy by some dominant habit of mind or ingrained prejudice. A striking illustration is afforded by Johnson, who was, according to his lights, an admirable judge of literature when he was in sympathy with his author's aims and principles, but quite the reverse of admirable when he had to deal with writers with whom, for one or another reason, he was out of sympathy. Thus we get the best of his work—and very good of the kind this is—in his lives of such men as Pope and Addison, who were exponents of the literary ideals which he esteemed; and the worst of it—and very bad this is—in his treatment of Milton and Gray, where his judgment was perverted, in the one case by political, in the other by personal and literary antipathies.[253]

In Coleridge, again, while in the faculty of insight and poetic intuition he is entitled to take rank with the greatest of English critics, the power to see things as they really are was often destroyed by metaphysical preoccupations and a veneration for certain chosen

---

[253]It will be noted that he handles Collins far more tenderly than Gray, even where the two men represent broadly the same, to him, objectionable tendencies in the poetry of the time. This is to be accounted for by his personal interest in Collins the man, and therefore furnishes another example of bias.

authors as irrational and superstitious as that of the pseudo-classic theorists of the seventeenth and eighteenth centuries for the literatures of Greece and Rome. He has been greatly praised for his criticism of Shakespeare; yet that criticism, stimulating and suggestive as it frequently is, is none the less characterised by the wildest extravagances. It is Coleridge, for instance, whom we in England must hold primarily responsible for the long-standing unhistorical and wholly 'subjective' treatment of Shakespeare, and for the popularity of the nonsense which is still talked about Shakespeare's 'universality,' or complete independence of all conditions of time and place. 'When Coleridge writes a criticism of Shakespeare,' says Mr Arthur Symons, 'he is giving us his [Coleridge's] deepest philosophy.'[254] True. But we must never forget that it is his philosophy that he is thus giving us, not Shakespeare's. In following his interpretations we must always be alive to the importance of distinguishing sharply between what he reads out of Shakespeare and what he reads into him. We shall thus often find it necessary to clear Coleridge's 'deepest philosophy' altogether out of the way in order to see the work of Shakespeare, the Elizabethan dramatist, as it really is—as the product of his genius and his age.

A third case in point is provided by none other than Arnold himself, and this is, of course, particularly instructive, because Arnold made it his mission to preach disinterestedness, and certainly did his utmost to practise it. Yet even in him traces of a distinct bias are frequently apparent—a bias due mainly to his early Oxford training and his rather too narrow academic culture. This led him to exaggerate the value of the Greek masters[255] and to overstate the claims of classical studies as a school of taste. It even caused him at times to revert to the older notions of absolute criteria and of

---

[254]Introduction to *Biographia Literaria*, in *Everyman's Library*.

[255]His remark in a letter to Miss Arnold, that Homer leaves Shakespeare 'as far behind as perfection leaves imperfection,' may be cited as a curious bit of extravagance (*Letters*, i, 148).

finality in literature; as when he called Scott's poetic style 'bastard epic,' though, as he ought to have remembered, it is not 'epic' at all, and tested the Wizard's narrative poems by what he termed the 'highest standards'—meaning the standards furnished by the epics of classical antiquity—in defiance of the fact that *Marmion* and *The Lady of the Lake* are poems of an entirely different kind from the *Iliad* and the *Odyssey*, and that, as Mr Moulton would have told him, the 'laws' of their composition are therefore to be sought in themselves, and not in the practice of Homer.

It is unnecessary to adduce further examples of the disturbance in judgment caused by the various kinds of bias, which are apt at times to interfere with the steadiness of a critic's vision and the impartiality of his views. Enough has been said to enforce the principle laid down, that in our study of a critic's writings it is important to take stock of his prepossessions, to observe their influence upon his thought, and, in estimating the value of his work, to make due allowance for them.

A critic's qualifications do not, however, depend only upon his natural gifts, and thus a second question arises in regard to his equipment for his work. Most of us have known persons of meagre scholarship and no technical training, whose instinctive feeling for what is good in literature has none the less given them a surprising power of discernment and appreciation. The honest judgment of a capable general reader on a book, like the honest judgment of a capable amateur on a picture, is never to be despised; it has often in fact a great value if only because it is fresh, independent, and free from the insidious influence of that perhaps most widespread of all forms of bias—the professional. At the same time, for systematic criticism, scholarship and technical training are clearly requisite. 'No more in literature than elsewhere,' writes one of the ablest of modern French critics, 'has the chance-comer the right to pronounce upon the value of work done, nor, whatever one may say about it, to judge of art without a long and laborious education of his taste. If aptitudes are not necessary'—though it is difficult to see how their necessity can, upon any hypothesis, be denied—'at least an apprenticeship is.'[256] This, perhaps, is rather too strongly put, and smacks a little too much of the tendency of the academic critic to regard literary appreciation as the business of an exclusive 'Brahmin caste.' But the general truth of the statement cannot be questioned. For the critic of literature, as for the critic of art, a special education is essential; and by education we must here understand, as always, both acquisition of knowledge and discipline of mind. The critic needs knowledge to give him breadth of view and to provide a proper basis for his judgment. He needs discipline of mind to make that knowledge serviceable. Other things being equal, his competence as interpreter and judge will be in proportion to his knowledge and discipline; and if these are lacking, his opinions, however interesting and suggestive, will carry little weight.

Thus, to illustrate by extreme cases, though we cannot go with Addison in his belief that the *Iliad* and the *Æneid* furnish the final rules of all epic poetry, we must still hold that a writer is but poorly qualified to discuss the art of *Paradise Lost* who is not himself familiar with the work of Milton's own masters; while a thorough and comprehensive acquaintance with the world's greatest productions in drama and prose fiction may safely be postulated as indispensable for anyone who would undertake to pass formal judgment on a play or a novel.[257] We can hardly dissent from Arnold's view that a knowledge of 'one great literature, besides his own, and the more unlike his own the better,' is the irreducible minimum of scholarship

---

[256]Brunetière, *L'Évolution des Genres*, p. 127.

[257]It must not be forgotten that inadequate knowledge of the real principles of the Greek drama and of Aristotle's criticism was in large measure responsible for the psuedo-classicism of the seventeenth and eighteenth centuries. This was triumphantly proved by the greatest of eighteenth-century critics, Lessing. Herbert Spencer's frequently perverse and some- times grotesque judgments on poetry and painting, while to some extent due to his temperament and his constitutional love of opposition, may also be explained in part by reference to his want of knowledge and training in these particular subjects.

necessary for a critic's preparation; while there is nothing really extravagant in his further contention that a 'proper outfit' must comprise a knowledge of what is best in all European literatures, ancient and modern, and even of the literature of Eastern antiquity.[258] Too exclusive devotion to any one kind of literature is certain to result in narrowness and obliquity of judgment.

It is worthwhile to insist upon the critic's need of training and discipline, for the matter has a practical bearing. One of the most curious and discouraging features of current newspaper and magazine criticism, at any rate in England and America, is its general want of measure, sobriety, and perspective. A new novel is published—a book perhaps with various admirable qualities and well deserving a word of cordial recognition. We turn to a notice of it in this or that journal, and we find the reviewer almost beside himself in a frenzy of wonder and excitement. The work is hailed as a masterpiece, its author pronounced on the spot a consummate artist compared with whom—if we are to take his language at anything like its literal meaning—Scott was a bungler and Dickens a mere novice. A few years go by; the great book and its author disappear from sight or drop back into the rank of the ephemerals; and the reviewer, who seems incapable of learning from experience, unblushingly breaks forth into another paean over the arrival of another masterpiece from the pen of another genius of the first order. These vagaries of periodical criticism point, of course, to a general laxity in contemporary taste. The average reviewer is so little impressed by the responsibilities of his office, and so little solicitous for the true interests of literature, that he does not pause to weigh his words or to consider the real significance of his opinions; while a public which reads current literature with the object (if the signs do not mislead us) of getting through as much as possible as quickly as possible and then forgetting it, naturally imposes no restraint upon him. It cannot, of course, be alleged that this deplorable laxity would be overcome merely

---

[258] *Function of Criticism at the Present Time*, in Essays, First Series.

by an increase of knowledge and discipline in those who set up as guides to popular taste in literary matters. But increase of knowledge and discipline would certainly help to secure some sense of that measure, sobriety, and perspective without which criticism is worse than useless.

In the systematic study of the work of any critic there are thus several points to be kept in view. We have to inquire into his personal qualities and equipment, and the extent to which they are likely to have aided or impeded him in his task of adjudicating upon a particular book or author; we have to watch for every indication of bias, and to consider both its sources and its bearings; we have to examine the foundations of his judgments and the standard to which, expressly or by implication, he makes his appeal. Nor must we overlook the important question of the general spirit of his work. A critic may write with an honest desire to understand his author, to interpret him, to do justice to him; or he may write with the too evident purpose of exhibiting his own learning and cleverness at his author's expense; he may be sympathetic, temperate, and anxious chiefly to see what is good; or he may be carping, censorious, and deter- mined to hunt out faults and dwell on failings. Whatever otherwise we may think of Addison's criticism, for example, we must at least acknowledge that its tone is admirable. Holding, as he did, that the 'true critic' ought to seek rather 'excellencies than imperfections,' he regarded it as his principal duty 'to discover the concealed beauties of a writer, and communicate to the world such things as are worth their observation.'[259] The tone of Lord Jeffrey's criticism, on the other hand, is too frequently the reverse of admirable; his idea apparently being, as Prof. Saintsbury has put it, that 'an author necessarily came before the critic with a rope about his neck, and was only entitled to be exempted from being strung up *speciali gratia* '—an idea, Mr Saintsbury rightly adds, which, 'as presumptuous as it is foolish, is not extinct yet, and has done a

---

[259] *Spectator,* No. 291.

great deal of harm to criticism, both by prejudicing those who are not critical against critics, and by perverting and twisting the critic's own notion of his province and duty.'[260] No one will deny that there are many cases in which critical severity is amply justified, or that, if arrogance is always wrong, mere weak and undiscrimmating clemency can never be right. But this is not now the question. For the moment we have only to insist upon the importance of including the spirit of a critic's writings among the characteristics of his work, and of observing the way in which it enters into and often colours his judgments.

IV

In the study of criticism, as in the study of other kinds of literature, we shall proceed next to extend and render more definite our knowledge of the individual writer by recourse to comparison and contrast. We shall place his work beside that of other critics who have dealt with the same subjects—the same books, authors, periods, or classes of literature; and in this way we shall seek to realise, more fully than would be possible were they considered separately, the powers and limitations of each. No longer satisfied, as in casual reading we are apt to be satisfied, merely to note agreement or dis- agreement in the judgments pronounced, we shall examine carefully all points of similarity and difference in the things which lie behind judgment—in personal attitude and proclivities; in the line of approach adopted; in the particulars emphasised or neglected; in methods, manner, standards, temper, taste. The results achieved by such comparative study will be found not only interesting in themselves, but will also be of special value in helping us to trace the qualities of each critic's work to their ultimate sources in character, education, and aims.

The further we go afield in this comparative study the more certainly we shall be struck by the extraordinary diversity of critical opinions, and by what I have already described as the failure of the

---

[260]*History of Nineteenth Century Literature*, p. 175.

critics to come to any agreement among themselves in respect of even essential matters. It is this which, as I have said, has been largely responsible for the contempt with which criticism has frequently been treated, and for the odium which it has incurred. Particularly perhaps has the widespread notion of the fundamental futility of all criticism received a certain amount of justification from the notorious fact that contemporary judgments concerning new works, whether in the way of praise or condemnation, have failed so signally in giving any true measure of the permanent value of such works that they have often been completely reversed by posterity.[261]

In many cases, of course, these differences in critical opinion are personal differences only; as such they must be accepted; as such, it is scarcely necessary now to add, they are in themselves interesting. But it will also be found, as might be anticipated, that differences and agreements alike often fall into groups. A certain amount of general conformity—of approximation to unanimity—is commonly observable among critics of the same epoch and school, and a certain amount of general nonconformity, or want of unanimity, among critics of different epochs and schools. Individual characteristics may thus to some extent be subsumed in the characteristics of the class to which each critic belongs. This is only the inevitable result of that

---

[261]It is well known that contemporary judgments of now acknowledged masterpieces furnish matter for a curious chapter in literary history. It is hard to say whether we ought to be more pained or amused, when, for example, we find the *Edinburgh Review* speaking of Coleridge's *Christabel*, as 'a mixture of raving and drivelling,' and pronouncing Wordsworth's *Ode on the Intimations of Immortality* 'illegible and unintelligible.' Prof. Dowden has collected some telling illustrations of critical obtuseness and perversity in his essay on The Interpretation of Literature (*Contemporary Review*, 1886). It is noteworthy that many critics who show the finest taste and sagacity in dealing with the literature of the past often fail to perceive or acknowledge the claims of the literature of their own time. Thus Arnold, who was so keenly alive to the value of Wordsworth's 'criticism of life,' spoke of Tennyson as 'deficient in intellectual power.' A tendency to discredit the present in favour of the past in literature, as elsewhere, is a very common kind of bias.

dependence of literature upon the life of the age which produces it, of which I have spoken at length in a former chapter. No less than all other kinds of literature, criticism, while never ceasing to be the vehicle of personality, is also in part the expression of the spirit of the epoch out of which it comes.[262]

We are thus led from the consideration of individual critics to the historical study of criticism—a field of immense interest, because the history of criticism contains the record of the changes which from age to age have come over men's conception of literature, of its aims and principles, its matter and methods, of the things which are to be sought and avoided in it, and of the standards by which it is to be judged.

A simple plan, and one which will naturally suggest itself to every student, is that of following and collating the variations which have taken place in critical opinion about particular representative authors. One most notable illustration—that furnished by the history of Shakespeare criticism from the restoration to the time of Coleridge, or even later—stands ready to hand; but this has been so often used that I prefer to set it aside for one less familiar,[263] but not in its own way less instructive. This is provided by the case of Bunyan.

---

[262]I do not think it necessary to burden the text with any discussion of racial qualities in criticism (see chapter 11, § 1). That—to mention a single example— the French and English points of view in regard to all questions which enter into critical consideration will generally be markedly different, and often quite opposed, will be evident to every reader. It is equally clear that the study of their differences as expressive of differences in racial ideas, both of literature and of life, will be found extremely suggestive. It has frequently been said that the contemporary foreign judgment of a book or author anticipates the judgment of posterity; but history yields little to support, and much to invalidate this daring proposition, which even on general grounds would appear to be quite untenable. Nonetheless, if we desire to cultivate the temper of disinterestedness we can hardly do better than to study carefully the writings of good foreign critics who have dealt with our own literature—such critics, for instance, as Sainte-Beuve, Scherer, and Brunetière.

[263]A sketch of the history of Shakespeare criticism will be found in the introductory chapter of Moulton's *Shakespeare as a Dramatic Artist*.

The eighteenth century, with its dominant notions of dignity in literature, its narrow conceptions of art, and its general inability to recognise the value of naturalness and simplicity, as a matter of course gave little critical attention to the Elstow tinker; so far as professed students and exponents of taste took cognisance of him at all, they regarded him (with few exceptions, of whom Swift and Johnson may be reckoned the most important) as a writer for the 'illiterate' and the 'vulgar' only. Thus, for example, Young, in one of his satires, links 'Bunyan's prose' with 'Durfey's verse'—a proverbial type of sheer doggerel; Hume indulges in a passing expression of contempt for him;[264] Burke talks about the possibility that a certain class of readers might perhaps enjoy the *Æneid* 'if it were degraded into the style of *The Pilgrim's Progress*'; in the reprint of this work in Cooke's *Pocket Library* (1797), it is distinctly stated that 'it cannot come under the Denomination of a Classic Production'; while Cowper testifies to the current taste of the time when in his *Tirocinium* he writes of its author:

I name thee not, lest so despised a name
Should move a sneer at thy deserved fame.

We pass abruptly into the thirties of the nineteenth century, and we find Macaulay eulogising Southey's edition of *The Pilgrim's Progress*, as 'an eminently beautiful and splendid edition of a book which well deserves all that the printer and engraver can do for it'; proclaiming it a 'wonderful' book, which 'obtains admiration from the most fastidious critics'; and speaking of its style—its 'depraved' style—as 'delightful to every reader'; after which, to cite only two

---

[264]"Whoever would assert an equality of genius and elegance between Ogilby and Milton, or Bunyan and Addison, would be thought to defend no less an extravagance, than if he had maintained a mole-hill to be as high as Teneriffe, or a pond as extensive as the ocean. Though there may be found persons who give the preference to the former authors, no one pays attention to such a taste; and we pronounce, without scruple, the sentiments of these pretended critics to be absurd and ridiculous' (*Essay of the Standard of Taste*).

from among recent enthusiastic critics, Mr Gosse pronounces this style 'perfection' in its kind, and roundly declares that Bunyan's 'allegory is successful above all other allegories in literature'; while Mr Stopford Brooke writes of his best-known book: 'Its form is almost epic: its dramatic dialogue, its clear types of character, its vivid descriptions, as of Vanity Fair, and of places, such as the Valley of the Shadow of Death and the Delectable Mountains, which represent states of the human soul, have given an equal but a different pleasure to children and men, to the villager and the scholar.'

How shall we explain the immense general change of attitude and judgment thus exemplified—for a general change it manifestly was? Clearly, the explanation is not to be found in the idiosyncracies of this or that particular critic. It must ultimately be sought in a consideration of all the influences within literature which during a century and a half had combined to transform its methods and spirit, and of all the forces outside literature which had done much to generate these influences through the immense alteration which they had wrought in the moral and religious ideals and temper of the English people. So intimately are all the phenomena of literature and life bound up together that it would thus be impossible to set out in full the story of the rise of this once-neglected writer in critical estimation to the rank of an acknowledged master, without continual reference to the history both of English literature and of English society.

Professor Saintsbury has touched in a suggestive way on the interesting problem of Bunyan's posthumous fame. *The Pilgrim's Progress*, he writes,

> 'has long been, and it may be hoped will always be, well enough known in England. But for something like four generations after its first appearance, its popularity, though always great, was, so to speak, sub-terranean, and almost contraband. It is probable that even when it was most sniffed at by academic criticism, it was brought by means of nursemaids to the knowledge of children. But it was not till quite the end of the eighteenth

century, or even the beginning of the nineteenth, that it was free of the study as it had long been free of the cottage and the nursery. Orthodoxy objected to Bunyan's dissent; dissent to his literary and artistic gifts; latitudinarians to his religious fervour; the somewhat priggish refinement of Addisonian and Popean etiquette to his vernacular language and his popular atmosphere; scholars to his supposed want of education. And so the greatest prose-book of the late seventeenth century in England had, for nearly a hundred and fifty years, the curious fate of constantly exercising influence without ever achieving praise, or even notice, from those whose business it was to give both.'[265]

This brief epitome of some among the many causes which long stood in the way of Bunyan's recognition by the critics, itself, as will be seen, indicates the nature of the changes in many directions which had to be effected before his standing in our literature could be made so secure that a place was found for him in the series of *English Men of Letters*.

The history of critical opinion thus broadens out on every side until it becomes a comprehensive supplement to the history of literary production. It is as such a supplement that we may therefore study, for example, the criticism of the eighteenth and the first decades of the nineteenth centuries, in its connection with the whole movement of literature from the period of dominant classicism to that of established romanticism and naturalism. In the gradual shifting and final reversal of judgment concerning Pope, the central figure of our Augustan age, and what Pope pre-eminently had stood for in poetry, we may follow in the clearest possible way some of the main lines in the great transition. For Dr Johnson, the doughty champion of the Augustan ideals at a time when the attack upon them had already begun, Pope's work, though after his manner he picked innumerable holes in it, was still the last word in poetic art.

---

[265] *Short History of English Literature*, pp. 516, 517.

'New sentiments and new images others may produce, but to attempt any further improvement in versification will be dangerous. Art and diligence have now done their best, and what shall be added will be the effort of tedious toil and needless curiosity. After all this,' the writer concludes, 'it is surely superfluous to answer the question that has once been asked, Whether Pope was a poet, otherwise than by asking in return, If Pope be not a poet, where is poetry to be found? To circumscribe poetry by a definition will only show the narrowness of the definer, though a definition which shall exclude Pope will not easily be made. Let us look round upon the present time, and back upon the past; let us inquire to whom the voice of mankind has decreed the wreath of poetry; let their productions be examined, and their claims stated, and the pretensions of Pope will be no more disputed.'[266]

These sentences, it will be noted, have the ring of apology. Why? Because the pretensions of Pope had already been disputed, and the question to which Johnson alludes, and which he deems it superfluous to answer save by a rhetorical counter-question, had been definitely raised by Joseph Warton (who, as a poet, takes an important place among the early romanticists) in an *Essay on the Genius and Writings of Pope*, the first part of which was published in 1756, or only a dozen years after Pope's death.[267] Warton strikes a distinctly new note by boldly declaring—the point is of the utmost importance as indicating a change of view concerning the essence of poetry—that Pope was a great wit rather than a great poet, since the largest part of his work 'is of the *didactic, moral,* and *satiric*; and, consequently, not of the most *poetic* species of *poetry*; whence it is manifest that *good sense* and *judgment* were his characteristical excellences rather

---

[266]*Life of Pope.*

[267]Boswell records that this was more than once praised by Johnson, who explained Warton's delay in publishing the second volume by the supposition that he found himself 'a little disappointed in not having been able to persuade the world to be of his opinion as to Pope.' Part II did not appear till 1782.

than *fancy* and *invention*.' Lowell describes this essay as 'the earliest public and official declaration of war against the reigning mode.' In the sense that it was the first open attack upon the great master of the reigning mode, this is correct. But ten years before, in his preface to a volume of poems published when the writer was only twenty-four, Warton had written in the same strain:

'The public has been so much accustomed of late to didactic poetry alone, and essays on moral subjects, that any work where the imagination is much indulged, will perhaps not be relished or regarded. The author therefore of these pieces is in some pain lest certain austere critics should think them too fanciful or descriptive. But as he is convinced that the fashion of moralising in verse has been carried too far, and as he looks upon invention and imagination as the chief faculties of a poet, so he will be happy if the following odes may be looked upon as an attempt to bring back poetry into its right channel.'

Indirectly, this is, of course, a challenge to the followers and admirers of Pope. From these utterances we learn that while a few poets at the time were more or less unconsciously experimenting in various kinds of poetry different in matter and manner from that to which Pope had given vogue, romantic criticism was making a preliminary attempt to formulate principles and outline a programme of its own. Without entering into details we may now see why the steady decline of Pope's reputation during the second half of the eighteenth century, and the acceleration of that decline as the century ran its course, are facts of capital importance for the student of literary history. They are unmistakable signs of the rise of the new school of poetry. As we enter the nineteenth century we find the battle waxing hot about the claims, qualities, and position of this long-acknowledged master of English verse. In this battle nearly all the leading critics took part on one or the other side; but the issue was the rout of the, supporters of the Augustan tradition. Bowles's severe strictures—the first shot in what has been called a 'thirty years' war'—drew forth the angry reply of Byron, the last of Pope's 'uncompromising devotees'; but in Byron's untempered eulogy 'we already recognise the note of half-conscious exaggeration usual in the defenders of a no longer tenable cause.'[268] With the triumph of the new school all along the line, the last vestiges of the eighteenth century superstition of Pope's supremacy were destroyed, and Warton's heterodoxy passed into the orthodox literary creed. Then, as Macaulay's essay on Byron (1831) suffices to show, extravagant admiration gave place to depreciation almost, if not quite, as un-critical. 'The time has gone by,' says a most judicial writer, 'for Pope to be ranked among the master-geniuses of our literature.'[269] From this judgment few would now dissent. Yet it is to be regretted that, as a consequence of such sweeping reaction, it is difficult today, as for many years past it has been difficult, to appreciate properly Pope's many substantial merits. In 1756 he stood at the zenith of this fame, and Warton had to be cautious in calling attention to his defects. A hundred years later he was at his nadir, and men like Garruthers, Mark Pattison, and, more recently, Professor Courthope, have found it hard work to convince their public that there is anything deserving praise in him.

Other lines of inquiry running parallel to this, and throwing light repeatedly upon it, will naturally suggest themselves to the student of the same period of our literature. Let me indicate just one of these. Among the most important movements in English poetry during the eighteenth century are those which are known as the Spenserian and the Ballad Revivals. Both of these did much in helping to bring the romantic spirit back into our literature, while the latter also exercised a powerful concurrent influence in breaking down the Augustan ideals of poetic style, and spreading a taste for naturalness and simplicity. Now each revival was, as might be anticipated, accompanied by a great deal of critical theorising and discussion, out of which came here and

---

[268] A.W. Ward, *Introductory Memoir* to Globe Edition of Pope's *Works*.
[269] *Ibid.*

there some work of real and permanent significance; such as Thomas Warton's *Observations on the Faerie Queene*, and (instructive if only on account of the editor's timidity in introducing what proved to be an epoch-making work) Percy's preface to his *Reliques*. If we want to gain a clear idea of what these two movements meant, therefore, it will be an excellent plan to consider carefully the praise and blame which they incurred, the help they received and the opposition which they encountered, the questions to which they gave rise, the controversies about literary principles and ideals which they precipitated, among the critics of the time.

It would be easy of course to multiply illustrations; but enough has, I think, been said to make good the thesis that the history of criticism as a record of changing ideas concerning every aspect and quality of literature provides an almost indispensable supplement to, I may even go so far as to say a valuable commentary upon, the history of literary production. It is, in fact, to the history of criticism that we must often turn if we would discover the rationale of the changes which we have to follow in studying the history of literature.

Several general considerations of some importance may here be mentioned. Criticism, as I have said, has habitually been conservative; it has sought guidance mainly in the past; it has rarely favoured experiments or new departures; its power has commonly been exercised to hamper and restrain. In every period of change, therefore, a struggle has of necessity arisen between the forces of production and those of criticism. This struggle is only one phase of the conflict which is ever going on in all departments of life and thought between liberty and authority, originality and tradition, individuality and rules, the old and the new. In literature as elsewhere, therefore, times of concentration and quiescence, during which the critical spirit predominates and men move only along well-beaten ways, alternate with times of expansion and adventure, during which the creative energy reasserts itself, and impatient genius goes forth in quest of 'fresh woods and pastures new.' In literature, as elsewhere, too, while critical opinion always tends to harden into dogmatic creeds, the process is repeatedly interrupted by the rise and spread of heresies, which, denounced in one generation, become accepted tenets of orthodoxy in the next. And in literature as elsewhere, as we must not fail to remember, if the abuse of authority ends in despotism, liberty may too easily run into licence. Again and again history has proved that the best interests of literature have been subserved by open defiance of the critic's 'this will never do.'

Yet the influence of criticism as a controlling power is not therefore to be despised. If the critics had had their way, there would have been no Shakespearean drama and no Romantic movement. But, on the other hand, no one will deny that some of the conspicuous excesses which characterised both the Shakespearean drama and the Romantic movement might have been checked, and with much advantage, had more attention been paid to the rules of the critics.[270]

It must, however, be borne in mind that, save in the way of restraint and guidance, criticism has played little part in the development of literature. It has seldom given any originative impulse or broken new ground. Occasionally, a fresh movement has been accompanied or even preceded by a critical programme, as was to some extent the case with the Romantic movement in France. But generally creative genius leads the way, and criticism follows. Indeed, when this relation is reversed, the results are seldom very satisfactory, since literature written to order and in accordance with a definite code, is almost certain to be characterised by a certain quality of premeditation and strain. Even where a poet is critic as well as poet, it may be laid down as a general law that he works as a poet best when he works on the natural promptings of his genius, and without thought of illustrating any preconceived theory; as such writers as Wordsworth, Matthew Arnold, and Walt Whitman may be cited to prove. In the general

---

[270]I have elsewhere pointed out that at the time when Shakespeare himself could in *The Winter's Tale* so clearly exemplify the dangers of romantic excess, there was ample warrant for Jonson's propaganda in favour of unity and restraint in the drama (see *Introduction to The Winter's Tale*, in *The Elizabethan Shakespeare*).

evolution of literature, therefore, criticism will be found habitually to lag behind production. Each new movement is likely at first to meet with more or less pronounced critical opposition. But by little and little, theory overtakes practice. Thus criticism gradually adjusts itself to the new ideas and principles; and then it becomes one of the critic's chief functions to draw them out and formulate them, to investigate their foundations, and to explain their meaning.

V

I have now indicated some of the main lines of inquiry which have to be followed in the methodical study of criticism, and some of the principal questions to be considered along the way. It remains for us to deal with the problem of the valuation of literature in its practical bearings.

Two facts stand out clearly. On the one hand, despite all modern theories as to the possibility of a purely 'scientific' kind of criticism in which no effort will be made to pass from interpretation to appraisement, judgment, universal in the past, must still be regarded as one of the proper functions of criticism. On the other hand, the results attained by the exercise of judgment have, on the whole, been so variable, uncertain, and inconclusive, that while its title cannot be impugned, its utility may well be called in question. In view of these facts we cannot be surprised if a very common idea about criticism comes somewhat to this—that every critic has of course a perfect right to hold his own opinion, and to do what lies in his power to persuade other people to agree with him; but that as, in the words of one of Montaigne's favourite mottoes, 'to every opinion an opinion of equal weight may be opposed,' criticism as a whole has proved a mere 'self-cancelling business,' and has accomplished little or nothing towards any final establishment of literary values. It is well enough to talk about a critic's 'judicial' faculty. But, it may be asked, is a critic, strictly speaking, a judge? Is he not rather, and in the very nature of the case, an advocate?

We are thus brought round to the full significance of the

contention, often urged, that all judgment in literature is, whether avowedly or not, necessarily personal in source and character.

> Now, who shall arbitrate?
> Ten men love what I hate,
> Shun what I follow, slight what I receive;
> Ten, who in ears and eyes
> Match me; we all surmise,
> They, this thing, and I, that: whom shall my soul believe?

If I express a certain view concerning the value of a book I have just been reading, this, it is said, is my view, and no more. If someone else expresses a view which absolutely contradicts mine, then we have only one person's individual judgment set against another's. If a third person intervenes in the discussion and agrees with either or neither, he only adds one more individual judgment to increase the confusion. Now here, it may be argued, we have an illustration in little of the processes of criticism at large. 'No two persons ever read the same book,' and each one can talk only of the book that he has read. The professional critic may pose in a judicial role, employ a technical language, and make a vast parade of principles, standards, and authorities. But as he can never escape from himself, his opinions, like those of the first man we may find airing his ignorance and philistinism in a railway carriage, may ultimately be traced back to a purely personal origin. And can criticism ever be redeemed from the charge of mere arbitrariness and caprice which thus rests upon it? Can it ever be more than the registration and formal statement of tastes, likes, dislikes, which fluctuate with the critic's changing moods, and depend on temperament, education, bias? *De gustibus non est dispulandum.*

Among critics themselves, there are not wanting those who take up the position that, however much principles and criteria may be invoked, whatever efforts may be made to eliminate the personal factor, all criticism is fundamentally subjective and impressionistic. Thus Mr Andrew Lang declares that the only criticism worth reading is that which 'narrates the adventures of an ingenious and educated mind in contact with masterpieces'; and thus M. Anatole France insists that a lecturer on literature, if he were really honest, instead of using the time-honoured exordium—'Gentlemen, I am going to speak to you today about Pascal, or Racine, or Shakespeare,' should rather begin his discourse with the words—'Gentlemen, I am going to speak to you today about myself in relation to Pascal, or Racine, or Shakespeare.'

Here, undoubtedly, we come face to face with a real difficulty. Yet it must be observed that even if the extreme view so cleverly put by the brilliant Frenchman be accepted—even if, for the sake of argument, we decline, with him, to acknowledge the existence of any principles which are not mere products of individual taste, and may therefore be of service in controlling and guiding it—we are not necessarily committed to universal nihilism. Looking at the subject for the moment in the broadest possible way, we may fairly maintain that in the vast majority of cases there is an appreciable difference in value between judgment and judgment, for the simple reason that there is an appreciable difference in value between judge and judge. This, indeed, has already been made clear. Every man may be entitled to his own private opinion on questions of literature, as on all other subjects; but there is no subject (and if there be, that subject is certainly not literature) on which one man's opinion can be deemed as good as another's. Mr Lang's likes and dislikes in the matter of books may often seem to some of us a trifle whimsical and even perverse; but they are always worthy of more consideration than those of the man in the street just because he is Mr Lang and has 'an ingenious and educated mind,'; and we listen with greater attention to M. Anatole France when he talks of himself in relation to Pascal, or Racine, or Shakespeare, than to some chance acquaintance who talks of himself in relation to the same theme, because, knowing M. France as we do, we feel assured to begin with that whatever he may have to tell us about his personal impressions will be marked by exceptional insight and sagacity. 'As the object of poetry is to give pleasure,' wrote Lord Jeffrey in one of his essays on Scott, 'it would seem to be a pretty safe conclusion, that that poetry must be the best which gives the greatest pleasure to the greatest number of readers'; after which the critic proceeded to argue (rather feebly it must be confessed) against what he called this 'plausible' proposition. But is any argument required to exhibit its absurdity? Is it really in the least plausible? A hundred persons may enjoy *The Absent-Minded Beggar* for one who enjoys Lycidas; but would any one of the hundred have the temerity to draw the inference to which the suggested 'safe conclusion' points? No one, I think, would venture to apply the Benthamite maxim to matters of art; no one would undertake seriously to contend that popularity is the final test of merit, or that a piece of literature, or a picture, or a musical composition, is to be estimated by its power of appeal to the uneducated multitude rather than to the educated few.

It is reported that at the present time one of the most widely-read of English novelists is a certain manufacturer of sporting stories, whose works are probably devoured by a public fifty times larger than that which knows and esteems *The Egoist* or *The Ordeal of Richard Feverel*. But is our confidence in the immeasurable superiority of Mr George Meredith in the least shaken? On the contrary, our comment simply is—so much the worse for the fact. Those who emphasise most strongly the infinite variation of taste in regard to all æsthetic questions must therefore admit that the element of quality enters into the variation, and that a distinction is to be drawn between trained and untrained taste, between good taste and bad.

These considerations help to clear away some misapprehensions which certainly exist, and often crop up in conversation, about the problem of the valuation of literature. It is true that they leave untouched the old difficulty of the differences in judgment among the experts themselves. To this we will return directly. One important point in connection with our own personal attitude to literature must first be made.

If I express a certain view as to the value of a book I have been reading, then—as I put it just now—it is sometimes argued that this is my view, and nothing more. In that view, it is, moreover, assumed, I must rest, and whatever importance it possesses it possesses only as an indication of one person's individual taste. But here a question arises which at once puts this fact of individual taste under a fresh light. Is the opinion I have formed about the said book necessarily final, even for me? Is it an opinion which I myself have to accept as, so far as I am concerned, completely satisfactory? I say—I have enjoyed this book; it has amused, pleased, touched me; and there the matter ends. But does the matter end there? Certainly not. As Sainte-Beuve pointed out, the real question to be examined is, not whether we have enjoyed a particular work of art, whether it has amused, pleased, touched us, but whether we were right in enjoying it, in being amused, pleased, touched by it.

Beyond the question of our pleasure in a given piece of literature, there lies therefore the further question of the justification of that pleasure and the quality of it. We have our likes and dislikes, and these, when analysed, may be found to strike their roots so deep down into the subsoil of temperament, and to be so closely entangled with all the intellectual and moral elements which make up character, that to control them may seem difficult, to eradicate them, impossible. Yet which of us does not realise that there is a world of difference between liking or disliking a thing, and feeling satisfied that we ought to like or dislike it? The majority of people think so lightly of their relations with the various forms of art, and are so apt to assume that their own immediate pleasure is for them the final criterion of value, that they will hardly pause to note the implications of the distinction. But once noted, they open up a wide field for consideration. We know perfectly well that when we pronounce judgment upon a book in terms only of our private likes and dislikes, and without making any attempt to transcend these, we are really passing judgment not so much upon the book as upon ourselves. In this case, then, M. Anatole France's view of the significance of our judgment is entirely sound. But we know also, though it may require some courage to confess it, that in such judgment we often define our own limitations. Thus we may recognise the existence of great qualities in a given piece of literature even when we are unable to enjoy it; indeed, it may frequently happen (and of this too we are all aware), that it is by reason of its great qualities that a piece of literature may fail to amuse, please, touch us—may even baffle and repel us; for the enjoyment of greatness in art needs strenuous effort which, through indolence or apathy or want of preparation, we may be unwilling or unable to put forth; and we may, therefore, prefer to rest among lower things—among the things which, because they are lower, give us less trouble to understand and enjoy. But if we think of literary culture as a matter of serious import in life, it is not among these lower things—these things which give us the least trouble—that we shall be content always to rest.

Now, if we make a practice of looking back at what we have read, with the determination to detach ourselves from the feelings aroused at the time of reading, we shall find it possible to examine these feelings critically, to weigh them, and to decide whether we are satisfied that they were aroused with good cause, and whether the pleasure we have taken in a book was worthily taken in worthy things. A further test—a test proposed centuries ago by one of the earliest critics—may also be applied: if the longer we read a book the less we think of it, and if the effect it produces is 'not sustained beyond the mere act of perusal,' then we may be certain that, however much we may have enjoyed it at the moment, it is after all a slight and trivial thing.[271] The truth, which can never be too often repeated, will thus be brought home to us, that our personal pleasure is one thing and our estimate of our personal pleasure another. They may correspond; but also, they may not; and where they do not, it is clearly our duty to make a resolute and systematic attempt to overrule the one by the other. To start

---

[271]Longinus, *On the Sublime*, trans., H. L. Havell, c. vii.

with the assumption that we must take our likes and dislikes as we find them, and allow them, unchallenged, to dictate to us, is to negate in advance all hope of growth in critical power, insight, appreciation. In matters of literature as in all other matters, we stand in imperative need, as Mr Bosanquet has said, of 'training in enjoyment.'[272] That to a certain extent we are bound to acknowledge the reality of some standards of value, even for us, outside of our own personal feelings and independent of them, is now evident. Our great aim must therefore be to read with these standards always in mind, to appreciate frankly our deficiencies and limitations, and by submitting ourselves patiently and wholeheartedly to the discipline of the things which we recognise as best worthy of our attention, however far they may, for the time being, seem to lie beyond us, to lift ourselves little by little towards their level, and so to educate ourselves in judgment and taste. Such self-culture in the enjoyment of literature is possible for those who will take themselves seriously in hand; and no one who from experience has learned anything of the results will deny that, if the labour is often great, great also is the reward.

So much for this question of tastes and standards as it directly concerns ourselves. We have still to consider the problem, so frequently referred to already, of the continual and often astonishing differences in judgment which we find among the professed critics and arbiters of taste.

Thus far we have tacitly taken it for granted that the commonly accepted extreme view is correct and needs no qualification; that criticism is a 'self-cancelling business'; that its history is little more than a record of quarrels and contradictions, assertions and denials, standards set up only to be knocked down again. But is this really a fair statement of the facts? Are the results attained by the exercise of judgment in literature quite so variable, uncertain, and inconclusive

---

[272]See the admirable essay on this subject in *The Civilisation of Christendom and Other Studies.*

as they are often alleged to be and may at first sight appear? The answer must be, that though the commonly accepted extreme view contains a great deal of truth, it does not by any means contain the whole truth. Nothing is easier than by a judicious selection of telling examples (and they may be found by the score) to make out a strong case against the utility of criticism. But it must never be forgotten that while the history of criticism does exhibit the strangest oppositions of taste and the most violent fluctuations of judgment even in regard to subjects of fundamental importance, it exhibits also from time to time a well-marked tendency among the critics to come to a substantial agreement on essential points, and here and there, even more notably, a long-standing and almost complete unanimity as to the significance and value of particular 'masterpieces' of literature. If divergences are picked out and made much of, agreement and unanimity, wherever they are found, must surely not be left out of account.

Let us try to understand exactly all that is implied by the existence in certain cases of a practical concensus of critical opinion.

I am, we will suppose, anxious to substantiate or correct the judgment which I have privately formed concerning a particular book, or perhaps, finding it difficult to form any judgment, I feel in need of help in coming to a decision regarding it. I therefore lend the book to half a dozen friends successively, asking each to give me honestly his own opinion upon it; and in order to make my experiment as broad and searching as possible, I am careful to choose persons whose views I shall necessarily hold in respect, but whom I know to be most widely divergent in temperament, interests, ideas of life and literature, and training. Now the chances are that when my six reports come in, I shall find them almost hopelessly at variance with one another, and that therefore, though they may be of interest and assistance to me as expressions of individual tastes, they will have little value in any other way. But suppose that of the six readers who, according to our hypothesis, have studied the book from six very different points of view, and have brought six markedly different types of minds to bear upon it, five, though their reports may vary much in matters of detail, practically agree in their sense of its value, and lay their emphasis upon the same qualities of matter and treatment. In this case I shall feel, and rightly feel, that to some extent the element of mere personality and bias has been eliminated, and this feeling will grow stronger in proportion as the agreement is more and more close among those whose individual differences of taste are the most pronounced. As for the one dissentient, though, if it were a question of setting him individually against any one of the other five, I might hold his opinion at least equally worthy of my attention, the weight of the authority of the other five being against him, I shall most probably treat him merely as a dissentient, and perhaps at my leisure shall proceed to inquire into the grounds of his nonconformity. I have here, then, to work upon a general consensus of opinion where difference rather than agreement was to be looked for; and whether such opinion harmonises with my own or not, I shall accept it as a substantial indication of the real qualities of the book under consideration.

What is the moral of this suppositious case? It is so clear that it hardly needs to be pointed out. The experiment which I have imagined to be made on a very small scale, has actually been made on an immense scale, and the general concensus of opinion among those who might be expected to disagree, which I have conceived as possible, has in sundry cases in fact been reached. In other words, in regard to the value of a certain amount of literature, we are neither left to the isolated judgments of individual authorities, speaking each only for himself, nor confounded by the contradictions of supporters of rival creeds. We have instead a practical concord among critics, not only of very different characters and education, but also of different nations, epochs and schools; and against such general concord all occasional utterances of dissent, though often not to be ignored, avail but little. What is the inference? Such literature has been tried repeatedly, and by the most various tests and standards, and under every fresh scrutiny it has only revealed some hitherto unperceived elements of strength and beauty. It has maintained its place amid the most sweeping fluctuations of taste. The rise and fall of critical dynasties have left it almost untouched. Its qualities, therefore, are no longer matters of mere personal opinion. Its greatness has been proved. For the secret of such stability and persistence, of such universal and permanent appeal, can be found only in essential greatness—in transcendent vitality and power.

We have, therefore, to recognise as one fact of capital importance in the history of literature what Hume describes as 'the durable admiration which attends those works that have survived all the caprices of mode and fashion, all the mistakes of ignorance and envy.' The perennial life of the *Iliad* and the *Odyssey* may be cited in illustration. 'The same Homer who pleased at Athens and Rome two thousand years ago, is still admired at Paris and at London. All the changes of climate, government, religion, and language, have not been able to obscure his glory.'[273] These words were first published in 1742, and how completely our whole conception of literature in general and of Homer in particular has been transformed since then, is made clear if we remember that to us today Pope's 'drawing-room versions' of the Homeric poems seem almost like some eighteenth century travesty of the originals. Yet the declaration remains as true now as it was when Hume penned it. We may therefore read the Iliad and the Odyssey, or we may set them aside in favour of the last new novel, hot from the printing press, the talk of the hour, and certain to be forgotten, tomorrow; if we read them, we may enjoy them or not as the case may be; we may consult this critic and that, and discover multitudinous differences in detail in the opinions expressed; we may make the most ample allowance for that academic bias which, as I have said, still leads a particular class of writers to attach an exaggerated importance to anything and everything that has come down to us from Greek and Latin antiquity.

But one fact stands out. The imperishable interest of these

---

[273]Hume's *Essays*, Part I, No. XXIII, *Of the Standard of Taste*.

poems furnishes overwhelming evidence of their real greatness and supremacy. And of the real greatness and supremacy of other bodies of literature—of the Greek drama, for example, and the plays of Shakespeare, and the work of Dante and Milton—we have similar evidence almost as overwhelming.[274] These works, then, so tried and so proved, we may accept as 'classics'; for a 'classic' may be simply defined as a book which has stood the test of time, and by its stability and permanence, and the universality and persistency of its appeal, has given unmistakable assurance of immortal life.

A principle of the utmost significance in the valuation of literature is thus established—the principle of *Quod ubique, quod semper, quod ab omnibus*. 'In general,' as Longinus wrote, 'we may regard those words as truly noble and sublime, which please all and please always. For where the same book produces the same impression on all who read it, whatever be the differences in their pursuits, their manner of life, their aspirations, their ages, or their language, such a harmony of opposites gives authority to their favourable opinion.'[275]

I need not take space to show in what sense this principle of 'catholicity' has to be understood, and what qualifications have to be introduced into the statement of it in order to prevent any careless confusion of the truth on which it rests with the wholly false notion, already mentioned, that the value of literature can in the least degree be inferred from its popularity with certain classes of readers at any given time. One point, however, calls for special attention. A chief 'note of catholicity' in literature is, as we have now seen, its lasting power—its power of continued life. But this power of continued life depends upon qualities quite different from those which commonly ensure immediate general success. This fact has some important implications.

---

[274]In the case of Shakespeare, as we have already had occasion to remark, there has been much dissent. But this dissent is easily explained, and when explained, is found to have little value.

[275]*Op. cit.*, c. vii.

Throughout the whole range of life, as we all know, the struggle for existence results in the survival of what is fittest to survive. The persistence of any organism in this struggle is possible only through its capacity for adaptation to its environment; where an organism fails to adapt itself to a changing environment, it perishes; while the higher the organism the greater its power of adaptation to perpetually changing and increasingly complex surroundings. These are familiar biological truths, and I recall them now because of their bearing upon the problem of survival, and therefore of fitness, in literature. A book, like any other organism, succeeds in the first instance by reason of its adjustment to its conditions; in other words, it succeeds by its power of interesting the particular body of readers to whom it is addressed; and its immediate success is, of course, to be measured by the extent of the interest which it arouses. A book which enjoys an enormous vogue does so because, as we say, it hits the popular taste; because, that is, for one or another reason, it falls in with and expresses the mood of the hour, deals with the things which people are thinking and talking about, and is in consequence exactly the kind of book for which the public is ready, and which it is most eager to read. But the adaptation which thus secures immediate success may be an adaptation only to conditions which are local and transitory. If so, then, when the mood has passed, when the things which people were thinking and talking about at the time have ceased to interest them, the book becomes obsolete; they no longer read it, and very probably, if they concern themselves about it at all, they marvel greatly at the enthusiasm with which it was first received.[276] Any piece of art which is merely timely must sooner or later perish of its timeliness, for having nothing in it

---

[276]One frequently recurring problem for the literary historian is that of explaining by reference to the conditions of the time of production the immense success of various works (such as Lillo's *George Barnwell* and Schiller's *The Robbers*), which are now little more than curiosities. In dealing with the historical study of literature I have already shown the vital interest which may still belong to many of these books (Chapter II, §3). But this is not now the question.

which transcends the fashions from which it drew its nourishment, it inevitably dies with them. Thus the very causes which gave it a temporary popularity operate against its continued life. Such is the history of many books which have flourished for a season, but whose place a new generation knows no more. But there are other books which, as I have said, possess the power of surviving all changes of fashion, taste, and even civilisation. Why is this? Because they are capable of continuous adjustment and re-adjustment to the ever-developing conditions of our moral and intellectual life. They had a message and meaning for their own age; they have a message and meaning for us still. Such books may have been, in a large number of cases they undoubtedly were, in the narrowest sense of the word, timely. But they do not survive in virtue of their timeliness, but rather in despite of it; for whatever they carry with them which belonged only to the place and time of their birth, is an obstacle to their endurance and not a help, though it was very probably a help to their first success. They survive because, however much they may originally have appealed to interests which in the nature of things could not but be local and transient, they contain elements which, now that these special interests are long since dead, have still the power to delight, move, inspire.

And here, perhaps, the analogy between the phenomena of biology and those of literature partly fails. For the literature which survives all changes of fashion, taste, and civilisation does so, not so much because it actually adjusts itself to new modes of life, thought, and speech, as because in its essential composition it was from the outset adapted to what is primary, elemental, and uniform in human nature and experience, and therefore to conditions which persist, independent of place and time. It is certain that, save in a very few instances, such literature was produced by men whose thought was fixed, not upon posterity or the things which are permanent in life, but upon their own public and the facts and problems of the hour. To the making of such literature, therefore, has always gone a large amount of purely local and temporary matter. But it is the peculiar mark of the books which are endowed with the secret of continuous life that in them even the local and temporary is so handled, and with such insight, and grasp, and power, that it is made to partake of the significance of the universal and permanent.

It has been said of Herodotus that he had the knack of taking interest in the things which have continued to interest people for twenty-three hundred years. This statement is true not only of the Father of History; it is incontestably true of all those who have written books which live; for it is just because their books deal with unrivalled insight, grasp and power, with the things which are universally and permanently interesting—with the experiences, motives, and passions, the struggles, joys and sorrows, which belong to the common foundations of human life, everywhere and at all time—that 'age cannot wither' them 'nor custom stale' their 'infinite variety.' What is merely accidental in a great book—what appertains only to the trappings of life, to the circumstances and conditions of the age and society out of which it came—will interest us in it just as such things interest us in any other piece of literature. But when we penetrate beneath these, we come upon the explanation of its enduring vitality in its wonderful adaptation to all that is most essential and stable in life at large. To measure the distance in everything but the essential and stable which separates us today from the *Book of Job*, the *Divine Comedy, Paradise Lost*, the Homeric poems, the tragedies of Shakespeare, is to gain some sense at least of what it is in the world's greatest literature which has lifted it above the reach of the destroying influences of time.

In the light of this somewhat protracted discussion of the problem of survival in literature, we ought to be able to understand the full meaning of the statement that there is a considerable amount of literature which we may regard as lying outside the region of personal opinion, and the greatness of which has been proved. To this statement we will now return since, as will doubtless have been anticipated, it provides us with a certain sure footing amid all questions and controversies concerning literary valuation.

The principal test of greatness in literature—that of its lasting power—is manifestly one which it must be left to time to apply. But meanwhile, what of the literature which has not yet been so tested? We cannot venture to forecast the result of the sifting processes of the centuries, nor can we say with any degree of certitude how this or that now famous work may look when, like Shakespeare's plays, it has stood the wear and tear of three hundred years. Only as we are able to step away from a piece of literature, and to see it in perspective, is it in the vast majority of cases possible to distinguish between essential interest and accidental interest, between the success which is merely timely and that which has in it the promise of endurance. It is difficult for us to conceive that what appeals intensely to us may not perhaps outlast our generation, for that which at the moment seems most vital will hardly fail to assume in our minds the characteristics of universality and permanence. In respect of the literature which still lies near to us, and in respect especially of contemporary literature, we are necessarily left to ourselves and to the guidance, such as it is, offered by our critics. Yet let it be said emphatically that such literature—the literature which grows out of the life that we our- selves live, is fed by all the influences which belong to our surroundings, and deals with the facts and problems which directly concern us as creatures of our own place and time—must inevitably have an interest for us quite different from that possessed by even the greatest literature of the past, and in many ways much deeper and keener than this. The advice that when a new book is published we ought to read an old one, is therefore not advice that any of us need take seriously. No man can properly be said to belong to his own generation who is not eager to keep abreast of its literature. Even the books which, as we may feel assured, are of merely ephemeral significance, may thus often have a real claim upon our attention. None the less, entirely justified as is our interest in all kinds of contemporary literature, since that literature is enormous in quantity and of varying degrees of excellence, and since, moreover, every reader should regard it as part of his duty to encourage what is good and discourage what is bad, it is of fundamental importance that we should read 'the new works of new days' with a constant sense of relative values, and a desire always to discriminate so far as possible between what is genuine and what is factitious.

And here, as I believe, a knowledge of the 'classics' may be of practical help to us. If in them we have recognised examples of literary greatness in various forms, and if there- fore they admittedly possess a certain rank and authority, we ought to be able to use them as standards of comparison. By this I do not in the least mean that we should seek to employ them in the narrow, pedantic, and inflexible way in which the Greek and Latin classics were employed by the academic critics of the seventeenth and eighteenth centuries. Nor do I propose that we should try to make systems and rules out of them. Above all, I do not suggest that we should invoke them to check originality, hamper experiment, or define in advance the lines which the literature of our own time should or should not follow. To imply that even the greatest things of the past are to be set apart as models for the present and the future would be against the whole drift and spirit of my argument throughout this chapter. The literature which really counts, as I have more than once insisted, is the literature which is made, not out of other literature, but out of life; and for a living literature no models will suffice. If, therefore, on the one hand, we must never allow ourselves to be misled into exaggerated estimates of contemporary productions by the noisy approbation of the general public or the injudicious praise of reckless reviewers, on the other hand we must not fall into the opposite error of supposing that all the great work in literature has been done, that there can be no new prophet in our own generation and country, and that the acknowledged masterpieces of bygone ages spell finality. What I mean, and all that I mean, by saying that we can use these acknowledged masterpieces as standards of comparison, is this: as their qualities are not matters of speculation, but, as we believe, of feat—as their greatness has been proved—we can by analysis of them discover something at least of what constitutes essential greatness, power, and beauty in literature, and can utilise the knowledge so gained in a practical way in our examination of the merits and defects of other pieces of literature belonging to the same general class.

We are thus brought back to a point already made—that a thorough and comprehensive acquaintance with the world's greatest work in poetry, the drama, and fiction may safely be postulated as indispensable for anyone who would undertake to pass judgment upon, or, as we may now add, would seek to appreciate the real qualities of, any poem, or play, or novel. In this work of comparison we shall seldom, in all probability, be able to proceed by any formal methods, nor is it necessary that we should try to do so. Our interest is in the spirit, and not in the letter; and it is enough for us to know that familiarity with great and good literature will quicken in us an instinctive feeling for what is great and good, wherever we may meet with it, and in whatever new forms it may be embodied.

Matthew Arnold's theory of the use of 'touchstones' of poetry— of selected lines and passages by which to try 'the presence or absence of high poetic quality, and also the degree of that quality, in all other poetry which we may place beside them'[277]—will probably seem to most readers, as it seems to me, rather fantastic and unconvincing. But the underlying idea is incontestably sound and fruitful. It is not by abstract theorising about power and beauty, about standards and tests, but by simply living as much as possible, and as sympathetically as possible, with the best that the world's literature has to give us, that our taste will be attuned to excellence, and our judgment trained for its appreciation.

Difficult as this whole question of the valuation of literature admittedly is, and superficial as our present treatment of it has necessarily been, it may still be hoped that we may now close upon certain positive results. An admirable French exponent of the doctrine

---

[277] *The Study of Poetry*, in *Essays in Criticism*, Second Series.

of discipline in art, M. Nisard, in the spirit of extreme revulsion from the anarchy threatened by the spread of mere impressionism, once asserted that the true purpose of criticism is to free literature from the tyranny of the notion that there is no disputing about tastes. There is not the slightest ground for hope that this purpose will ever be completely achieved. Criticism cannot be reduced to a science; it cannot be made into 'a sort of botany applied to the works of man.' We talk, with Arnold, about 'seeing the thing as it really is.' But this is only a fashion of speech. To see the thing as it really is, is impossible; for we can see it only in our own minds; and since our minds are 'steeped and infused in the humours of the affections,'[278] we can see it only through the atmosphere of our own temperaments and characters. We can clear away the mists of prejudice; we can make due allowance for predisposition; we can do a great deal of correct bias. But that is all. Literature grows out of personality, and addresses itself to personality. It deals with many subjects in many forms. It is of its very essence that it should enlist sympathy, stir feeling, arouse passion. Thus it appeals to variable elements, and variation must inevitably characterise our response to it. From this conclusion there is no escape. We cannot eliminate the individual factor from criticism, and the differences which arise from the play of many minds upon the same phenomena must be accepted as matters of course. I see no reason to regret this; rather I am glad that a colourless uniformity in literary appreciation is never likely to be reached. Yet though in the last analysis we are thus thrown back upon our own taste and judgment, the great fact remains that to a large extent, I would venture to say to an extent quite incalculable, taste may be trained and judgment controlled, disciplined, and directed. Thus in our own relations with the problem of literary valuation, we have, after all, a principle of practice to start with, and to this we shall certainly look for illumination and guidance, if we desire to make our study of literature of the utmost possible service to us as a means both of enjoyment and of life.

---

[278]Bacon, *Advancement of Learning*, I, i, iii.

Appendix

I. *On Personality in Literature*. The Communal Element in Early Literature—Mediæval Impersonality—The Study of Communal Personality. II. *On the Treatment of Nature in Poetry*. The Question of Fidelity—Ways of Using Nature—The Poetry of Simple Delight in Nature—The Poetry of Nature's Sensuous Beauty—The Metaphorical Use of Nature—Nature as Background—The Poetry of Association—The Poetry of Set Description—Nature Contrasted with Man—The Indifference of Nature—The Sympathy of Nature—The Subjective Treatment of Nature. III. *The Study of the Essay*. Various Types of Essay—General Features—The Personal Factor in the Essay—The Study of the Essay. IV. *The Study of the Short Story*. The Story and the Novel—What is a Short Story?—Principles of Composition: (1) Concentration; (2) Unity—Details of Composition—The Germinal Idea—Illustrations.

I

ON PERSONALITY IN LITERATURE
(SEE PP. 14–16, 40–42)

In a very valuable review of this book in the *Manchester Guardian* (for which I believe I am indebted to one of the foremost of our living English scholars), it was suggested that in emphasising the personal element as the foundation principle in literature I had apparently neglected the fact that there are considerable bodies of literature in which the personal element does not exist. The matter is one which perhaps deserves a little further attention.

Every student of literary evolution is, of course, aware that very early literature, even when it assumes what seems to be a lyrical form, is not in our sense of the term a literature of self-expression. This is because the emergence of the individual unit from the mass is a relatively late result of advancing social life. The common view, set forth by Victor Hugo with characteristic energy in his famous preface to *Cromwell*, that the 'primitive' ages of the world were ages of 'colossal' individualism, is grotesquely unhistorical. They were, on the contrary, ages in which group-life and group-consciousness were in the ascendant; while it is only 'in the movement of civilisation—a movement by no means regular, but often spasmodic, back and forward, forward and back, though on the whole forward'—that 'personal character comes to stand out more and more distinctly from the general crowd.'[279] The importance of these considerations in the study of early literatures is seldom recognised by general readers. One of the most fertile sources of error in our common interpretation, or rather misinterpretation, of the Old Testament, is our habit of reading back into it ideas derived from our modern highly developed individualism and entirely out of keeping with its own real spirit and bearings. The centre of interest in most surviving Hebrew literature is, in fact, not the individual but the family or the community, and no true understanding of that literature is possible unless this is kept always in mind. I have already noted that the greater part of Hebrew lyrical poetry is communal and not personal in character (pp. 97, 98, 100). The entire Hebrew attitude towards life, Hebrew patriarchal notions of family continuity as against personal immortality, and early Hebrew moral theories concerning corporate and hereditary responsibility and vicarious suffering,[280] were also based

---

[279]Posnett, *Comparative Literature*, pp. 70, 71.

[280]As summed up, for instance, in the famous proverb against which the more

upon the conception of the community as the centre of life and the point of departure. In other early literatures, also, the origin of the lyric must be sought in efforts to express the emotion of the group, not that of the individual singer. 'In the rude beginnings of literature among loosely federated clans, we find,' as Mr Posnett says, 'the communal 'lyric' reflecting the corporate organism and ideas of contemporary life. Even in Pindar, the communal, as opposed to the individual characteristics of the 'lyric,' are still visible, the victor of the games being often merely a centre round which the achievements of his clan or city are grouped.'[281] The very conception of personal authorship arose only with the change from communal to personal life, and so little indeed, during the earlier stages of literary evolution, was the integrity of any composition regarded, that every new generation felt free to deal with it as it chose. Hence a piece of early literature may best be likened to a mediæval church, which grew gradually into the shape in which we know it under a succession of master-builders, and now bears little distinctive trace of any one mind.[282] In later times, a backward movement in civilisation has occasionally brought about a repression of individuality, with the result that personality has again almost disappeared from literature. I have lately had reason to lay stress on this in dealing with the effect of mediæval conditions on literature and art. Having shown how all these conditions were 'fatal to the free development of individuality,' I have said:—'One curious result which followed in the domain of literature and art is worth attention—the almost complete want of individuality in the works produced, the absence

---

individualistic later prophets protested, 'the fathers have eaten, sour grapes, and the children's teeth are set on edge.'

[281] Op. cit., p. 40.

[282] Note, for example, the obvious tamperings with the text of Ecclesiastes and The Book of Job; also the different 'layers' in the Iliad (for which see Leaf's Companion to the Iliad). The objectivity of most early narrative poetry, in part at least the poetry of composite authorship, is very marked; as in the Homeric poems (with which compare the highly personal Æneid), Beowulf, and the Nibelungenlied.

of the distinctively personal note. Everywhere we meet with what Brunetière calls the spirit of anonymity. There is nothing in poem or painting to reveal the character of the poet or artist behind it. One *roman* is just like another *roman*; one mystery-play just like another mystery-play; one trouvère or minnesinger just like another trouvère or minnesinger; one Madonna or Crucifixion just like another Madonna or Crucifixion. Individual genius had been swamped by tradition and convention.'[283]

The points upon which I have above touched were neither forgotten nor intentionally ignored by me when I wrote the pages in the text to which this note refers. I passed them over simply because I did not wish to burden my exposition with what might seem to most of my readers somewhat extraneous matter. Their bearings upon the general principles of literary interpretation will, I think, be fairly obvious. Where the purely individual element does not exist in literature it will be idle of course to look for it; and it would, therefore, be correct to say that in our study of an early lyric poem or play, or of a mediæval romance or miracle-play, we cannot be concerned about the factor of individuality, as individuality is understood today. Yet the lyric, play, romance, or miracle-play, as the case may be, is still the product of human energy seeking the channels of literary form; it still stands for human thought and feeling; and behind it necessarily lies, if not the power of the individual unit, at any rate, that of what we may call generalised or communal personality. In such circumstances, then, it is with generalised or communal personality that we have to get into touch. What I have said on pp. 17 and 18 of the text may thus, with slight change of wording, be applied to the study of the literature which expresses group-consciousness rather than the mind of the individual maker. That in analysing such group-consciousness we are in fact inquiring into the significance of literature as a revelation of race and age (see pp. 31–33) will be equally apparent. Moreover, as 'the progressive

---

[283] *The Story of the Renaissance*, pp. 5, 6.

deepening and widening of personality' is, as Mr Posnett rightly insists, the central fact in the evolution of literature, the development of personality is manifestly a problem of capital importance in the study of literature on the historical side.[284]

II

ON THE TREATMENT OF NATURE IN POETRY

On the Treatment of Nature in Poetry on p. 126 I have suggested this as a special topic for study. It is one so rich in interest that a little space may fittingly be devoted to its further consideration.

Clearly, the first test to be applied is that of poetic truth. With this I have already dealt at some length (pp. 80–82), and have now only to insist upon the fundamental difference between the faithful and the unfaithful or conventional treatment of natural facts. Even to the uncritical reader, the contrast is apparent between the first-hand knowledge and the specific accuracy of Wordsworth, or Keats, or Tennyson, each of whom wrote (in Wordsworth's own phrase) with his eye 'steadily fixed upon his object,' and the bookishness, the vague generalised statements, and the neglect of detail, which characterised Pope and his school. The occasional carelessness and conventionalism of Milton have already been noted. Elsewhere we may find illustrations without number of the difference in question. Thus the May morning and the garden landscape, which were partly conventional even with Chaucer, are entirely so with his fifteenth century imitators; while on the other hand, in the writings of some of their Scottish contemporaries (in Gavin Douglas's prologues to his translation of the *Æneid*, for instance), there is a marked tendency to

---

[284]When once attention has been directed to the existence of this problem, we shall find it cropping up in all sorts of unexpected places, and even in connection with quite recent literature. To give one example: the decline of the drama and the rise of the modern novel are in part results of growing individualism, while such growing individualism is again one factor in the evolution of prose fiction itself.

break away from mere literary formulas and to attempt the realistic reproduction of things actually seen. In the pastoral poetry which from the time of the Renaissance onward was written on classic models, the treatment of nature is almost wholly imitative and conventional.

This question of fidelity settled, we have next to consider the poet's emotional response to nature, and, more broadly, the manner in which, and the purposes for which, nature is employed by him. It is evident that while poetic truth is a characteristic which Wordsworth, Keats and Tennyson have in common, the emotional response of each of these poets is strikingly different from that of either of the other two. It is equally evident that nature is used in one way, let us say, in John Dyer's *Grongar Hill*, in another way in Scott's *Marmion*, and in another again in Arnold's *Dover Beach*. So much is clear. Yet, as this is a matter in regard to which some definite guidance may be useful, I will here indicate a few of the most important ways in which poets may deal with nature; though it must be understood that the subject is too large for full treatment within a small space and too complex to admit of exact classification. What follows is based on Principal Shairp's suggestive chapter on the subject in his *Poetic Interpretation of Nature*. I do not, however, adopt his analysis in all particulars, and I have added a good deal to it in various places.

To begin at the beginning, we may find in poetry the expression, in Mr Shairp's words, of 'that simple, spontaneous, unreflecting pleasure which all unsophisticated beings feel in free open-air life.' We get this 'fresh child- like delight in nature' very often in Chaucer (as we may see by going no farther than the opening of the *Prologue* to the *Canterbury Tales*), and often, too, in snatches, in our old ballads; as in the charming lines:

When shaws beene sheene, and shradds full fayre,
And leaves both large and longe,
Itt is merrye walking in the fayre forrest
To heare the small birdes songe.

There is again the same note of simple pleasure, uncomplicated by intellectual or moral considerations, in the following passage which I translate from Walther von der Vogelweide, the most famous of the minnesingers:—'When the summer was come, and the flowers sprang up wonderfully through the grass, and the birds were singing, then came I passing over a long meadow, where a clear well gushed forth; through a wood it ran, where the nightingale sang.' In the very nature of things, such expressions of unreflecting pleasure must be sought chiefly among the older poets, for in our modern enjoyment of the open air and the freedom of the fields, even though the occasion be a picnic expedition, intellectual and moral elements are almost certain to intrude. Yet now and then, even in our analytical and sophisticated age, the poet will abandon himself wholeheartedly and unspeculatively to the mood of the moment, and then we catch again, though with unmistakable suggestions of deeper passion, the simple rapture of earlier times. Keats's sonnet, *To One Who Has Been Long in City Pent*, and Lowell's glorious *Prelude to the first part of The Vision of Sir Launfal*, may be cited as illustrations.

Superficially somewhat akin to this simple enjoyment of nature, though essentially quite different from it, is that love of nature which we may best describe perhaps by the epithet sensuous. Mr Shairp has left this altogether out of his survey—a serious omission, since poetry is full, as we should expect, of the artist's feeling for the material beauty of nature considered as material beauty only. In describing the development of his own relations with nature, Wordsworth has shown how, after leaving behind him the 'coarser pleasures 'of his 'boyish days,' he passed into a stage in which

> The sounding cataract
> Haunted me like a passion; the tall rock,
> The mountain and the deep and gloomy wood,
> Their colours and their forms were then to me
> An appetite—a feeling and a love
> That had no need of a remoter charm
> By thought supplied, nor any interest

Unborrowed from the eye.[285]

These lines exactly describe the pure artist's sensuous love of natural beauty—a love which has no need of 'any interest unborrowed from the eye.' In Wordsworth himself we do not find many expressions of this love, because, as he goes on to tell us, even this stage was in turn presently outgrown. But we find it in many modern poets; notably, for example, in Keats. As I have elsewhere said:

> 'Keats did not love nature as Wordsworth and Shelley loved it. There was nothing spiritual or mystical in his feeling for it; he had little sense of those unseen realities which speak to the contemplative soul out of the external show of things. His was a sensuous love of natural beauty just for its own sake—the beauty of field and forest, of flower, and sky, and sea; and in the interpretation of this beauty, in this simple and direct passion for nature...no English poet takes a higher place than Keats.'[286]

Wordsworth's reproof of Peter Bell might indeed have been addressed to Keats, for of him it was in fact perfectly true that

> A primrose by a rive's brim
> A yellow primrose was to him,
> And it was nothing more.

But then Keats's reply would have been—why should it be anything more? Why should we probe it for moral or spiritual meanings? Is not its simple beauty enough?

We may next note, though Mr Shairp has not done so, how nature may be used merely as a source of imagery and illustration. Metaphors and similes from nature are common in all poetry; at times, poets have seen and handled nature only in the metaphorical way. Thus it has been pointed out that though the Hebrew poets generally show great fidelity in their treatment of nature, they

---

[285] *Lines Written above Tintern Abbey.* Compare, for a fuller account of the transformation of the poet's feeling for nature, *The Prelude,* Books I and II.
[286] *Keats and his Poetry* (in the *Poetry and Life* series), p. 35.

nowhere suggest any real love of nature as such: nature being for them, as Canon Cheyne puts it, mainly 'a magazine of symbols,' bearing upon human life. Homer's similes from nature are justly famous, and the fact that while they are all manifestly taken at first hand from the things described, they have often been elaborately imitated by modern poets (as by Arnold in *Sohrab and Rustum*), brings us back again to the difference between the genuine and the traditional and bookish treatment of nature on which I have already insisted. It is, of course, important under this head to trace all metaphors and similes to their sources, whether in nature or in other literature, and to inquire both into their accuracy and into their propriety.[287] Interesting details will often come to light. It is, for example, a point worthy of attention that, though many of Virgil's similes are fashioned directly upon Homer's, the poet's own intimate knowledge of nature is often revealed; as in the passage in which (evidently recalling what he had seen on his father's farm when a boy) he likens the labours of the men of Carthage to those of bees in their hive.[288]

Another way in which nature is often employed in poetry is as a background or setting to human emotion or action. This was a common way with those poets of the eighteenth century in whom the reviving love of nature was conspicuous, but who still fixed their attention chiefly on man. Thus, for instance, Gray uses landscape in the *Elegy* and Goldsmith in *The Deserted Village*. This too is the way in which nature has been employed by narrative poets from Homer down to our own times. That in the evolution of narrative poetry the tendency has been towards the greater and

---

[287]The question of propriety, or 'keeping,' is an important one. Note that Arnold, while adopting Homer as his model, 'took a great deal of trouble to orientalise 'his similes in *Sohrab and Rustum* (see his *Letters*, i. 37), and that Tennyson was equally careful to make all the similes in *Enoch Arden*' such as might have been used by simple fisherfolk' (*Memoir*, by Hallam Tennyson, ii, 8).

[288]*Æneid*, i, 430 ff. Virgil's father was, among other things, a bee-keeper. The passage has often been imitated; notably by Milton in *Paradise Lost*, i, 768–75.

greater elaboration of the landscape setting—that, in other words, description has become increasingly important and has encroached more and more upon story—is a fact the significance of which no reader is likely to overlook. Even in the *Iliad*, as Mr Shairp notes, 'there is little or no description of the scenes in which the battles are fought. The features are hinted at by single epithets, such as many-fountained Ida, windy Ilion, deep-whirlpooled Scamander, and the presence of nature you are made to feel by images fetched straight from every element'; Homer, as the writer says in another chapter, being 'so full of business and of human action, that he cannot stay for description.' There is more pure description in the *Odyssey* and again in the *Æneid*, as in Hebrew literature there is more pure description in *Esther* than in *Ruth*; and in each case its greater prominence is to be interpreted, in general terms, as evidence of changing methods of narrative art.

But it is only in quite modern literature that its immense development has become a persistent feature. In any case in which a recent poet has retold an ancient story we shall be certain to find ready to hand an illustration of the striking difference between the naïve and the highly elaborated manner of using nature for narrative purposes. In speaking of the famous tale of *Cupid and Psyche* in the *Metamorphoses* of Apuleius, Professor Mackail remarks: 'The version by which it is best known to modern readers, that in the *Earthly Paradise*, while, after the modern poet's manner, expanding the descriptions for their own sake, follows Apuleius otherwise with exact fidelity.'[289] Here, as will be seen, the expansion of description is more suggestive because of Morris's general adherence in all other particulars to his original. There is a similar contrast between Malory and Tennyson. Malory is satisfied with the bare statement that a certain knight was riding through 'a wood,' and then passed on at once to the adventure which he met with there. Tennyson pauses to give a picture of the wood. Nor is this all.

---

[289] *Latin Literature*, p. 243.

Another, and more important, mark of the general change which has come over our attitude towards nature is to be found in the fact that whereas the older poets habitually used nature merely as a detached background, modern poets tend to relate such background to the human drama which is played out against it, thus exemplifying the characteristic subjectivity of modern art. This method of using nature is a conspicuous feature of Tennyson's narrative poetry. The whole tragedy of the *Idylls of the King* is worked out amid scenes which are made to correspond with each stage of the story as it is reached. Thus in the spring setting of *Gareth and Lynette*; in the late autumn setting of *The Last Tournament*, and so on throughout, nature is brought in to sustain by sympathy the inner significance of the human drama. But such human drama may be thrown into relief by contrast as well as by sympathy; as Tennyson again shows us in *Enoch Arden*. When Enoch lands, and the sea haze gathers about him, turning the world to grey, nature responds to his own rising doubts and becomes prophetic of his approaching doom; but when, earlier in the poem, Tennyson paints his gorgeous picture of the tropical island on which Enoch has been cast, it is clear that he does so to intensify by contrast with the exotic fertility of the landscape the loneliness and despair of the 'shipwrecked sailor waiting for a sail.'

Arnold makes a very fine use of contrast when he closes the tragic story of *Sohrab and Rustum* with the description of the river Oxus, flowing out through the darkness and leaving the petty hum of human life behind it in its majestic passage through vast solitudes to the Aral Sea.

Again, natural scenery may be interesting to a poet because of its association with human events. Mr Shairp is wrong in thinking that the nature poetry of historical association is entirely modern, for the, learned and antiquarian Virgil puts much of it into the *Æneid*.[290] But it is unquestionably a kind of nature poetry which grows with the growth of historical studies and the historical imagination, and

---

[290]See, in particular, the discourse of Evander in Book VIII.

it must therefore be regarded as the product of modes of thinking which are possible only in relatively advanced periods of culture. We have many striking examples of such poetry in Byron's *Childe Harold's Pilgrimage*; but for its fullest development we have perhaps to turn to Scott. It is not only, as Mr Shairp says, that Scott

> 'has in his romantic epics described the actual features of the fields of Flodden and of Bannockburn with a minuteness foreign to the genius of the ancients. He has done this. But besides, wherever he set his foot in his native land—not in a battle-field alone, but by ruined keep or solitary moor, or rocky seashore or western island—there rose before his eye the human forms either of the heroic past or of the lowlier peasantry, and if no actual record hung among them, his imagination supplied the want, and peopled the places with characters appropriate, which shall remain interwoven with the very features of the scenes while the name of Scotland lasts.'

Landscape with Scott is, in fact, habitually seen through a haze of historic or romantic associations. He himself has touched upon this characteristic aspect of his attitude towards nature in the introduction to the third canto of *Marmion*.

While thus recognising the poetry of historical association, Mr Shairp has failed to perceive that there is a poetry of personal association as well. Indeed, the memories which colour landscape or otherwise affect our relations with it, will on analysis be found to be far more frequently of an individual than of a general character. Goldsmith's *Deserted Village*, Tennyson's *The Daisy* and (for the most part) *In Memoriam*, Arnold's *Obermann* poems and *Stanzas from the Grande Chartreuse*, and William Watson's *Wordsworth's Grave*, may be mentioned as examples, under various forms, of this kind of poetry. Under this same head a singularly interesting line of study of both kinds of association—general and personal—is provided in Wordsworth's three Yarrow poems—*Yarrow Unvisited, Yarrow Visited*, and *Yarrow Revisited*. Of the second of these Prof. Veitch says: 'We have there the truest Yarrow, the truest Yarrow that ever was pictured; real yet not literal; Yarrow as it is for the spiritual sense made keen, quick, sensitive and deep through the brooding over the stories of the years and living communion with the heart of things.'[291]

The poetry of set description, in which the poet undertakes to do with his pen what the landscape painter does with his brush, may next be referred to. Of such pictorial poetry Thomson's *Seasons* is a familiar example. Its essential feature is, that while human life is often introduced into it (as figures are put by a painter into his landscape), nature is the first consideration and humanity is merely subordinate. Hence the difference between this poetry and the poetry in which, as in the *Deserted Village* and the *Elegy in a Country Churchyard*, nature is used as a background to human life. Of course, passages of set description are usually found embodied in narrative and meditative poetry, where they are so often interwoven with other elements that it is impossible to say just where pure description ends and a human interest in nature begins. But descriptive poetry has still to be recognised as a division of the poetry of nature. Questions of method and success, of course, arise here; and these, pushed home, will be found to entail a large and complex æsthetic problem—the problem, namely, how far, in what ways, and under what conditions the poet is able to paint at all. At this point the student will be well advised if he turns to Lessing's masterly treatise, *Laokoon*. Lessing, indeed, carried his condemnation of descriptive poetry much too far, and neglected considerations which the reader of modern nature-poetry will readily provide for himself. At the same time *Laokoon* remains one of the foundation books on this, as on many other subjects connected with the relations of poetry and painting.

In principle at least descriptive poetry is entirely objective. We have now to note some of the uses to which nature may be put in poetry of a highly subjective kind.

Nature may be set in sharp contrast with the life of man, to

---

[291]*History and Poetry of the Scottish Border*, ii, 316.

the end that the pathetic brevity and littleness of that life may be brought out and emphasised. Sometimes the contrast is between that totality of things which we call nature—nature conceived as the vast and undying—and the tiny span of our personal existence or of the passing generations, which come and go, in Homer's phrase, like leaves on the trees of a forest. So the voice of nature speaks to Arnold;

> Race after race, man after man,
> Have thought that my secret was theirs,
> Have dream'd that I lived but for them,
> That they were my glory and joy.
> They are dust, they are changed, they are gone!
> I remain.[292]

Sometimes the contrast is between some phenomenon or aspect of nature and man's life. So Catullus sings that, while suns set to rise, for us, while once our brief light is extinguished, there is nothing left but eternal night.[293] So Keats contrasts the life of the individual man with that of the nightingale figured as an 'immortal bird'; and Tennyson finds a message in the babbling of the brook:

> For men may come and men may go,
> But I go on for ever.

This note, as we might expect, is often heard in elegiac poetry. It is heard, for instance, in Longfellow's *The Warden*:

> Meanwhile, without, the surly canon waited,
> The sun rose bright o'erhead,
> Nothing in nature's aspect intimated
> That a great man was dead.

---

[292] *The Youth of Nature.*
[293] Soles occidere at redire possunt.
Nobis, quum simul occidit brevis lux,
Nox est perpetua una dormienda.

It is a recurrent note in Arnold's Thyrsis and in *Watson's Wordsworth's Grave*.

Again, special stress may be laid on the indifference of nature—an indifference which, if we are to continue to apply words of human connotation to purely natural processes, we may even describe as cruelty. The sense that nature, though we may by a trick of the imagination personify it as the Great Mother, has, after all, no care for man and his welfare—that, in fact, there is nothing in the universe about us save impersonal, eternal, and inexorable law—weighed heavy on the thought of the noble old poet Lucretius. But it is, of course, within recent times that, under the ever growing influence of science, it has come specially to the front. Among our great English poets Tennyson in particular saw nature 'red in tooth and claw with ravine,' and realised to the full what our deepening knowledge of cosmic processes portended on the spiritual side. The vastness of the universe, in time and space, as revealed by science, appalled him:—

> Many hearth upon our dark globe sighs after many a vanish'd
> face,
> Many a planet by many a sun may roll with the dust of a
> vanish'd race.[294]

Another Victorian writer of immense power dwelt on the modern scientific conception of nature as a further argument in favour of his all-comprehensive pessimism:—

> I find no hint throughout the Universe
> Of good or ill, of blessing or of curse;
> I find alone Necessity Supreme.[295]

In this way we are brought round to the scientific interpretation of nature, which I have already sufficiently considered in the text (pp. 84–87).

On the other hand, men may discover, and most of our modern

---

[294] *Vastness.*
[295] James Thomson, *The City of Dreadful Night*, xiv.

poets have discovered, in nature, not indifference, not cruelty, not sensuous beauty only, but sympathy, companionship, and infinite spiritual significance. As every poet responds to nature according to the peculiar qualities of his own temperament, the poetry of emotional interpretation takes many different forms, as in the poetry of Wordsworth, for whom nature was divine, and who sought communion through nature with nature's indwelling soul; of Shelley, to whom nature was a mystical revelation of that eternal spirit in whom all modes of life are one; of Byron, who found in nature the passionate freedom which the conditions of the human lot denied to man; of Arnold, to whom, on the contrary, nature's calm was a refuge and a solace to the fretful and troubled heart. The deeply religious quality of this kind of nature poetry will be specially remarked; as pre-eminently in the case of Wordsworth, who has shown, as Mr Myers has put it, 'by the subtle intensity of his own emotion, how the contemplation of nature can be made a revealing agency, like love or prayer—an opening, if indeed there be any opening, into the transcendent world.'

Not to carry this analysis any farther, I may finally note that most highly subjective kind of nature poetry in which all nature is steeped in the poet's personal feeling. Very much of our modern poetry comes under this head, and modern readers, as a rule, find it extremely sympathetic. In fact, the ability to see and describe any natural phenomenon without reference to personal feeling, is very rare in recent literature. By way of example, let me suggest a comparison of Keats's *Ode to Autumn* and the *Autumn* of Mr William Watson. The former is almost completely objective; the poet has looked steadily at his subject, and no disturbing sentiments affect his picture. In the latter, the poet's eye is turned inward upon himself rather than outward upon the world, and it is not with the simple facts of the autumnal landscape but with the melancholy reflections which the season inspires, that he is really concerned. Such subjective treatment of nature brings us at once to the question of the pathetic fallacy, which has already been discussed in the text (pp. 82, 83).

It will, of course, be understood that the foregoing inquiry is by no means exhaustive. It is intended only to open the way. Nor will the student assume that the different kinds of nature poetry which have been named are to be regarded as mutually exclusive. One kind insensibly merges into other kinds; no fixed line can anywhere be drawn; and the different kinds will be found side by side, or overlapping, or blended, not only in the work of one poet, but often even in the same poem and passage. Outstanding features and dominant tendencies, however, are generally fairly clear. Speakly broadly, we may say that the interpretation of nature is fundamentally a matter of temperament and mood, and that the investigation of it thus forms part of the personal study of literature. But the subject has its historic aspects also, and in any large survey the spirit of the race and the age will always have to be taken into account (op. pp. 35, 36).

III

The Study of the Essay

The essay fills so large a place in modern literature and is so attractive a form of composition, that attention must necessarily be given to it in any course of literary study. At the same time, its outlines are so uncertain, and it varies so much in matter, purpose, and style, that systematic treatment of it is impossible. The question may indeed be raised whether the essay is to be considered as an independent and settled form of literary art at all. The force of this question becomes apparent the moment we compare a number of representative essays by different writers, and observe, as indeed no one can fail to observe, how little they have in common in respect either of theme or of method.

An essay by Bacon consists of a few pages of concentrated wisdom, with little elaboration of the ideas expressed; an essay by Montaigne is a medley of reflections, quotations, and anecdotes; in an essay by Addison, the thought is thin and diluted, and the tendency is now towards light didacticism and now towards personal gossip; Locke's

Essay concerning Human Understanding is a ponderous volume close-packed with philosophic matter; the essays of Macaulay and Herbert Spencer are really small books. In these cases, cited hap-hazard and for purposes of illustration only, it is evident that we have to do with totally different conceptions of what the essay is and what it should aim to accomplish. If now we turn to attempted definitions we shall find little in them to clear up the confusion. According to Johnson, for example, an essay is 'a loose sally of the mind, an irregular, undigested piece, not a regular and orderly composition'—a view which certainly does not tally with the highly-evolved essay of more recent times; while Murray's *Dictionary*, taking note of modern changes in the meaning of the word, speaks of the essay as 'a composition of moderate length on any particular subject or branch of a subject,' adding—'origin- ally implying want of finish, but now said of a composition more or less elaborate in style, though limited in range.'

Manifestly, then, the word essay is very loosely used, and any attempt to fix rigorously its forms and features must perforce end in failure. Yet if Murray's definition be scrutinised, it will, I believe (and this notwithstanding the fact that it is so ingeniously qualified that at first it seems almost meaningless), be found to help us at certain points. For the sake of a clearness in thinking we may emphasise as characteristics of the true essay the comparative limitation both of length and of range which is brought out in it. When the so-called essay grows in bulk and comprehensiveness to the proportions, let us say, of Spencer's *Essay on Progress*, the proper term for it is rather 'dissertation' or 'treatise.' That the essay is not intended to be exhaustive, then, is one aspect of it that should be kept in mind. Another aspect is suggested by Murray's further remark that it originally implied 'want of finish'—that it was, in Johnson's delightfully characteristic phraseology, 'a loose sally of the mind.' Etymologically, the word essay connotes this, for it is the same as assay, and therefore means a trial of a subject, or an attempt towards it, and not in the least a thorough and final examination of it. It was in that sense that it was employed by our first modern essayists, Montaigne and Bacon;[296] and when Locke used it for his massive treatise it must be assumed that it was extreme modesty and the sense that, after all, he had only broken ground on his subject that prompted him to do so. Vast, as has been the transformation of the essay since the time of Montaigne and Bacon, the original signification of the word has not altogether been outgrown.

The essay, then, may be regarded, roughly, as a composition on any topic the chief negative features of which are comparative brevity and comparative want of exhaustiveness. It was to these two features that Grabbe referred the extraordinary vogue of the essay. 'The essay,' he declared, 'is the most popular mode of writing,' because 'it suits the writer who has neither talent nor inclination to pursue his inquiries farther, and...the generality of readers who are amused with variety and superficiality.' This is obviously a very narrow view; but I quote it in part because it is a view which must be considered, and even more because it serves to introduce a contrasted conception of the essay which is much more important. Crabbe, it will be noted, thought the essay easy because (as he alleged) it is necessarily superficial. Sainte-Beuve, on the other hand, held it to be one of the most difficult, as well as delightful, forms of literary expression, because for him it implied (as his own fine essays show) the power of condensation, or of saving much in little. In other words, he would not admit that brevity entails superficiality. He believed rather that a good essay should be characterised by that combination of conciseness and thoroughness which is possible only when a man is absolutely master of his subject. An important distinction is thus suggested. It will always be well, in the case of any given essay, to consider to which standard it seems to approximate—to that of Crabbe, or that of Sainte-Beuve. Is it brief because the writer knows little of his subject and therefore soon comes to the end of what

---

[296]So Bacon writes in the dedication of the 1612 edition of his Essays; 'The word essay is late, but the thing is ancient, for Seneca's *Epistles to Lucilius*, if one mark them well, are but essays, that is, dispersed meditations.'

he has to say? Or because his wide and intimate knowledge enables him to disengage and present both concisely and adequately those special aspects of it with which for the moment he wishes to deal? As practical clues, these questions will be found to take us farther than might at first be supposed.

Comparative brevity, then, must in any event be admitted as a formal feature of the essay, and it would therefore seem to be a necessary condition of a good essay that it should not attempt too much. Artistically, it will inevitably suffer from overloading. Both the amount of material introduced and the method employed in dealing with it must be adjusted to the restrictions imposed. Selection and the proper distribution of emphasis will therefore be found among the elementary principles of essay writing. At the same time, while an essay must generally be confined to aspects only of a subject, it should, despite its fragmentariness, impress us as complete within itself.

Another commonly accepted canon is, that the method of the essay (as distinguished from that of the dissertation and the treatise) is marked by considerable freedom and informality. This brings it well within Johnson's definition—'a loose sally of the mind, an irregular, undigested piece.' A certain want of organic quality, and the absence of that orderly and logical mode of procedure which we look for in the more ambitious kinds of literature, may be reckoned among the essay's most pronounced structural peculiarities. In the early stages of its evolution, indeed, such irregularity and (in Murray's words) 'want of finish,' were fundamental; in fact, the essay arose because men had come to feel the need of a vehicle of expression in which they could enjoy something of the freedom of conversation. Thus Bacon's essays are, as he himself tells us, 'brief notes set down rather significantly than anxiously,' while Montaigne's discursiveness and habit of going about his subject in a series of 'hops, and skips, and jumps,' are notorious. Charles Lamb's amusing reference to the schoolmaster who offered to instruct him in the art of regular composition, will be recalled at this point. In the abstract, therefore, we may consider the essay as relatively unmethodical as well as relatively short. The well-marked tendency among modern essayists towards greater logical consistency and regularity of structure is only one among many signs of the transformation of the essay into something different from the original and genuine type.

Thus far I have dealt only with the formal aspects of the essay. Passing from form to substance, we have specially to note that whatever its theme—and the range of its subject matter is, of course, practically unlimited—the true, essay is essentially personal. Like its verse analogue, the lyric, it belongs therefore to the literature of self-expression. Treatise and dissertation may be objective; the essay is subjective. Montaigne said of his essays that they were 'consubstantial' with their author, and if few essayists have ever been so out- spoken and so unabashed in their egotism as this wise old Frenchman, the vital relationship between their work and themselves may usually be detected just beneath the surface of what they write. The central fact of the true essay, indeed, is the direct play of the author's mind and character upon the matter of his discourse.

It is evident, then, that in our study of the essay there are several things which have to be kept in view. In the first place, we have to consider the writer's personality and stand- point, his immediate attitude towards his subject, and incidentally, towards life at large. While thus disengaging the personal qualities of his work, we have also to follow the evolution of his thought, marking what aspects of his subject he has selected for treatment, how he introduces his ideas, how he handles and enforces them, and how he brings them to a conclusion. Under this head we have, moreover, to examine his whole art of presentation, exposition, and illustration, and, manifestly, to estimate the value of what he says. Finally, we have to pay particular attention to his style which, on account of the strong personal element in the essay, will be found of great importance. On this matter, however, nothing remains to be added to what has been said in the text (pp. 27–30) about style in general as an index of personality.

An historical study of the essay will, of course, include a

consideration of its growth and transformation, and of the way in which it has influenced, and been influenced by, other forms of literature. Its connection with the novel, of which it was one of the affluents, and into the composition of which it still often enters, is a point of special interest.[297] Let me add that what I have said about the transformation of the essay must be taken simply as the statement of a fact. No judgment upon the fact is suggested. We may regret the tendency of the modern essay towards greater elaboration and formality, and may feel that this implies loss of freedom and personal charm. Yet literary types must necessarily evolve in response to changing conditions, and their evolution is, at bottom, a sign of continued life.

IV

THE STUDY OF THE SHORT STORY

The short story has firmly established itself as a favourite form in modern literature. Its immense vogue is the result of many co-operating causes; among them, the rush of modern life, which has made men impatient of those 'great still books' (as Tennyson called them) over which readers were glad to linger in more leisurely ages, and the enormous development of the magazine, in which a large field is naturally afforded for tales complete in a single number.

So popular, indeed, has the story become that extraordinary claims are at times put forth in its behalf. We are even told that it is the 'coming form' of fiction, and that ultimately it will displace the novel entirely. Such claims, however, may be safely set aside. The story is not in the least likely to displace the novel for the

---

[297]The reference is to the part played by the 'social essay' of the early eighteenth century, especially the *Spectator* papers, in the development of the novel, and to the fact that in the works of many modern novelists (as in those of Thackeray and George Eliot) essays are frequently incorporated in the story. (*Op.* what has been said on p.: 65 about the novelist's use of direct commentary and explanation.)

very good reason that it cannot meet the novel on the novel's own ground, or do precisely what the novel does. It cannot, for instance, exhibit life in its variety and complexity, for this needs a larger canvas than the story provides. Nor, for the same reason, can it deal with the evolution of character, which, as we have seen (pp. 148, 149), is one of the most important problems of modern prose fiction. Quite manifestly, to cite extreme cases, the spiritual history of Levin in *Anna Karenina*, and the study of Tito Melema's moral downfall in *Romola*, would be impossible within the framework of the short story. It is a matter of common experience that we have to live for some time with men and women and to see them in different relationships and circumstances before we really get to know them; and this, I take it, is as true of men and women in fiction as it is of men and women in actual life. But in the short story we meet people for a few minutes and see them in a few relationships and circumstances only; and while it is indeed true that concentration of attention upon a particular aspect of character may result in a very powerful impression,[298] still, as a rule, such impression is not exactly comparable with that left by an ampler, more detailed, and more varied representation. Hence those characters in fiction who dwell in our imaginations as fully portrayed and completely alive, are, if I mistake not, generally characters in novels. So long as people are interested in the intricacy and many-sidedness of life and in minute studies of character in the making or the unmaking, we may thus safely conclude that the novel will hold its own as the representative type of modern literary art. The tendency of the short story to run into sequences (as in Stevenson's *New Arabian Nights* and Sir Arthur Conan Doyle's *Sherlock Holmes* books) is itself suggestive of a desire on the part of its writers to escape from its formal limitations. We may interpret such examples of emancipation

---

[298]It may be noted that Maupassant, one of the greatest masters of the short story, was far more successful with his characterisation when working in the story than he was when he essayed the novel.

as attempts to combine the brevity and concentration of the story with something of the sustained interest of the novel on the side either of character or of plot.

We are here concerned with the short story, therefore, not as a rival to, or as a substitute for, the novel, but as another kind of prose fiction, which has grown up beside the novel, and has now its recognised and important place in literature. Some inquiry into its objects and methods is, for this reason, desirable.

For working purposes we need a rough definition to start with, and that suggested by Edgar Allan Poe will do well enough: a short story is a prose narrative 'requiring from half an hour to one or two hours in its perusal.' Putting the same idea into different phraseology, we may say that a short story is a story that can be easily read in a single sitting. Yet while the brevity thus specified is the most obvious characteristic of the kind of narrative in question, the evolution of the story into a definite type has been accompanied by the development also of some fairly well-marked characteristics of organism. It is now very commonly recognised that a true short story is not merely a novel on a reduced scale, or a digest in thirty pages of matter which would have been quite as effectively, or even more effectively, handled in three hundred. The older forms of story, indeed, exhibit in general a very imperfect differentiation of the growing type from the parent stock. Thus, for instance, Dickens's *Christmas Books* are in organism simply novels, though novels-in-little. This statement of fact does not, of course, imply any adverse judgment upon these ever-delightful and, in their own way, quite admirable examples of the storyteller's art. It is made only to illustrate the distinction, which since Dickens's time has been emerging into greater and greater clearness, between the materials and method of the novel and the materials and method of the story. Even today we meet with innumerable indeterminate productions the place of which is on the border- line between the two classes of fiction. But, on the whole, the increasing popularity of the story has brought with it an increasing sense that considerations of art involve various specific requirements of matter and treatment. In other words, as the story differs from the novel in length, so it must of necessity differ from it in motive, plan, and structure.

Of such requirements the first may be very easily formulated. The subject of a story must be one that can be adequately and effectively developed within the prescribed limits. On this point the reader's own feeling of satisfaction or dissatisfaction will provide a sufficient test.[299] Whatever its particular theme and object, a story should leave us with the conviction that, even if nothing would have been lost, at least nothing would have been gained, by further elaboration. It should impress us as absolutely clear in outline, well proportioned, full enough for the purpose yet without the slightest suggestion of crowding, and within its own framework complete.

This first principle of composition is not to be interpreted too narrowly. I do not mean that a story must necessarily be confined to a single incident or moment. A story may be little more than an anecdote worked up into literary form, and its success may depend entirely upon the skill shown in the telling. It may deal with some one phase of character or experience, or with a detached critical scene. But, on the other hand, it may cover a wider field of time and involve a larger sequence of events than many novels. Yet even in these last-named cases the principle before us will still be exemplified. In Washington Irving's *Rip Van Winkle*, for example, we have the tale of a lifetime; yet as even the least critical reader will instinctively feel, the effect is greatly enhanced by that concentration of interest which inevitably results when such a subject is put into so small a space, and in particular, by the fact that no extraneous matter is allowed to intrude between the moment of Rip's falling asleep and that of his waking.

Again, to take a very different illustration, Maupassant's grim little masterpiece, *La Parure*, contains the long-drawn-out tragedy

---

[299]Compare at this point what has been said about plot and characterisation in the novel and the drama respectively on pp. 183–185 and 187–189.

of many years; yet once more an enormous artistic gain is achieved by the focusing of attention throughout upon the single motive on which the story turns, and by the rigorous exclusion of everything not directly connected with it. When, therefore, we insist that the subject of a short story must be one that can be adequately and effectively handled within the limits of the short story, we must not forget that in this, as in all other forms of art, the question of subject is vitally bound up with that of treatment.

A second fundamental principle of composition thus comes to light—that of unity; under which head we include unity of motive, of purpose, of action, and, in addition (in regard to results), unity of impression. It may be laid down as a rule to which, so far as I see, there can be no exception, that a short story must contain one and only one informing idea, and that this idea must be worked out to its logical conclusion with absolute singleness of aim and directness of method. It is this essential kind of unity which will be found to characterise every really good short story, whether it belong to the highly concentrated type, like Hawthorne's *Dr Heidegger's Experiment*, Poe's *The Cask of Amontillado*, and Stevenson's *The Sieur de Maletroit's Door*; or the highly expanded type, like Maupassant's *La Parure*; or to any type (like, say, Bret Harte's *The Luck of Roaring Camp*) the place of which is somewhere between the two extremes.

In the case of the novel, so many different elements may be woven into the texture that it may be difficult to detect any central organising principle, while at times analysis may reveal two or more quite distinct pivots of interest. No such scattering of attention can be permitted in the story. Here, on the contrary, the germinal idea must be perfectly clear and the interest arising out of it must never be complicated by any other consideration. Singleness of aim and singleness of effect are, therefore, the two great canons by which we have to try the value of a short story as a piece of art.

Attainment of this unity is one of the principal difficulties of short story writing; and in passing it may be noted that it is largely because the art of the story is so much more exacting than that of the novel that many critics rate it higher than the novel, and that perfection of workmanship in it—the complete adaptation of means to end—gives peculiar æsthetic pleasure to the thoughtful reader. As Poe said:

> 'A skilful literary artist...having conceived, with deliberate care, a certain unique or single *effect* to be wrought out, he then invents such incidents—he then combines such events—as may best aid him in establishing this preconceived effect. If his very initial sentence tend not to the outbringing of this effect, then he has failed in his first step. In the whole composition there should be no word written, of which the tendency, direct or indirect, is not to the one pre-established design. And by such means, with such care and skill, a picture is at length painted which leaves in the mind of him who contemplates it with a kindred art, a sense of the fullest satisfaction. The idea of the tale has been presented unblemished, because undisturbed; and this is an end unattainable by the novel.'[1]

This must, of course, be taken as a counsel of perfection; but it is useful as indicating that theoretic standard of excellence which we shall do well to keep in view. By reason of its brevity and concentration, the short story manifestly demands particular care in all the details of composition. Far more than in the novel, everything superfluous and redundant must be omitted, the proper perspective must be maintained, the emphasis justly distributed, necessary values given to the successive movements of the narrative, and the separate parts strictly subordinated to the whole. Technical defects in the story, it should be noted, stand out with much greater clearness than the same defects in the novel; Scott's clumsiness in getting his plots started, for instance, while bad enough in *Waverley*,[300] nearly ruins *My Aunt Margaret's Mirror*.[301]

At the same time, it is obviously impossible to lay down

---

[300]Review of Hawthorne's *Twice-told Tales*.
[301]See p. 137, note.

any abstract rules for construction. Here, as always, method must ultimately depend upon matter and purpose. A story may, for example, contain little or no dialogue, or it may be nearly all dialogue; and while in the great majority of cases the amount of description introduced must be small, occasionally, as in Cable's *Old Creole Days* and Stevenson's *Island Night's Entertainments*, local colour is an essential feature and the expansion of description is therefore fully justified.

The great principle of all true art is thus again applicable; details can be rightly estimated only be reference to the total design. In regard to the nature of the germinal idea, again, generalisation is equally out of the question. Provided that the elementary conditions which have been emphasised are fulfilled, a story may deal with any kind of motive and material. In Washington Irving's *The Stout Gentleman*, a whimsical fancy is worked out with admirable skill, and the very slightness of the substance is an element in the impression produced. Poe's *Gold Bug* turns on a puzzle; his *Mystery of Marie Roget* aims at sensation; his *Purloined Letter* is a 'tale of ratiocination'; his *Masque of the Red Death*, pure impressionism, or (in his own classification) a 'tale of effect.' Hawthorne's *Wakefield*, with its attempt to reconstruct a character on the basis of a bare fact, is, like Gogol's marvellous *Madman's Diary*, and Stevenson's *Olalla*, an excursion into morbid psychology; the *Minister's Veil* is a piece of mysticism; *The Great Stone Face* is an allegory; *The Maypole of Merry Mount* and *The Grey Champion* roughly resemble Riehl's *Kulturgeschichtliche Novellen* and Strindberg's *Svenska Öden och Aventyr*, in being primarily representative pictures of the past. To the last class the wonderful little story, *When Father brought Home the Lamp*, of the Finnish novelist Aho, may also be said to belong. Stockton's *The Lady or the Tiger* and Aldrich's *Marjorie Daw* are contrived expressly for the dramatic surprise of their endings—in the one case the conundrum, in the other, the sudden shock of disenchantment. Stevenson's *Bottle Imp* is pure fantasy. In Tolstoi's *Polushka* the whole interest hinges on the workings of the moujik's mind, while many of the same writer's later tales are either expanded anecdotes illustrative of the Russian peasantry, or moral and religious parables. These are examples, which I cite as they occur to me, and wholly for the purpose of suggesting the immense range—the practically unlimited range—of the short story in respect of theme. A dramatic incident or situation; a telling scene; a closely co-ordinated series of events; a phase of character; a bit of experience; an aspect of life; a moral problem—any one of these, and innumerable other motives which might be added to the list, may be made the nucleus of a thoroughly satisfactory story.

A glance at the actual practice of two accomplished masters of the art of the story may at this point be interesting. Hawthorne's *Note Books* contain many suggestions for stories, and they show us that in his case the first conception—the germinal idea, as I have called it—came to him generally in the form, not of an incident or of a plot, but of a detached situation, or of a particular manifestation of character, or of an abstract thought which had to be put into concrete shape. Considering the peculiar character of Hawthorne's genius we are certainly not surprised to find that with him the starting point of a story was often some curious fancy or speculation regarding the obscurer workings of motive and feeling. The strange tale already mentioned—*Wakefield*—is an instance, and I will give another.

In the *American Note Books* of 1840 there is an entry which runs: 'A person to be the death of his beloved in trying to raise her to a more than mortal loveliness; yet this should be a comfort to him for having aimed so high and holily.' This was the origin of *The Birthmark*. The very emphatic declaring of Stevenson concerning the three great types of story, is equally illuminating. I quote from a conversation which he once had on the subject with Mr Graham Balfour: "There are, so far as I know, three ways, and three ways only, of writing a story. You may take a plot and fit characters to it, or you may take a character and choose incidents and situations to develop it, or lastly—you must bear with me while I try to make this clear'—(here he made a gesture with his hand as if he were trying to shape something and give it outline and form)—'you may take a certain atmosphere, and get actions and persons to realise it. I'll give you an example—*The Merry Men*. There I began with the feeling of one of those islands on the west coast of Scotland, and I gradually developed the story to express the sentiment with which that coast affected me."[302]

Here, even if the classification given is not quite so final as Stevenson thought, we have a most useful clue in our study of the story. Our first business will always be to disengage the initial conception and foundation interest; and in our search for this we shall be greatly helped by keeping in mind the distinction here brought out between the story of plot, the story of character, and (in a larger sense than Stevenson himself perhaps attached to the term) the story of impression.[303]

It is scarcely necessary to add that in the foregoing brief discussion of the short story I have taken no account of the elements which enter into its composition. Such elements are the same as those which constitute the raw materials of the novel, and the canons by which they are to be evaluated are the canons which have already been considered at length in our chapter on prose fiction in general. We have here been concerned only with the characteristics and requirements of the short story as a specific form of literary art, having, like every other specific form of art, its own organism and its own laws.

The reader does not need any introduction to the best English and American storywriters. He will be well advised, however, if he carries his studies farther afield, for much of the finest work in the story has been done by the great continental masters. The list of these is a long one; but special mention may perhaps be made of Mérimée, Gautier, Daudet, and Maupassant among the French; of Paul Heyse, who holds the pre-eminent place among the Germans;

---

[302]Graham Balfour's *Life of Stevenson*, ii, 169.
[303] In theory, Poe held strongly to the superiority of the story of impression, or effect, as he called it.

and of Pushkin, Tolstoi, Gorki, and Chekhov among the Russians. As always in such cases, the wider the range of our interest, the more opportunity we get for a comparison of essential differences, personal and racial, in matter, method, and aims.